Making it Real: Sustaining Knowledge Management

Adapting for Success in the Knowledge Based Economy

Annie Green

Making it Real: Sustaining Knowledge Management
Adapting for Success in the Knowledge Based Economy

First published: April 2013

ISBN: 978-1-909507-08-1

Copyright © 2013 The authors

All rights reserved. Except for the quotation of short passages for the purposes of critical review, no part of this publication may be reproduced in any material form (including photocopying or storing in any medium by electronic means and whether or not transiently or incidentally to some other use of this publication) without the written permission of the copyright holder except in accordance with the provisions of the Copyright Designs and Patents Act 1988, or under the terms of a licence issued by the Copyright Licensing Agency Ltd, Saffron House, 6-10 Kirby Street, London EC1N 8TS. Applications for the copyright holder's written permission to reproduce any part of this publication should be addressed to the publishers.

Disclaimer: While every effort has been made by the editor, authors and the publishers to ensure that all the material in this book is accurate and correct at the time of going to press, any error made by readers as a result of any of the material, formulae or other information in this book is the sole responsibility of the reader. Readers should be aware that the URLs quoted in the book may change or be damaged by malware between the time of publishing and accessing by readers.

Note to readers.
Some papers have been written by authors who use the American form of spelling and some use the British. These two different approaches have been left unchanged.

Published by: Academic Conferences and Publishing International Limited, Reading, RG4 9SJ, United Kingdom, info@academic-publishing.org

Available from www.academic-bookshop.com

Contents

List of Contributors iii

Foreword v

Narrative Intelligence Perpetuates the Learning Organization 1
    By Madelyn Blair and Denise Lee

Optimize the Flow of Knowledge 30
    By John Hovell

Cultural Identity and a Global Mindset: Awareness to Knowledge, Skills to Competence 55
    By Iouri Bairatchnyi

Bringing Order to Chaos: Knowledge Architectures that Sustain Knowledge Practice 86
    By Denise A. D. Bedford

Transferring Tacit Knowledge with the Movement of Employees 115
    By Bonita Best Coppedge

Managing Critical Knowledge Assets: Achieving and Sustaining Organizational Competitive Advantage 149
    By Milena Ristovska & Michael A. Stankosky

Success Factors from the Frontline of Knowledge Management (KM) 174
    By Steve Newman

KM Strategic Execution: How to Get Executive Attention 219
    By Patrice "PJ" Jackson

Employee Participation, and Increased Organizational Performance – Building a Collaboration Network 231

    By Patrice "PJ" Jackson

The Cognizant Organization 251

    By Annie Green

Keeping Abreast: A Knowledge Management (KM) Challenge for Information Technology Service Providers 275

    By Richard Donnelly and Christopher Durney

Transformational Leadership and Knowledge Management: It's Effect on Organizational Innovation and Performance 308

    By M. Birasnav, Mirghani Mohamed & Anjum Razzaque

Cyber-and Semantic Technology Integration for Knowledge Awareness 324

    By Lakita Conley-Ware

Improving Healthcare Quality Using Web 4.0 Decision Making 354

    By Anjum Razzaque[1], Mirghani Mohamed[2] & M Birasnav

Afterword 369

List of Contributors

Iouri Bairatchnyi, Kent State University, Kent, OH, USA
Denise A. D. Bedford, Kent State University, Kent, OH, USA
Madelyn Blair, Pelerei Inc, Jefferson, MD, USA
M. Birasnav, New York Institute of Technology, Adliya, Manama, Kingdom of Bahrain
Francesco A. Calabrese, The George Washington University, Washington D.C., USA
Bonita Best Coppedge, Virtual PM, LLC, Ruskin, FL, USA
Lakita Conley-Ware, New York Institute of Technology, Vancouver, BC VTY1KB, Canada
Richard Donnelly, George Washington University, Washington, DC, USA
Christopher Durney, George Washington University, Washington, DC, USA
Annie Green, George Washington University, Washington, DC, USA
John Hovell, HovellCreative LLC, Chantilly, VA, USA
Patrice "PJ" Jackson, Lockheed Martin, Bethesda, Maryland, USA
Denise Lee, Price Waterhouse Cooper, McLean, Virginia, USA
Mirghani Mohamed, Applied Knowledge Sciences, Inc., Leesburg, VA, USA
Steve Newman, NASA (retired), Arlington, Virginia, USA
Anjum Razzaque New York Institute of Technology, Vancouver, BC, Canada
Milena Ristovska, George Washington University, Washington, DC, USA
Michael A. Stankosky, George Washington University, Washington, DC, USA

Foreword

Dr. Annie Green has always taken a practical and applied approach to her studies, research, and work. She excels in this, and the results are included in the authors and their insights. Even her title choice reflects this: "Making It Real."

Somehow, Knowledge Management (KM) is still a struggle within a lot of organizations. They embrace the concept, without even knowing what it is. They apply it, without even knowing how. They speak of it, as if they have a proven definition and framework; yet they do not. KM is one of these 21st century phenomena, where a lot of people would prefer to ignore it, but realize they cannot. It is like the air we breathe: it sustains our economic, social, and personal well being. We are a knowledge-intensive global economy, which is defined as one in which data/information/knowledge are the major inputs to agriculture, manufacturing, and services. By some estimates, over 70% of the global economy inputs (factors of production to use an industrial term) are knowledge based. On a micro level, we can see this in the recent iPad: it costs approximately $500, and the majority of these costs and profits are knowledge-related: the design, the software, the marketing, the maintenance, and logistics.

So, given this state of affairs, what are we to do next in reference to KM? It is incumbent on organizational leaders to both recognize these facts and educate themselves in an active way in the language, framework, and solutions that KM offers. One former CEO (Lew Platt of HP) said that if HP only knows what it knows, it would be three times as more profitable. Of course, he was talking the essence of KM: leveraging knowledge assets/capital to improve effectiveness, efficiency, and innovation.

In academia, where I have spent my last 14 years, we still do not have a unified curriculum in KM. In fact, most universities have no focus area or degree-related KM research and studies. There is no global KM professional group to research and advance the theory, practice, and certification of KM. Our efforts are, at best, singular and non focused. Efforts are underway to change this, but they advance at a snail's pace. Lack of concentrated funding drives a lot of this neglect.

When I visit organizations and talk to their executives, I ask if they have an inventory of their assets. They often reply that they do. However, the ones that they have are of their physical capital and people. But, they do not have a true inventory of their knowledge assets. How can one manage assets they are not aware of? And, we still use economic models for pricing and risk that are industrial based. We have no standard names for our knowledge assets, let alone a way of valuing them. Someone said you can't manage what you can't measure. I go further, and say you can't measure what you can't name. We work in a globally integrated environment, and common names and values are essential to governance and management. How we function without agreement in knowledge-intensive industries is a mystery to me. We do muddle well, don't we?

Enough of my preaching! We need action now, and my wish is that this book, so artfully brought together by Dr. Green, will serve as a platform for concerted action by you, the readers. Anne is an excellent point of contact, since she is a leader of the KM Educational Forum and a member of The George Washington University's Institute for Knowledge and Innovation, both of whom are dedicated to advancing the discipline and practice of KM. My wish is for all of us to add to our wealth by leveraging the relevant knowledge around us for both the common good, as well as our own.

Michael Stankosky, DSc
Professor, George Washington University
Co-director, Institute for Knowledge & Innovation
October 2012

Narrative Intelligence Perpetuates the Learning Organization

Madelyn Blair[1] and Denise Lee[2]

[1]Pelerei, Inc., Jefferson, MD, USA
[2]PricewaterhouseCoopers, Virginia, USA

Introduction

Knowledge Management (KM) is about making information and knowledge accessible to staff so that they can do their jobs better. KM can be implemented either through capturing knowledge in databases and making it available to other employees who need it, or through facilitating the conversations between and among employees. Whether the conversation occurs within an organized Community of Practice (CoP) or whether it occurs in informal, casual conversation between two people, the knowledge is most often transferred through stories.

Historically, stories have been around since before language. "Humans have told, used, and relied on stories for over 100,000 years (Haven 2007, 4)." Only a few hundred years ago, before written language became common, oral stories gave us the news, history, values, and culture. Stories have been around for so long that our brains have been formed to help us see, tell, and understand stories. This chapter examines story – this smallest unit of knowledge – and translates that into why narrative intelligence is essential to an effective KM strategy. Let's begin with what is a story.

What is Story?

Madelyn Blair and Denise Lee

"Stories interpret raw facts and proofs to create reality... In this ocean of choice, a meaningful story can feel like a life preserver that tethers us to something sage, important, or at the very least more solid than disembodied voices begging for attention"

(Simmons 1997).

John Seely Brown says that a story is the smallest unit of knowledge. Why? Because a story contains the context of the knowledge nugget and we only learn through context (2003). If we, as listeners, can't place the story into our own situation or our own context, then it means little to us. If we can see the context in which it rests and relate it to our own, then the nugget of knowledge is understood and fixed in our memory. In the end, having access to knowledge is necessary but not sufficient for applying it in our work. It must be one that is implanted in our thinking as a whole so that we can relate it to our own situations and apply as appropriate.

People have been using stories to communicate information for thousands of years. We often meet stories for the first time in our own lives when we listen to the parables from sacred scripture – simple little stories that convey deep truths without ever mentioning the truth itself. For example, the parable of the Good Samaritan allows us to take in the fact that there is good in people who appear, on the surface, to be evil and despised and doing this without ever saying it explicitly.

Sometimes these kinds of stories are called fairy tales. Yet their creation is founded in the desire of societies to convey important values to the next generation. For example, the story of Little Red Riding Hood was a story meant to help young girls understand the challenges of womanhood according to Bettelheim (1989). In both this case and the parable, the story is approachable. We can see ourselves in related situations. In both cases, the story contains the seeds of a greater meaning. But this still doesn't say why story works so well.

Every great storyteller knows that when he or she tells a story, the real story is in the mind of the listener. The power of story comes from the connection we make to the story as it is being told. We may recognize the setting. We may realize that we have a similar character in our own lives. We may have experienced the very same dilemma as the protagonist in the story. In each of these cases, we begin to bring the story into ourselves, making the story our own. And, because of this ability to link to the story so intimately, we are open to learn from it. Story contains within it the mechanism for generating the force that empowers our learning. Talk about power!

How Does a Story Work?

Every story contains within itself a setting, a point of tension, and a resolution – the beginning, the middle and the end. A story begins in a certain place, at a particular moment in time, involves certain characters -- the setting. It then shifts and provides us with the sense of discomfort that something is not perfect in this setting – the point of tension. (For example, the client is unhappy with the solution that had been offered, the project produced an unexpected result, or there is tension among the team members.) Lo and behold, the story then moves on, telling us actions and events -- the resolution. This movement from setting to point of tension to resolution is called the story arc and can be seen in Figure 1.

Madelyn Blair and Denise Lee

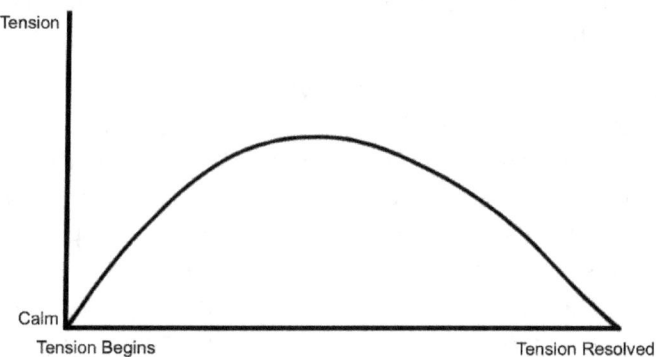

Figure 1: The Story Arc

Each story contains these three elements whether they are obvious or not. The setting helps us relate to the story by giving us an image of where, when, and what is happening. The point of tension offers us a reason to continue to listen to the story. We are drawn by our own curiosity to see how things work out and so we continue to listen. The resolution offers us the ease of mind that at least things seemed to get fixed or settled so that there no longer is a sense that something needs doing, and we relax. The next time you watch a great movie; look for the setting as it is laid out for you. Identify when you feel a sense of tension that things are not quite right. Watch to see how the movie makers bring you to the resolution.

Take a moment and think of a time when you were part of a story yourself. Perhaps the challenge was that your boss asked you to look into using Twitter (setting) and you have no idea how to use Twitter or why anyone might use it given workloads and time limits (point of tension). You called three colleagues to get their ideas, and on the last call, you were told about a person who has a simple strategy for using Twitter to gather knowledge that makes sense and doesn't take a great deal of time. Suddenly, you see the potential for your situation. You lay out a strategy for posting and reading Tweets to test for yourself, and it works (resolution). You're feeling a real sense of satisfaction as you offer this approach to your boss.

This is an example of a lived story. You might tell this story to someone else. You might write the story down so that others can read it and learn. You might even decide to do something very creative and create it all in cartoon form. In any case, it is a story, because it contains those three elements.

In business, the recognition of story as an effective means to convey information, share insights, motivate, or build teams has been recent. Steve Denning's book (2000) started opening business minds about how effective story can be. His use of the springboard story to help the World Bank understand why knowledge management was important is now a classic of the business application of story. Annette Simmons had been writing on the topic long before Denning, but her emphasis was on the power of the personal story not necessarily within the business setting (1997). After the initial introduction to the business world, such authors as Peter Gruber who wrote, "Tell to win" (2011) and others have moved the concept along. Today, there are many voices that speak about the use of storytelling in business.

Narrative Intelligence: Eliciting Stories and Story Listening

Let's get a sense of the difference between narrative and story. We experience many stories in a day, yet the day itself forms into a narrative for the day. For example, you might say that you began your day with an unexpected opportunity to arrive at work early due to traffic that was particularly light. This delightful event seemed to follow you throughout the day with a chance to talk with a particular client who had been hard to reach yet received your call with enthusiasm and agreement. In the end, the day could be described as a successful campaign. We call the sum of all the little stories of the day as they weave in and out of each other, the larger story or the narrative of the day. Thus, knowing how narrative is created and what its structure is helps us better understand the meaning of the day as we put it all together. Within an organization, the many stories of the people of the organization also weave together into the larger story or narrative of the business. And the more effectively we understand this phenomenon, the better we can interpret what is happening in the business, learning from it at a deeper level. So, you see, beginning with story is essential to appreciating why organizational learning occurs at all.

There are those who say, no, it's not about story, it's about narrative. Yet there are others who equate story and narrative – believing they mean the same thing. To resolve this apparent paradox is to look at the relationship between the two words. In this chapter, we view story and narrative as different and intertwined within each other. Every day, we live in stories – our own and within others. Every day, our stories enter the weave of the narrative of our organizations, our work, and our lives. In the previous section the concept that stories represent threads of contexts, emotions, characters and conflicts was introduced. Also introduced was that story represents "the smallest unit of knowledge".

Stories are threads of knowledge being shared within the organization. They are the way people exchange experiences. As people connect, they create webs across the organization called social or organizational networks, a term made popular by Dr. Robert Cross at the University of Virginia (2004). As these threads are woven together across the networks they represent the braid of the narrative. A narrative is a braid of stories sharing knowledge through the social networks.

> Helping people identify their own stories is sometimes a challenge. Many techniques can be used to help in this process. For example, you can tell them your own relevant story. Or, you can suggest they look at a list of words that relate to the work and see if any of them stimulate a story. Or, you can use images such as a Dialoogle card (Figure 2). Or, you might have a series of objects from which they can select to tell their story. Don't be surprised at how simple the key can be to unlocking some of the best stories.
>
>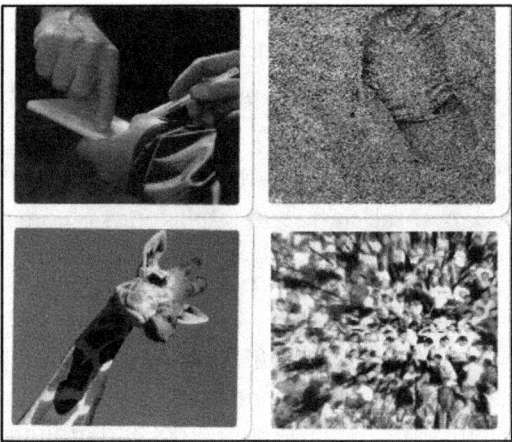
>
> **Figure 2: Dialoogle Card**

The term "Narrative Intelligence" was developed by Michael Travers and Marc Davis to describe work at the emergence of Appreciative Inquiry (AI) (2003, 27-38). Other researchers, David Blair and Tom Meyer used this term to mean, specifically, human ability to organize experience into narrative form (2002). These collective uses of story produce specific behavior - storytelling - that humans interpret as narrative. Within the Organization Development discipline, narrative has long been a theme in AI and has recently experienced a surge of popularity. Researchers in various subfields, including system design, story generation and understanding agent architecture, and interface agents have all taken independent forays into narrative, finding it a fruitful way to rethink some basic issues in their disciplines. Examples include:

- Narrative as a system design principle: If humans often make sense of the world by assimilating it into narrative, then it makes sense to design our systems to allow people to use their well-honed narrative skills in interpreting these systems.
- Narrative as a way of structuring agents: Conversely, since humans make sense of the world via narrative, perhaps artificial systems should also employ narrative in understanding the world. Thus, for example, two artificial agents may want to organize their experience as stories they can share.

At its most fundamental, narrative intelligence is concerned with narrative as a way of understanding the world. Turning experience into a story is considered by many as a fundamental mode of sense-making. The narrative weaves together stories that help people within the organization with broader sense-making of the whole. For example, as a new leader joins an organization, the stories that are told through the networks and around the water cooler begin to create a narrative of what this leader is about such as he is a good listener. In addition, the telling of stories is one way that an organization's procedural knowledge is understood and shared. Many types of story and storytelling combine to create narratives. For example, the basic types of business storytelling, include oral and written stories, documentaries, oral histories, organizational myths and legends, case scenarios, training scenarios, encoded and embedded business rules, gossip and business conversations.

Narrative intelligence is a critical tool that helps a learning organization to strengthen its organizational vision, enhance organizational communications, capture and transfer organizational knowledge, externalize and internalize tacit knowledge, encourage innovation, build communities; and to develop effective training, mentoring and learning strategies. In fact, these are the critical elements of a KM program. Being able to work effectively with narrative and story is a critical competency in a learning organization. Therefore, the relationship between knowledge, learning and narrative intelligence is the linkage that represents the post- modern understanding of what sustains a vibrant learning organization.

Today's workforce does not accept the autocratic style often adopted by leaders that follow the industrial management model and embrace the more collaborative model that understands the power of collective stories. Leadership has to evolve to match this growing sense of democracy and independence in the workforce especially with the baby boomers retiring and the younger generation expecting to have more of a voice. For example, when developing a training course that rolls out a new strategic initiative in which story is going to be used by the presenter, there needs to be an understanding of how to link the stories into the narrative of the new strategy. When using video, there needs to be awareness that all of these story threads must connect to make a comprehensive point, or they are just disjointed videos that are confusing rather than enhancing the training session. If the staff cannot relate to the stories told in the videos, they are out of context and do not build on the narrative the presenter is trying to portray.

A narrative process is about listening, sense-making, and engagement. Now, consider if you were developing a new strategy, what stories would you need to share? Narrative intelligence is about listening and not just telling. It is about sense-making and not just accepting at face value. Strategic communications is a critical part of rolling out any new initiative in the organization. The communication artifacts are not just branded so they look pretty but should contain a comprehensive narrative. A phased narrative process engages people into a change process.

Narrative Intelligence is a fundamental organizing principle of human experience that builds on narrative as a carrier of knowledge and is a fundamental organizing principle of human experience. Many different disciplines recognize the importance of narrative. In fact, work in narrative intelligence has drawn on conceptions of narrative from many of these sources: art, in which narrative is understood as a form of representation; psychology (especially narrative psychology), in which narrative is thought of as a way in which humans make sense of the world; cultural studies, in which narrative is studied as a way in which a culture structures and propagates knowledge. This last awareness of narrative as a braid of stories carrying and, thus, sharing knowledge through the social networks opens new possibilities for transformation about the way organizations not only share knowledge but learn.

Narrative Intelligence in the Real World

Building on the common terms and understanding developed from reading the last two sections we will now set the use of story and narrative intelligence in real world examples. In order to really understand the intersection between the way organizations are managed and the impact of the introduction of narrative, we need to look back in history. Business management and what we know of hierarchies and command and control began with the work of Frederick Taylor. His work, "Scientific Management," was written during the Industrial era set in the 19th century (2006). Even as we have evolved in so many ways in the work place, this fundamental "factory model" point of view still dominates the management and structure of our organizations and ultimately our work. Unfortunately, this model does not evoke the potential and high performance of human behavior (Taylor 2006). People are not motivated by mechanistic models

Narrative Intelligence Perpetuates the Learning Organization

or environments. People do not communicate and share knowledge through the boxes of the organization chart. Rather, people communicate through networks and in the white space between the boxes. What do they share through these networks? Stories!

A landmark book was published in 2006 - "Wake Me Up When the Data is Over - How Organizations Use Stories to Build Results." This book was written by a collection of experts in the use of story to include Michael Margolis, Ashraf Ramsey, Susan Sites and the esteemed authors of this chapter. The chapters are drawn from the prime areas of application ranging from strategy, to marketing, project management, training, and research. Specific examples of the application of story were richly woven through the chapters. We will share a few of the notable cases. One in particular was the application of story at NASA. In 2000, Dr. Edward Hoffman and Dr. Alexander Laufer piloted the use of story to share knowledge in the Academy for Program and Project Management (APPM). The premise of the pilot was to address the business problem NASA was encountering with project management capability across the agency being inconsistent in response to the Challenger Investigation Report. The goal was to identify excellent project managers and capture and share their stories to push learning and unique practices across the agency. The specific methods included knowledge sharing conferences called Masters Forums and a storytelling magazine called Ask Magazine. The power of the stories shared within these Forums resonates. For example, let's look at the story shared by renowned NASA program manager Martin Davis from Goddard Space Flight Center.

Imagine what happens to relationships if you are asked to restart a project because your predecessor performed poorly. Martin Davis from NASA shared this story widely to communicate his learning. "Three "project managers" were to solve a problem. One guy was managing the project. Another guy, for the parent contractor organization, was helping him. I was from the customer, the funding agency, so I felt I was in control. They weren't doing a great job of working together (when I took over). One day I saw elephant rides being given at a nearby strip mall. It hit me. "The three of us need to get on that elephant." He dragged his two fellow managers down to the mall. Did it work? "Sure it worked. There is a picture to prove it happened and afterwards we worked more closely and moved beyond our differences." After three men get on an elephant together things can never be the same (Silverman, 2006, 66).

Stories about real life experiences provide the hook to alter behaviors and stick in people's memories. They engage people and help them understand lessons and expectations. These Forums enable leading project managers to tell their experiences in live storytelling settings where discussions would follow the storytelling in order to further embed the learning's. Stories with the most impact would be selected for publication in ASK Magazine. This magazine was recognized as one component of taking NASA to 'green' status in the Human Capital metrics of the President's Management Agenda scorecard and continues today.

Another example of the application of story is in the area of strategy. Organizations need to move beyond written plans to inspire and communicate strategies. In this era of information overload only the well-crafted and memorable messages make their way through the noise to the target audience. Significant speeches from leadership launching the strategy rarely make an impact and are usually forgotten before the audience files out of the auditorium. Take for example one of the speeches we are all familiar with - the President's State of the Union. An enormous amount of discussion by the pundits and hype lead up to it but rarely do individual citizens remember much of what they heard. But - we do remember the stories. When the young military officer stands up and is recognized for bravery, or the fire fighter that saved the child's life or the nurse that worked during the hurricane recovery. We remember those stories and those people because they inspired and were memorable. Leaders need to inspire in order to bring business strategies to life and have people execute to success.

As leaders begin to incorporate, more intentionally, the use of story in their strategies and purposefully set the goal to increase the narrative intelligence of their organizations, they will increasingly see results. An excellent example of the application of narrative intelligence practice in a business setting is provided by Robert Allen. He created i.d.e.a.s., a former Disney operation that became an independent creative content studio. Allen wrote a future story about what an enterprise looked like that was working the way he envisioned. He told that story to himself over and over. He then wrote a business plan and it became the structure and architecture for the business. He initially used the story as a vision for the company and then went on to use it with staff, prospects and existing customers. The story keeps everyone focused and prevents distraction from the core purpose and gives the company a heart and soul. Allen shared, "Don't confuse story making with strategic planning or analytics. Working with stories is a fearless act of creation. Once the story is compelling, you can bring the analytics and information to the passionate framework of the story and give it life" (Silverman 2006, 142).

Oral Histories – A Deeper Example

The core of oral histories is the spoken word. For the purpose of this section, we will discuss oral histories as the gathering of the founders' stories. The founders' stories can create an everlasting narrative braid that informs the actions and behaviors of members of the organization. The gathering begins with a deep exploration of the stories that live in the organization.

Anyone who has worked with Disney has heard a story about Walt. The story might be about how he used up the entire budget to assure that the product allowed for the imagination to flow freely. The story might be about a time when he spent more hours than could be counted to assure that the product incorporated the best creativity. It didn't matter which story was told, the listener always knew that Walt valued creativity. Even today, the most valued Disney staff is called an Imagineer. And, when you have stories like these of the founder that live on through the retelling, the values of Walt remain alive and well in the organization.

Oral histories are a specific type of narrative in an organization. They are collections of stories about particular events or moments in the history of an organization, spoken from individual experiences, each spoken from a different perspective, in a different voice. For example, when a founder is leaving, gathering his or her stories along with those who played roles in the early formation of the organization can illuminate the early energy, direction, and values of the founder. Another might be the stories of team leaders at the time of an important process change and how each experienced it. Where one team leader remembered capitalizing on one new feature of the process change, another might talk about the time when the new system led to confusion. Each story adds to the overall lessons and intelligence to be learned from the change. Yet another example might be the stories from a cross-section of staff about a time when the organization moved to its new headquarters building. The story from the economist is different from that of the auditor and from that of the sales force. Together, it gives a more nuanced picture of the move than a list of names into spaces with x number of boxes.

Before we talk about how these collections of stories might be used, a few words about gathering the stories are useful. Key to oral histories is that they remain personal. The teller should be telling the story from her or his perspective, using the first person pronouns, I and me and never 'they' for example. Creating an inviting and safe place to tell the stories is essential. A great deal of thought and attention must be given to the interviewing team, where the interview takes place, and how the interview is conducted. The team should be small and except for the interviewer, should be out of sight to the teller. The location should be one that is familiar to the teller or at least one that has familiar aspects to put them at ease. The interview itself should be guided by the desire to help the teller to move beyond the 'normal' stories he or she has told in the past and is reminded of stories they have not told before. The challenge is to prompt the teller's memory without being intrusive. At the same time, the interviewer looks for stories that present value (perhaps through a challenge to norms) to the overall objectives of the oral history project.

The overall objectives of the organization are to guide the selection of those who tell their stories. Broader perspectives are usually considered better, but the purpose may demand depth and, thus, call for a more narrowly defined group of tellers. Likewise, how the narrative is presented is an important, early decision. Should it be in the form of knowledge nuggets in a data asset database? Is it summary input into strategic planning? Is it a standard handout at every organization orientation session accompanied with a digital story of the organization, or something else? All of these points should be considered from the start of the project so that stories are gathered appropriately and efficiently. Lastly, oral histories must be approached with the time, patience, and care alluded to in this section. It is a serious undertaking. It is more than a series of interviews, and it offers a different set of results and benefits.

The next challenge begins once the stories are gathered. Within the stories are threads that must be found, examined, and understood without unravelling the braid of the narrative – the collection of stories. This means that the stories may be broken into smaller pieces and tagged for speaker, time, subject matter, place, and any number of pre-selected key words. Done electronically, it is possible to examine the items from many voices yet preserve the stories as a whole. Thus, listening again to the items from the various stories, the threads that are distinguished can be seen. Yet the stories can still be reassembled.

In some cases, these little snippets of stories are used to demonstrate underlying norms within an organization. For example, a project team addressing a related issue might not have heard the stories. (That said care and attention must be paid to the agreement on confidentiality given to the tellers.)

Understanding these threads gives insight to braiding new forms that allow new capabilities in the future. Participants in oral history projects are never the same after such an experience. The structure of the stories told and how they weave into the narrative leave lasting impressions. As participants listen to new stories, they are already seeing the weaves and turnings. Just being a part of such a storytelling exercise builds narrative intelligence.

The Dynamic Narrative

Just as oral history examines and creates a broader understanding of the essence of the organization, networking through social media can create an environment where broader and deeper sense-making is created dynamically and continuously. Social media is a force for sharing ideas, shifting perceptions, breaking down barriers, and transforming the group, the organization and the world. Tech book publisher Tim O'Reilly coined the term Web 2.0 in 2003. In the process, he provided a name for the thread that connects many different ways people are now communicating such as blogs, wikis, social networking, bookmarking and mashups. Web 2.0 refers to social software that enables people to interact and share knowledge. This social software provides over 1,000 platforms that now exist for communication activities such as sharing stories. In the past, Web 1.0 represented the static websites or brochure-ware of the 20th Century. Now, the

Narrative Intelligence Perpetuates the Learning Organization

interactivity of Web 2.0 provides the opportunity for two-way conversation and a method by which people can add their own thoughts directly to what someone else has shared. This ability to collaborate changes what used to be a one-to-one or a one-to-many information flow into a many-to-many information flow. These collaboration activities have spurred the growth of businesses to support the growing needs of people to share and communicate. They include such social networking platforms as MySpace, Second Life, and Facebook, as well as standalone services such as Blogger, Wikipedia, Blog lines, Google Maps, Digg, and Yahoo! Pipes.

As seen with activities in the Middle East referred to as the 'Arab Spring' where social media played a major role, the need for people to share and communicate is what has made Web 2.0 so popular for consumers. The need for people to connect goes way beyond teenagers chatting online. When organizations understand the connection between the need for people to share stories and the amazing tools that are now available to facilitate that interaction, we start to get to the core of how to facilitate narrative intelligence. These tools can help flatten the organization and push authority down through the organization to empower the workforce, and dissolve the barriers between disparate networks.

With the ever increasing message to noise ratio getting out of hand, leaders need to find a way to communicate strategy and tactical execution guides in order for people on the front lines to make the right decisions. Decisions can no longer be made from the top. The world is global and moving fast. The chain of command decision making is a thing of the past for day- to- day work interactions. Otherwise, realizing the goal of being a learning organization is in jeopardy of not being achieved because flexibility, agility and quick decision making are critical components. Leveraging narrative intelligence through these new tools is only possible for organizations that are focused on the cultural change that must complement the adoption of social media technology as part of the new way of working. This implies a strategy that understands the road to shift human behavior is a long, consistent path. Only then can we realize the benefits of the interactive Web.

Web 2.0 has been in existence for more than five years and has changed how people interact with a startling growth of popularity never seen before. For example the adoption of the telephone from its invention in the 1870s only became widely used in the US in the 1940s. By contrast in December 2007, MySpace and Facebook were ranked fifth and ninth, respectively, in audience share among the top 20 Web sites in the US, according to Hitwise. Neither service existed six years before. MySpace began service in late 2003, and Facebook, in early 2004. By January 2008, hundreds of millions of people worldwide had joined the current generation of social networking sites*(PricewaterhouseCoopers Technology Forecast Fall 2010, www.pwc.com):

- MySpace led the rest, with more than 200 million users.
- Chinese site 51.com had more than 90 million.
- Facebook reached 63 million.
- Bebo, popular in the UK, claimed 40 million.*

Given these numbers, the current generation of Web 2.0 services is a communications phenomenon with implications beyond the online communities that preceded them and identifies a clear human need that organizations need to seek to understand and leverage.

If people make sense of the world by assimilating it to narrative, then it makes sense to design our organizations and tools to enable people to use their well-honed narrative skills in interpreting business problems, making decisions and doing work. For example, Don (Don 1990) borrows concepts from the oral storytelling tradition to organize the interface for a multimedia knowledgebase.

As previously discussed in this section, information overload is a primary concern in organizations today (Blair 2010). A component of this is document management and the need to access documents to support specific conversations or work. The research conducted by Don focused on three properties of oral storytelling that she believed can guide interface design of knowledge bases that could be tapped during conversation:

- The first property she examined is the trait that storytellers adapt the story to the reactions of the audience. In this case, as individuals react to documents or individuals, they can grade or rank them. (For example Amazon has used this technology remarkably well for products and is seen as a pioneer in this area.) Obviously specific guidelines and change management activities would need to be developed in order for people to understand what and why they were ranking people and knowledge assets.
- The second property is the use of information such as names and lists that are embedded within the storyline such that the audience experiences this information as events are unfolding in time. This connects to the use of keywords or search where individuals have the ability to connect the right documents or artifacts together to get to the right information and then use it to deepen the discussion.
- Finally the third property, Don points out that characters with predictable traits are used to prime expectations as part of the oral story. In the organization the need for robust person profiles and the need to identify, connect and engage these specific individuals in order to have the right conversation with the right people in the organization are critical.

So the sharing of stories and knowledge has to be with the narrative context of the right content, the right people and enable the ability to use social media tools to share with the larger organization the value of those documents, conversations or people to the specific topic.

Ethics of the Use of Story

By now, you, as the reader, are beginning to feel the ever-present and ever powerful use of story and narrative in our work – in our lives. We have talked about using story in specific business situations, as an effective learning tool, as a way to understand the organization as a whole – either statically or dynamically. If this is true, you are beginning to acquire the competency of narrative intelligence. As a person using narrative intelligence, you are called to an ethical standard that begins from a position of respect for the story itself and for the teller of the story. Once the power of story is recognized within the organizational setting, there is the temptation to use stories with only the business goal in mind. This section looks at the ethics of how stories should be treated in any setting, including organizational.

> - Ground rules for story circles.
> - Tell your story in the first person. The story must be true for you.
> - When someone is telling his or her story, listen. Do not interrupt the teller during the telling.
> - At the completion of the story, offer an appreciation for the story. Avoid telling them the story that came to your mind as a result of their story.
> - Agree to not share the stories of others unless they give you express permission to do so.

The principle force behind the ethics stems from the reality that when a person shares a personal story, they are sharing a part of themselves. Thus, the story is as important as the teller. It be-

Narrative Intelligence Perpetuates the Learning Organization

longs to the teller[1]. Given freely, the story is easily taken on by others and retold. In some cultures, it is anathema to do so unless you have been given permission to tell the story – and usually with reference to the person to whom the story belongs. In organizational settings, telling the stories of others is not frowned upon. Yet, narrative intelligence calls us to recognize that a story belongs to the original teller. Even after permission is granted to tell the person's story, it is important to identify the owner when it is told. Even in the sometimes chaotic environment of social media, stories have an owner.

Another more subtle aspect of ownership is to be prepared to assure that a representative is present when the story is related. Let us explain what we mean. Let's assume that the organizational change being sought is to make the knowledge assets of the organization available to employees who are blind. Telling the story of a blind person's delight in being able to hear or read the information is best told by someone who is blind. At the very least, let the owner or an appropriate representative of the story be present.

Narrative intelligence calls us to recognize who owns the story. But even before the story is told, it is incumbent on you to declare how you wish to use the story that you are asking for. Is it for a marketing campaign? Is it to help build a team? Is it to spot common threads for lessons learned? The teller should be aware of why you are asking for the story.

No one should be forced to tell his or her story. It should be an active and informed decision on the part of the teller. This becomes less obvious when the person feels obliged to tell the story because there is an imbalance of power between the re-

---

[1]There are ownership issues even around created stories that become the professional possession of the writer, for example, for stage storytellers or fiction writers. This segment is not about this aspect of story ownership

quester and the teller. Make it explicit that the story is their choice to share, and nothing untoward happens if they decide not to share. Also, if there is any danger in their telling their story, it is the requester's responsibility to alert the teller of this and protect them, if necessary. In the dynamic world of social media, it remains important to remind tellers of their rights and 'listeners' of their responsibilities. From a recent talk given by Thaler Pekar presented on Worldwide Story Work, December 8, 2010, on the subject of the Ethics of Narrative in the arena of social media where individuals tell their stories to an unknown audience, the responsibilities of the listener or reader of the stories of others remain. Ignorance of these responsibilities is particularly challenging in this arena.

Once informed permission is given, the teller has an appreciative environment in which to tell the story. In face-to-face telling, there should be at least one person actively listening to the story during the telling. This is a sign of respect for the teller and the story. A more powerful way to offer such an environment is in story circles of 3 to 5 people where each person shares their story with the others. It provides the listening environment and allows the story to become known to the community as well. It requires some ground rules for the participants.

In the organization setting, it is important to think of the stories that are not being told. The person using narrative intelligence must think about who is 'in the room' and who should be. If you are trying to understand what makes a good project successful, are you hearing stories from the projects that were not as successful? If you are trying to introduce change in the organization, are you hearing the stories from the assistant staff as well as the senior staff? Are you hearing stories from the technical staff? Are you hearing stories from the janitorial staff? No one has the full story. More voices are important to get closer to the full story. When designing story collection processes, be certain that all the voices you need have the invitation and opportunity to share their stories. Recognize that everyone is in some way in another's story. Narrative intelligence demands that you recognize that you exist in the stories of others and be conscious of this as you explore the threads of the other stories. Our own assumptions and our own part in the stories can blind us to the most important threads. Begin by being aware that you are a part of the other stories.

When given permission to use the stories, there remain further obligations in deciding how the stories are shared. Care is taken to not prescribe the context of the story by saying, for example, the following stories are from women. That simple description can set off a series of assumptions on the part of the readers/listeners. This is especially important when the group that is tagged is disenfranchised in some way. Once the story is categorized, the context is changed and with it, the meaning that is derived. Help your audience to always hear/see/listen to the story with an open mind. Only then does the meaning have a chance to be at its fullest.

Narrative Intelligence is about sense- making at the broader level. Respecting the stories – the individual threads of the braid – are foundational. Applying ethics when gathering lessons learned through stories is essential and not onerous. The guidelines for gathering lessons learned through narrative are:

- Respect the story and the teller.
- Remember the story always belongs to the teller.
- Be clear about why and how you will use the stories.
- Seek to have all relevant voices heard and represented.
- Offer the opportunity to share the story without any strings for not doing so.
- Create an appreciative environment of active listening.
- Be aware of your own assumptions (to the best of your ability).
- Share the stories respectfully and without bias.

In exploring ethics and the use of any story that 'stories-over' or 'stories-out' the people that the story is most likely to effect, is narratively speaking, unethical and therefore as stated above - not innocent. As Paul Costello goes on to point out the voice of the person most effected, whose interests are most at stake, needs to be in the story of the decision (2008). It is also important to understand that we have to claim and win narrative authority over our lives from those who assume they know our story or who have the power to impose it on us. The narrative ethical position is always, "I must be able to tell the story in front of the people most likely to be affected by it."

Narrative Intelligence in the Learning Organization

You have been introduced to narrative intelligence and how it weaves throughout the learning organization – through formal and informal structures. It is important to recognize the link of this chapter to the concept introduced by Peter Senge 20 years ago of the learning organization (1990). As the 21st century knowledge workers struggle to provide value and be effective under 20th century managerial structures of the current work environment, the need to pursue the evolution to a post-modern learning organization is even more pressing.

Narrative intelligence promotes sense-making at all levels and informs the tacit understanding and knowledge for guiding action. A learning organization is the structure and ways of working that is at the heart of the ability of the individual, the organization, and society as a whole to process knowledge and maintain continuous learning. You can't grow, evolve, or respond to change without the ability to effectively learn – to be aware, to understand, to integrate new insights. Narrative intelligence offers an entry point to the source of integration and sense-making through the braid of stories that makes up the narrative network across the organization.

Narrative Intelligence Perpetuates the Learning Organization

With the ever increasing demands on our attention, leaders need to find a way to communicate strategy and tactical execution to effect decision making across the learning organization. People make sense of the world by assimilating it to narrative so it makes sense to design our communication strategies to enable the use of well-honed narrative skills in interpreting business problems to do work. The sharing of stories and knowledge has to be with the narrative context of the right content, the right people and enabling the ability to use social media tools to share with the larger organization the value of the leader's vision. Narrative Intelligence in the post-modern learning organization is about sense-making at the broadest level. Respecting the stories – the individual threads of the braid – but understanding and appreciating the weave of the narrative.

Conclusion

We explored the relationship between knowledge, learning and narrative intelligence. This linkage that represents the post-modern understanding of what sustains a vibrant organization has as its life blood the knowledge being shared and created by the people. Knowledge management as a discipline is about making information and knowledge accessible to staff to impact performance. KM is implemented through facilitating the conversations and connections between and among employees. Whether the conversation occurs within an organized community of practice or whether it occurs in informal, casual conversation between two people, the knowledge is most often communicated through a story. The structure of the stories told and how they weave into the narrative leave lasting impressions. As participants listen to new stories, they are already seeing the weaves and turnings. Just being a part of such a storytelling exercise builds narrative intelligence and the successful facilitation of these interactions represents a component of a successful knowledge management program. This chapter concludes with three exercises for practice and further learning to make narrative intelligence real to you.

Practical Exercises

Exercise 1 - Identify the three components of a story.

> *Step 1*: Think of a time when you were really feeling successful in your work.
>
> *Step 2*: Tell about this time in the form of a story (make sure that your story is no longer than 3 minutes.).
>
> *Step 3*: Tell the story to at least 3 other people (tell them that you are conducting an experiment, and ask if they could give you 10 minutes of their time).
>
> *Step 4*: Observe how your story changes as you tell it each time.
>
> *Step 5*: For each of the 3 people, jot down where in the story they gave you the impression that they were enjoying the story.
>
> *Step 6*: Now, look at the story and see if you can define the various elements of the setting, the point of tension, and the resolution.

Exercise 2 - Deciding whether oral history can add to organizational learning.

> *Step 1*: Ask 6 people, individually, to tell about a time when they felt they were learning something through their work.
>
> *Step 2*: Ask each of them individually to think about it for a while and then tell a specific story of that time.
>
> *Step 3:* Help them to locate their story by telling them one of your own.
>
> *Step 4*: Gather the seven stories, including your own,

Narrative Intelligence Perpetuates the Learning Organization

Step 5: Identify what threads are clearly woven through the seven stories.

Step 6: Ask yourself what more might you learn about how to create a learning organization if you were to employ some of the lessons from these threads.

(Note: A variation of this exercise would be to have the six individuals who shared their stories with you to join you or create another team to do this together and explore the lessons from all the stories of the team.)

Exercise 3 – Using story to understand a recognized issue in your organization.

Step 1: Inform your management that you would like to do an exercise from a book you are reading on KM which involves asking people for personal stories. Remember:
- to keep the results of your exercise to yourself
- to that any stories you hear are not to be shared beyond you and the teller
- to let management know you just want them to be aware as they may hear from folks who have told you their story
- if management asks what issue you are exploring, try to avoid identifying it
- to be clear that the exercise is too small to offer anything definitive for management purposes as your goal is simply to better understand the ethics of using narrative in the workplace

Step 2: Develop an approach for asking people to tell you a story that relates to the issue. This is the really hard part of this exercise. You need to develop a question that does not preclude the answers you will get. For example, if the issue is the new time system, you might ask them to tell you a story about how they have brought the new system into their work day. Thus, your question does not suggest that you think the new system is good or bad.

Step 3: Help them to locate their story by telling them one of your own --if people are having difficulty finding a story.

Step 4: Select a group of people, at least six, that represent the ones that have the best insight into the issue and invite them individually to tell you their stories. Be sure to tell them exactly why you are asking for these stories and what you plan to do with them.

Step 5: Listen to the stories and thank them for their participation in your learning.

Step 6: Think of a way in which you might have shared their stories had that been part of your intention.

Step 7: Think of the form that the story should take.

Step 8: Think of who should tell their own stories rather than you relating it for them.

Step 9: Think of what this might mean for a larger story collection project.

References

Don, Abbe. 1990. Narrative and the interface. In The Art of Human-Computer Interface Design. Ed. Brenda Laurel. Reading, MA: Addison-Wesley

Bettelheim, Bruno. 1989. The Uses of Enchantment: The Meaning and Importance of Fairy Tales. New York: Vintage Books.

Blair, David and Tom Meyer. 2002. Narrative Intelligence. In M. Mateas, & P. Sengers, Narrative Intelligence. Advances in Consciousness Research

Blair, Madelyn. 2010. Riding the Current: How to Deal with the Daily Deluge of Data. Chagrin Falls, OH: Taos Institute Publications

Brown, John Seely. 2003, pp. 02 01. Narrative and Knowledge Sharing. (S. Kahan, Interviewer

Costello, Paul 2008. The Presidential Post. Washington, DC: Storywise Publications

Cross, Robert. 2004. The Hidden Power of Social Networks: Understanding How Work Really Gets Done in Organizations. Cambridge: Harvard Business School Press

Denning, Steve. 2000. The Springboard: How Storytelling Ignites Action in Knowledge-Era Organizations. Boston: Butterworth Heinemann

Gruber, Peter. 2011. Tell to Win: Connect, Persuade, and Triumph with the Hidden Power of Story. New York: Crown Business

Haven, Kendell. 2007. Story Proof: The Science Behind the Startling Power of Story. Connecticut: Libraries Unlimited

Pekar, Thaler. (n.d.). Ethics of Narrative [Online]. Retrieved from http://thalerpekar.com [Accessed: March 1, 2012]

Senge, Peter. 1990. The Fifth Discipline: The Art & Practice of The Learning Organization. New York: Doubleday

Silverman, Lori et al. 2006. Wake Me Up When the Data is Over. New York: Jossey Bass

Simmons, Annette. 1997. Whoever Tells the Best Story Wins: How to Use Your Own Stories to Communicate with Power and Impact. New York: AMACOM

Taylor, Frederick, W. 2006. The Principles of Scientific Management, New York: Cosimo

Travers, Michael and Marc Davis. 2003. A Brief Overview of the Narrative Intelligence Reading Group. In M. Mateas, & P. Sengers, Narrative Intelligence (pp. 27-38). Amsterdam: John Benjamins Company

Optimize the Flow of Knowledge

John Hovell

HovellCreative LLC, Chantilly, VA, USA

Introduction

Organizations are collections of people. These people are gathered to serve a purpose. Once an organization grows larger than 150 people, it is exceedingly difficult for everyone to 'know everyone' within that organization. Normally at this point, smaller teams and organization charts begin to form and this tends to be the beginning of organizational silos. However, there are approaches to ensure that the organization is operating as a high performing team, regardless of its number of employees. These approaches are a blend of mindsets, processes and technology. This blended approach strives to continuously answer three questions:

- Who knows who?
- Who knows what?
- Who does what?

The goal of this chapter is to provide an approach to continuously answer the three above- listed questions. Having the ability to quickly and accurately answer these questions, positions the organization to optimize the flow of knowledge inside and outside of its boundaries. An organization that provides a framework to continuously answer these three questions and aligns them with their strategy is better prepared to experience a competitive advantage.

Who Knows Who?

In 1992, British anthropologist Robin Dunbar theorized that most people can only maintain 148 social relationships. This number is often rounded to 150 and known as Dunbar's number. Dunbar's number holds true in most cases. Groups such as the Roman armies or farming villages or nomadic tribes all follow Dunbar's number. Once these groups grow larger than 150 people, they tend to begin splitting into multiple groups (Dunbar 1993).

There are many organizations larger than 150 people. These organizations tend to create hierarchies and organizational charts, or a hierarchical arrangement of people. The organizational chart is a depiction of who reports to whom. It makes visible the organization's groups of its people. Hierarchies and organizational charts offer an understandable way for people to remain in groups of 150 people. These approaches tend to organize people based on function or project. Given these hierarchies and reporting structures, it is common for a culture of "managing up", "managing down" or "managing across" to begin (Hill et al. 2011). "Managing up" refers to a person's motivation to take direction from their supervisor. "Managing down" refers to a person's motivation to give direction to direct reports. "Managing across" refers to a person's motivation to give or take direction from their peers in other groups. "Managing across" is rare and, most often, the incentive and reward systems focuses on managing up and managing down more than managing across. Also, even with the most recent technology, there tends to be a time constraint, and often a culture and motivational issue, to manage across.

Despite their best efforts and intentions, it is difficult for managers to know all of the tasks and projects that are being addressed in the organization. Over time, managing up and down can lead to organizational bottlenecks and redundancies. However, work is being done and progress is occurring. Often, there are serendipitous conversations that help separate groups to realize that they are working on similar projects or that they could benefit from working together. These conversations happen between people that know each other, have worked together in the past or just happen to meet each other. Therein is an opportunity -- an opportunity to build a different kind of organizational chart. An organization can build an organization chart that depicts the people that have conversations with each other versus a chart that depicts who reports to whom.

This new type of organization chart gives the organization a different perspective of their organization. It would allow the organization to visually depict the people that talk to each other. This chart is known as a social network analysis (SNA) or an organizational network analysis (ONA). An ONA is a map of "who knows who" within an organization or even beyond the organizational boundaries (Cross & Thomas 2009).

The SNA and/or ONA give the organization an opportunity to see its flow of information and knowledge. It also provides insight into the "trust networks". Trust networks are groups of people that communicate on a frequent basis, they trust each other. It is very common for many trust networks to exist within an organization and it is very common for organizations to be unaware of their trust networks. Insight and visibility into these trust networks could provide untapped potential for organizational teamwork and learning.

Who Knows What?

Dave Snowden teaches us that "we know more than we say and we say more than we write". He is reminding us that we are experiencing a filter between what we think, what we speak and what we write. We have a lot more thoughts than we can say and we say a lot more than we can write. If we only rely on the written word, or even the spoken word, then we are missing the most abundant resource which is knowledge.

Most organizations do not experience the full benefit of the knowledge of their employees. Organizations tend to assign people to jobs or roles. After a person is assigned to a job or a role or a project, it is often overlooked by manager and co-workers that the person has much more knowledge than they need to complete their daily work. Often, the person focuses on their job or project and unintentionally withholds knowledge from the organization. Organizations have an opportunity to reach into this untapped potential of their employees' knowledge. Employees' knowledge is much broader than what they say or what they write. It is quite common for organizations to focus on assigning employees to jobs and tasks while overlooking the vast amount of knowledge that is available to them.

Optimize the Flow of Knowledge

The organizations that create cultures and processes that maximize the flow of knowledge have a competitive advantage over those organizations that focus too much on assigning employees to projects. Knowledge changes and continuously improves faster than information. Sharing conversations is one way to share knowledge as opposed to documenting thoughts and sending them to another person. Since most companies have employees that are working in different locations, this flow of knowledge is often enabled by tools and technology. Each employee will feel a different level of comfort or preference towards certain tools, so it is important to consider these preferences when developing an organizational approach to maximizing the flow of knowledge.

With the appropriate blend of a knowledge- sharing culture, processes and tools, an organization can become more aware of "who knows what." In an ideal situation, an organization would have the ability to quickly find the very best answers, decisions and approaches that they can deliver. This ability to rapidly solve problems and improve situations would continually improve over time as the employees become better and better at sharing knowledge and improving their results.

Who Does What?

During the Industrial era, our scarcest resources were land, labor and capital. It was difficult to find land, at a reasonable price, that met the requirements of an organization. It was also difficult to find people, at a reasonable price, which met the requirements of the organization. Borrowing money or earning cash was also extremely difficult.

Now we are in the Knowledge era. In the Knowledge era, the scarcest resources are no longer land, labor and capital; the scarcest resources are time and attention. The most effective organizations will increase focus on how their employees spend their time and attention.

All employees have tasks. In most organizations, there is tremendous overlap between the tasks being accomplished by disparate employees. Organizations have an opportunity to increase the focus and awareness on how employees spend their time and attention. If employees knew what other employees were working on, then there would be an increased opportunity for partnering and sharing critical knowledge. As it stands today, most employees are unaware of similar tasks or who to ask for help as they work on their projects. At a macro level, this lack of awareness results in inefficient operations and repetitive time spent solving business problems. Inefficient operations and repetitive time has a direct cost to the organization.

The organizations that best align their knowledge with their customer needs have a tremendous competitive advantage over those organizations that do not have this alignment. It is critical for an organization to know "what does what" within their organization so that problems and projects are not repeated over time.

The Approach to Answer the Three Questions

There are at least three approaches that can help us continuously answer the three key questions of who knows who, who knows what and who does what. Those three approaches are:

- Employee Profiles
- Knowledge Markets
- Talent Markets
- Employee Profiles

Most organizations maintain at least local phone lists, if not enterprise-wide phone lists. Many organizations have employee profiles. Some organizations expand the standard phone list data from name, location, phone number to reporting relationships and job title. However, very few organizations further expand the employee profile to include current projects, past projects, past companies, hobbies, interests, personality type, passions, skills, trusted colleagues, and knowledge.

Expanding the employee profile and making it online and searchable can offer extensive benefits to an organization. First, it gives employees an opportunity to quickly and easily find other employees that can help them with their tasks. Second, it gives groups an opportunity to partner on shared business objectives. Third, it gives the organization the opportunity to begin to optimize the flow of knowledge.

Optimize the Flow of Knowledge

There are challenges in gathering and maintaining this expanded employee profile data. One option is for the profiles to automatically update based on employees' emails, documents, and online activity. However, this option does present certain privacy and security issues. The automation of this employee profile data can often be intimidating to employees because it can give them the perception that someone is watching them.

A second option is to allow employees to manually maintain their employee profiles. However, this option often results in minimal data and updates because it is usually placed at a low priority for most employees.

A third option is to allow all employees to manually maintain their profiles as well as other employee's profiles. However, this option often results in similar challenges identified in both option one and two above.

Each organization is different when it comes to employee profiles, but there should be an acceptable balance of manual and automatic profile input and maintenance. Opening this data and information to all employees has business impact and can help organizations answer all three key questions.

Knowledge Markets

Knowledge markets are rarely implemented in organizations. In fact, knowledge markets are rarely even discussed or documented in knowledge management literature. The concept is that a market is created to optimize the supply and demand of knowledge. The idea is that someone somewhere has a need, or a demand, for knowledge and someone somewhere has the corollary supply of knowledge. The market provides a mechanism to reach equilibrium for the supply and demand of knowledge.

The demand side of the knowledge market usually comes in the form of a question. The supply side of the knowledge market comes in many different forms. One example of the supply side is a text based response. Other examples include pictures, photographs, videos, face-to- face conversations, virtual conversations and many other avenues of communication.

Talent Markets

Talent markets are similar to knowledge markets in that they provide a marketplace for finding equilibrium for the supply and demand of talent. It is common for organizations to have internal job boards, but it is exceptionally uncommon for organizations to have true talent markets. The internal job board lists available jobs, but there is usually quite a bit of related politics and perception that goes along with applying for internal jobs.

The supply side of the talent market is not only jobs, but projects and tasks. The supply side of the talent market provides insight into 'who's doing what' and what needs to be done. It gives employees an opportunity to not only apply for jobs, but increase awareness of exactly what is being accomplished across the organization.

The demand side of the talent market is employees and their interests, passions, experiences and knowledge. The demand side of the talent market gives employees an opportunity to see what knowledge exists in the organization.

The talent market can automatically match people to tasks and tasks to people. When a job, project or task is posted, the talent market can automatically search the profiles and supply side of the market to recommend best matches. From the supply perspective, when an employee updates their profile, it can recommend related knowledge, jobs, tasks or projects that might further engage the employee.

Employee profiles, knowledge markets and talent markets provide an opportunity for organizations to begin to optimize their flow of knowledge. It is the combination of these approaches that begins to deliver the most noticeable business impact. The combination of these approaches helps to foster a culture of awareness, collaboration and knowledge sharing.

Technology to Enable the Three Approaches

Tools and technology are required to implement employee profiles, knowledge markets and talent markets. It is important to keep in mind that technology enables processes. Technology by itself is not a process or a solution. It is common for organizations to place their emphasis and focus on technology. However, in most cases, when an organization focuses on technology, the business process becomes ambiguous and people are less likely to use the tool.

Technology and Employee Profiles

Most, if not all technologies, provide the capability to establish employee profiles. Many organizations have profiles on their intranet, within their human resources tool, their help desk or support tool, their email system and many other business tools. A profile can be as simple as a username and password. The first challenge of an employee profile system is to integrate all these distinct profiles. There are at least three strategies for solving this integration problem: centralized, decentralized and federated:

- The Centralized Model is a single employee profile where all other profiles would pull data directly from the single profile system. The challenge to the centralized approach comes from the difficulty of modifying and maintaining tools to receive data through an interface to a central source.
- The Decentralized Model allows all profile systems to maintain their own, separate profiles systems. The challenge with this approach is that with multiple systems, there is duplicated data and the systems need to be synchronized to ensure the integrity of data in all systems.
- The Federated Model comes from a database perspective. In the federated model, a central database is created to maintain all employee profile data. The central database does not contain duplicate data. It only stores each data field one time, similar to the centralized approach. Similar to the decentralized approach, the federated model allows each tool to have its own profile, but the data is pushed and pulled to and from the main database. The

federated approach allows organizations to blend all of the profiles together and make them available from a single location. It also allows the organization to create new fields that may not be stored in any profile in any system. For example, most systems do not store hobbies, interests, passions, previous companies worked for, projects currently working on, knowledge, skills, abilities, personality assessments, etc. When companies store all of this information in a federated employee profile system and then allow the data to be tagged and indexed, it can have a profound impact on the business. The problem with the federated model is that it can be difficult to get data in and out of disparate systems.

Technology and Knowledge Markets

Knowledge markets are "question and answer" sites and prediction market software. Question and answer site examples include experts-exchange, Google answers, Yahoo answers and Innocentive. The goal of these sites is typically to find a bartered equilibrium between the supply and demand of questions and answers. In other words, people can ask questions and other people can answer questions. There is usually a fee or cost of some sort to ask or answer questions. The problem for these sites is that the entire Internet is a less-direct-cost mechanism for asking and answering questions. The positive perspective is that sometimes it is easier and faster to obtain abstract or difficult answers.

Prediction markets provide an opportunity for people to spend real or virtual money on answers to questions. If you buy an answer and it turns out correct, then you earn more money. If you buy an answer and it turns out incorrect, then you lose that money. Prediction markets have been found to be very accurate in answering future-based questions due to the wisdom of crowds.

Knowledge markets generally take on a blended form. What appears to be the best approach is to have a single, centralized starting point for the market. The starting point then points to many different approaches depending upon the preference and requirements of the user. The starting point could offer a simple enterprise search and/or a question and answer site. Inside an organization the question and answer site does not ask for real money as an exchange, although it could ask for virtual money. Another form that is better than money is to barter or exchange, such items as badges or points, preferably on the integrated employee profile. The starting point could also offer prediction markets. Yet another option could be simple phone lists or points of contact.

The concept of the knowledge market could be applied through a blend of numerous technologies. As employees begin to find benefit from asking and answering their colleagues throughout the organization, the use of the system could grow.

Technology and Talent Markets

Talent markets are our hiring, recruiting and staffing systems. Often these systems have mastered the capability of posting and finding jobs. Rarely have these systems mastered the posting and finding of tasks, skills, competencies or knowledge. Hiring managers and recruiters often have an easy time posting a job, but then a much more difficult job finding great candidates. This is partially due to the availability and existence of great candidates as jobs change quickly. Moreover, this is due to the void of employee profile data that might allow the system to automatically match people to jobs and jobs to people.

A talent market system maintains the job posting aspects of current staffing systems. It adds a feature of integration with the employee profile. Jobs could be posted and the system could automatically find and recommend jobs to specific people. From the user perspective, the talent market allows the user to update their profile and then automatically recommend jobs for them based on their updated profile. This integration increases engagement and utilization of both the employee profile and talent systems.

Beyond the job level, a talent market also dives into the task, project or knowledge level. At the knowledge level, a talent market is similar or identical to a knowledge market. At the task or project level, a talent market could be used to find and setup short-term goals. These short- term assignments would result in a more agile, efficient and effective organization. In most organizations today, a manager becomes aware of a task and assigns it to one of their direct reports. Imagine if tasks and projects were crowdsourced and accomplished by not only the best fit person in the organization, but possibly the best-fit person in the world.

Other Factors to Consider When Optimizing the Flow of Knowledge

There are many factors to consider when an organization begins the journey to optimize the flow of its knowledge. Along with the aforementioned questions and answers, there are additional critical factors to consider such as expertise location, culture, leadership, mindset and organizational behavior. These factors work together in what we call a learning organization. It is these learning organizations that enjoy the sustainability and viability of a long- term successful enterprise.

Expertise Location

Expertise location is a complex problem that requires complex management. It can be approached differently by each organization. An expertise location system could consist of employee profiles, enterprise search, tagging and searching as well as online collaboration tools, or it could be as simple as lists of points of contact for high level knowledge domains of the organization. And, yet, another part of an expertise location system could be enterprise-wide communities of practice.

Expertise location systems have multiple facets and multiple entry points. Each person looks for expertise in a different way and it is important to have multiple paths to better accommodate each person's approach to finding knowledge. The business is more effective and efficient when its staff can find the knowledge they need on-demand, in the moment and context that it is needed.

The Culture, Leadership and Organization

As we know, every person is different and every organization is different. While we are all different, there is value is discussing some of the similarities. There is also value in discussing the differences. All organizations have a culture which can be defined as a set of expectations, norms and acceptable behaviors. When organizations talk about changing their culture, they are normally referring to changing these expectations, norms and acceptable behaviors. Implementing employee profiles, knowledge markets and talent markets introduces change in the workplace, which is residence of the organization's culture.

Mindset

There are many misconceptions about knowledge. For example, knowledge is power. Loose lips sink ships. Loose tweets sink fleets. If I share what I know, then I am less powerful because others then know everything that I know. I don't have time to share. I don't think others will share critical knowledge with me. Now is the time to address these misconceptions. A mindset to consider is knowledge shared is knowledge squared. When people share their knowledge, everyone involved has the opportunity to learn, grow and improve. Shifting the traditional mindset of knowledge is power is a fundamental and critical change to that needs to happen.

Lead by Example

Given that most of our organizations follow a traditional hierarchy, one of the best ways to begin shifting cultures and mindsets is for leaders to lead by example. Leaders can learn, discuss and practice collaborative behaviors. Leaders leverage technology for information sharing, setup communities of practice or knowledge transfer processes and are active participants in them. Even in traditional hierarchies, in this context, all employees can be considered leaders. All employees can practice knowledge sharing and collaborative behaviors.

Organizational Behavior, Dynamics and Structure

On a broader scale, there are organizational behaviors, dynamics and structure to consider. Organizational behaviors are the specific actions taken by employees in the context of their organization. It is these behaviors, along with values, expectations and norms, that come together to form the perception of an organization's culture. Organizational dynamics are the changes or the conversations and decisions that are made on a daily basis. These dynamics affect the organizational behavior and the culture. Organizational structure is the approach that an organization uses to conduct task allocation, coordination and supervision.

Most organizations have grown comfortable with hierarchical structures or matrix structures. Hierarchical structures offer a simple approach for all employees to report to a single manager. The matrix structure offers a way for employees to be organized by tasks and projects. Although there are advantages and disadvantages for all organizational structures, it is important to note that new organizational structures are becoming available. These new structures offer more non-linear approaches. They are mostly unproven techniques, so it is our responsibility to consider them wisely.

One example of a new organizational structure is known as a "wirearchy". This new approach is a dynamic two-way flow of power and authority. This two-way flow of power and authority is based on knowledge, trust, credibility and a focus on results. This approach is enabled by interconnected people and technology. The concept is that roles and responsibilities should emerge and change as quickly as they arise. Leadership is intended to be emergent in this approach and strong teamwork is critical to its success.

There are other organizational structures to consider as well. The point here is to always have an open aperture to new ways of organizing. It is time to check our assumptions with regard to our culture, our mindset, our behaviors and our organizational structures. If we're looking to gain a new competitive edge in a chaotic and quickly changing environment, these concepts of agility, openness and transparency are critical to success.

Case Studies – Optimizing the Flow of Knowledge in Organizations

Companies in the Aerospace and Defense industry practice knowledge management (KM). They practice KM for the benefit of their internal employees as well as their external customers. Their primary customers are the Department of Defense and other federal government agencies. These federal agencies request KM in several ways. Some customers and programs specifically ask for KM, while other customers and programs request KM approaches, techniques and tools without directly calling them "knowledge management" requirements.

The KM Journey of a Mid-Size Government Contractor Organization

A mid-size government contractor began an enterprise-wide knowledge management journey in 2006. Up until 2006, there had been pockets of KM related efforts throughout the less-than-10,000 employee company, but zero of those efforts had been known as a knowledge management effort.

A new Chief Operating Officer (COO) was promoted from within the company. He formed a corporate university and created the first Chief Learning Officer (CLO) position in the company. Once the CLO position was filled, the new CLO started his job by focusing on formalizing a learning organization. His vision is to increase productivity and efficiency and save the company money.

The CLO's initial project is the implementation of a Learning Management System (LMS). The LMS serves as the central repository and system of record for all formal learning within the organization. In the CLO's search for team members for the LMS project, he found and hired several employees who were passionate about knowledge management and the importance of informal learning. Informal learning is the type of learning that an employee defines, opposed to formal learning that the organization defines. An example of informal learning is talking to your mentor or colleague about solving a business problem. An example of formal learning is attending a course in a classroom or completing an online web-based training program.

These new project members were offered the opportunity to create strategies for informal learning. This opportunity resulted in one of the project team members creating an Enterprise KM strategy. This KM strategy is a simple one-page proposition that explains three critical problems within the organization. These three critical problems are:

- Knowledge is too critical of an asset to not be managed.
- Decisions are made and executed on a suboptimal level.
- Mistakes and inefficiencies are resulting in avoidable costs.

Senior executives of most companies often say "our people are our greatest asset." This is true as companies and organizations could not exist without people. It is far too common for organizations to overlook the importance of the knowledge of their employees and this was the case within this organization. This organization was divided into three lines of business and each line of business had their own senior leadership. The lines of business were defined by their products and services versus their customers or internal employee skill sets. Employees of this organization were often retirees from the organization's customer. Thus, some of the employees had intimate knowledge of the customer because they had previously worked for the customer. Unfortunately, it is common for the organization to solicit and win business without understanding their employees who had customer knowledge, experience and a past relationship.

In the organization, decisions are made by small, local teams under the assumption that it is the best way to make decisions. Within the organization, decisions are being made and executed on a suboptimal level. Dr. K. Anders Ericsson is a Swedish psychologist and his research explains that it takes approximately 10,000 hours of experience to become an expert. An expert has the ability to make better judgment and better decisions on a particular topic than someone without the 10,000 hours of experience. In the case where there are limited choices available, then the expert would make the same decision as a non-expert, but the expert would make that same decision faster than the non-expert. Either way, the expert provides business value in terms of improved decisions and time savings. It is exceedingly rare for decision makers to search for experts and their expertise for improved decisions. In fact, there were very few processes, procedures and tools for finding these experts inside or outside the organization.

Optimize the Flow of Knowledge

Mistakes and inefficiencies result in avoidable costs in this organization. While it is important to realize that mistakes do happen and sometimes efficiency is the only lever to consider, it is a competitive disadvantage to repeat mistakes and inefficient results that drive unnecessary costs to the business. For example, this organization invested in external training courses. The decision to purchase the training courses is made by each business area. Each made a decision to purchase their courses from the vendor they determined to be the best available vendor. As it turns out, each business area purchased their courses from the same vendor. If the organization had taken a centralized approach, more than likely, the organization could have negotiated with the vendor to get a better price due to number of courses purchased, as well as identified duplicate courses. There is a good possibility that the organization would have experienced significant savings on the purchase of the courses. This kind of decentralized decision making is common in organizations and can often lead to costly mistakes and inefficiencies.

The COO and CEO presented the three key points, resulting in the senior leaders agreeing that there is business value in creating the Director of Knowledge Management position. The goal and objectives of Director of Knowledge Management is directly related to improving the three key points.

The Director of Knowledge Management begins by developing a strategy to optimize the flow of knowledge across the enterprise. Across the organization, several strategy sessions are held and several group discussions are conducted. A decision is made to start the initial solution framework with three core elements:

- An Enterprise Wiki
- A Leadership Development Program
- Enterprise Communities of Practice (CoP)

The Enterprise Wiki is available to all internal employees and they have the opportunity to create simple WebPages to share their knowledge. Hundreds of pages are created in a short period of time and immediate business impact is experienced. The organization is successful in implementing a new enterprise-wide web application.

As an example, the Enterprise Wiki was used to help provide clarity on a different enterprise-wide web application. There was confusion regarding the roles within the tool because the system administrator used one set of role definitions, while the training materials and screens in the tool used different sets of role names and definitions. The Enterprise Wiki was a simple webpage that lists all three sets of role names and definitions. The page that contained an explanation of the role names and definitions resulted in instant clarity of those role names and definitions. After broadly communicating the ability to provide clarity like this, the wiki had increased usage and business value.

A leadership development program is initiated to address the discovery that managers and leaders across the business have been "thrown into" leadership positions without proper training and understanding of their new roles and responsibilities. The leadership development program offers an opportunity to build cohorts and the capability to share talent and knowledge across the enterprise. The leadership development program begins with an expertise location system to provide these cohorts of new leaders ways to connect their networks and create avenues for knowing and finding each other.

Enterprise communities of practice also begin with the implementation of an expertise location system. Based on the enterprise strategic plan, a dozen community topics were chosen. As advocated by Etienne Wenger, each community is a volunteer-based group where employees with shared passions could share practices and hold conversations about their passions. For example, the Enterprise Knowledge Management Community of Practice had monthly phone calls as well as conducting online conversations. The community grew from two initial participants to over 50 participants in just a few months. The group had discussions about the enterprise knowledge strategy and these discussions led to continuous improvement of the plan and an improved capability for the organization to quickly find its experts on the topic of knowledge management.

Optimize the Flow of Knowledge

The enterprise knowledge strategy of this midsize government contractor facilitated a positive business impact for the organization. This initiative has positioned this organization to make better and faster decisions. The organization experiences fewer mistakes as experts and leaders are more readily available across the enterprise. Increased business and decreased cost are the results of these improvements within this organization.

A Large Government Contractor Organization Practicing KM

A key strategic hire is made early in the 21st century and this person triples the revenue in a particular line of business in less than three years. A large government contractor starts practicing knowledge management, where enterprise communities of practice and a culture of increased openness and transparency are among the triggers to triple the organization's business.

Given the success of knowledge management in the one business area, additional knowledge management hires are made throughout the organization. The large size of this organization made it easy for "pockets" of expertise and approaches to exist with little knowledge or understanding of them. Knowledge management begins to grow throughout the organization without it being overly aware of its growth and impact.

Another early KM success in this organization is an annual event focused on "improving collaboration across the enterprise." This annual event brought people that shared a passion for KM to gather and engage in discussions on KM. A similar annual event also provided an opportunity for all employees to gather and discuss a broad range of passions. Although technology has come a long way over the years, there still does not seem to be a technology that can replicate the speed of knowledge flow that occurs at face- to- face events.

Over time, at this large organization, several functions led to the creation of full-time knowledge management positions. The Information Technology group created a position focused on the technologies that support knowledge management. The Human Resources (HR) group created a knowledge management position that focused on the learning aspect of KM. The Communications group created a position that focused on the two-way flow of knowledge. Also, several programs created positions that focused on mission-specific aspects of knowledge management to support customer requirements. In just a few years, there were numerous knowledge management approaches being leveraged within the organization. Each of these approaches is valuable in their own right, no one overarching strategy for these efforts surfaced.

Human Resources (HR) function has an HR strategy, which was used by KM professionals to create the format and structure of an enterprise knowledge strategy. The structure respectfully included "key platforms", "key initiatives", "key projects", and "measurement and metrics". The key platforms align with the stages of the knowledge lifecycle: knowledge creation, knowledge transfer, knowledge sharing and knowledge application. Many of the knowledge management approaches were listed under the key initiatives in alignment with their overarching key platform. For example, enterprise communities of practice were listed under the key platform of knowledge sharing.

Each of the approaches is best described in the categories: people, process and tools. People are the behaviors, culture, expectations and norms that an organization demonstrates. Processes are the formal and informal approaches to execute the expected behaviors. Tools enable the people and the process to conduct business. These approaches are described as follows:

- Peer Assists - Peer assists are a knowledge management technique that is used to elicit feedback from specific experts or a group of peers on a problem, project, or activity, and to collect lessons from the participants' knowledge and experience. Similar to face-to-face events, peer assists offer a powerful way to move forward as efficiently and effectively as possible through the re-use of expertise.
- Enterprise Wiki - Enterprise wikis are approaches used to gather the wisdom of crowds. As experienced in Wikipedia.com, enterprise wikis provides the capability for individuals to edit simple WebPages and further define a word, topic or concept. In a large

organization, this reaches a critical mass as many people create pages and edit others' pages. Each company creates its own set of acronyms and project names and enterprise wikis are an excellent approach to document their acronyms and project names. The enterprise wiki helps employees to know when acronyms have multiple meanings thereby improving clarity and understanding when employees work together.

- Collaboration Behaviors - The concept of collaboration has different definitions and expected behaviors. To improve clarity and understanding of collaboration, there were several KM initiatives. One initiative is a board game with the purpose of explaining and clarifying the meaning of collaboration. Another initiative is an online 'wizard' that helps employees to know where they can begin their collaboration journey based on the type of collaboration they are seeking.
- Talent Management - Talent management is the process of putting the "right people in the right jobs at the right time." Talent management is full of KM opportunities. In this organization, a process for sharing knowledge was implemented to help people moving from job to job to prepare for their transition. There was a period of major transitions happening in the organization and the pre-defined knowledge- sharing process provided the organization the ability to quickly codify, transfer and apply knowledge that could have been lost, which has happened in some prior transitions that were external to the organization.
- Alumni Network - The organization established an alumni network for those who were transitioning out of the organization. This alumni network allows the organization to reach back to its retirees and alumni to brainstorm and engage in conversations where they were valuable and appropriate. This channel for communications is critical during a time of mass transition. The customer should not experience a decrease in quality because an organization goes through a major change.
- Mentoring - When in a period of change, a mentoring program is another valuable KM approach. Mentoring is traditionally viewed as a one-way communications approach for an expert to teach a

mentee. Typically, the mentor is older than the mentee and has more years of experience. In this organization, mentoring is viewed as a two-way communications approach for mentors to teach mentees and vice versa. More recently, mentoring has taken on a two-way flow of knowledge where everyone plays a role in learning from each other. In fact, this organization changed the construct from mentor and mentee to learner and advisor. These words were intended to imply that all employees are both learners and advisors.

- Discussion Threads - Discussion threads are generally email-based listservs that allow participants to communicate. Discussion threads may not be the newest approach, but they allow the participants to easily interact, which can result in a high usage. Discussion threads should meet the participant where they already are doing work, so it does not feel like additional work to the participant. This organization uses many discussion threads, especially along its critical line of business. Their experts in their critical line of business found it very easy to stay in touch and keep on top of the most recent advances in their field.
- External Tools - The organization informally uses an extensive set of external tools such as Facebook, Linkedin, Youtube, Wikipedia, Slideshare, Flickr and many other public websites. These external tools give the organization the ability to not only connect their employees to each other, but also connect their employees to other thought leaders in the world. Often times, the most insightful questions, observations or suggestions come from folks that do not see the problem every day and, therefore; bring a set of fresh ideas and approaches to the problem. Being open to the use of external tools provides a valuable resource to an organization and its continued success. This organization used external social media tools, purchased social media tools for internal use and designed their own social media tools. These tools provided employees the opportunity to choose their preferable approach. Several tools are available to employees and each has its own level of engagement and success. However, it appears that the newest tools tend to have the greatest usage and following. By

keeping in touch, using the newest tools, employees are aware of which tool is going to be available for use next. These tools resulted in many employees quickly finding each other and solving difficult business challenges in a timely manner.

- Business Processes - This organization had several specific KM business processes. Some KM processes were designed for knowledge creation; some were designed for knowledge sharing; while others were designed for knowledge transfer or knowledge application. In this organization, an example of a knowledge creation process is the idea management system. The idea management system is used to create and brainstorm new ideas to be considered for internal funding through the internal research and development program. An example of a knowledge application approach is the enterprise coaching program. Coaches are internally trained and certified in how employees solve their own problems by asking the most poignant questions.
- Storytelling - Storytelling is considered the secret language of leadership. As social beings, we are hardwired to listen and learn through stories. There are many great storytelling approaches on the market today. This organization follows the SUCCES model as described by the Heath brothers. Stories are crafted using the model, videotaped and shared online. Career discussions are also videotaped and shared in a similar fashion. There are communities of practice dedicated to storytelling. By telling better stories and consistently sharing stories, the organization is able to retain and engage employees as well as continually learn from mistakes and capture best practices.
- Expertise Location - Each person looks for an expert in a different way. Some people walk down the hall to ask their neighbor for help on a problem. Some people pick up the phone and call someone that might be able to help. Some people write emails or post questions online to try and find help. It has been documented that most of our time at work is spent looking for answers to our questions and our problems. Expertise location is a KM approach used to increase the effectiveness and efficiency of finding people that have the answers to questions needed in the

moment that they are asked. It is usually not enough to find documents and information about a problem, quite often a person needs specific context or adaptation to the situation. This context and adaptation is best found in conversation, dialog or expertise from another person. There are several ways to establish an expertise locator system. This organization uses these three approaches:

- White Pages - White pages are an online directory of all employees. Traditional white pages simply contain a person's name, email address and physical location. In this organization, the white pages system includes employee's interests, hobbies, passions, previous employers, names of projects/programs that they have worked on, biographical information, recent activity on the network and many other data points. In conglomeration, these data points help an employee find another employee that might be able to answer their question.
- Enterprise Search - An enterprise search tool further enables the ability to find expertise. This organization tied the white pages to the enterprise search tool. The enterprise search tool searched millions of documents across hundreds of sites. The enterprise search tool also searched the white pages. For example, if you searched for a specific computer programming language, the enterprise search tool would return documentation about that programming language, enterprise wiki pages for that programming language, as well as people that have that programming language listed in their white pages entry and other data points.
- Social Media Tools - Social media tools are web sites or web applications that enable people to find each other and communicate with each other. There are several approaches that these social media tools tend to leverage. One approach is the 'follow' method, where you can connect to other people and watch their content without their explicit permission. Another approach is the 'friend' method, where you can enter into relationships where both parties agree to share their content with each other. The final method is a blended method sometimes called 'circles' where you can join a group or create a group and the group ei-

ther publically or privately agrees to communicate with each other. This organization implemented a blend of all three approaches. There were separate tools for each approach which allowed employees with certain preferences to have tools available to meet their needs.

All of these KM approaches and examples are intended to optimize the flow of knowledge. A way to approach this complex situation is to create an architecture that continuously facilitates ways for all employees to be able to answer three questions: 1) "Who knows who?", 2) "Who knows what?", 3) "Who does what?", and a fourth question might be 'How do they do it?.'

Conclusion

Organizations in the 21st century have tremendous challenges to face. Not only is the global economy presenting a challenging environment, the shift from an Industrial era to a Knowledge era is yet another challenging environment. It seems as though everything is not only changing, but changing at an ever increasing rate. For the foreseeable future, those companies that can answer 'who knows who', 'who knows what' and 'who does what' will enjoy a competitive advantage over those organizations that cannot answer these questions.

One strategy for answering these questions is to consider how your organization can best approach these three specific challenges:

- Perfect Storm
- Connect the Dots
- Decision Advantage

The Perfect Storm refers to the first time that organizations have had four generations working at the same time. Not only are there generational differences and preferences, there is also a war for talent as very few "Gen X" employees exist. Connect the Dots refers to an organizations' ability to strategically know what all of its groups and employees are doing. An organization that connects the dots enjoys the benefits of very little overlap between groups' efforts. In addition to connecting the dots, organizations should also "focus on the noise" which refers to the ability to see how employees are creatively solving problems. The balance of connecting dots and noise will result in an agile and successful organization. Decision Advantage refers to an organization's ability to make the best decisions or the same decisions in a shorter period of time than its competitors.

The three key solutions to consider in this strategy are talent markets, knowledge markets, and employee profiles. Talent markets ensure that the right people are working on the right tasks and projects at the right time. This approach is much different from the traditional hierarchical approach. Knowledge markets ensure that the right people have the right knowledge at the right time. Knowledge markets are specifically designed to optimize the flow of knowledge. Employee profiles are a simple approach to ensuring that employees have the opportunity to find each other and connect for any purpose. Communities of practice, hierarchies, expertise location, and storytelling are further solutions to consider. An organization that understands these approaches, and implements them in the best fit and balance with their culture and strategy, will be well on their way to optimizing the flow of knowledge.

Organizations that follow this solution architecture will demonstrate a competitive advantage. This competitive advantage of optimal knowledge flow will result in a more viable, sustainable and successful organization in the increasingly complex times that we face today.

References

Dunbar, R.I.M. 1993. Co-evolution of neocortical size, group size and language in humans, Behavioral and Brain Sciences 16 (4): 681–735.
Cross, R. L. and R. J. Thomas. 2009. Driving Results Through Social Networks: How Top Organizations Leverage Networks for Performance and Growth. California: Jossey-Bass
Hill, L.A. et al. 2011. Harvard Business Review. Publication date: Dec 08, 2011. Prod. # 11126-SBC-ENG

Cultural Identity and a Global Mindset: Awareness to Knowledge, Skills to Competence

Iouri Bairatchnyi

Kent State University, Kent, OH, USA

Introduction

The relation between the notions of cultural identity and global mindset might seem somewhat counterintuitive because of the semantics of the terms: "identity" is meant to differentiate; "global" implies a certain degree of standardization and moves our mind across (local) differences. At the same time, "cultural" implies belonging to a group, while "mindset" is rather unique. However, with a closer look, it becomes evident, that both terms, when considered together, might exhibit a high degree of compatibility and even complementarily. This combination seems to provide a natural equilibrium for knowledge acquisition and management: the competing forces of differentiation and integration stimulate analysis, evaluation, knowledge creation, and further exploration.

Another layer of ambiguity is added by the dual nature of culture – it is as personal as it is collective. This triggers the assumption that cultural identity and global mindset could be attributed to individuals and groups, and arguably to organizations and societies.

Given these considerations, we intend to examine the competing values of cultural development of individuals and groups, and the role of knowledge management (KM) in merging explicit and tacit knowledge of culture. In more concrete terms, we will try to understand and demonstrate the scope and nature of cultural identity formation and the role (or maybe a function?) of the mindset in the context of globalization and conscious KM.

Why is it important? For the sole reason that the formation of one's cultural identity is an enigma – it is a largely intuitive and semi-conscious process that never ends and only becomes explicit and fully conscious when the mindset is stretched by a threat or new and utterly unfamiliar information or circumstances. Therefore, increasing awareness of new knowledge formation that impacts self or group identity is important under any circumstances. It is critical, however, in times of accelerated globalization, when the speed and quality of decision making is of a survival nature.

Further in this chapter, we outline a framework for analyzing and modelling knowledge acquisition and use in forming (1) cultural identity as a mechanism of integration within any type of social or professional setting and (2) the development of a global mindset as the means of adaptation to external challenges. The framework is a result of research and practical application of a holistic learning approach to achieve understanding of "self," "others," and "self and others" together in the context of multinational professional settings and international development.

Acquiring knowledge and learning of "self" and "self through others" contributes to the development of a multicultural perspective. The conceptualizing of "self and others" together in a given context leads to the development of particular communication and interaction competencies and, ultimately, overall global competence.

What is cultural identity?

Culture hides much more than it reveals, and strangely enough what it hides, it hides most effectively from its own participants (Hall, Beyond Culture, 1977).

Cultural identity is an integral, if not the most essential, part of human identity. Evidently, a holistic consideration of human identity would

Cultural Identity and a Global Mindset: Awareness to Knowledge, Skills to Competence

require biological, philosophical, and psychological analysis. That would be outside the purpose of this chapter. However, in order to outline the premise and preserve the context of cultural identity, we start with an obvious assumption that there is a common denominator for all humans, both biologically and, to a smaller extent, psychologically, which creates a relatively steady, mostly genetically predetermined and contextually refined frame for the development of one's cultural identity.

So, what is cultural identity? How is it formed and how does it develop? In simple terms, cultural identity is an achieved sense of belonging. The formation of cultural identity is a sequential path to a level of comfort and competence in relating to others and the surrounding environment. Ultimately, it results in an ability to identify with a desirable and feasible social or professional setting by an individual or a group. Contextual changes invariably test identity and are usually inconsequential; lasting environmental changes, on the other hand, can cause substantial identity adjustment.

A common, somewhat simplified but still largely adequate way to present the frame of human development is a pyramid with "human nature" as a common and constant base, "culture" as the main variable of human development in the middle, and "personality" on top as a partial variable (Figure 1).

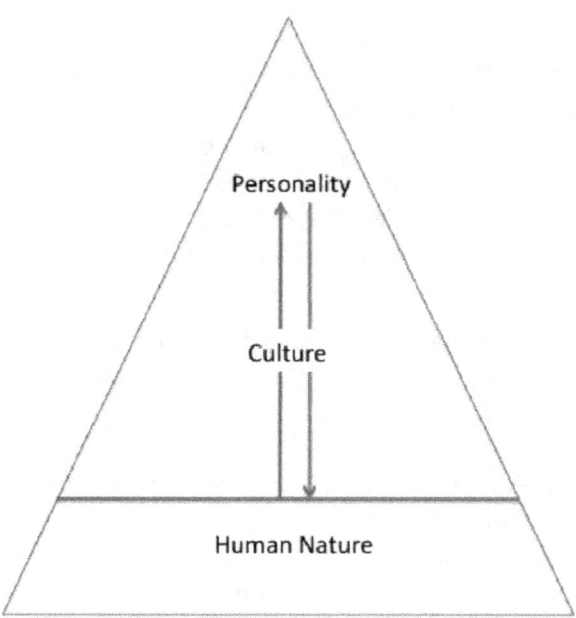

Figure 1. The positioning of cultural development as the only true variable of human identity.

Figure 1 presents the interplay of the three basic components of human development. The main assumption is that human nature is inherited, personality is both inherited and developed (or learned), and culture is only developed (or learned). In other words, while human nature is a constant and personality is somewhat variable, culture (or one's cultural identity) is variable to a very large extent. Leaving biology, physiology, and psychology aside (philosophy as well), let's take a look at the path of cultural identity formation and the role of knowledge formation and management in this process.

The formation of cultural identity is an incremental and open process through the maturation and life span of an individual or a group. The incremental feature is determined by a sequential nature of knowledge, skills, and competence acquisition. The openness of the process is determined by the very nature of culture: we learn how to adapt (1) to the environment and (2) to others within our current environment.

Cultural Identity and a Global Mindset: Awareness to Knowledge, Skills to Competence

As long as both are changing and presenting new challenges, we will learn how to deal with them and how to retain and reuse knowledge acquired during learning.

This process is best presented as a cumulative sequence of stages in cultural identity formation and development.

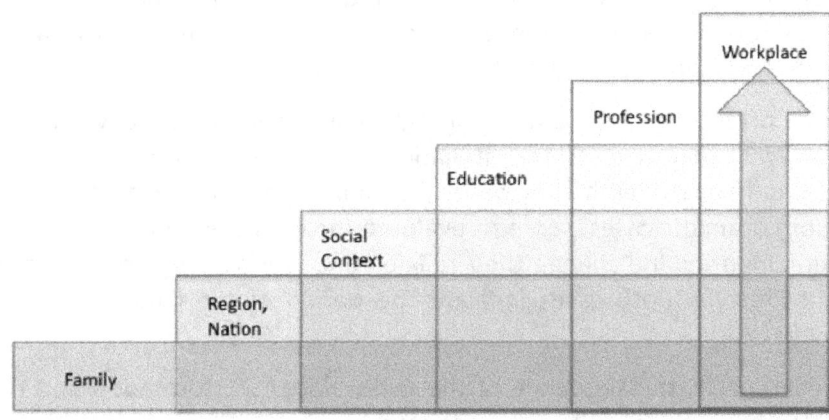

Figure 2. Cumulative progression of cultural identity formation.

Obviously, there is not much we can do about being born into a certain ethnicity (or a mixture of two or several). Also, there is not much we say during the first stage of our enculturation - through the teen years. What happens during this period is a cultivated process of one's upbringing where family and society "impose" most attributes of a potential cultural identity on a child; there are practically no options to deviate – our values, attitudes, preferences regarding using space and time, communication and interaction patterns are prescribed (usually passed down through generations) and are strictly and methodically reinforced in accordance with the status of the family in society (gender, class, income). Even though the progression seems normal, there is a significant potential break in the underpinning of the cultural identity formation – a point in time comes when "cloning" by the parents and those in possession of knowledge becomes less and less viable. When does it happen? When is it when that initial formation starts to wind down? The most common time frame cited is puberty – that's the time to deviate and start searching for one's own path. Further in life, depending on successes and failures while learning different aspects of life and self, we make our own choices in affiliation with others and educational and professional paths. This transition stage in the development of one's cultural identity indicates the beginning of the knowledge ownership transfer and formation of skills necessary to become an independent and accepted member of a desired social and possibly professional setting.

Very often this stage is not a straight line – people rediscover themselves, change professions, affiliations with interest groups, etc. Usually it happens within previously acquired values and attitudes. In more dramatic cases, some re-evaluate the core elements of their cultural identity and change their religion and worldview, adopt a different lifestyle. Both cases indicate the period of the cultural identity ownership.

In summary, the sequence of the cultural identity formation and development includes the following stages:

- The formative stage is the initial knowledge acquisition and conceptualization in the process of cultural identity formation (through puberty). By this time values and beliefs are formed as an initial version of worldview. A sense of self and cultural identity is, however, just beginning to evolve, mostly intuitively and almost subconsciously. Jumping ahead, we must notice that this stage is called "formative," because even dramatic changes in life don't cancel it out – it is the heritage to carry through life, either as a reference or a safe haven to escape from trouble or wrong choices; or sometimes as a curse.
- The transition to "preferred self" is the stage of (e)valuation and norm formation during the transition from knowledge imposition by the society (family, school, community, church, older friends) to selective acquisition of "one's own path" - one's deviation into certain educational, professional, and social settings (from puberty through the end of one's education.) This is a stage of active and intentional formation of cultural identity.

Cultural Identity and a Global Mindset: Awareness to Knowledge, Skills to Competence

- The (re)evaluation of the "preferred self" is a cyclic stage of adapting to new environments and discoveries; it is a stage of constant differentiating, integrating, and identity adjustments. The cumulative character of culture and cultural identity is the key factor in its further development. While adjusting our preferences to deal with the environment and other people, we don't reject the values and beliefs of our early upbringing (that means mostly of our parents or caretakers) and "preferred self" from the past – they are in a state of suspended judgment, so to speak.

The sequential and cumulative nature of cultural identity formation is beneficial in two ways: (1) it widens the options (instead of replacing them) and (2) creates a safety net of a more or less established cultural belonging, which enables us to have a more open mind towards experiencing new values, beliefs, and worldviews of those quite different from us.

Furthermore, a fluid transition from one stage to another naturally ensures a proper preparation for one's explorative interactions with the world. In turn, the interaction with other cultures becomes a powerful source of an explicit self-discovery. For instance, when you ask people when they first realized what their cultural identity is (what it means to be American or French), most say, "When I first went abroad (or moved to a different area)." A natural follow-up question (what it means to be American or French) poses a different kind of difficulty – there are too many potential answers; and most of them are very personal. This kind of realization is a clear indication of self-awareness and a transition from intuitive knowledge acquisition and use to an explicit attempt to understand how to manage that knowledge intentionally while widening a horizon of interaction. Equally important, it teaches us how to learn not just about ourselves but also about others.

Is cultural identity an individual or group phenomenon? While individual cultural identity clearly has anthropological roots and sociological refinement, identity of a group has a much heavier sociological colouring, especially in a professional environment, and can be formed above individual cultural preferences. In other words, cultural identity of an individual has a dual nature due to belonging to a certain "anthropological source" – an ethnic or national group - and being a member of various, sometimes completely different, social or professional affiliations. Imagine three teachers from the same school and the same age group – Jane, Michael, and Frieda. Jane and Michael are white, while Frieda identifies herself as Latina. As opposed to a common generational and professional denominator, the ethnic and possibly national components of their identities are clearly different. It might be easy to assume that Michael and Jane would have the same or similar cultural core, but it may be that they have different ethnic backgrounds (Jane identifies herself as an Irish American, Michael has mixed European roots). They also might belong to different social levels of the society and would have different affiliations and interests. Michael and Frieda had a similar upbringing even though in different ethnic contexts – it is likely that they would have common interests (gardening, art). Jane and Frieda could share a religious background as a commonality. This example illustrates that sometimes people appear similar on the surface, but their life experiences vary widely. As a consequence, their cultural identities have become cumulative sets of various integral parts, which allow a variety of options to identify with different subgroups of a society or an organization (Kennedy, Zion, and Kozleski 2005).

The current challenge of the increasingly global environment is that the impact of national, cross-national and especially virtual environments on human experience in communicating and interacting with each other happens without sufficient and adequate formative or transitional preparation (Kapp and O'Driscoll 2010).

While it is possible and very useful to "study" different cultures one at a time, which would most certainly contribute to one's cross-cultural competence, it would be rather naïve to assume that global competence and the related mindset would develop by itself. Globalization of human interactions doesn't equal the sum of participating cultures – it goes beyond existing boundaries, not just across them (Adler 1998).

Cultural Identity and a Global Mindset: Awareness to Knowledge, Skills to Competence

Developing global competence and a global mindset requires utilization of meta knowledge in skill and competence development without explicit formalization of real experience. In other words, country-specific cultural knowledge is tangible and can be kept in a form of usable knowledge products: description of values, beliefs, depiction of communication and interaction patterns – for example, presentation styles, listening habits or audience expectations and negotiation patterns, depiction of time and space use, motivation factors, etc. Furthermore, it is possible and useful to do a comparative analysis of two cultures within the same categories. It would be rather unfeasible though to apply the same approach to "measure" the global level of cultural competence. In a narrow sense, global means all countries and cultures, without exception, and entails development and application of knowledge products. In a wider sense, global means above or even in spite of the lines and borders drawn often by will to separate cultures; it transcends usual understanding of how things are done here or there and requires not fixed knowledge products but flexible knowledge structures, capable of interpreting ambiguous and conflicting environments. It is not just being aware of what to do in a particular situation, but rather knowing how to do it anytime anywhere, which is often intuitive and requires a higher level of abstraction. How do we acquire such knowledge? That brings us to the notion of the global mindset formation.

What is a global mindset?

Knowledge shall be sought throughout the world so as to strengthen the foundation of the Imperial rule.

(Japanese imperial slogan, Charter Oath of 1868)

The current state of social and economic development is heavily marked by the increasing pace of globalization and decreasing time for decision making. How successful a person or an enterprise is depends on how well they observe, process, and learn from the dynamic world. Creating an adequate mindset to meet the ever-coming challenges and emerging opportunities is crucial for both individuals and business enterprises.

It is equally important to possess a knowledge structure flexible and adequate enough to reflect the complexity of human interaction across borders and continents.

The term mindset refers to a certain type of information filtering cognition determined by several factors. The most obvious are as follows:

- Ambiguity and uncertainty of the information in the surrounding environment.
- The cumulative and iterative nature of human ability to process and acquire new information – we accept it if it is consistent with previous knowledge, and either reject it or adjust previous knowledge to acceptable extent.
- Natural propensity for subconscious information processing at the individual level (we conveniently call it intuition).
- Heavily influenced (by authority) information processing at the organizational level (cognitive compliance, in a sense).
- Rigidity of personal cognitive habits (we tend to believe the familiar and routinely struggle to embrace the new or unusual).
- Complexity and flexibility of collective cognition (too many variables, such as group composition, power structure, purpose, etc.).

In summary, a mindset is an ability to manage (even if subconsciously) existing knowledge under the influence of a changing environment and to learn from it. The emphasis here is on "to learn." An ability to accept or reject new information, or to use it in a given context, does not create a mindset, even though it could contribute to its formation. On the other hand, the ability to learn from your decisions in a systematic and hopefully self-conscious manner is the way mindsets are crafted. In a way, it is a sign of personal or organizational mastery achieved through continuous interplay of learning, change management, and resulting knowledge.

At the organizational level, a collective mindset is less of a historic phenomenon – it is much more determined by circumstances and the current purpose of a business. Changes in management, organizational structure, social context and, last but not least, in the composition of an organization, can visibly change its mindset. There is a natural overlap of influence areas of individual and collective mindsets. A good example would be changes of leaders when not the society or businesses have to change dramatically, but a different mindset is needed (Gupta and Govindarajan 2002). On the other hand, there are many examples when great leaders managed to change minds of organizations and nations (Gardner 2004).

How is global mindset different from a "local" (or parochial) mindset?

Given social, economic, political, and intellectual idiosyncrasies of any culture, it is not difficult to imagine how overloaded a mind could be, even within the comfort zone of a single cultural identity. It becomes exponentially more complex when we encounter cognitive set ups of slightly or significantly different cultures, where the cultural identity formation is filled with a different content throughout all stages – formation, transition, and re-evaluation. A bi-cultural exploration would be a starting point and often presents plenty of challenges and rewards for both sides, where not just the strength of one's mindset is tested but also one's intellectual and psychological capacity, as well as social agility. Understanding others (of a different culture) requires intellectual curiosity and psychological strength – to embrace new knowledge while balancing the ambiguity of new information and uncertainty of new environments. It shouldn't be perceived as a threat but as a promise of a closer understanding as a relationship progresses. In other words, maturing within one's cultural domain and mostly familiar identity (or identities) is a relatively less challenging task than crossing a border. To have any hope for success, one would have (1) to study – to gain explicit and tacit knowledge for conditioning one's usual mindset, and (2) to practice - to condition one's mind to be at peace with unanswered questions without feeling threatened or be intellectually, emotionally, or psychologically blocked, from further exploration and learning. Gradually, it becomes a serendipitous journey from ethnocentricity to ethno-relativity, from being constrained by one's own cultural identity to being freed by an open mind and a global mindset.

As mentioned before, increasing the "repertoire" of discovered unfamiliar cultures paves the road to a formation of a more flexible mindset but is unlikely to result in a global mindset. A transition from being multicultural savvy to being globally competent requires a qualitative leap – at large, it's the ability to see the world through different eyes. In basic cognitive terms, it means a high ability to analyze and synthesize, to differentiate and integrate information and behavior patterns in cognitive settings where cultural variables are highly ambiguous - socially, psychologically, and intellectually.

Generally, as a premise, a global mindset could be defined as a combination of "openness to and awareness of diversity across cultures and markets with a propensity and ability to synthesize across this diversity" (Gupta and Govindarajan 2002).

We do not think that there is any cognitive diversity in the way mindsets function locally or globally. After all, there is plenty of diversity in any society to condition one's local mindset in adversarial situations. The basic process of the cognition in information processing and decision making remains the same across cultures. However, the interpretation and resulting knowledge acquisition and re-use - in a form of a changed mindset or related knowledge products - should be naturally different. It's not the facts, it's how we interpret them and what conclusions we make that defines us as different. So, an effective and efficient global mindset should be relatively high on both the ability to analyze and differentiate, as well as synthesize and integrate in unfamiliar environments. Problems appear when a local mindset rules on a global stage. The ubiquitous Swedish furniture retailer IKEA is a classic example of applying its Swedish cultural lens and a parochial mindset to global markets and learning the hard way not to fail and develop a more integrative perspective on the global market.

The following example exhibits a compelling case of a simultaneous focus on understanding the diversity and an ability to synthesize across this diversity. The CEO of a young and successful US-based company, an immigrant from China, succinctly summarized his strategy for comparative advantage in the global market as "combining Chinese costs with Japanese quality, European design, and American marketing. There are other Chinese competitors in the market, but along with Chinese costs, what they bring is Chinese quality. On the other hand, our American counterparts have excellent product quality but their costs are too high. We can and do beat both of them" (Gupta and Govindarajan 2002).

The interplay of cultural identity and global mindset

> *"The test of a first-rate intelligence is the ability to hold two opposed ideas at the same time and still retain the ability to function. "*
>
> - F. Scott Fitzgerald

Everybody's cultural identity is unique. Everybody has a mindset, and there are no two mindsets completely alike. However, the way they became different is very much the same. A cultivation of both begins with small and safe steps – through discovering diversity within the safety net of one's own culture. From early on we are "forced" to play the game of choosing friends, affiliations, and alternatives of an intuitive nature or acquired taste (fashion, food, hobbies, etc.). Very often, without proper reflection, when the options are benign and not mutually and finitely exclusive, one's current mindset remains unchanged, because there is no "threat" or pressure to battle anything new. When it is "either or" with lasting consequences, everything changes. Compare the difference in choosing between two meat dishes (beef or chicken?) and making a decision not to eat meat at all. The basic cognition process is the same – "either or," the consequences for one's identity and mindset are very different. The choice in the first instance is circumstantial and non consequential. The choice in the second instance is defining. When the options are mutually exclusive, finite, and entail lasting change, the mind has to go beyond the comfort zone of the usual. Consider a nine year-old deciding not to eat meat anymore. That would be not just out of the comfort zone, but straight to a mindset stretch - for both the child and the parents (if they are not vegetarians). Ironically, it is somewhat easier for the child – decisions of this type don't happen ad hoc; when this happened in my family, I backtracked my daughter's history of decision making and was not very surprised – she started recycling at age 5, (with the most consistency of the family of four, even though she was the youngest), donated some of her allowance to good causes at the age of 7, and decided to make peace with the animals for good at the age of 9 (as my inquiries attested, it is not unusual, even if not that common). All three decisions resulted from differentiating the options and integrating the choices into self-image (partially new identity) and a chosen worldview (a potential for new affiliations). The ability to make an educated (through formal learning or practice) choice, in a situation where the options are mutually exclusive and have lasting consequences, is a safe sign of a different or, for a better term, open mindset development, which essentially is one of the foundations of a global mindset. It is not something new to learn, it is something new to handle. In fact, I have spoken with a number of kids who turned vegetarian – the answers were generally similar: they felt comfortable being a vegetarian and saying that. The transition from the old comfort zone to the new one is usually smooth when the mindset is well prepared.

With more exposure to the diversity in one's own society and, further, to the diversity of cultures in the world, our mindsets continue a journey towards becoming more flexible, agile, and tolerant as a result of constant pressure from the surrounding environment and changing circumstances. At the same time, the forces of our cultural identity, directed towards the environment, on a collision course with everything new and unusual, equip our mindsets with stability, persistency, and a sense of safe curiosity.

A good description of staying true to your beliefs and having an open mindset was given by Percy Barnevik, the CEO of ABB, in an interview in 1991 (Gupta and Govindarajan 2002). "Global managers have exceptionally open minds. They respect how different countries do things, and they have the imagination to appreciate why they do them that way. But, they are also incisive: they push the limits of the culture. Global managers don't passively accept it when someone says, 'You can't do that in Japan because of the Ministry of Finance'. They sort through the debris of cultural excuses and find opportunities to innovate." The key word in this citation is "innovation" – in this case, it is the ability to consider competing, sometimes opposite, points of view and find a harmonizing solution.

The interrelation between the notions of cultural identity and global mindset is somewhat more complicated when attributed to organizations. While it is conceivable that organizations have cultures (as a metaphor for organizational behavior) and we can speak of cultural identity of an organization, it seems more difficult to attribute a cognitive process to an institution and speak of a collective mindset transcending the ones of its members. For this reason, some scholars prefer the terms "global corporate culture" or "global identity;" all three terms seem to be almost interchangeable or at least overlap largely. When we talk about "a global mindset of an organization," we mean mostly people who make decisions around the world (global managers) as well as a (global) strategy and policies that promote and allow global practices. The baseline of business has its role as well – there would be no strong global culture in an organization if its members didn't accept it as a feature of their personal cultural identity (Beechler, Taylor, Boyacigiller, and Levy 1999).

Another factor is that organizations become global over time, they mature by expanding and dealing with new circumstances and environments, they learn how to make faster and smarter decisions in unfamiliar contexts. Just like individuals preserve their identity, organizations try to retain their brand, image, and reputation.

Overall, the competing interplay of cultural identity and global mindset creates an equilibrium of constant personal or collective knowledge management reinforcing the complementary value of two opposites – consistent cultural identity and a mindset to "build cognitive bridges" anywhere.

From multicultural perspective to global competence

By nature and definition, cultural identity is a process of dynamic attribution to a set of preferences consciously or subconsciously owned by individuals and groups. It is an evolving process, as it is constantly under revision due to a changing environment. The revision is enabled by a mindset which, by definition as well, is a fixed way to interpret and evaluate the environment. In a sense, it is a condition or a set of conditions for developing a cultural identity. A global mindset has to do with the way we interpret the world and adds a new dimension to a fixed mindset – it allows different, sometimes opposite points of view to be held and considered at the same time.

In fact, the reconciliation of opposites is one of the fundamental principles of intercultural and multicultural development. Fons Trompennars and Charles Hampten-Turner offered compelling examples of converting potentially vicious circles of opposing values into virtual circles of meaningful balance between "individualism and communitarianism," "universalism and particularism," "status achievement and ascription," etc., (Trompennars and Hampten-Turner 1998). Together, the reconciled opposing values and practices form a dynamic knowledge (management) structure that enables individual development of intercultural sensitivity. While discovering self and learning about others, we move from ethno-centricity to ethno-relativism: from denial, through defense and minimization, to acceptance and adaptation, and finally to integration of initially foreign and unacceptable values, worldviews, and practices into the current operating environment (Bennet 1998).

Further development results in a formation of a multicultural perspective, cross-cultural and, ultimately, global competence. Let's take a look at this process.

As Figure 3 depicts, the initial step on the way to developing a multicultural perspective is the realization of what we need to know. The very starting point is, not surprisingly, our own self – (Who am I? What am I doing here? – eternal questions).

Cultural Identity and a Global Mindset: Awareness to Knowledge, Skills to Competence

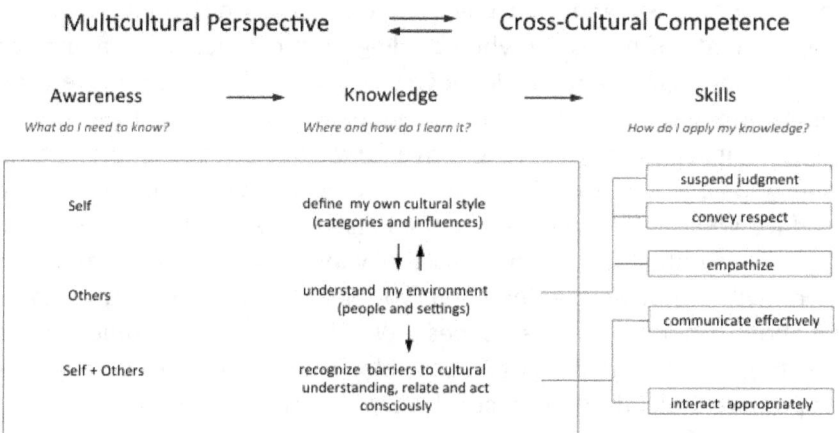

Figure 3. A framework for developing multicultural perspective and cross-cultural competence.

As mentioned earlier, culture hides very efficiently, and it hides from its carriers most successfully. That happens because the acquisition of cultural identity is mostly intuitive and rather seldom conscious (in a sense, it is like language acquisition – it is equally painful to explain the values, beliefs, and deep assumptions of your own culture as to explain the grammar of your mother tongue, unless you study). The most common definition of culture, especially of organizations, is concise and ambiguous: "It's just the way we do things around here." Another, equally non-obliging definition underlines the process of culture formation: "Culture is a loosely structured and incompletely shared system that emerges dynamically as cultural members experience each other, events, and the organizations contextual features (Martin 2005)." Both definitions clearly imply the intuitive, almost passive, and largely tacit nature of cultural knowledge formation.

The most common visual for presenting the culture of individuals and groups is an iceberg with artefacts above the water and intangibles below. This naturally results in a disproportionate balance between explicit and tacit knowledge of one's cultural identity. To understand why we do things in a certain way takes efforts of various types: intellectual curiosity, psychological strength, and social courage. Learning about yourself is sometimes painful and is usually postponed in life to the moments of necessity when dealing with conflicts and failures or overcoming significant challenges. It is naturally easier to rely on common assumptions about participants of your own culture. Unfortunately, it is hardly possible to move forward and learn to understand others, unless we learn how we are seen and what impression we produce while interacting with others, especially of different cultures. Therefore, unfortunately or not, the way to global competence is paved with iterative learning about yourself through others and learning about others "from their shoes." We all know that it's much easier said than done, but it's not impossible, and in the next part of this chapter we look into two practical examples of such learning.

The awareness stage on the way to global competence is critical because it determines the direction and outlines the value of personal development towards understanding one's personal cultural style beyond familiar boundaries. It is worth repeating here that a cultural style, or cultural identity, is not equal to one's cultural heritage and/or national identity. As described earlier, the national "layer" in the formation of cultural identity comes rather early in life and becomes an important part of one's culture, but it is just a part. There are many more important and sometimes decisive choices to make throughout life that ultimately shape the way we choose to live our personal and professional life.

Understanding what we need to learn leads to the next step – realizing how we learn it and where. Raising awareness is a great way to deal with tacit knowledge in terms of getting a direction, but finding and acquiring the needed knowledge is a taller order. For example, having learned that my communication style; in particular, in making presentations, doesn't have the same response with different audiences (from different cultures), I realized that there is no standardized way to present to culturally various audiences; and, evidently, I am not fully aware of what kind of impression I leave behind. Finding resources to understand that; in particular, learning about listening habits of different cultural types would be the next step. Furthermore, exploring these issues with representatives of other cultures, unveils the barriers to understanding, "disarms" misunderstandings and makes them impersonal helps evaluate the situation with an open mind and act consciously. If you think about it, it is a significant and necessary step forward - you become accustomed to learning about yourself through the eyes of others.

It is a leap forward when you and others try to learn together. The difference is essential; when you learn about other cultures, you learn how to relate, how to act in a single context. When you learn along with others (consciously and in a targeted fashion), you learn the art of communication and interaction that is acceptable throughout cultures and conducive to developing meaningful relationships – you learn how to suspend your judgment without being submissive, how to convey respect while remaining your natural self, how to exude empathy and positive regard, how to listen actively, etc. As Edward T. Hall summarized it, "You learn how to make friends" (Sorrells 1998).

Moving from awareness to knowledge involves two basic aspects of knowledge management: the process of knowledge creation and the practice of knowledge acquisition. Using cultural counterparts as a reflection mechanism for better self understanding leads to the creation of explicit knowledge products: sets of values, patterns of communication and interaction, taboos and empathy techniques, etc. What is arguably more important though, is the meta knowledge of the existence of types of knowledge – cognitive knowledge containers, so to speak. While learning about audience expectations, negotiation patterns, or value structures in particular cultures, we develop a steady mental model for each type of human communication and interaction.

The following diagrams (figure4) are rather compelling examples of such knowledge creation (Lewis 2008).

Iouri Bairatchnyi

Cultural Identity and a Global Mindset: Awareness to Knowledge, Skills to Competence

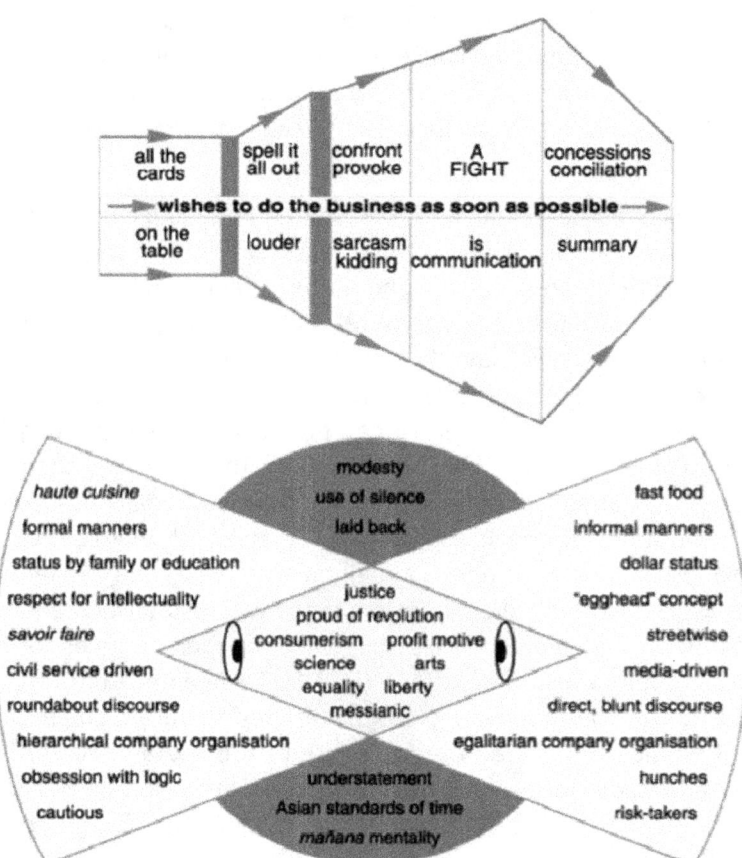

Figure 4. Examples of value comparison, speaking patterns, and audience expectations.

Learning together with those who are culturally very different provides an opportunity to tap into the realm of tacit knowledge – in a sense, it is like building a community of practice to learn how to be or work together, with all differences accepted as a starting point. This ultimately allows a student of culture to bridge the knowledge (values and beliefs, worldviews, communication patterns, etc.) and separate skills (listening, being positive and optimistic, being open to differences, etc.). The ultimate outcome of this effort would be the evolving competence to make the right choices without checking the reference - you know the appropriate thing to do or not to do, and you know how to handle it. Moreover, with exponential exposure to various cultures it becomes a part of your way to deal with others, no matter who they are; it becomes a part of your personal cultural identity ... unconscious competence, as some like to call it, which leads towards a global mindset.

There are two pivotal points in the presented knowledge management and collective learning structure. The first point is that the formation of cultural identity goes beyond the national level – no one fits a national stereotype. In the context of learning this means searching for cultural characteristics above known nation-states and trying to find similarities at a higher level of abstraction, i.e., certain types of people who choose to behave, relate and communicate in a certain way irrespective of their origin. The second point is that learning about self and others requires the same point of reference. Ideally, one model and a consistent approach should be used for analyzing self, others, and groups of people. It doesn't really matter what the model is, as long as it's tested and valid. There are many well-established and truly useful models and tools for assessing cultural types or styles for individuals, groups, and organizations (Hall E. T., Beyond Culture 1977) (Hall E. T., The Silent Language 1973) (Hofstede 1980) (Schein 2010). While it would be outside of our purpose to provide a review of such models and tools here, we use one model with related web-based tools and two cases as an example of building the foundations of global competence.

A practical approach to discovering cultural identity and diversity

In 1976, Edward T. Hall offered a somewhat simplified but not simplistic dichotomy of cultures in the world. He divided the world's cultures into two main categories – high context cultures, where many things remain unsaid and communication is to a large degree implicit and indirect, and low context cultures, where communication is much more explicit and direct. Earlier, he had proposed a time-related dichotomy to view cultures as "polichronic" vs. "monochronic," which distinguishes the preference to multitask or to be sequential. This four-point framework became the foundation of cross-cultural communication studies. Hall's ideas had quite a few followers. The most noticeable of them is Richard D. Lewis, who furthered Hall's vision and extended his model. Additionally, he created a comprehensive web-based tool, called CultureActive, for assessing cultural preferences of individuals and groups, as well as for learning about national, regional, and global cultural specifics and tendencies. The underpinning principle of the model and the tool is that the same framework is valid and useful for assessing the cultures of individuals, groups, countries, and regions.

Lewis redefined "low context and monochronic" cultures as "Linear-active" (cool, factual, decisive planners); further, he split "high context and polichronic" into "Multi-active" (warm, emotional, loquacious, impulsive interrelators) and "Reactive" (courteous, amiable, accommodating compromisers and harmonizers) (Lewis R. D., When Cultures Collide, 1996). Visually, the model is represented as a triangle where the multi-active corner is colored red, the linear-active corner is colored blue, and the reactive corner is colored yellow.

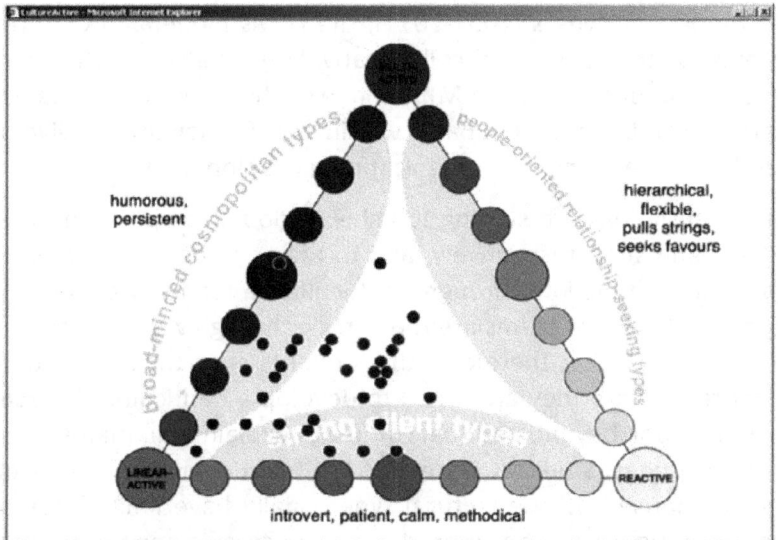

Figure 5. A group profile based on the Lewis model and produced in CultureActive.

Based on the results of individual surveys, which are designed to elicit both explicit and tacit knowledge of one's cultural preferences against

15 categories, individuals and groups are placed within the triangle where the position indicates one's varied preferred affiliation with the three types. In most cases, individual and group profiles possess features of all three types, usually with one or two dominants, e.g., an individual or a group could be predominantly linear-active with quite a few multiactive and just some reactive features. Both individual and the aggregated group feedback profiles provide a score and a detailed feedback on the composition and implications of identified cultural preferences.

The combination of an abstract model with three broad categories and a tool for detailed cultural analysis and differentiation provides a powerful framework for learning about culture in general, for discovering cultural identity of individuals and teams, and for creating the foundations of global competence and a global mindset.

Creating new knowledge through managing diversity at the Duke Fuqua School of Business and the World Bank

Over the last ten years (2001-2011), the Lewis model and CultureActive have been actively and collaboratively used at Duke University's Fuqua School of Business (in MBA and Executive and now Global MBA programs) and the World Bank within the framework of diversity, cross-cultural learning, and organizational development.

Both organizations are striving to achieve global competence of their students and staff, respectively, and to foster global leadership. Both organizations function through multicultural teams. At the Fuqua School, multicultural teams are the vehicle through which much of the learning takes place; therefore, the students start their education in the context where they are urged to develop a multicultural perspective and to look beyond national culture to explain teammates' behavior and attitudes. Students learn that the team composition is critical: teams comprised of one cultural type usually have limited perspectives and insights and an unproductive sense of competition; mixed teams, on the other hand, offer a variety of views and preferences. In their teams, the students "are urged to use the diversity as a source of innovation and learning rather than conflict and dysfunctional behavior. A Linear-active team might have too much reliance on facts without paying sufficient attention to relationships. A Multi-active team might lose focus and waste time in digression, and a wholly reactive team might spend so much effort on face considerations, harmony, and gradual solutions that little can be accomplished. A multicultural team would allow for a much broader perspective and a more balanced and interesting approach to teamwork, but time is needed for members with different assumptions about behaviour to learn from each other." Therefore, students are given the opportunity to learn from each other as individuals with a set of certain cultural preferences, not members of a certain national culture. (Gates et al. 2008).

The main benefit from the efforts to discover and leverage individual and group cultural differences and similarities at the Fuqua School is the creation of an environment conducive to further individual and collective learning and development of capabilities to be successful globally. Here are the main takeaways:

- Certain behaviors can be attributed to certain cultures; however, national culture does not determine individual behavior.
- No one is a perfect representative of a national culture – stereotypes are convenient lies.
- Diversity must be managed so that it produces creativity, innovation, and sound decisions.

The success in preparing the MBA students to learn about their cultural styles and to deal with and benefit from diversity in their future work certainly paves the road to their future professional success.

The World Bank faces a similar but much larger two-fold challenge: (1) managing the diversity and global development of its staff, and (2) managing diverse, intricate, and often culturally challenging relationships with its clients – in over one hundred countries. The World Bank, as a development agency with a mission to alleviate poverty and deprivation in the developing parts of the world, faces the utmost challenge to contextualize its efforts locally and globally. Decontextualized efforts to export a Western way of thinking and development failed in earlier years of international development. Now, when not the loans but the knowledge is the most valued currency of international development, the ability to think globally and act locally underlines the importance of the two cultural challenges.

The first challenge - raising awareness of cultural diversity beyond national cultures and helping staff to develop a global mindset had a similar approach and impact at the Fuqua School, even though the demographics of the World Bank staff is obviously different than in a graduate school. Most of the World Bank staff are hired in their mid-career, both in headquarters in Washington DC and in more than one hundred country offices around the globe, are well educated and internationally experienced. Most, if not all, teams are multinational – it is not unusual that 10 members of a team would represent 5-10 countries, speak two or three languages and have first-hand experience of seeing most of the world and working abroad. Does it guarantee success across cultures when interacting with colleagues, counterparts, and, most importantly, clients? Not exactly, as practice and the results of various surveys show. The challenge of managing diversity, and raising awareness of diverging but complementing cultural styles, was met in a similar way as, at the Fuqua School – several thousand staff from many units and teams in Washington, D.C., and country offices participated in cross-cultural training events or retreats designed around the Lewis model and the survey results from CultureActive. Occasionally, clients and counterparts participated in such events as well. The impact of these efforts proved to be very positive and similar to the one at the Fuqua School. In general, the impact was evaluated as high on awareness, moderate on skill building, and substantial in creating positive changes in the workplace. Detailed results are presented in an Impact Evaluation Study (WBI Evaluation Studies 2007).

The second challenge – bringing cultural knowledge and global skills into operational work is quite significant; mainly, because it assumes not only preparedness of both sides (Bank staff and clients) for a global dialogue, but also requires a well-designed knowledge management system to be in place, where tacit knowledge is as important as facts and numbers.

Cultural Identity and a Global Mindset: Awareness to Knowledge, Skills to Competence

The initial solution for this challenge was found in supplementing culture-related events (workshops and retreats on both country-specific and country-neutral issues) with systematic attempts to elicit tacit knowledge through peer-learning events, as well as communities of practice and social networks by professional (e.g., financial specialists, economists, environmentalists, etc.) or regional interests (working in Africa, South or East Asia, etc.).

Over the years, the Lewis model and related cross-cultural framework provided thousands of staff with a unique opportunity to examine cultural preferences in their work environment and suggest how to work with others in diverse cultural settings capitalizing on others' values and beliefs while gaining better insight into their behavior patterns. It helped distinguish between appearance and reality in team members' behavior, identify commonalities and strengthen synergies.

The advantage of using a one-model approach is in its viability for assessing individuals and groups through the same lens – a hybrid of three cultural types that are abstract and intuitive enough to present a credible (according to validation studies) and compelling (according to the results of hundreds of workshops and learning sessions) outline of people's cultural preferences in terms of what they value, how they relate to others and the environment, how they communicate and interact, and how they plan and carry out tasks. The value of this approach, however, is in its complementary nature: each of the three proposed cultural types has something unique to offer that would be beneficial for other types –so, we need them all! For example, we need linear-active types to organize, plan and see problems, analyze consequences, hold consistent policies, access rational thought, generate data, and challenge us objectively. We need multi-active types to generate enthusiasm, motivate and persuade, create a positive social atmosphere, generate dialogue, access emotions, and challenge others personally. And we need reactive types to harmonize, act intuitively, be patient and see a big picture, think and act long-term, assess feelings, listen, empathize ... and not to challenge anyone. As we can see, a combination of the three types and what they have to offer provides a balanced and complete environment for success across cultures. In other words, it offers both differentiation and integration of cultural idiosyncrasies.

Finally, cultural profiling based on the Lewis model is not correlated with national profiles – there is not a shadow of one's cultural origin in the profile, even though the national profiles of countries are described in the same way. This allows observing a deviation of an individual profile from a national stereotype (described in Lewis terminology). In fact, in most cases individual profiles do not fully correspond to "the colors" of a national profile. At the end of the day, one's cultural identity remains personal, complex and multifaceted.

Conclusion

The aim of this chapter has been to offer a framework to encompass the seemingly incompatible notions of cultural identity and global mindset. We discovered that these phenomena are interdependent because of the necessity to balance existing knowledge and highly ambiguous incoming information.

Operating within a familiar cultural environment refines cultural identity and conditions the mindset. Expanding into culturally unfamiliar environments validates the cultural identity and stretches the mindset, mostly through the challenge of matching new explicit and new tacit knowledge. For example, aligning foreign communication and interaction preferences with the reasons why they are the way they are (i.e., with the underlying values and beliefs) requires intellectual efforts, psychological stamina, as well as social courage and agility. Ultimately, this type of inter-cultural practice leads to multicultural competence and the ability to operate in a new environment with adequate preparation, mainly through the use of (1) tangible knowledge products (data, visuals, depictions, stories, etc.) and (2) adequately designed learning and competency frameworks to elicit acquisition of tacit knowledge (an example of such a framework was described in this chapter).

The biggest challenge in operating in today's world, however, is not related to the number of cultures in the world (many more than nation-states). It is caused by the increased speed of globalization and the changing socio-economic paradigm.

The pressure from globalization for human interaction (social and commercial) is to develop the ability to transcend the national worldviews and to learn how to handle global challenges in new harmonizing ways, preserving national identities. This ability would be a result of developing a global mindset, a new type of cognition with a new capacity to accommodate contradictions of today's world, to harmonize and innovate. The development of a global mindset requires, in turn, new knowledge management practices that rely not on fixed knowledge products but on flexible knowledge structures. Another attribute of a global mindset is its enigmatic intuitive nature, not in a sense of the intuition during the formative stages of one's cultural identity, but in a form of a seasoned (tested, refined and stretched) mindset.

The socio-economic landscape of today's world is changing as well. The scarcity model of modern economic theory is being challenged by the increasing value of information. Unlike currency, information is non-appropriable and can be shared without being given away. Information travels from place to place based on an individual's desire to interact with it and sustains human interaction: while Google is set out to organize the world's information, Facebook is leveraging information to organize better interaction between people. Both approaches are having a profound impact on human interaction throughout the world (Kapp and O'Driscoll 2010).

In summary, the challenges of globalization combined with the co-evolution of society and technology are not just a fascinating subject for academic research, but a formidable challenge in managing knowledge, as well as a great opportunity to learn how to make sound and timely decisions and sustain meaningful relationships across and beyond borders.

References

Adler, P. S. 1998. Beyond Cultural Identity. In: Basic Concepts of Intercultural Communication. Yarmouth: Intercultural Press.

Barnevik, P. 1991. Harvard Business Review. (W. E. Taylor, Interviewer)

Beechler, S. et al. 1999. Building Global Mindset for Comparative Advantage, Annual Meeting of the Academy of Management Meetings. Chicago.

Bennett, M. J. 1998. Intercultural communication: A current Perspective. In M. J. Bennett (Ed.), Basic concepts of intercultural communication: A reader (pp. 1-34). Yarmouth, ME: Intercultural Press.

CultureActive. 2001. [Online]. Retrieved from http://www.cultureactive.com [Accessed: July 1,2012]

Gardner, H.2004. Changing Minds. Boston: Harvard Business School Press.

Gates, M. J., et al. 2008. Use of the Lewis Model to Analyze Multicultural Teams and Improve Performance by the World Bank. The International Journal of Knowledge, Culture & Change Management , V8, N12: 53-60.

Gupta, A and V. Govindarajan. 2002. Cultivating a Global Mindset. Academy of Management Executive, V1.16, N1: 116-126.

Hall, E. T. 1977. Beyond Culture. New York: Anchor Books.

Hall, E. T. 1973. The Silent Language. New York: Anchor Books.

Hofstede, G. 1980. Culture's Consequences: International Differences in Work-related Values. Beverly Hills: Sage.

Kapp, P. M. and T. O'Driscoll. 2010. Learning in 3D, Adding a New Dimension to Enterprise Learning and Collaboration. San Francisco: John Wiley and Sons, Inc.

Kennedy, K., Zion, S., and E. Kozleski. 2009. Report: Cultural Identity and Teaching [Online]. Retrieved from http://ea.niusileadscape.org/lc/Record/605?search_query=Zion%20 [Accessed. March 1, 2012]

Lewis, R. D. 2008. Cross-Cultural Communication: A Visual Approach. Wanford: Transcreen Publications.

Lewis, R. D. 1996. When Cultures Collide. London: Nicholas Brealey.

Martin, J. 2005. The Organizational Culture: Pieces of the Puzzle. In: Classics of Organizational Theory. Belmont: Thomson.

Nonaka, I and H. Takecuchi. 1995. The Knowledge-Creating Company: How Japanese Companies Create the Dynamics of Innovation. New York: Oxford University Press.

Schein, E. H. 2010. Organizational Culture and Leadership. San Francisco: Jossey-Bass.

Sorrells K. 1998. Gifts of Wisdom: An Interview with Dr. Edward T. Hall. The Edge: The E-Journal of Intercultural Relations, 1(3): 1-12. [Online]. Retrieved from http://www.interculturalrelations.com/vli3Summer1998/sum98sorrellhall.htm [Accessed: October 20]

Cultural Identity and a Global Mindset: Awareness to Knowledge, Skills to Competence

Trompenaars, F. and C. Hampten-Turner. 1998. Riding the Waves of Culture: Understanding Cultural Diversity in Business. New York: McGraw-Hill.

WBI-Evaluation-Studies. 2007. Developing Multicultural Perspectives: An Evaluation of the World Bank's Cross-Cultural Training.

Bringing Order to Chaos: Knowledge Architectures that Sustain Knowledge Practice

Denise A. D. Bedford

Kent State University, Kent, OH, USA

Introduction

Three major trends are affecting the way we work and our working environment in the early 21st century. The first trend is the shift from an industrial to a knowledge economy fueled by the increase in and economic value associated with learning, innovation and intellectual capital. The second trend is the rapid advance in semantic and knowledge technologies. And, the third trend is virtualization of the working environment and work. The way that knowledge workers work is changing – where they work, how they work, who they work with, how they find and manage knowledge all are evolving, and continues to evolve for at least the next decade.

Trends Affecting the Way We Work

Over the past several decades we have learned much about knowledge and knowledge management (KM). We have grown a profession and professional practices around some fundamental principles – that knowledge is a valuable asset, that it should be captured, shared, mobilized, reviewed and preserved. These trends present significant opportunities for the knowledge management profession. If leveraged, these opportunities have the potential to move us closer to the exposure and capture of tacit knowledge, to afford greater access to all types and forms of knowledge, to enable access regardless of where the producer or consumer lives and works, and to represent and verify

Bringing Order to Chaos: Knowledge Architectures that Sustain Knowledge Practice

knowledge as encoded rules and processes. These trends also challenge the knowledge management (KM) profession. The primary challenge is that while the environment is rapidly moving forward, the essential architecture has not kept pace. Most knowledge management initiatives and projects today are still very much anchored in late 20th century architectures. To take advantage of the new knowledge management opportunities, we need 21st century architecture.

How do we take advantage of the changes to expand and grow the profession? How do knowledge principles and practices translate to this new working environment? What does it mean in terms of access to knowledge sources? And, perhaps the most fundamental question – What does the knowledge foundation look like in a dynamic and continuously evolving work environment? What does the architecture of this new foundation look like? How do we design to a continuously changing environment? Let's consider how to take up the challenges by understanding how each trend affects knowledge.

Trend 1: Shift from Industrial Capital to Intellectual Capital Assets

The first major trend influencing our working environment is the shift from an industrial to a knowledge economy. A knowledge economy is an economic system which is grounded on knowledge or intellectual capital (Benbya and Van Alstyne 2011). In the knowledge economy, intellectual capital rather than physical or financial capital, becomes a primary factor of production. Knowledge is both a product that is consumed and produced, and it is a tool that fuels business and economic activity in the form of procedural knowledge, know how, expertise, and relational capital. Our ability to create, grow, share, capture, discover, use and preserve knowledge is a critical capability in the knowledge economy. As a product and a tool in the knowledge economy, knowledge takes on new value and new forms. Today, the range of knowledge sources, the types of knowledge that are available and the granularity in which knowledge can be accessed and used are all rapidly expanding.

This increased complexity and richness of knowledge products creates a demand for new knowledge services – personalization, recommender engines, filtering and other forms of user-assisted "computation". Essentially, knowledge becomes "computable" in the new working environment – computable and consumable by both machines and human beings. "Computable" or machine consumable knowledge products and services means that machines produce it according to an individual's specifications and requirements, and that machines can consume it to reason, solve problems, and support more intelligent processing.

Coupled with the rise of semantic technologies, in the early 21st century we are able to capture knowledge at an earlier stage in the knowledge life cycle – moving the bar for knowledge management closer to the "tacit" and informal, un-reviewed stages and forms. The pervasive use of social networking and collaboration technologies now make it possible for us to more readily access the most important of all sources of knowledge – the people and communities who hold knowledge in their brains. The advances in technology create an opportunity to develop new methods for knowledge elicitation, representation, transformation and exchange for use in semantic technologies. In the early 21st century tacit knowledge is encoded into enterprise resource planning systems as tacit knowledge. And, we have the capabilities to affordably and effectively reverse engineer knowledge and information products into "chunks" which machines can leverage.

These new capabilities further increase the value of knowledge simply by opening up what Marshall Van Alstyne and his co-researchers refer to as knowledge markets (Bell 1974, Machup 1962, Benbya and Van Alstyne 2011). Open knowledge markets support knowledge transactions and allow knowledge producers and consumers to establish the value of knowledge based on a particular context. Tracking and capturing knowledge earlier in the life cycle may be easier thanks to the new social media, but the volume, nature of knowledge types, stages and overall "management" of knowledge products and services is now exponentially more complex and challenging. Thus, while markets are more open and transparent, so is the risk of now finding and using poor quality knowledge markets.

Bringing Order to Chaos: Knowledge Architectures that Sustain Knowledge Practice

These trends present several challenges for knowledge professionals. Is there an emerging structure of knowledge itself? Are there types of knowledge structures that are now visible? How do we involve subject matter experts and knowledge workers in the quality assessment of "computable" knowledge? How do we ensure reliability when knowledge is designed into the "From Searching to Knowing" technologies that (Bell 1974) refers to?

Trend 2: Emergence of Semantic Technologies and Intelligent Systems

The second major trend is the rapid development of semantic and knowledge technologies. According to Mills Davis, a thought leader in the semantic web:

"Internet innovation has a direction. It is towards greater bandwidth, more intense social connectedness, smarter applications and devices, and pervasive adaptability. The broad sweep of internet evolution we call the semantic wave. The semantic wave embraces four stages of internet growth. Web 1.0, was about connecting information and getting on the net. Web 2.0 is about connecting people — putting the "I" in user interface, and the "we" into webs of social participation. The next stage, Web 3.0, is starting now. It is about representing meanings, connecting knowledge, and putting these to work in ways that make our experience of internet more relevant, useful, and enjoyable. Web 4.0 will come later. It is about connecting intelligences in a ubiquitous web where both people and things reason and communicate together (Bell 1974).

Web 3.0 is commonly referred to as the Semantic Web. It is about semantics and semantic technologies. Semantics deals with the study of meaning, changes in meaning, and the principles that govern the relationship between sentences or words and their meanings.

Semantic Technologies encode meanings separately from data and content files, and separately from application code. This enables machines as well as people to understand, share and reason with them at execution time. With semantic technologies, adding, changing and implementing new relationships or interconnecting programs in a different way can be just as simple as changing the external model that these programs share. Semantic technologies have the potential to capture and leverage more knowledge and expertise. They have the potential to improve the efficiency and effectiveness of our work and working environment (Bell 1974). But, they can only do so if they reflect and interact with human knowledge. As machines move us closer to the capture and interaction with tacit knowledge, it is important to ensure that knowledge practices and principles are built into their design and use. Some of the semantic technologies that Davis has identified as semantic are something also referred to as "Knowledge Technologies." Davis has identified and mapped 16 categories of semantic technologies which are critical to our realization of Web 3.0 (Figure 1). Of the 16 categories, six have knowledge as a central focus. The six categories include: (1) Knowledge Representation; (2) Knowledge Based Applications; (3) Semantic Content Tools; (4) Intelligent Systems; (5) Semantic Architectures; and (6) From Search to Knowing.

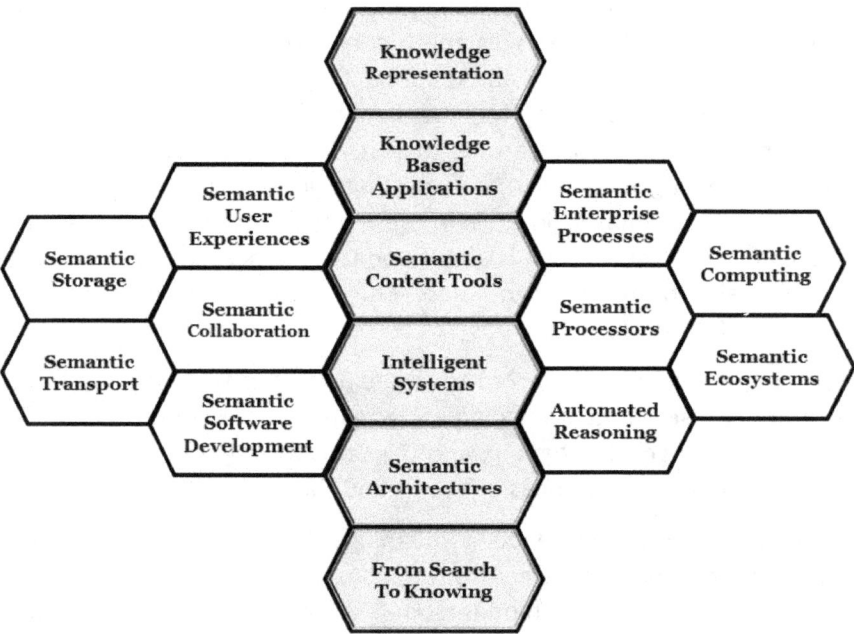

Bringing Order to Chaos: Knowledge Architectures that Sustain Knowledge Practice

Figure 1. Recreation of a Knowledge-Based Representation of Mills Davis Semantic Technology Map

These knowledge-centric technologies will have a significant impact on our daily work. The risk for knowledge professionals is that these knowledge-centric semantic technologies will move forward without a strong knowledge foundation. Knowledge professionals must work to ensure that these knowledge-centric technologies reflect the current or future state of human knowledge, and that they are designed in a way that ensures they can be used and maintained by knowledge workers. This means designing a knowledge architecture that integrates knowledge, knowledge practices and processes, applications and technologies.

Trend 3: Virtualization of the Working Environment and Workforce

This new environment is both a "knowledge factory" and a knowledge market. This is where knowledge is continuously produced and consumed. In the future, and to some extent today, people will work where and when they want to work. Workers will do their work in an environment that is designed for them. Workers will have personalized agents that find information for them regardless of where it lives. The new virtual environment will support dynamic people-to-people connections. It will support collaboration and facilitates the development of knowledge-centric cultures. Smart, adaptable workflows leverage both explicit and tacit knowledge, and have built in mechanisms for peer review. Machines will take on some of the knowledge work in a virtual working environment. And, all of this must ride above any one institution's information management or information technology infrastructure. This means that a virtual set of knowledge management support function needs to be embedded into the working environment. This virtual working environment is likely to take the form of both internal and external cloud architecture.

The implication of this trend is that we need to think entirely differently about our application and technology environment. Today's information technology environment will soon be a supporting foundation, rather than a primary working environment.

Denise A. D. Bedford

The challenge this trend presents for knowledge professionals is fundamental and significant, though perhaps less obvious than the opportunities referenced above. Essentially, knowledge management principles and practices through the first decade of the 21st century have been supported by and built on information management technologies. This made sense because the emergence of the knowledge management profession occurred simultaneously with the IT wave of the 1990s and early 2000s. In most cases, though, the design and functionality of information management technologies reflects a pre-web perspective and capability in Davis' evolutionary timeline.

It is a fundamental truth that knowledge workers must have access to the full breadth and depth of an organization's data and information assets to do their work. This generally means having full access to all of the organization's information management technologies and repositories. However, information management technologies focus first on applications and technology, only on data and information from a storage or processing perspective, and rarely if ever on knowledge. Information management technologies "own" and "secure" the information that they store. Data and information are the focus and subject of the applications – they are not independent entities in their own right. Information management technologies are designed to support a well-defined and linear final product management life cycle.

In comparison to semantic and knowledge technologies, information management technologies are designed around simple and straight forward linear processes, principles and practices. Both information management and information technology provide support for predefined and "hard wired" data formats. Data structures and program logic are physically embedded into systems making dynamic change or adaptation extremely cumbersome and painful. This approach to management and technology is not the support environment needed for the knowledge future we just described.

Information technology architectures are not well designed to support the dynamic nature of knowledge work, to manage computable knowledge or the extensibility of knowledge objects. Where information architectures have been centrally controlled and managed,

Bringing Order to Chaos: Knowledge Architectures that Sustain Knowledge Practice

knowledge architectures will be user controlled, loosely coupled, user selected applications. Information architectures and technologies will continue to play a critical role in the new environment. However, the nexus of control shifts from enterprise information repositories to knowledge objects that flow across applications.

In addition, information technologies focus more on formal or secondary information products and packages, rather than on primary sources of knowledge such as people and communities. These sources are key to capturing tacit knowledge and knowledge at an earlier stage in the knowledge life cycle. In an information technology and a Web 1.0 environment, we find people through their data and information products. People and communities are only treated as accessible sources of knowledge when we reach Davis' Web 2.0 – the connected web. With Web 2.0's social and professional networking technologies, knowledge professionals have the capability to represent people as entities and sources of knowledge. Today, knowledge workers access knowledge resources by interacting with other people, communities and groups directly or through multiple channels. Knowledge technologies, on the other hand, are designed to support knowledge as an independent entity wherever it may be used. In a virtual environment, access to other people and communities must be seamless and easy. The virtual knowledge working environment involves a fundamental shift in how knowledge is captured, shared, mobilized, productized, disseminated and evaluated. It will become "knowledge-centric" rather than "information technology application-centric." The new virtual working environments need to support the knowledge life cycle for all participants and all sources, wherever they live or are stored.

Denise A. D. Bedford

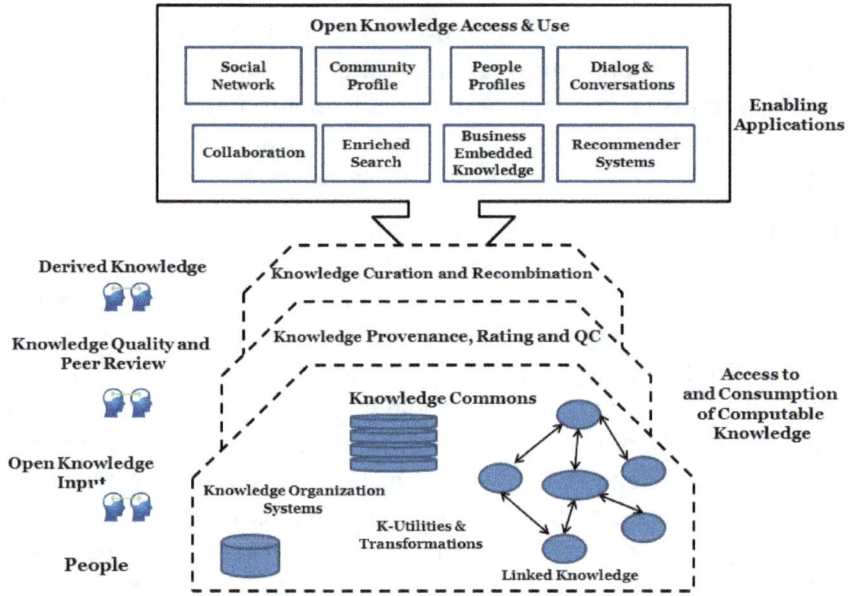

Figure 2. Open-Knowledge Working Environment

The new semantic or knowledge technologies require the support of an abstraction layer above existing IT technologies. This layer enables bridging and interconnection of data, content, and processes. Semantic technologies provide the capabilities that support a more intelligent, relevant, user-controlled and user-responsive interaction than our current information technologies.

In contrast to industry-standard processes for information management and information architectures, knowledge technologies and architectures are user and business driven, designed to suit the way an organization works and to support its business goals. They respond to interactions and business needs, rather than drive the way the business works. Semantic and knowledge technologies are just evolving. We do not have the benefit of thirty-years experience with information technology to fall back on. In contrast to IT standards and best practices, good practices for knowledge technologies are defined at the organization, group or individual level – not the industry level. What becomes a standard in a knowledge environment is the need to

Bringing Order to Chaos: Knowledge Architectures that Sustain Knowledge Practice

have an established or consistent way to define what the knowledge environment looks like and how it links to and interoperates with the business and information technology foundation.

Essentially, the challenge for knowledge professionals is to ensure that when knowledge work is moved to the virtual environment, we not only sustain the gains that have been made at the information management and information technology level, but that there is a new knowledge architecture layer to support knowledge-rich business practices and processes. This brings us to two fundamental questions – what does the knowledge architecture of the future look like? And, how do we design it?

Architecture and the Architecting Process

There are many facets to these challenges. One theme which we can speak to is the need in the future for knowledge architecture. A knowledge architecture which is grounded on knowledge principles, managed through established architecture methodologies, and which is aligned with and supports the organization's business goals, strategy, and its knowledge strategy. Knowledge architectures, unlike information management architectures, should not drive the way a knowledge organization works. Rather, they should be designed to support the way that people work and where they work, to reflect the value of knowledge in the new economy, and to treat knowledge, rather than applications, as the primary asset.

Architecture is the art and science of designing an environment to suit its purpose. Enterprise architecture is the art and science of designing an organizational environment to suit its strategic business performance. A good enterprise-architecture design ensures that the whole digital environment supports the way the organization works best. Enterprise architecture provides the design guidance for the environments that support the day-to-day work activities within an organization; taking into consideration business capabilities and processes, information and data architectures, software applications, and technology infrastructures.

There are several enterprise architecture frameworks and models in use today, including the Zachman Framework, The Open Group Architecture Framework (TOGAF), Federal Enterprise Architecture (FEAF) and the Department of Defense Enterprise Architecture Framework (DoDAF). Figure 4 below illustrates what is commonly referred to in most of these models as an "architecture stack."

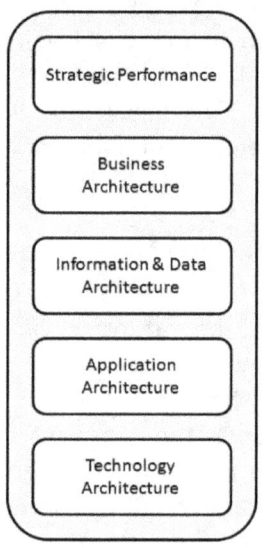

Figure 3. Enterprise Architecture "Stack" Example

Each layer in an enterprise architecture stack is made up of components or segments. For example, the business architecture includes all of the business objects, capabilities, processes and vocabularies. The information & data architecture describes how the enterprise data stores are organized, the data assets of the organization, the organization's vocabularies and the access controls. The application architecture describes the applications that are used, their alignment with business capabilities and processes, and how they interact with one another. The technical architecture layer describes the actual hardware infrastructure that supports applications and the communication across those applications there are as many enterprise architecture methodologies as there are frameworks and models. Drawing upon

Bringing Order to Chaos: Knowledge Architectures that Sustain Knowledge Practice

what is common to all, is that each of the methodologies takes into consideration some key elements, including:

- Design Principles – knowledge principles;
- Business Requirements – knowledge practices and how knowledge workers work;
- Types of Entities and Assets – knowledge assets and typologies;
- Supporting knowledge technology requirements in the form of supporting applications and technologies,
- Knowledge principles, practices, typologies and supporting knowledge technology requirements provide the design requirements for knowledge architecture. Figure 4 illustrates the relationship of these principles to the knowledge strategy and to the information-architecture foundation and provides examples of what would be covered in each of the design elements.

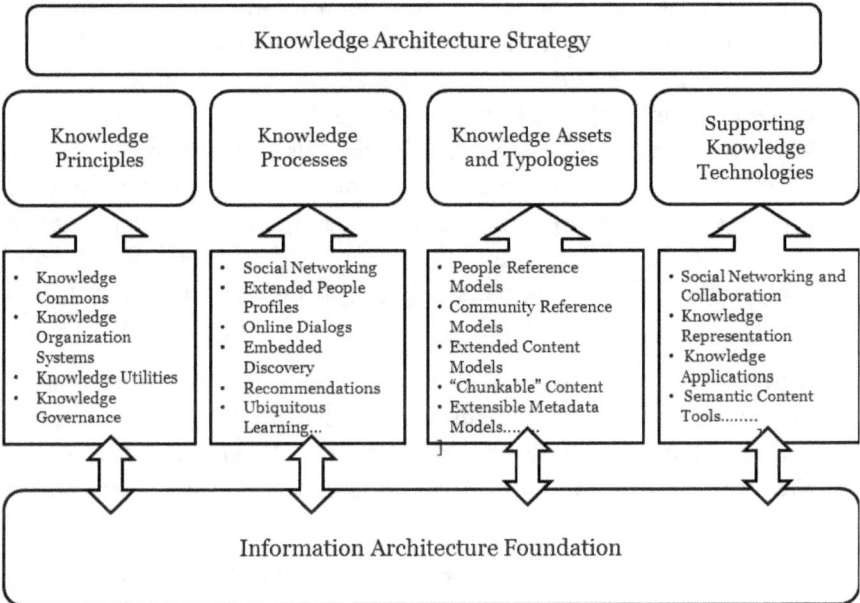

Figure 4. Designing a Knowledge Architecture

Denise A. D. Bedford

Knowledge or Information and Data Architecture

While knowledge architectures have been referenced and discussed within the KM community, it is generally in the context of data and information architecture and information technology methods. Enterprise architects generally assume that knowledge architecture is supported by information architecture principles, processes, and designs. However, practical experience would suggest that there are some key distinctions between data and information architecture, and knowledge architecture. What are some of those distinctions? What does a conceptual model of knowledge architecture look like? What does it include? Let's begin with a discussion of knowledge principles which would guide a knowledge architecture design.

Knowledge Principles

Architectures must always be grounded on principles and aligned with practices. Information principles are fundamental and necessary, but they are not sufficient to support a knowledge environment. They do not speak to the fundamental characteristics of knowledge and knowledge work. Information management is typically centrally controlled, predictable, and linear in nature. This perspective is generally reflected in information management principles. An environment that supports knowledge work, on the other hand, may be managed at the group or individual level, must be open, support broad access to resources, and allow for variant configurations suited to the task at hand.

A knowledge-architecture should be designed around seven principles which are specific to knowledge and which supplement the information architecture principles. Knowledge is: (1) Open, (2) Collaborative, (3) Transparent, (4) Interactive, (5) Perishable, (6) Embedded, and (7) Extensible.

Knowledge is Open - the architecture is designed in a way that lowers barriers to knowledge creation, access, use, reuse, contribution, discovery and collaboration, and is grounded on the adoption of open standards, open source, and open knowledge and data as core elements of a modular and sustainable design.

Bringing Order to Chaos: Knowledge Architectures that Sustain Knowledge Practice

Knowledge is Collaborative - the architecture should support community based review and curation of knowledge assets to maximize relevancy, quality and reliability, supports feedback and recommendations regarding knowledge assets, metadata and knowledge services, and enables any user to comment upon, review, assess and rate the quality of knowledge assets.

Knowledge is Transparent - the architecture provides a clear description of the methods, sources, assumptions, outcomes and other information that allow a user to understand how the knowledge asset was designed or produced (its provenance), and it affords traceability and facilitates end-user contribution of new knowledge assets, to edit or reconfigure metadata or to create linked associations among knowledge asset.

Knowledge is Interactive - the architecture supports interaction whether face-to-face or virtual as an opportunity to acquire and share knowledge.

Knowledge is Perishable - means that the architecture now supports the full life cycle of knowledge and prevents loss in the early deliberative stages.

Knowledge is Perishable – knowledge is a fleeting commodity that achieves its greatest value when it is shared, transferred, exchanged and mobilized. This means that the knowledge architecture needs to be both robust in capturing knowledge and unobtrusive in the way that it does this. It cannot introduce barriers or impediments to knowledge transactions.

Knowledge is Embedded - the knowledge architecture supports embedding knowledge assets wherever business is conducted and wherever staff and teams are working – all environments.

Knowledge is Extensible - the architecture must support the building of complex knowledge assets through the creation, bundling, and linking of individual components as well as the disaggregation of existing knowledge assets for the purpose of more relevant and targeted reuse.

Denise A. D. Bedford

The three trends provide a good picture of the business requirements, the entities and the technology support requirements needed to design knowledge architecture. The knowledge principles suggest that today's current data-information architecture layer and its segments provide suboptimal support in the future knowledge economy. Walking through that design process, there are four essential segments in knowledge architecture (Figure 5): (1) People; (2) Communities; (3) Knowledge; and (4) Knowledge Processes. Knowledge is the property of people. People create, share, and discover knowledge in communities. Knowledge organizations support knowledge processes which accelerate the creation, sharing, and discovery of knowledge. And, by definition, knowledge is the key asset of knowledge architecture.

From an enterprise architecture perspective, we may be able to place these components in an existing enterprise architecture framework. However, placement would be suboptimal and not address the centrality of knowledge over applications in the future. By defining a new "Knowledge Layer" in the architecture framework, we raise awareness of new and distinct principles, new types of entities, and new processes not currently referenced. A knowledge-architecture layer fits into the overall design between the business-architecture and the data-/information-architecture layers.

Bringing Order to Chaos: Knowledge Architectures that Sustain Knowledge Practice

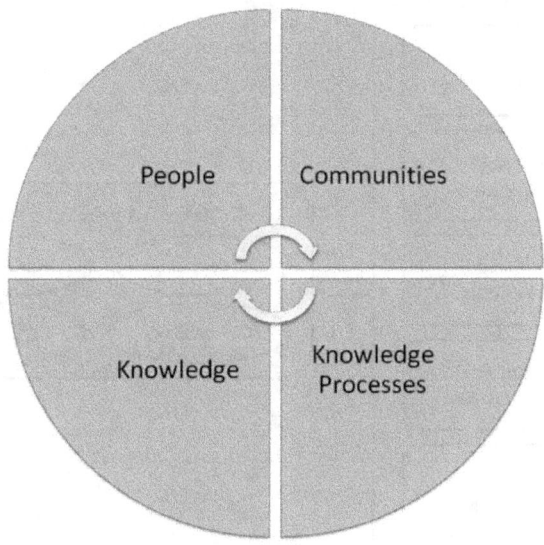

Figure 5. Knowledge Architecture Segments

A New Knowledge Architecture Framework

A new layer in the enterprise architecture stack is needed to support the knowledge environment of the future. Figure 6 illustrates the traditional enterprise-architecture "stack" with the addition of a knowledge-architecture layer, and its four proposed segments.

Each layer in an architecture "stack" has distinct segments and components. The four segments of the knowledge architecture provide the context for building out the components to support the segments. The following sections discuss the components of each of four segments in knowledge architect.

Denise A. D. Bedford

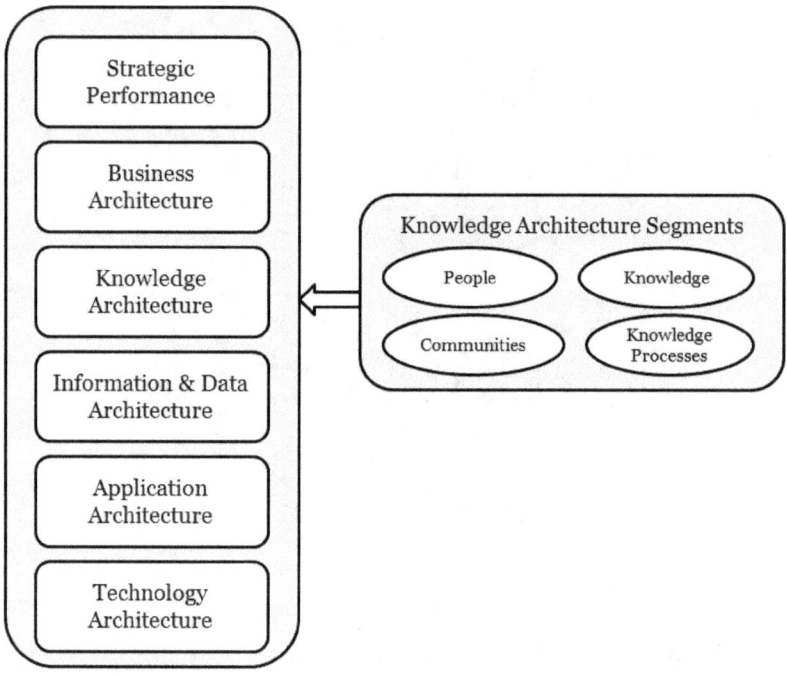

Figure 6. Knowledge Architecture in the Enterprise-Architecture Stack

The People Segment

Through the people segment, the knowledge architecture provides opportunities to represent people as a key source of knowledge. This segment allows one to capture, synthesize, surface, review and enrich the existing information about people. In addition, it provides them a space in which to expose, mobilize and manage their own knowledge. Today, there is an emergent form of a People segment in Web 2.0 social networking applications. But, consistent with our characterization of the "information technology approach" earlier – this data is embedded in an application. If that application disappears, so does all of the information that was created about the people who "used the application." The People segment should also provide the foundation for persistent metadata warehouse about a person, for locating and reviewing expertise, for defining intellectual capital indicators, and to develop "knowledge dashboards" that help individuals to improve their own knowledge behaviors.

For people, persistent data models can be enriched by leveraging the information generated in social networking and collaboration contexts. Enriched People Profiles can be used to improve expertise discovery, social networking, knowledge sourcing, personalization, recommender engines, and content syndication. The People Segment also provides a key starting point for looking for knowledge and information by tracking it to the people who created it. Figure 7 describes four people sub-segments: (1) the people data model, (2) expertise locator, (3) people data warehouse, and (4) intellectual capital dashboards. T

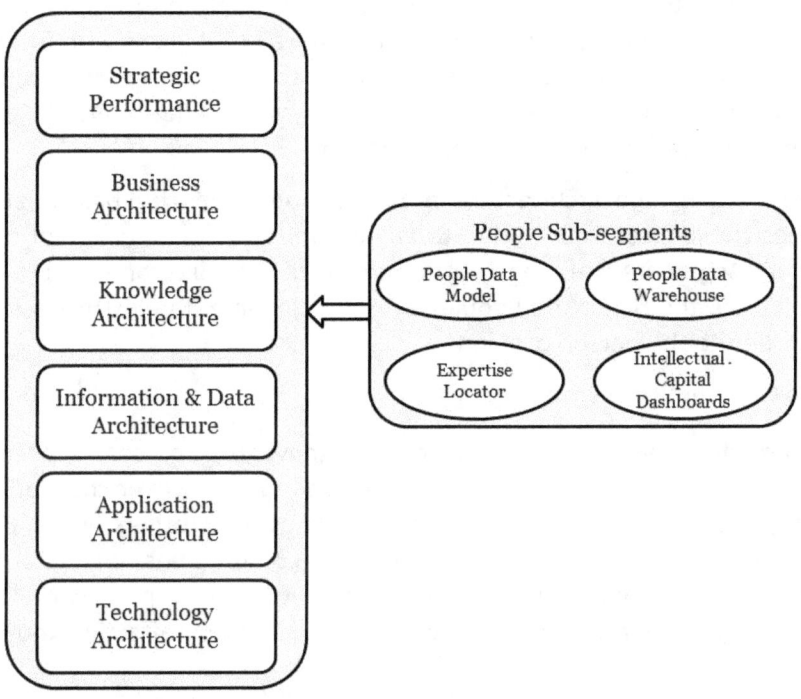

Figure 7. People Architecture Components

he people data model provides the foundation for a robust profile of people, essentially an extensive metadata description of all aspects of an individual and their intellectual capital. An expertise locator leverages the people data model, but provides a broader expertise architecture that supports discovery, review, verification and use of expertise. People data warehouses are the equivalent to information and document repositories but with several important variations. Information and documents change slowly or infrequently after they have been formalized. People are continuously growing, learning and changing. People data warehouses will have to be far more flexible in their design and operation than are any of today's information repositories. Intellectual capital dashboards are the components that leverage people data models and people data warehouses. They serve many purposes, including enabling individuals to grow and manage their own intellectual capital. They also enable organizations to measure, monitor and manage those assets in a way that aligns with future needs. Intellectual capital dashboards are similar to performance dashboards, with the exception that the assets being managed are intellectual rather than financial or physical.

While knowledge architecture provides many opportunities, it also raises challenges. One caution to any organization in building out the people segments is the need for an institutional policy on privacy. By definition, the richer the People segments become, the less privacy is afforded to the person profiled.

The Community Segment

Communities are where many of the knowledge processes occur. Communities are where individuals ask questions, discover knowledge gaps, learn from others, share what they know with others, engage in collaborative work processes, etc. Finding communities, understanding what a community is all about, and capturing and preserving the knowledge generated by communities are all key to effective knowledge management.

Most enterprise architecture frameworks treat a community or a group as a formal organizational entity – as an administrative fact

Bringing Order to Chaos: Knowledge Architectures that Sustain Knowledge Practice

rather than a complex and rich source of knowledge. Modelling a community as an entity-relationship model fails to grasp the dynamic and more complex knowledge ecosystem that a community truly represents. The other way that communities are represented in enterprise architecture is as a controlled source of values - master data.

Informal or transitory communities are generally not "managed" or "supported" within organizations. This perspective must change in a knowledge future. With the increase in professional and social networking due to the availability of collaborative environments and social networking, there is a need to define a community data model, to define essential types of communities and attributes, and to define methods for capturing knowledge that is generated by communities for exposure beyond the community. Knowledge is exchanged and transacted in these contexts which are essentially dynamic knowledge ecosystems. These are critical elements in the knowledge architecture. Figure 8 describes four community sub-segments: (1) the community data model, (2) community director, (3) people-community linkages, and (4) community knowledge.

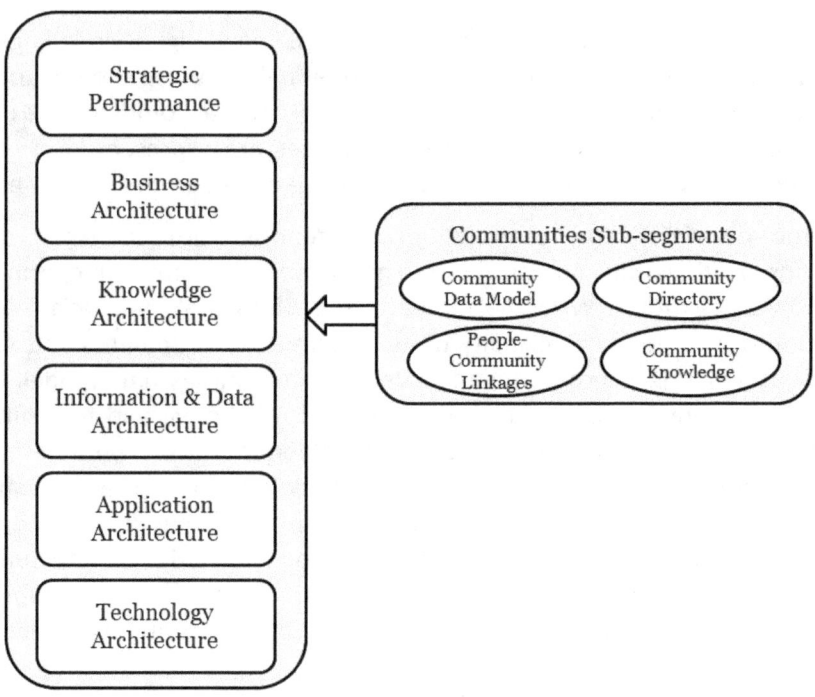

Figure 8. Communities Architecture Components

Community data model serves a similar purpose to the people data model. The community data model, though, is not a mirror or an aggregate of people data models. The community data model is a complex model which includes individual people models, relationships between people, and attributes of the community as a single entity. The community director is represented by a single people data model, as well as its particular business roles and linkages to other members in the community. People-community linkages are like links in a network structure. In the new architecture, though, links not only connect two other entities but they are entities in their own right. Links have attributes and take on meaning in knowledge architecture. Community knowledge is represented as both the sum of the knowledge of the community members, and as knowledge the community creates or holds collectively. The community segment is dynamic and continuously changing, just as is the people data model. The level of change in a community is as great as that for a single individual.

The Knowledge Segment

Knowledge is dynamic, cumulative, connected, and contextual. Knowledge is consumed in small chunks—ideas, concepts, discussions, annotations, comments, critical reviews, smart lessons, and lessons learned, for example. This is a very immature environment, though it is developing rapidly. The need to look at knowledge differently than data and information is great. For example, "raw" or un-reviewed knowledge in the form of dialogs, ideas, or results does not receive formal attention in the enterprise architecture framework. Accessing parts of information products is now a manual human process. There are no standard processes for peer review of knowledge. Neither are there processes that capture and track the provenance of knowledge as metadata nor meta-information. Of all of the challenges, though, the need for a comprehensive typology for knowledge assets tops the list for the knowledge segment of knowledge architecture.

To address some of these needs, the knowledge segment (Figure 9), includes six components: (1) Knowledge Topologies, (2) Knowledge Capture and Tagging, (3) Information Asset Reverse Engineering, (4) Knowledge Structures, (5) Knowledge Peer Review, and (7) Knowledge Metrics:

- Knowledge Typologies which enable classification of knowledge for use and management;
- Knowledge Capture and Tagging including the structure and architecture of knowledge content itself, as well as its description and surrogation;
- Information Asset Reverse Engineering which involves retrospectively adding structure and explicit meaning to content that was either born as print or as flat content for display;
- Knowledge Structures or the semantically enhanced architecture of an otherwise flat content object to make it understandable and computable by machines;

- Knowledge Peer Review which offers an important validation and verification process for tacit or raw knowledge in an open environment, and draws heavily from social media platforms and processes;
- Knowledge Metrics which includes a wide range of indicators about knowledge in all phases of its life cycle.

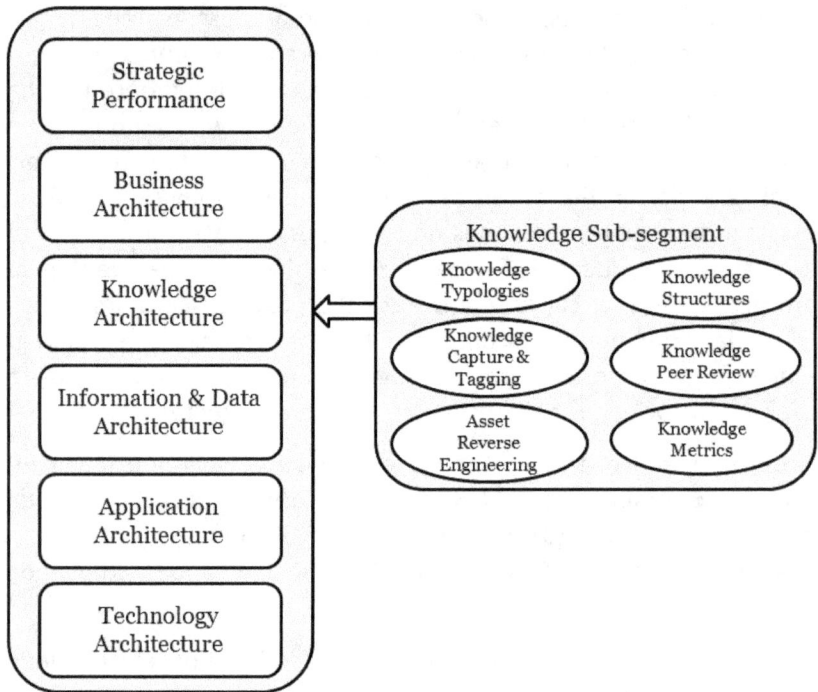

Figure 9. Knowledge Architecture Components

The Knowledge Segment provides support for the other three and provides the critical functionality to operationalize knowledge practices and processes.

The Knowledge Processes Segment

Knowledge Architectures must support the new environment in which knowledge workers work. Referring back to the knowledge principles, the platform should be designed for open access, interoperability and

Bringing Order to Chaos: Knowledge Architectures that Sustain Knowledge Practice

integration, and the unobtrusive capture of knowledge. The architecture must enable knowledge workers to discover new sources of knowledge and expertise; create, encode, and circulate new knowledge; reuse existing knowledge; and to validate or repudiate knowledge. It must support community and group work, dialog and open communication, the ability to capture knowledge at any stage of its life cycle, and to create "knowledge traps" which prevent loss. Architecture must support building trust through provenance tracking, feedback, and quality control. A knowledge-friendly work environment also allows relevant knowledge to rise to the surface in business context and enables users to embed their know-how and procedural knowledge in business processes.

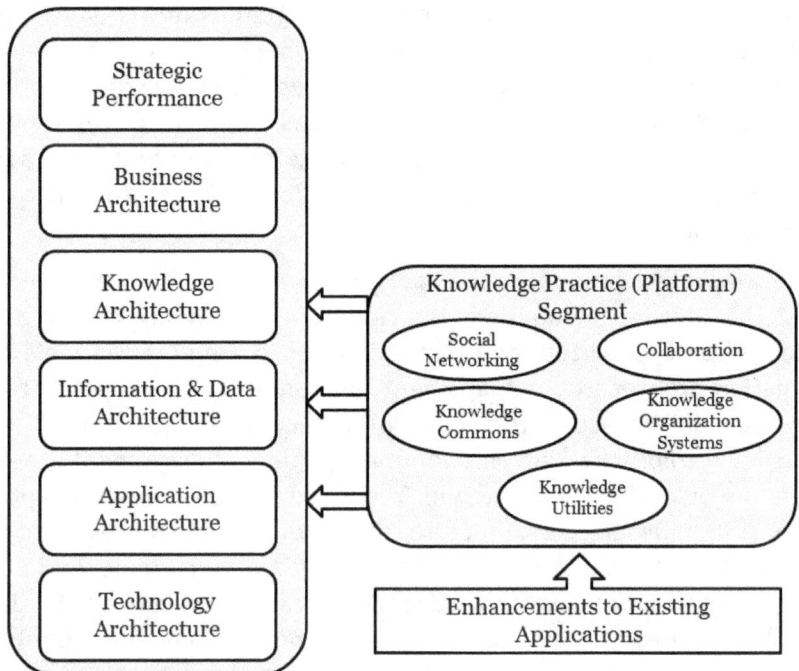

Figure 10. Knowledge Process Components

The knowledge process segment speaks to the essence of "knowledge principles"—i.e., it must be open, collaborative, interactive, connected, agile, and user-defined. The knowledge architecture is designed to function above and across existing applications – a level of access is elevated to virtual working environments. This new knowledge processing environment also is inherently semantic – it speaks directly to the inclusion and seamless integration of supportive knowledge technologies referred to by Mills Davis.

The Knowledge Processing Segment leverages some key semantic technologies including: (1) Knowledge Commons; (2) Knowledge Organization Systems (KOS); (3) Knowledge Utilities; (4) Social Networking; and (5) Collaboration Applications.

The Knowledge Commons

The knowledge commons provides an open grid and transparent access to all knowledge assets at the level of granularity required. The knowledge commons must be accessible directly to any knowledge practices. The knowledge commons leverages knowledge organization systems (KOS)—a backbone of ontologies, controlled references sources, and knowledge maps and networks used to organize knowledge. Knowledge utilities support the creation and use of the knowledge commons and the KOS.

The knowledge commons is the heart of the new knowledge architecture. The knowledge commons is a cloud of linked and linkable metadata and data—a virtual grid that exists above the organization's information and records management environment. This represents a significant shift in access to and use of metadata, structured data, and KOS. In a traditional information-management environment, these sources would be encapsulated in "record structures" housed in applications. In knowledge architecture, these sources are represented as open statements represented in Resource Description Framework RDF (Bell, 1974) or Simple Knowledge Organization System SKOS (Bell 1974) structures—accessible to any user who can find them (Benbya and Van Alstyne 2011). This trend is also a fundamental component of current open-linked data portals, eScience, and other open research initiatives. The knowledge commons and KOS may, in part, derive from the Bank's enterprise-information repositories, but it does not connect or interfere with them.

Bringing Order to Chaos: Knowledge Architectures that Sustain Knowledge Practice

The knowledge commons enables:

- Any user to create links or add knowledge objects
- Any service provider or end user to extend or supplement knowledge, metadata and meta-information to enrich our understanding of a resource
- The creation and definition of new kinds of links and relationships
- The creation and management of links as distinct knowledge assets with their own metadata
- Linking of all kinds of knowledge—including people, communities, conversations, references, concept maps, etc.
- Programmatic linking based on similarity or other business rules
- The addition and retention of context, other use meta-information, and provenance to allow users to decide whether they trust the knowledge or can improve it
- The addition of review and quality-control information about a resource

Access to assets that live outside the organization

- Quality control and "curation" of all knowledge assets
- Discovery of all knowledge assets produced for the new knowledge assets
- Provides an easy capture point for new knowledge assets
- Allows end users to directly explore and exploit knowledge assets without jeopardizing the security or integrity of the enterprise's knowledge assets

Another significant change in the knowledge common is a shift from single-source institutionally created metadata to the integration and extension of metadata from personal collections, from end users. In essence, the creation and extension of metadata from any source that contains knowledge relevant to the organization's work. This metadata is enriched through user curation—i.e., the ability of users to augment existing metadata to reflect their perspectives, domains, evaluation, or use of the assets.

Denise A. D. Bedford

Knowledge Organization Systems (KOS)

The open knowledge commons provides the flexibility for knowledge processing. KOS provides backbone support for links and access points. Backbone KOS supports:

- New knowledge discovery capabilities
- Knowledge classification schemes and taxonomies
- Knowledge metadata and meta-information standards
- Linked data rich relationships
- User tagging

User Feedback and Ranking Structures

Current controlled reference sources also take a virtual form in the new knowledge architecture. Where these sources are maintained in a virtual and open environment, organizations may encourage stakeholder involvement in managing these structures. A new approach to governance would ensure that stakeholder and institutional views are aligned.

Knowledge Utilities

Knowledge utilities support the creation, management, and governance of the knowledge commons, the creation and use of the knowledge organization systems (KOS), and all end user access and functions. Knowledge utilities include:

- Metadata Harvesting and Transformation from enterprise applications and working environments
- Relationship and Link Management
- Provenance Tracking and Quality-Control Structures
- Authorization and Authentication Services required to access content
- Automated Content Profiling
- Automated People Profiling

Knowledge utilities may leverage functionality that is already available in other enterprise-architecture domains. However, these utilities are fundamentally semantic, whereas existing technologies may not have any inherent semantic capabilities. Today's information technologies are generally predefined and "hardwired."

Social Networking Collaboration Applications

Enhancement of existing application architecture domains

The Knowledge Processing Segment introduces new requirements for the application layer, for example, the upgrade and institutionalization of social networking and collaboration technologies. Security and identity access management become much more important applications in knowledge architecture because the capabilities must now be embedded in and travel with knowledge assets. Privacy policies must be upgraded and aligned with more extensive profiling of people and communities. And, workflow and business process management applications must now be "knowledge rich" with knowledge embedded at the machine level. Perhaps the greatest impact is today's design of search. As Mills Davis noted, in a new knowledge environment, search transforms "From Search to Knowing."

Conclusion

All that we have learned in knowledge management over the past two decades is good preparation for meeting the challenges of the knowledge economy, the new knowledge working environment, and the world of semantic technologies. But, they are not sufficient to ensure that our principles and practices carry forward into the future. Knowledge professionals need to step up and take an active role in designing the components of the future knowledge architecture. This involves working for change in many different domains, in different standards organizations, and in our own working environments.

The critical task for sustaining the gains that have been made in knowledge management in the past twenty years is the definition and adoption of a knowledge architecture framework and methodology. A knowledge architecture framework and methodology enables enterprise architectures to better design architecture to support future knowledge environments. Without a knowledge architecture framework and methodology, engineers and architects continue to design information management and information technology principles and standards. Knowledge professionals need to lead the discussion out of the 1990s and into the 21st century. The knowledge architecture is rich in components – there are opportunities for everyone to contribute.

References

Bell, D. (1974). The Coming of Post-Industrial Society: A Venture in Social Forecasting. London: Heinemann.

Machup, F. (1962). The Production and Distribution of Knowledge in the United States. Princeton: Princeton University Press.

Benbya, H. and Van Alstyne, M. (2011). "How to Find Answers Within Your Company," MIT Sloan Management Review, Reprint No. 52212 (Winter 2011), Vol. 52, No. 2.

Davis, M. (2008). Semantic Wave 2008 Report: Industry Roadmap to Web 3.0 & Multibillion dollar Market Opportunities [Online]. Retrieved from http://www.eurolibnet.eu/files/Repository/2009050/165103_SemanticWaveReport2008.pdf [Accessed Nov. 7, 2011].

Transferring Tacit Knowledge with the Movement of Employees

Bonita Best Coppedge

Virtual PM, LLC, Ruskin, FL, USA

Introduction

Leaders of today's organizations are surprised to learn that valuable organizational history sometimes resides only in their employees' brains and when employees leave an organization, a portion of the organizational corporate knowledge leaves as well. An organization's most valuable asset is knowledge that is located in employees' minds (known as tacit knowledge) and contains approximately 90% of an organization's corporate knowledge (Baumard 2002; Stenmark 2001; Vera-Munoz Ho, and Chow 2006). In the past, many projects failed because of incomplete or poor knowledge transfers. Thus, transferring corporate knowledge among employees within an organization is essential for promoting best practices, maintaining a competitive advantage, and enhancing corporate capabilities.

By reading this chapter, entrepreneurs building a business, seasoned managers overseeing global expansions, government officials overseeing multi-agency initiatives, consultants providing professional services to clients, gain insights on successful ways to transfer tacit knowledge with the movement of employees. Knowledge Management (KM) practitioners are able to expand their knowledge about influencers and barriers to knowledge transfer to improve their outcomes. Industry leaders and KM practitioners are introduced to the application of the TKT Cycle© model (Figure 1), a theoretical model that contains a 10-step process for transferring tacit knowledge from one employee to another.

The Movement of Employees

According to scholars, moving employees result in knowledge transfer (Argote and Ingram 2000). De Gregori (1987) noted that organizational knowledge and capabilities might lose value when shared over time. However, Lado and Zhang (1998) argue that value from corporate capabilities increase when shared internally. Lado and Zhang (1998) further state that corporate capabilities are specific to the organization and are path-dependent processes that are not available in the competitive marketplace, making them difficult to copy and nurture through continuous learning.

The TKT Cycle© evolved from Coppedge's (2010) expert panel regarding the movement of people in the transference of tacit knowledge. The model is based upon knowledge-based, resource-based, agency, and actor-network theories. It offers practical insights on transferring tacit knowledge and enhancing the organization's ability to grow its organizational knowledge.

The knowledge-based resources are difficult to imitate (Lado and Zhang 1998) and organizations with diverse knowledge bases and knowledge capabilities contribute to the organization having a competitive edge (Barney 1991; Peteraf 1993). The resource-based theories acknowledge the role of knowledge within organizations that achieve a competitive edge. The ability to identify, share, and apply corporate knowledge contributes to organizational performance. Knowledge is an essential asset for growing and sustaining organizational performance (Grant 1996; Nonaka 1996). Organizations exist because leaders create an environment within the organization to leverage the knowledge integration process (Camass, Darning, & Lana 2005). An organizational environment that utilizes the knowledge integration process incorporates common knowledge shared by individuals (i.e., employees) and the organizational structure (Grant 1996).

The agency theory is used to study organizations (i.e., multinational corporations) to explain the headquarter-subsidiary relationships (e.g., global firms and federal agencies). It addresses the challenges that occur in agency relationship, such as conflicting goals. According to agency theory, organizations may appoint employees, consultants, and other resources to fill the knowledge gap (Khosrowpour 2000). In general, organizations such as small businesses, large government agencies, and global firms benefit from having the skills and knowledge internal to fill strategic roles in implementing a project, establishing a business unit, or building a business.

The actor-networks theory is derived from Latour's (1987, 1999) idea of human and non-human resources having the ability to enroll new actors into the network to mobilize knowledge between locations (e.g., the movement of people such as scientist, engineers, consultants, and project managers). The perspective of actor-networks solves the compartmentalized knowledge conduits (artifacts and people) approach as mutual constituting entities (Barnes, Sheppard, Peck, and Tickell 2003). The actor network theory asserts that things happen only by enrolling a large number of entities within a larger network, making them work together to produce the desired outcome (Barnes et al., 2003). The actor network theory provides insight into how mobile knowledge networks function through interdependencies between people (e.g., employees and consultants) and things (e.g., tacit knowledge or corporate knowledge).

Characteristics: Knowledge-Based, Resource-Based, Agency, and Actor-Network Theories

Characteristics from the knowledge-based, resource-based, agency, and actor-network theories serve as principles to leaders, entrepreneurs, and practitioners, who could include these characteristics into corporate plans (e.g., strategic, global expansion, interagency agreements, and knowledge transfer) when transferring tacit knowledge from one location to another with the movement of employees.

Knowledge

Employees generate knowledge within an organization regardless of the size or location of the organization. Organizational knowledge is a blend of evolving experience, contextual information, expert insight, and values. People and firms are carriers of knowledge dynamics (Biggiero 2006). Knowledge dynamics are due to an organization's continual process of learning. Leaders view an organization's ability to expand or grow its corporate knowledge and employees with embedded organizational knowledge as vital assets and capabilities.

Tacit Knowledge

Tacit knowledge is the individual's expertise or know-how and individuals are inclined to know more than they can tell (Polyani 1996; 1983). Tacit knowledge is "heuristic, subjective and internalized, and is not easy to communicate" (Evans, Hodkinson, and Unwin 2002, 133). It is personal and hard to communicate using language, articulate in words, or share with others. Tacit knowledge includes both intellectual and practical knowing (Polyani 1996). A person's experience, actions, insights, values, beliefs, perceptions, and intuitions are categorized as tacit knowledge.

Proximity is critical when transferring tacit knowledge because it requires the movement of people (Biggiero 2006). Leaders in the private and public sectors seek ways of working within the United States and internationally with the use of knowledge transfer (e.g., to support military missions and to relocate business units). However expanding a business globally or completing an international mission, leaders need to develop strategies for transferring knowledge using tactics such as member-to-member knowledge transfers.

Explicit Knowledge

Explicit knowledge is explained using written formats and/or people transmitting the knowledge in a formal language (Sun & Scott 2005; Vera-Munoz, Hoe and Chow 2006). Explicit information that is shareable via a formal, systematic language (Simmie 2003). For instance, operational manuals are explicit knowledge. Although knowledge transfers include the exchange of tacit knowledge and explicit knowledge, in this chapter, the focus is on tacit knowledge because of the complexity surrounding its transfer.

Transferring Tacit Knowledge with the Movement of Employees

Knowledge Management (KM)

KM focuses on the processes of creation and transfer of organizational knowledge and the development of tools to manage organizational knowledge (Easterby-Smith, Burgoyne, and Araujo 2001). Views of KM have been on a micro- or macro-level. At the macro-level, individuals who embrace KM leverage knowledge with an objective of productivity and competitiveness (Misra 2007), that includes knowledge transfer and knowledge creation within an industry or within a nation (Guzman and Wilson 2005). The micro-level of KM involves the organizational, social, cognitive processes by which people transform, transfer, and create knowledge (Guzman and Wilson 2005; Nonaka and Takeuchi 1995). Within the micro-level of KM, organizational process involves the mechanisms and capability that support the management of knowledge and the attainment of knowledge (Guzman & Wilson, 2005). The focus of this chapter is on KM at micro-level.

There is a considerable amount of research on KM; however, there are areas of KM that remain vague (e.g., organizational knowledge transfer). Many researchers tend to focus on either explicit or tacit knowledge separately, and do not address the method of transferring tacit knowledge (McLaughlin n.d.). Coppedge's (2010) Delphi study is focused on a method of transferring tacit knowledge (i.e., moving people with a goal of transferring tacit knowledge).

Transferring Tacit Knowledge

The ability to transfer tacit knowledge from one person to another is not well understood. As previously stated, proximity is critical when transferring tacit knowledge because it requires moving people to interact with one another via meetings and onsite visits (Biggiero, 2006; Maskell and Malmberg 1999). Leaders are challenged with figuring out how to recognize, generate, share, and manage tacit knowledge (Levinson 2007). Recognizing knowledge or intellectual capital involves perception. Leaders or other team members can recognize an employee's knowledge, skills, and abilities and begin to shape their perceived value of the employee's expert knowledge.

People acquire and/or develop their tacit knowledge through hands-on experiences and observation; not exclusively from formal education or training. The process of transferring tacit knowledge is embedded contextually (Kostova, 1999) and does not occur in a vacuum. According to Kostova (1999), there are three ways knowledge is embedded in context: 1) organizational embeddedness, 2) social embeddedness, and 3) relational embeddedness.

Organizational embeddedness is where the knowledge transfer outcome can be positive or negative as organizational culture could affect the transference of tacit-knowledge (Kostova 1999). Supporting Kostova is the suggestion of Szulanski (1996, 748) that "the success of transfer will be affected by the compatibility between the values implied by the particular practice and the values underlying the culture of the organizational unit".

Social embeddedness has country-level effects on the success of tacit-knowledge transfers (Adler 1995; Riusala and Suutari 2004). Leaders with a goal of global expansion may want to consider the country-level effects on knowledge transfers before moving the knowledge sender to the knowledge recipient's location as some countries provide more favorable environments and others present an array of challenges that may negatively influence tacit knowledge transfer. Leaders and practitioners are encouraged to investigate the country's institutional profile (e.g., country rules, laws, regulatory, and norms) before moving employees.

They should also be cognizant that knowledge transfers can fail when the social and organizational context are favorable because of the relationship between the knowledge transfer participants (i.e., knowledge sender and knowledge recipient) (Riusala and Suutari 2004). Transferring tacit knowledge depends on the ease of communication and the relationship between the knowledge sender and knowledge recipient, which requires numerous individual exchanges (e.g., onsite visits and telephone calls).

Transferring Tacit Knowledge with the Movement of Employees

The Knowledge Transfer Process

Knowledge transfer is defined as a process in which an organizational is affected by the experience of another (Argote and Ingram, 2000). The knowledge transfer process involves five high-level steps:

1. Creating the Knowledge
2. Sharing the Knowledge
3. Assessing or Evaluating the Knowledge
4. Disseminating the Knowledge
5. Adopting the Knowledge

Using the knowledge transfer process to create knowledge or generate new ideas, employees should be encouraged to think outside of the box and problem solve. This new knowledge or idea is the basis for sharing knowledge that introduces the credentials of the employees or knowledge transfer professionals. Employees or knowledge transfer professionals, who share, need to be knowledgeable in the technical or functional area and be able to communicate using a common language such as English, French, German, Arabic, or Spanish. Once knowledge is shared, leaders, practitioners, and employees should be able to assess or evaluate the new knowledge through practice or application of the new knowledge. The knowledge transfer participants (i.e., knowledge recipient, knowledge sender, and leader) are then able to make a decision to disseminate and adopt the new knowledge based on the assessment or evaluation.

Although organization leaders oversee and facilitate the transfer of tacit knowledge within an organization, tacit knowledge transfers are generally discretionary activities that are dependent on the complexity and interdependencies that exist, recipient's comprehension and absorption, and the sender's capability to transfer the knowledge. The success of transferring tacit knowledge depends on the ease of communication and the relationship between the source and recipient. In addition, the effectiveness of transferring tacit knowledge is dependent upon the sender's motivation to transfer the knowledge.

The transference of knowledge is affected by four characteristics (Szulankski 1996):

1. Characteristics of the Knowledge Transferred
2. Characteristics of the Source of Knowledge
3. Characteristics of the Recipient of Knowledge
4. Characteristics of the Context

Stickiness is a term used to describe the success of transferring tacit knowledge, because the challenge is to get the knowledge to stick to the recipient (Szulanski 1996; von Hippel 1998). There are three key origins of stickiness (Szulanski 1996): the lack of absorptive capacity of the recipient, causal ambiguity, and strenuous relationship between the source and recipient. Tacit knowledge is personal and requires the knowledge source or transferor to share his/her knowledge as well as the recipient to understand and absorb the new knowledge.

Knowledge Transfer Importance

Continual attention to knowledge transfers reflects the growing recognition that transferring knowledge among employees is the primary intangible source of sustained competitive edge, economic growth, and corporate value (Vera-Munoz et al. 2006). Organizations are most successful at sustaining a competitive edge when leaders understand how to transfer and integrate knowledge within the organization (Lui 2004).

The transference of tacit knowledge is important for maintaining a competitive edge because the continued success of a business often depends upon the distinctive experience of the predecessor (Cabrera-Suarez, De Saa-Perez, and Garcia-Almeida 2001; Chrisman, Chua, and Sharma 2005). To sustain a competitive edge in the global marketplace, leaders need to facilitate the organization's ability to generate knowledge, transfer knowledge, and effectively leverage collective expertise (Lucas 2005).

An organization's most critical asset is knowledge and knowledge gains value when shared with others (Vera-Munoz et al. 2006). However, transferring this critical asset across organizational units is a challenge for leaders (Bjorkman, Barner-Rasmussen, and Li 2004). Organizational members may recognize and perceive the property as symbolic capital (i.e., knowledge or intellectual capital); and then place value on this symbolic capital.

The perceived value of an employee's embedded knowledge is not automatic and requires the application and reproduction of this knowledge (Lyon, 2005). In simpler terms, the perceived value to an organization of the corporate knowledge embedded in an employee's mind increases when the employee shares his/her knowledge with another employee. Employees create knowledge, however, leaders within organizations create the organizational environment that influences how employees create and transfer knowledge (Nonaka & Takeuchi, 1995).

Grant (1996) refers to knowledge as an organizational asset that is transferrable, receivable, and usable between and among employees. Knowledge transferability is important within an organization (Grant, 1996). Organizations as well as employees acquire knowledge from others through the transferring of people with specialized expertise from one unit to another (Lyles and Salk 1996). As employees work together, employees become co-creators and innovators of new organizational knowledge (Lyon, 2005). When an employee improvises or applies his or her personal expertise, the knowledge is probably highly context specific, yet valuable for the organization (Morris 2001). Transferring tacit knowledge requires several individual exchanges (Bethoin, Lenhardt and Rosenbrock 2001; Nonaka 1994; Szulanski 1996).

It is argued that movement of knowledge between different geographical locations is important to the process of adding value in knowledge development and tacit knowledge transfers (Grant, Almedia and Song 2000). Also, it is stated that relationships between two individuals depend on what he or she contributes as well as what he or she has done to create and maintain a relationship (Newcomb, Turner and Converse 1996). Of significant importance to tacit knowledge transfers is trust, an organizational culture trait (Lyles and Salk, 1996).

Knowledge Transfer Influencers: Human Resources

In general, people influence tacit knowledge transfers. The people involved in the transference of tacit knowledge include knowledge senders, knowledge recipients, and leaders. Influencing the transfer of tacit knowledge can be positive and negative. A positive influence may result in employees sharing knowledge and a negative influence may result in employees not sharing tacit knowledge. The 4-factor framework of knowledge transfer (i.e., 4C Framework) proposes that credibility, capability, communication, and culture are sources that influence knowledge transfers (Sarker et al. 2005).

The 4C Framework highlights that the knowledge source or sender's credibility and communications skills are important factors that influences transferring knowledge. A knowledge sender needs to be trusted, viewed as reliable, and available for frequent communications with the knowledge recipients. In addition, the knowledge sender's culture is an important factor, which may influence the extent of the knowledge transferred (Bresman, Birkinshaw, & Nobel 1999; Sarker et al. 2005; Szulanski 1996). A knowledge sender should be a subject matter expert (SME), have the ability to adapt to the local culture, and have compassion for the knowledge recipient(s).

The knowledge recipient requires the ability to recognize, share, apply, and absorb knowledge, along with maintaining a relationship between the knowledge sender and recipient. Absorptive capacity can create challenges in the knowledge recipient's ability to receive and understand the transferred knowledge. In addition, the knowledge recipient must have the technical capability to carry out the knowledge transfer (Szulanski 1996). Knowledge recipients should have the appropriate soft and hard skills (i.e., listening, cognitive and technical skills), interest in receiving the tacit knowledge, and an understanding of the importance of the knowledge.

Leaders are vital knowledge participants because they are responsible or involved in the development and execution of the Human Resource Management (HRM). Leaders adhere to, execute or contribute to policies, practices and staffing procedures, performance-related awards, employee motivation, and hire resources, which are critical components to growing employees. Leaders are on the frontlines when dealing with employees and have a primary role in the transference of tacit knowledge; for instance, facilitating and fostering knowledge sharing, influencing the organizational culture and environment, eliminating obstacles for establishing and maintaining relationships, recognizing knowledge, moving or transferring employees, and examining or identifying knowledge gaps. Leaders are challenged with managing tacit knowledge or the knowledge in people's minds. They have to ensure that 'right employees' are involved in the transference of tacit-knowledge.

When ensuring that the right employees are involved in the transference of tacit knowledge, leaders might consider moving the knowledge recipient and sender geographically closer. Employees who are moved to a new location influence the transference of tacit knowledge and the tacit-knowledge transfer from the knowledge sender to the knowledge recipient is plausible (Coppedge, 2010).

Knowledge Transfer Influencers: Non-Human Resources
Both human and non-human resources contribute to successful knowledge transfers. Internal non-human resource factors such as the organizational environment, cost, and capabilities influence tacit knowledge transfers. Organizational environment factors that influence knowledge transfers include creating a repetitive atmosphere, maintaining an environment that is conducive, creating a learning environment, and supporting an open atmosphere for new ideas and change.

Transferring tacit knowledge between individuals can be costly, slow, and uncertain (Kogut and Zander 1992; Riusala and Suutari 2004). Organizational costs can influence tacit knowledge transfers. The cost savings from transferring tacit knowledge that increases the bottom line and reduces operational costs can be offset by such costs as the cost of knowledge senders traveling to/from the knowledge recipients' (or vice versa) location, which could be viewed as a financial loss. However, leaders should refer to these costs as investments.

Organizational capability refers to an organization being able to acquire, absorb, store, and renew corporate knowledge continuously (Wu et al. 2007). Organizational capabilities influence the transfer of tacit knowledge. Having the capabilities to use, integrate, and acquire knowledge to improve or sustain the organization's competitive advantage can definitely work in the favor of an organization's ability to transfer knowledge. Organizational performance illustrates how an organization uses, applies, and leverages its corporation knowledge.

Communication is vital during the transfer of tacit knowledge, and thus has significant influence. Tacit knowledge does not transfer well because it can be difficult to articulate (Kelly and Rice 2002). Language barriers and other difficulties of communication can influence tacit knowledge transfers. Knowledge senders and recipients have difficulty transferring knowledge when obstacles such as words having different meanings, no common language (e.g., speaking English, Spanish, or French), and inadequate writing skills exist.

Tacit Knowledge Transfer Barriers

Tacit knowledge transfer barriers includes organizational and learning (Sun & Scott, 2005), communication (Busch 2006, 2008; Kelly and Rice 2002; Sarker et al. 2005), motivation (Szulanski 1996), and personnel turnover (Droege and Hoobler 2003; Tsai and Ghoshal 1998). Organizational barriers may include differences in organizational cultures, values, and practices as well as geographic distances between the organization's headquarters and subsidiaries. Kostova (1999) confirmed that organizational cultural difference could cause conflict between organizations and reduce the knowledge transfer effectiveness.

In addition, the knowledge transfer participants may encounter cultural barriers. Cultural barriers are found at the organizational-level and people-level. The organizational-level includes the organizational culture. At the individual-level, knowledge transfer participants encounter power and ethnic differences. Other barriers include knowledge senders and recipients' characteristics, relationships between the knowledge senders and recipients, characteristics of the tacit knowledge (e.g., stickiness or complexity of the knowledge), knowledge recipients receiving the tacit knowledge, communications between the knowledge senders and recipients, and geographical distance between the knowledge sender and recipient, turnover of employees, and organizational practices.

Many times during the transference of tacit knowledge, knowledge recipients and senders encounter communication barriers when transferring messages, exchanging ideas and/or transferring information (e.g., words having different meanings to different people). There are barriers such as people withholding knowledge that serves in the transference of tacit knowledge; for example, a knowledge sender deliberately withholding information or selectively sharing information to ensure job security when in fear of losing his/her job, or knowledge blockage (Gregory, Beck and Prifling 2009). When organizations do not motivate their employees with rewards during knowledge transfers or if the knowledge transfer participants do not perceive being rewarded for sharing their knowledge, it causes an organizational-level barrier.

Transferring Tacit Knowledge Successfully

Although there is limited literature contributing to the successful transference of tacit knowledge, Coppedge (2010) identified several conditions. These conditions are categorized as people-level and organizational-level. People-level include leaders having the right employees involved in tacit knowledge transfers, fostering relationships among employees, and employees serving as mentors. The organizational-level includes having an ideal organizational environment, using technology, and properly handing stressful environments.

Social Networks or Relationships

Workplace relationships such as social networking or social relationships are vital conduits for knowledge transfers (Burgess, 2005; Szulanski 1996). Chen, Duan and Edwards (2002) states that the knowledge transfer infrastructure involves three networks: social, knowledge, and relationship.

Leaders and practitioners should view social and electronic networks as channels to facilitate organizational knowledge exchange (Chen, Duan and Edwards 2002). Social networking provides an opportunity for face-to-face communication, which contributes to building stronger relations between units through the application of trust and power (Chen, Duan and Edwards 2002). Trust and power works as a channel to transfer tacit knowledge. Electronic networks such as FaceBook®, LinkedIn®, and Twitter® may serve as another conduit to transfer knowledge between employees and business units.

Organization theory and KM literature highlights that cross coordination and informal networks are better fits than formal systems for knowledge transfer. Formal systems or planned knowledge exchange limits transfer between units (Grant 1996). Formal systems are not ideal when flexibility is needed in the knowledge transfer process (Willem and Buelens 2007).

Knowledge practitioners and leaders should use an agile, multi-layered, coordinated approach with minimum pre-planned activities (Willem and Buelens 2007). Cross and casual coordination results in more intense communication cooperation than formal systems (Nidumolu 1996). Informal coordination offers opportunities for cross-organizational boundaries because lateral coordination is easier than establishing formal links between units. Leaders are encouraged to have an open atmosphere and to allow spontaneity and voluntary knowledge transfer (Andrew & Delahaye 2000).

Technology

"Tacit knowledge exchange among team members could be enhanced through use of information technology" (Song 2009, 84). Using Information Technology (IT), helps leaders and practitioners facilitate knowledge creation, storage, and sharing (Ismail, Nor and Marjani, 2009). Leaders, employees, and practitioners can leverage electronic networks and group decision support systems, electronic mail (e-mail), Internet chat sessions, web-based discussions, and videoconferencing (Coppedge, 2010; Isamil, Nor and Marjani 2009; Kavur, 2010; Song, 2009).

Measuring Accomplishments

Knowledge transfers are quantifiable by measuring change in the knowledge recipients' knowledge (Argote 1999). Measuring tacit-knowledge effectiveness and efficiency is a main competence for an organization's long-term survival (Efteckharzadeh 2008). However, there are not many methodologies available to measure the success of tacit knowledge transfers (Foos, Schum and Rothenberg 2006). Measuring conditions such as increased productivity, consistent information, improved innovations, customers' perceptions, and other measurable elements beyond increases in the organization's financials can be used to assess or evaluate the successfulness of a tacit-knowledge transfer (Coppedge, 2010). Efteckharzadeh (2008) suggests measuring the social aspect of the tacit-knowledge transfer process (e.g., meetings, seminars, conferences, and social events).

TKT Cycle© Model

The TKT Cycle© (Figure 1) model evolved from a Delphi study conducted to address a gap in the literature related to the transference of tacit knowledge with the movement of people (Coppedge, 2010). Expert panellists provided their input on how organizations transfer tacit knowledge with the movement of people. Based upon the experts' input, the TKT Cycle© model evolved. The TKT Cycle© model illustrates that tacit knowledge is a vital aspect of a 10-step cycle, which involves human and organizational capabilities.

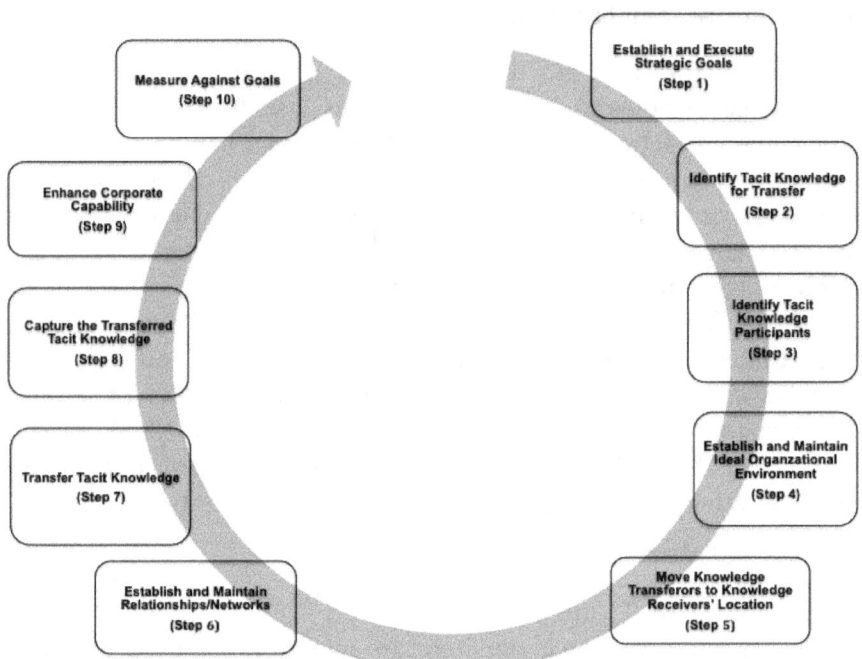

Figure 1. Coppedge's Tacit-knowledge transfer cycle (TKT Cycle©).

Step 1 - Establish and Execute Strategic Goals

Organizational strategic and (HRM) plans contribute to the success of the tacit knowledge transfer process. Leaders should establish strategic goals and incorporate tacit knowledge transfer into their strategic plans before executing the knowledge transfer process. They should consider the vital role of tacit knowledge when identifying and developing goals to be incorporated into their strategic and HRM plans and are encouraged to understand factors such as economic, social, and political issues that may influence the successful transfer of tacit knowledge. In addition tacit knowledge transfer goals should include strategic tactics that aid in organizational success and competitiveness.

Step 2 - Identify Tacit Knowledge for Transfer

To compete in the 21st century competitive global marketplace, organizations need to recognize the importance of identifying, sharing, and applying corporate knowledge (i.e., tacit knowledge). Employees with the ability to identify, share, and apply tacit knowledge contribute to an organization's performance. Members of the organization may be able to recognize tacit knowledge in specific employees when a "skillful performance is achieved by the observations of a set of rules which are not known as such to the person following them" (Polanyi 1962, 42).

Step 3 - Identify Tacit Knowledge Participants

HRM plans should be developed after conducting a thorough assessment of the organizational needs. This provides a path to identify the appropriate skills, personal characteristics, and knowledge of employees identified to participate in tacit knowledge transfers. The HRM plan should be a tool to facilitate the tracking of employees throughout an organization; for identifying skills or lack of skills, behaviors, and abilities within the organization, and for creating an organizational culture that fosters collaboration and teamwork within organizational units. Employees should be aligned with the organization's purpose, vision, mission, objectives, and goals.

It is important to identify the right knowledge source or sender and knowledge recipient when transferring tacit knowledge. Coppedge (2010) emphasizes that leaders and practitioners are responsible for determining the transfer participants' prerequisites (i.e., have competences) before engaging their participation in the tacit knowledge transfer process. For example, if a knowledge recipient needs to have technical expertise or needs to study a specific reference guide before participating in the tacit knowledge transfer process, the leadership and/or knowledge transfer practitioner should notify the knowledge recipient in advance.

Step 4 - Establish and Maintain an Ideal Organizational Environment

Tacit knowledge transfer participants need an organizational environment that fosters a positive learning experience and allows flexible working practices. Creating an ideal organizational culture is a vital factor because it affects employees' attitudes and communications. Leaders are encouraged to foster the desired organizational culture that ensures continuous transfer of tacit knowledge as the organizational knowledge matures.

Broad acceptance and understanding of the goal to transfer tacit knowledge is required for successful tacit knowledge transfers. Leaders should establish and enforce standards for tacit knowledge transfers (i.e., establish standards for a KM program). The well-designed KM program includes rewarding and recognizing employees who share tacit knowledge (Coppedge 2010).

Step 5 - Move Knowledge Transferors to Knowledge Receivers or Recipients' Location

In Step 1, Establish and Execute Strategic Goals, leaders define the staffing strategy for the tacit knowledge transfer based on the HRM plan and strategic goals as defined in the strategic plan. Leaders select the right employee with specialized tacit knowledge and temporarily move the employee to the knowledge recipient's location with the goal of transferring tacit knowledge. They should also select individuals who have the appropriate skills to transfer and receive the tacit knowledge.

Knowledge transfer conduits involve people, text, and/or artifacts. Knowledge makes resources such as people moveable. The need to expand the tacit knowledge to another location is a condition that is fostered by the leaders' decisions to move an employee. Tacit knowledge transfers are high in cost; however, face-to-face interaction is the preferred mode to transfer tacit knowledge because it involves language and communication in order to promote absorption. Movement of employees is a method to assist in knowledge transfers and to develop networks and relationships (Alavi and Leidner 2001; Welch and Welch 2008)

Step 6 - Establish and Maintain Relationships

There are potential barriers to transferring tacit knowledge among employees. Workplace relationships are a vital conduit for transferring tacit knowledge or sharing information. Communication is necessary when transferring knowledge especially since a significant amount of corporate knowledge is embedded in the employees' minds. Face-to-face meetings tend to be expensive when transferring tacit knowledge among employees; and the employees require frequent interactions. Therefore, leaders and practitioners should establish networks and embrace the act of building relationships when transferring tacit knowledge. Developing relationships is a predecessor to transferring and absorbing tacit knowledge (Johannessen, Olaisen, and Olsen 2001).

Step 7 - Transfer Tacit Knowledge

Once the value of transferring tacit knowledge is realized, leaders want to use, transfer and manage this corporate asset. At this point, knowledge participants are involved in the tacit knowledge transfer process. The process can be planned or be impromptu. Mechanisms for transferring tacit knowledge involve people and processes. For example, knowledge transfer participants may participate in demonstrations, working sessions, and presentations (both written and verbal).

Leaders may opt to leverage technologies to augment the tacit knowledge transfer process. Using technology to augment the tacit knowledge transfer can help bridge the geographic distance between the knowledge transfer participants as well as better facilitate the capture of the shared knowledge. However, the face-to-face interaction should not be replaced as technology could minimize the scope, variety, and richness of personal contact (Coppedge 2010; Roberts 2000).

Step 8 - Capture the Transferred Tacit Knowledge

People involved in transferring tacit knowledge need to have the ability to communicate, translate, convert, filter, and render the shared information. Member-to-member knowledge transfers are vital to an organization's competitive advantage because it involves people.

However, business knowledge (i.e., industry domain knowledge) and process knowledge (i.e., software development methodologies and working procedures) are difficult to codify as it is tacit.

Step 9 - Enhance Corporate Capabilities

Transferring tacit knowledge or sharing information is increasingly becoming more important for leaders as they attempt to gain greater levels of productivity and agility, and to make their organizations more successful. Although transferring knowledge across business units is still challenging for some leaders, an organization's ability to transfer knowledge contributes to organizational performance. Lado and Zhang (1998) asserted that leaders should refer to corporate capabilities in value, and the value increases when the tacit or corporate knowledge is shared internally.

Step 10 - Measure against Goals

Successful tacit knowledge transfer involves both human and non-human factors. As identified in Step 4, Establish and Maintain Ideal Organizational Environment, leaders need to acquire organization-wide acceptance of goals to have successful tacit-knowledge transfers. Coppedge (2010) suggested that leaders and knowledge transfer practitioners measure organizational accomplishments against the defined goals defined in Step 1 of the TKT Cycle©.

Real World Scenarios

This section provides two real-world scenarios to help facilitate the understanding and application of the TKT Cycle©. Scenario 1 is about a federal manager acquiring new employees to expand the program to become a federally operated Center for Operational Excellence. The federal manager needs to get the new employee up to speed to achieve results. Scenario 2 is about a domestic-based organization with an international customer. The executives of the organization are interested in expanding beyond the domestic borders.

Transferring Tacit Knowledge with the Movement of Employees

Scenario 1: Getting New Employees Up To Speed

Over the years, the program has provided lean processes, techniques, and tools to a government agency with the support of the private sector primarily. In order to accomplish the goal of becoming a federally owned and operated Center for Operational Excellence by fiscal year 2011, the federal program manager needed to get the new employees up to speed quickly. The federal manager had a contractor-employee who was supporting the federal manager for approximately five years and had gained significant corporate knowledge that needed to be transferred because the contractor-employee's contract period of performance was ending. The new employees had the basic knowledge, skills, and abilities to support the federal manager's goal to strategically position the program to become a Center for Operational Excellence; however, the new employees were not familiar with the program's processes, procedures, practices, and tools. The federal manager had a finite period of time to perform tacit knowledge transfer between the sender (contractor-employee) and recipients (new employees).

The federal manager provided the new employees with reference materials and access to the organization's information systems (i.e., explicit or captured knowledge). The federal manager asked the contractor-employee to share or transfer his corporate knowledge with the new employees. To get new team members up to speed, the federal manager, contractor-employee, and new employees have made several assumptions.

The federal manager assumed that the contractor-employee and new employees spoke the same language, and that the new employees had the knowledge, skills, and abilities to consume, understand, and apply the organizational-specific knowledge. The contractor-employee assumed that his corporate knowledge would be less valuable when more people acquired his knowledge and it would have an adverse impact to the contracting firm's financials (i.e., the profits). The new employees assumed that the employer-provided explicit knowledge was current or up-to-date and the contractor-employee would freely share his tacit knowledge prior to the contract's period of performance, which ended in fiscal year 2011.

Applying the TKT Cycle© model:

Step 1 – Prior to the federal manger initiating the TKT Cycle© model, the federal manager ultimately wanted to be a federally run and operated program; therefore, the federal manager hired new federal employees. The federal manager's strategic goal required the following objectives: get the new employees up to speed quickly before the contractor's period of performance ends and to keep the program operational seamlessly through this transitional period.

Step 2 - The federal manager identified the tacit knowledge within the program office, which was documented in some reference guides as well as embedded in the contractor's mind. The federal manager knew that some operational procedures, processes, and practices were not documented because the same contractors were supporting the program for a number of years. Not having the operational activities thoroughly documented was not a risk until the federal manager changed his strategic goals and objectives for the program.

Step 3 - The federal manager has a contractor who supported the program since inception and embedded the know-how about the program. In addition, the federal manager hired new employees based upon their professional experience gained at other government agencies and the ability to absorb information quickly.

Step 4 - The federal manager established an ideal organizational environment and culture to help facilitate knowledge sharing. For instance, the federal manager identified which meetings he wanted the employees and contractor to attend together as well as allowed the contractor and new employees adjust their schedules to spend more time together. In addition, the federal manager also incorporated knowledge transfer, milestone-drive incentives in the new employees' performance plans.

Step 5 - The knowledge participates were relocated in the same vicinity to aid in the transference of tacit knowledge (e.g., the contractor and new employee sat nearby each other). Since the contractor worked between his employer's offsite location and the client's site, the federal manager was invoiced for transportation costs during the knowledge transfer period.

Step 6 - The contractor and new employees leveraged the government agency's social network, used other tools, and periodically had lunch together to establish and maintain a relationship during this transitional period.

Steps 7 & 8 – The new employees gained access to tacit knowledge through various channels such as shadowing, interviewing, documenting information learned via a checklist, and validating and updated documented procedures and processes. The contractor shared his calendar with the new employees as well as forwarded any new meetings to new employees; this fostered the new employees' ability to shadow the contractor.

Step 8 - The new employees and contractor continuously validated and updated the program-level activities, practices, and processes. When the new employees discovered undocumented processes and practices, they documented the information and stored it on the program's web-based portal site.

Step 9 – Besides becoming a federal-employee operated program, the federal manager wanted to enhance the program's capabilities by improving its lean processes, practices, and procedures as well as tools. When the program becomes known as the Center for Operational Excellence, the federal manager wants to help other government agencies by allowing the agencies to leverage the program's service offerings.

Steps 8, 9 & 10 – Quarterly, the federal manager measured the tacit-knowledge transfer effectiveness and efficiency by measuring aspects of the processes and conducting meetings. The federal manager began marketing the program's service offerings to other government agencies via conferences and seminars in hopes of becoming recognized as the Center of Operational Excellence.

Step 10 – The federal manager evaluated the new employees' ability to perform specific tasks independently (as prescribed in their performance plans), conducting standing meetings, conducting independent audits or assessments of the documented processes and procedures, and surveying internal and external customers who have leveraged or used the program's service offerings.

Scenario 2: Going Global – Expanding Internationally

In calendar year 2009, the chief executive officer (CEO) of an organization expressed interest in expanding its service offerings beyond the domestic borders by calendar year 2011. The firm has clients internationally; however, the firm did not have offices in those other countries. A chief executive officer established a global expansion team to help with determining the likelihood of going global, identifying an ideal business model (e.g., franchising, licensing, joint venture, or acquisition), assessing the external factors (e.g., tariffs, regulations, and norms), developing a budget, assessing the internal resources required, and other key elements to aide in the decision making process. A representative from the HR department is a member of the global expansion team; the HR representative will help in identifying skills, abilities, and knowledge needed to support the global expansion effort. Based upon the global expansion team's due diligence, the firm was able to expand beyond the domestic borders.

The global expansion team and the executives identified the corporate knowledge that required transferring from the headquarters to the offshore subsidiary. The HR representative identified employees (now expatriates) who were willing and able to temporarily move to the offshore subsidiary to participant in the tacit knowledge transfer process. The HR representative also collaborated with a staff augmentation firm to aid in staffing the offshore subsidiary based upon specific requirements (e.g., language, technical competencies, and gender-specific job roles). Based upon the countries' norms and culture, the expatriates were aligned accordingly.

The executives released memorandums and expressed the organization's goals, objectives, and culture at town hall meetings and other venues. The executives set the organizational culture (i.e., set the tone at the top). In calendar year 2009, the executives established a knowledge management program to support the strategic goals and influence knowledge maturity at the headquarters as well as its domestic and international subsidiaries.

The tacit knowledge transfers began in calendar year 2010 and continue through the use of technologies as well as regular visits to and from the subsidiaries and headquarters. The knowledge transfer participants leveraged technologies to bridge the geographical gap; however, the expatriates from headquarters committed to supporting the knowledge transfer process for 12 months or longer. The expatriates were offered incentives; the longer the expatriate remained onsite the incentives increased. The expatriates' commitments to longevity fostered the relationships between the offshore employees and the expatriates.

With the expatriates and executives' commitment to apply, leverage, and improve upon the corporate knowledge, the firm's competitive edge in the global marketplace improved. The firm leverages web-based tools that foster real-time collaborations, knowledge management, virtual environments, and other tools such as online chatting, online telephone calls, electronic social networking, and teleconferences. The executives committed to sponsoring employees to temporarily move from their countries to the headquarters' location to continuously enhance the corporate capability.

Quarterly, the executives met with the global expansion team members as well as the expatriates to monitor progress as well as to discuss risks and issues. These quarterly meetings are open to the management team. Every six months the global expansion team members and executives measure against the strategic goals; at times the team had to make adjustments to the strategic plans.

Applying the TKT Cycle© model:

Step 1 – The CEO communicated his goal and objectives to go global by a specific timeframe. The CEO challenged the global expansion team to aid in developing a strategy to achieve this goal.

Step 2 – The CEO and global expansion team identified the organization's portable intelligence assets (i.e., corporate or tacit knowledge).

Step 3 – Representatives on the global expansion team identified employees with the embedded corporate knowledge and specific characteristics such as gender, language, and technical competencies.

Step 4 – The CEO and global expansion team communicated the leadership's philosophy, which sets the organizational culture. In addition, the executives communicated the corporate goals, objectives, and corporate culture at the town hall meetings and through other channels. In addition, the executives launched a knowledge management program in order to foster knowledge sharing, renewing, and growth throughout the organization.

Step 5 – The employees, identified by the global expansion team, were viewed as SMEs; the SMEs were temporarily transferred to the offshore location to transfer the corporate knowledge.

Step 6 – The SMEs temporarily moved from the headquarters to the offshore subsidiaries with the goal of transferring the tacit knowledge and, also, established relationships with the subsidiary employees (i.e., knowledge recipients) because they were together for at least 12 months. In addition, the knowledge senders or source and the knowledge recipients leveraged the corporation's technologies in order to maintain their relationships after successfully transferring the corporate knowledge from the headquarters to the subsidiary by using social networks, online and real-time communications, and web, video and telephone conferences.

Steps 4, 5, & 6 – The SMEs were offered incentives (i.e., the longer the SMEs stayed onsite their rewards increased). By the SMEs remaining onsite longer, they were able to foster relationships with the offshore employees.

Step 7 – The SMEs and offshore employees performed various activities to share knowledge; for instance, hands-on training and conducted meetings or learning workshops.

Step 8 – The SMEs and offshore employees recorded the shared knowledge through various channels; for instance, entering information into a knowledge management system, developing and updating Standard Operating Procedures (SOP), recording information in a presentation or briefing packet, and developing an operational manual.

Step 9 – The CEO and global expansion team sponsored employees to move from the offshore subsidiaries to the corporate headquarters (and vice versa) to continue to enhance the corporate capability through knowledge sharing tactics as such. In addition, the corporation strived to continuously absorb, renew, create, and grow knowledge throughout the organization. These are some of the activities that provided the firm a competitive advantage in the global marketplace.

Step 10 – The CEO and global expansion team monitored, measure, and reported on the knowledge transfer activities and knowledge management program periodically throughout the year. As required, the CEO and global expansion team realigned the organization to achieve its goal of going global.

Conclusion

For years, people cited the old cliché of knowledge is power; however, knowledge management and knowledge transfer scholars have emphasized the power and value of tacit knowledge. Within the workplace, corporate leaders and government officials have placed value on its intellectual asset (i.e., tacit knowledge or corporate knowledge) and are encouraging employees to share knowledge with each other and across business units. This chapter provided knowledge transfers practitioners, experts, leaders, government officials, educators, researchers and students an understanding on the differences between explicit and tacit knowledge; the focus of this chapter was on tacit knowledge.

Tacit knowledge is embedded knowledge or know-how and it resides with people. Organizations' leaders, despite the size, classification (for-profit, non-profit, or government), geographic location, and other characteristics, are interested in enhancing organizational capabilities. Organizational capabilities are based upon corporate knowledge and other capital assets. As cited within, approximately 90% of organizational knowledge or corporate knowledge is embedded in its employees' minds; and this tacit knowledge is difficult to transfer.

Scholars, noted within this chapter highlight that moving people such as employees, results in transferring knowledge. Therefore, this chapter contributes to the body of knowledge by identifying the influencers and barriers of transferring tacit knowledge transfers; leaders and practitioners who understand these influencers and barriers that may be able to help organizations successfully transfer knowledge, enhance organizational growth, and increase competitiveness in the marketplace. In addition, this chapter highlights organizational and people-level factors contributing to successful tacit knowledge transfers. Leaders, practitioners, educators, and students were provided two real-life scenarios to help demonstrate the application of the Coppedge's (2010) 10-step process, TKT Cycle© for transferring tacit knowledge process.

References

Adler, N. J. (1995). International dimensions of organizational behaviour. Boston, MA: PWS-Kent.Alavi, M., and Leidner, D.E. 2001. Knowledge Management and Knowledge Management Systems Conceptual Foundation and Issues. MIS Quarterly. Vol. 25. No. 1. March

Andrews, K., & Delahaye, B. L. (2000). Influences on knowledge processes in organizational learning. The psychosocial filter. Journal of Management Studies, 73, 797-810. doi:10.1111/1467-6486.00204

Argote, L. (1999). Organizational learning: Creating, retaining, and transferring knowledge. Norwell, MA: Kluwer.

Argote, L., & Ingram, P. (2000). Knowledge transfer: A basis for competitive advantage in firms. Organizational Behavior and Human Decision Processes, 82(1), 150-169. doi:10.1006/obhd.2000.2893

Barnes, T. J., Peck, J., Sheppard, E., & Tickell, A. (2003). Reading economic geography. Boston, MA: Blackwell.

Barney, J. B. (1991). Firm resources and sustained competitive advantage. Journal of Management, 17(1). doi:10.1177/014920639101700108

Baumard, P. (2002). Tacit knowledge in professional firms: The teachings of firms in very puzzling situations. Journal of Knowledge Management, 6, 135-151. doi:10.1108/13673270210424666

Berthoin, A. A., Lenhardt, U., & Rosenbrock, R. (2001). Barriers to organizational learning. In Dierkes, M., Berthain, A., Child, J., Nonaka, I. (ed.).

(2001). Handbook of organizational learning and knowledge. New York: Oxford University Press. pp. 865-885.

Bjorkman, I., Barner-Rasmussen, W., & Li, L. (2004). Managing knowledge transfer in MNCs: The impact of headquarters control mechanisms. International Business Studies, 35(5), 443-445. doi:10.1057/palgrave.jibs.8400094

Biggiero, L. (2006). Industrial and knowledge relocation strategies under the challenges of globalization and digitalization: The move of small and medium enterprises among territorial systems. Entrepreneurship & Regional Development, 18, 443-471. doi:10.1080/08985620600884701

Bresman, H., Birkinshaw, J. M., & Nobel, R., (1999). Knowledge transfer in acquisitions. Journal of International Business Studies, 30(4), 439-462.

Burgess, D. (2005). What motivates employees to transfer knowledge outside their work unit? Journal of Business Communication. October, 42, 324-348. doi:10.1177/0021943605279485.

Busch, P. (2006). Organization design and tacit knowledge transferal: An examination of three IT firms. Journal of Knowledge Management Practice, 7(2). June. Retrieved from http://www.tlainc.com/jkmp.htm

Busch, P. (2008). Tacit knowledge in organizational learning. Hershey, PA: IGI Global.

Cabrera-Suarez, K., De Saa-Perez, P., & Garcia-Almedia, D. (2001). The succession from a resource and knowledge-based view of the family firm. Family Business Review, 15, 37-47.

Chen, S., Duan, Y., Edwards, J. S., & Lehaney, B. (2002). Toward understanding inter-organizational knowledge transfer needs in SMEs: Insight from a UK investigation. Journal of Knowledge Management, 10(3), 6-23. doi:10.1108/13673270610670821

Chrisman, J. J., Chua, J. H., & Sharma, P. (2005, September). Trends and directions in the development of a strategic management theory of the family firm. Entrepreneurship Theory and Practice, 29, 555-576. doi:10.1111/j.1540-6520.2005.00098.X

Coppedge, B. B. (2010). Transferring tacit knowledge with the movement of people: A Delphi study. (Doctoral dissertation, University of Phoenix, 2010). Dissertation Abstract International, 72/05, 0850. Retrieved from ProQuest Dissertation & Theses database.

De Gregori, T. R. (1987). Resources are not; they become: An institutional theory. Journal of Economic Issues, 21, 1241-1263.Droege, S. B., & Hoobler, J. M. (2003). Employee turnover and tacit knowledge diffusion: A network perspective. Journal of Managerial Issues, 15(1), 50-64. Retrieved from

Easterby-Smith, M., Burgoyne, J., & Araujo, L. (2001). Organizational learning and the learning organization. London, United Kingdom: Sage.

Eftekharzadeh, R. (2008). Knowledge management implementation in developing countries: An experimental study. Review of Business, 28(3), 44. Retrieved from http://www.entrepreneur.com/tradejournals/article/186785396_4.html (accessed May 31, 2011)

Evans, K., Hodkinson, P., & Unwin, L. (Ed.). (2002). Working to learn: Transforming learning in the workplace. London, UK: Routledge Press.

Foos, T., Schum, G., & Rothenberg, S. (2006). Tacit knowledge transfer and the knowledge disconnect. Journal of Knowledge Management, 10(1), 6-18. doi:10.1108/13673270610650067

Grant, R. M. (1996). Toward a knowledge-based theory of the firm. Strategic Management Journal, 17, 109-122. Retrieved from http://www3.interscience.wiley.com/journal/2144/home (accessed date June 1, 2011).

Grant, R. M., Almedia, P., & Song, J. (2000). Knowledge and the multi-national enterprise. In C. J. Millar, R. M. Grant, & C. J. Choi (Ed.). International business: Emerging issues and emerging markets. (pp. 102-114). Basingstoke, United Kingdom: MacMillian. Retrieved from http://findarticles.com/p/articles/mi_hb020/is_3_18/ai_n28887106/ (accessed date June 15, 2011).

Gregory, R., Beck, R, & Prifling, M. (2009). Breaching the knowledge transfer blockage in IT offshore outshoring projects – A case from the financial service industry. Retrieved from http://www.wiiw.de/publikationen/protected/BreachingtheKnowledgeTransferB3013.pdf(accessed date June 1, 2011).

Guzman, G. A., and Wilson, J. The "soft" dimension of organizational knowledge transfer. Journal of Knowledge Management, 9(2), 59-74. doi:10.1108/13673270510590227Ismail, W. K., Nor, K. M. and Marjani, T. (2009) The role of knowledge sharing practice in enhancing project success, Interdisciplinary Journal of Contemporary Research In Business, 1, 7, pp. 34-52.

Johannessen, J. A., Olaisen, J., and Olsen, B. (2001). Mismanagement of tacit knowledge: The importance of tacit knowledge, the danger of information technology, and what to do about it. International Journal of Information Management, 21(1), 3-20. doi:10.1016/S0268-4012(00)00047-5

Kavur, J. (2010). Social networking unveils tacit knowledge: PWC. Computer World Canada. Retrieved from http://www.itworldcanada.com/news/social-networking-unveils-tacit-knowledge-says-pwc/139993-pg3 (accessed June 12, 2011)

Kelley, D. J., & Rice, M. P. (2002). Leveraging the value of proprietary technologies. Journal of Small Business Management, 40(1), 1-4. doi:10.1111/1540-627X.00034

Khosrowpour, M. (2000). Challenges of information technology management in the 21st Century. Hersey, PA: Idea Group.

Kogut, B., & Zander, U. (1992). Knowledge of the firm, combinative capabilities, and the replication of technology. Organization Science, 3, 383-397. doi:10.1287/orsc.3.3.383

Kostova, T. (1999). Transnational transfer of strategic organizational practices: A contextual perspective. Academy of Management Review, 24, 308-324. doi:10.2307/259084

Lado, A. A., & Zang, M. J. (1998). Expert systems, knowledge development and utilization, and sustained competitive advantage: A resource-based model. Journal of Management, 24, 489-509. doi:10.1177/014920639802400402

Latour, B. (1999). Pandora's hope: Essays on the reality of science studies. Harvard University Press. Cambridge: Massachusetts.

Levinson, M. (2007, March 07). Knowledge Management definitions and solutions. Retrieved from http://www.cio.com/article/40343/Knowledge_Management_Definition_And_Solutions

Lui, Y. (2004). A study of the perceptions of knowledge transfer in multinational corporations in China's information technology industry. (Doctoral dissertation, University of Minnesota, 2004). Dissertation Abstract International, 65/11, 4078. Retrieved from ProQuest Dissertation & Theses database.

Lucas, L.M. (2005). The impact of trust and reputation on the transfer of best practices. Journal of Knowledge Management, 9(4), 87-101.

Lyles, M. A. & Salk, J. E. (1996). Knowledge acquisition from foreign parents in international joint ventures: An empirical examination in the Hungarian context. Journal of International Business Studies, 27(5): 877-904.

Lyon, A. (2005). Intellectual capital and struggles over the perceived value of members' expert knowledge in a knowledge-intensive organization. Western Journal of Communications, 69, 251-255. doi:10.1080/10570310500202413

Maskell, P., & Malmberg, A. (1999). The competitiveness of firms and regions: "Unification" and the importance of localized learning. European Urban & Regional Studies, 6(1), 9-17. doi:10.1177/096977649900600102

McLaughlin, S. (n.d.). Is your approach to knowledge management helping or hindering innovation? Retrieved from http://www.gla.ac.uk/media/ media_68395_en.pdf (accessed June 24, 2011)

Misra, D. C. (2007). Ten guiding principles for knowledge management in e-government in developing countries. Retrieved from http://unpan1.un.org/intradoc/groups/ public/documents/UNPAN/UNPAN025338.pdf (accessed June 24, 2011)

Morris, T. (2001). Asserting property rights: Knowledge codification in the professional service firm. Human Relations, 54, 819-838. doi:10.1177/0018726701547002

Newcomb, T. M., Turner, R. H., & Converse, P. E. (1966). The study of human interaction. London, United Kingdom: Routledge & Kegan Paul.

Nidumolu, S. R. (1996). A comparison of the structural contingency and risk-based perspectives on coordination in software-development projects. Journal of Information Systems, 13(2), 77-113. Retrieved from http://www.jisonline.com/

Nonaka, I. (1994). A dynamic theory of organizational knowledge creation. Organization Science, 5(1), 14-37. Retrieved from doi=10.1.1.115.2590

Nonaka, I., & Takeuchi, H. (1995). The knowledge-creating company. Oxford, United Kingdom: Oxford University Press.

Peteraf, M. A. (1993). The cornerstones of competitive advantage: A resource-based view. Strategic Management Journal, 14, 13. doi:10.1002/smj.4250140303

Polanyi, M. (1962). Personal knowledge: Towards a post-critical philosophy. Chicago, IL: Chicago University Press.

Polanyi, M. (1996). The tacit dimension. London, United Kingdom: Routledge & Kegan Paul. Riusala, K., & Suutari, V. (2004). International knowledge transfers through expatriates. Thunderbird International Business Review, 46, 743-770. doi:10.1177/031289620703200207

Roberts, J. (2000). From know-how to show how? Questioning the role of information and communication technologies in knowledge. Technology Analysis and Strategic Management, 12(4), 429-443. doi:10.1080/713698499

Sarker, S., et. al. (2005). Knowledge transfer in virtual information systems development teams: An empirical examination of key enablers. Systems Sciences, 43, 322-335. Retrieved from http://www.tandf.co.uk/journals/tf/00207721.html (accessed date June 12, 2011).

Simmie, J. (2003). Innovation and urban regions as national and international nodes for the transfer and sharing of knowledge. Regional Studies, 37,

607-621. Retrieved from http://www.tandf.co.uk/journals/titles/00343404.asp (accessed date June 11, 2011).

Song, D. (2009). The tacit knowledge-sharing strateg analysis in the project work. International Business Research 2(1), 83-85. Retrieved from

Stenmark, D AND WINTER (2000). Leveraging tacit organizational knowledge. Journal of Management Information Systems, 17, 9-24. Retrieved from http://www.jmis-web.org/

Stenberg, R., Wagner, R., Williams, W., & Horvath, J. (1995). Testing common sense. American Psychologist, 50, 912-927. doi:10.1037/0003-066X.50.11.912

Sun, P. Y., & Scott, J. L. (2005). An investigation of barriers to knowledge transfer. Journal of Knowledge Management, 9(2), 75-90. doi:10.1108/13673270510590236

Szulanski, G. (1996). Exploring internal stickiness: Impediment to the transfer of best practice within the firm. Strategic Management Journal, 17(1), 27-43. Retrieved from http://smj.strategicmanagement.net/ (accessed date June 1, 2011).

Tsai, W., & Ghoshal, S. (1998). Social capital and value creation: The role of intrafirm networks. Academy of Management Journal, 41, 464-476. doi:10.2307/257085

Vera-Munoz, S. et al. (2006). Enhancing knowledge sharing in public accounting firms. Accounting Horizons, 20(2), 133-136. doi:10.2308/acch.2006.20.2.133

von Hippel, E. (1998). The sources of innovation. New York, NY: Oxford University Press.

Welch, D. E., & Welch, L. S. (2008). The importance of language in international knowledge transfer. Management International Review, 48(3), 339-360. doi:10.1007/s11575-008-0019-7

Willem, A., & Bullins, M. (2007). The effect of organizational characteristics on interdepartmental knowledge sharing. Journal of Public Administration Research and Theory, 17, 581-589. doi:10.1093/jopart/mul021

Wu, F., et al. (2007). Overcoming export manufactures' dilemma in international expansion. Journal of International Business Studies, 38, 283-289. doi:10.1057/palgrave.jibs.8400263

Recommended Other Reading

Baumard, P. (1999). Tacit Knowledge in Organizations

Capasso, A. Dagnino, G. B. & Lanza, A. (2005). Strategic capabilities and knowledge transfer within and between organizations. Cheltenham, Glos UK: Edward Elgar Publishing

Collison, C. & Parcell, G (2005). Learning To Fly: Practical lessons from one of the world's leading knowledge companies.

Dixon, N. M. (2000). Common knowledge: How companies thrive by sharing what they know. Harvard Business School Press.

Ericsson, K. (ed.), Charness, N. (ed.), Feltovich, P. J. (ed.), & Hoffman, R. (ed.) (2006). The Cambridge Handbook of Expertise and Expert Performance

Srikantaiah, T. K. & Koenig, M. E. (2004). Knowledge management lessons learned: What works and what doesn't. Information Today.

Managing Critical Knowledge Assets: Achieving and Sustaining Organizational Competitive Advantage

Milena Ristovska & Michael A. Stankosky

The George Washington University, Washington, D.C., USA

Introduction

With the rising complexity and the rapidly changing existing market environment, it is of the utmost importance that today's companies discover and effectively use "mechanisms" that provide them with a sustainable competitive advantage. Sources that provide this competitive advantage are found in innovative and knowledge-intensive practices that heavily rely on the efficient and effective creation, codification, transfer, storage and use of knowledge resources. Knowledge resources, comprised of human capital, structural capital and relationship capital, are the most important resources that companies own and can use to create a competitive advantage that is unique, difficult to imitate by others, superior in relation to competitors and are applicable in different situations. The characteristics of knowledge that are important to achieve and sustain a competitive advantage are its breadth and depth, complexity, transferability, tacitness, codifiability and ability to be diffused within and across companies.

Also important to achieve and sustain a knowledge-based competitive advantage is the system of processes for effective and efficient management of knowledge assets within an organization. This system consists of leadership/management, organization, learning, and technology. These four building blocks provide the structure and enable the functions of a KM system. All four must be present in any enterprise management-engineering framework that has knowledge assets as the prime factors of production because they are mutually dependable and supportive of each other.

In this chapter, we provide insights into the "schools of thought" related to today's sources of sustainable competitive advantage. We discuss the common approaches to the significance of knowledge and the knowledge management system (KMS) to gain a competitive advantage. Our aim is to enhance and extend the reader's knowledge on the significance and impact of knowledge assets and practices on creating and sustaining superior competitive advantage in the 21st century company.

This chapter provides a view of the process of generating a competitive advantage of companies as an endogenous process that happens within the companies themselves and is a result of having core competencies. The core competencies are a system of skills and resources that enable the company to deliver a certain benefit for its customers. What is important about this system of skills and resources is that it is developed through a process of continuous improvements over a longer period of time. Some authors also define them as integrated sets of behavior that are aimed towards a successful achievement of the company's strategic objectives: ability to coordinate, integrate and manage the technology, knowledge and expertise; managerial, organizational and operational skills; mediating and supporting mechanisms; systems of value and culture and understanding who the customers are, which markets should be attended and what are their potential. Therefore, the core competencies include all the dimensions of the organization that enable optimal results and delivery of quality products. In order to achieve that, it is necessary to identify the advantages of the organization which are interconnected and which could be managed by knowledge sharing with the intent of achievement of the organization's objectives. The starting point of the analysis of the core competencies is the fact that the competition between businesses is as much a race for competence mastery as it is for market position and market power. Companies' management cannot focus on all business activities and all competencies required to undertake them, but only on the competencies that really affect a company's competitive advantage.

The Knowledge Economy in Which Today's Companies Operate

Companies no longer operate in the manufacturing-based and capital-intensive industrial economies in which the market assumptions are stable, the business rules rigid, the command-and-control management model is adequate, competitors and customers are known and the future is almost predictable. In the 1970s, Bell (1973) announced the post-industrial society and; nowadays, are witnessing the knowledge economy[2] that produces a complex, dynamic and perpetually changing market landscape for which the twentieth-century organization structures and operations are neither designed nor able to deal with the challenges it imposes.

- The main features of the Knowledge era are summarized as follows: The economy is affected by a rapid technological change manifested in the rapid pace of innovation which cuts the half-life of companies' products and services, on one hand and the speedy diffusion of the new technologies, on the other. This technological change is embodied in labor- and capital-saving, as well as knowledge and information-intensive technologies. These tech-

---

[2] An economy is a knowledge economy if knowledge is acquired, created, disseminated, and applied to enhance its economic development. It is based on four pillars: 1) workforce dominantly composed of **educated and highly-skilled workers**; 2) modern and adequate **information infrastructure** that facilitates effective communication, dissemination, and processing of information and knowledge; 3) effective **innovation system** consisting of companies, research centers, universities, consultants, and 4) **institutional regime and a system of economic incentives** that allow for the efficient mobilization and allocation of resources, stimulate entrepreneurship, and induce the creation, dissemination, and efficient use of knowledge. A common view is that the knowledge economy is better performing because of its capacity to reconcile high growth and high employment with price stability (World Bank Institute, 2007).

nologies not only change the structure and manner of functioning of the entire production system, but also call for immediate and effective changes in the present management practices. The national economies are being transformed into learning economies prominent for their social process of creation, acquisition, transformation, accumulation, diffusion, sharing (and also destruction) of specialized knowledge. Currently, the emphasis is on the capacity to learn and to innovate as being crucial to the productivity and competitiveness of economic agents, rather than on the capacity to acquire and use new technical means. The contexts in which today's companies operate are no longer routine and they are burdened by huge risks. In order to survive in the business arena, companies must transform themselves into knowledge-driven, flexible and innovative systems. The famous economics of competitiveness based on Michael Porter's work was developed at a time when physical, tangible resources and goods dominated. What was important then was the notion of *competitive positions,* defined by the goods or services an organization produced and the markets it served. Today, information and knowledge are the key resources and goods being produced in most economies. To produce a product or serve a market, an organization needs to have knowledge, and use it more efficiently and effectively than its competitors. Products are just one aspect of the positioning. They are the visible, tangible realization of an organization's product/market position. But, most of what is important 'lies below the surface' and it is the knowledge that enables an organization to produce those products. Most economies are knowledge-based, in that the major source of growth and wealth is found in intangible assets such as knowledge, information, bands, patents, trademarks, copyrights etc. In terms of output this means a predominance of knowledge-intensive services over goods. In terms of inputs, this means that the primary assets of companies are intangibles, such as human, organizational, and relationship capital, rather than physical capital, such as land, machines, inventories and financial assets. Knowledge has become companies' key strategic resource, the new dominant driver of their profitability, competitiveness and long-term expansion and domination of the market. Digitization of data, information and knowledge, have had huge impacts on the capacity for transferring, storing and processing information and knowledge. It has opened new areas of competitive advantage. In the knowledge era, **Document Management** technology has transformed the way to manage content and knowledge by providing an organized conversion of documents to an electronic format at a cost effective rate, and in a quality controlled manner.

- New complex networks of human capital, technology, institutional regimes and modes of governance that determine the nations' developmental prospects have emerged. Actually, the economy is networked and global – there is unprecedented interconnectivity due to the development of new communication media and digitization of some of their major aspects. As a consequence, the formal organizations, altogether, as institutions for achieving coordinated action, have a declining role and there is a rapid development of virtual organizations.
- There is a growing need for shorter and quicker decision-making and decision-taking processes for which quality information is needed ex ante etc., (Grean, 2008 & Grant, 2000)

In contrast to the traditional emphasis on optimization, the focus now is on foresight, conversion, innovation and adaptation. Companies must maintain focus on their core business, while at the same time repositioning for the future if the markets get saturated. Also, they should be well aware of their clients' needs and problems, and continuously bring to market better and more affordable products and services "in no time." From knowledge perspective, the new knowledge economy "forces" companies to generate and leverage relevant, applicable and value added knowledge, so that they could achieve their goals efficiently and effectively (Bixler, C. H., 2005). What determines their position on the market is their ability to generate sustainable competitive advantages that distinguish them from their competitors and provide for their long-term success and ultimately, survival in the market competition.

Milena Ristovska & Michael A. Stankosky

The Nature of the Sustained Competitive Advantage of Organizations

The competitive advantage of companies is the advantage over their competitors for their offering to their customers from either lower prices for their products or supplying higher quality products and services at higher prices. Having a competitive advantage means that the company operates more efficiently or with higher quality than the rest of the market players, thus, resulting in higher benefits for the company. To be effective, the competitive advantage has to be:

- Difficult to be imitated by the competitors;
- Unique;
- Sustainable;
- Superior in relation to the competition;
- Applicable in numerous different situations.

A very common approach to analysis of the competitive advantages of companies is the paradigm of structure-conduct-performance initially elaborated by Michael Porter (1979) based on the economics of industrial organization, i.e., the approach of competitive strategy. According to this approach, the structural characteristics of the industry determine the conduct and the performances of the companies that operate within that particular industry. The aim of the company's competitive strategy is for the company to find its position in the industry from which it can best defend itself from the competitive forces (entry of new companies into the market, threats of substitution, the negotiation power of customers, the negotiation power of suppliers and the rivalry among existing competitors) or could influence them in its own favor. Companies gain competitive advantage by discovering innovation (new and better ways to compete within the industry) and making them effective in the market by anticipating the needs of the domestic and international market. The sources of innovation that change the competitive position of the companies are: technological change; discovery of new needs of customers or change of existing ones; discovery of new industry segments, changes in the costs or availability of the production inputs and changes in the state regulation of the market (Porter, 1998).

Managing Critical Knowledge Assets: Achieving and Sustaining Organizational Competitive Advantage

The main premise of this approach is that all the relevant industry-specific resources are homogenously distributed and are perfectly mobile. It means that the basis for the competition is not derived from the company itself, but from the characteristics of the industry. Hence, the superior performances within the industry or the strategic group are a result of this competitive advantage that is derived from the environment.

The second premise is that the terms of supply and the terms of demands are known, i.e., that the market conditions are relatively stable. When the demand is stable, the competition comes down to a "battle" for presence in the market among the current and potential companies which leads to a zero sum gain. Furthermore, because of the stable and predictable conditions on the demand side, the competitive advantage comes from the supply. The core of the formulation of the competitive strategy is for the company to connect with its environment.

The Postulates of the Resource-Based View of the Company Related to the Sustained Competitive Advantage

One of the most famous approaches to the sustainable competitive advantage of companies is the resource-based view. This perspective is a significant departure from the long dominant market-based view which, companies are largely seen as being homogeneous, and competition is seen as occurring via positioning in markets. With the market-based view, the strategic challenge is seen as identifying attractive markets to compete in - attractive markets being ones with characteristics identified by analysis of Porter's five forces. What is not asked in the market-based view is whether the market opportunity is one that can be exploited by the company in question, that is, does the company have the resources and competencies to compete in this market?

According to the resource-based approach, the competitive advantage of companies depends on the efficiency and effectiveness of the usage of an exceptionally valuable resource base that is internally available to the company and not on some external factors within the industry in which the company operates, the market position of the companies, etc. Companies are viewed as "clusters" of resources and capabilities[3] with the help of which they surpass their competitors and gain competitive advantage in the long run. The resources could be material (land, capital, labor, machines, equipment, technology, patents, etc.) or immaterial (know how, the reputation of the company, its organizational culture and knowledge). They are the foundation of the company and its competencies, i.e., they determine what the company is capable of achieving.

It is very important to give the basic interpretation of the main concepts employed by this school of thought. The most important concept is the one of resources which can be defined as "all assets, capabilities, organizational processes, firm attributes, information, knowledge, etc., controlled by a firm that enables the firm to conceive of and implement strategies that improve its efficiency and effectiveness"(Barney, 1991).

Some authors such as Amit and Schoemaker (1993) think that the encompassing construct previously called "resources" can be divided into resources and capabilities. In this respect, resources are tradable and non-specific to the firm, while capabilities are firm-specific and are used to engage the resources within the firm, such as implicit processes to transfer knowledge within the firm.

In order for the company to acquire competitive advantage, the resources have to manifest heterogeneous characteristics and to be imperfectly mobile. This means that the clusters of resources differ among companies and that the competing companies face certain difficulties when they try to obtain, develop or use the resources. This, subsequently, means higher costs compared to the company that already possess the resources.

---

[3] One of the main flaws of the resource-based view is that it does not make a clear distinction between the resources and the competencies. For the purpose of clarification, we consider here the resources as the inputs in the processes of value generation within the company i.e. the factors of production that the company owns and controls, while the competencies are the company's capacity to engage and use these resources.

Managing Critical Knowledge Assets: Achieving and Sustaining Organizational Competitive Advantage

These main postulates lead to sets of resources that are unique and specific for every company which then implies that these resources could not be easily traded on the market of production factors. This is the ground for achieving superior rents, i.e., sustainable and above-the-average yields. For the companies to achieve these kinds of results, the resources that they have, have to fulfill the following conditions:

- Provide strategic value for the company, i.e., help the company use its market opportunities or lower the threats and the risks that come from the market that could be achieved by lowering the costs;
- Be unique and rare;
- Not be easily imitated and
- Not have a substitute. (Madhani, 2009 & Ishikawa, 2006)

Other authors, like Peteraf (1993), for example, think that the necessary conditions for rent generation are: heterogeneity of the resources; their imperfect mobility, ex ante limitations of competition and ex post limitations of competition. Ex ante limitations of the competition mean acquiring resources in the absence of any competition which could lead to competitive advantage and the ex post limitations of the competition are isolating mechanisms which limit the equalization of the rents among individual companies. The isolating mechanisms include the aspects of corporate culture, the managerial capabilities, information asymmetries and the property rights that prevent the loss of competitive advantage once it is gained.

The critical resources and capabilities of the company are developed over a longer period of time during an evolutionary learning process that is path dependent. For the companies, the resources that they manage to internally develop and create a competitive advantage are more important than the resources that they can obtain in the markets.

Milena Ristovska & Michael A. Stankosky

The Importance of Knowledge for the Sustainability of Competitive Advantage

A common view of the competitive advantage that is closely related to the resource-based view of the company is the knowledge-based approach which emerged as an extension of the previous one. According to this approach, the companies are agents that develop superior capacities for protection of the knowledge they own or for integration and application of the knowledge that individuals within the companies possess. Only recently, the knowledge-based approach has evolved towards a more dynamic analysis of the company so that it brings insights into the processes of value creation. The company is viewed as an institution that integrates the knowledge and it possesses mechanisms through which it develops the abilities to flexibly respond to the dynamical conditions on the hyper-competitive markets and even as a generator and incubator of knowledge.

The most important resource for production of goods and services are the immaterial resources whose combination and usage depend on the current level of knowledge within the company. This knowledge is embedded and is transmitted through the individuals, as well as through the organizational culture, identity, routines, and systems. These knowledge resources can create a long-term sustainable competitive advantage for the organization because they are socially complex, are difficult to be figured out by other organizations and are almost impossible to imitate.

Knowledge assets have dynamic and complex natures and are embedded in various aspects of the organization and have different types of characteristics depending on the context within which they are embedded. They are typically embedded in:

- All the stakeholders of the organization including all the employees, shareholders, customers, suppliers, regulators and all other involved parties;
- The cognitive processes on different levels are often expressed in process models and organizational structural models. Collectively, this knowledge is embedded into the organization's culture

(Boisot, 1998) and is ultimately manifested in the behavioral elements such as politics, processes and collective meaning (Fiol, 1991).
- The organization's explicit content which might be formal-like policies, directives, position papers, blueprints, strategies, reports and governance and informal content like blogs, documented frequently asked questions, socially collaborative software like chat rooms and peer-to-peer applications like video conferencing and even externally based social communities.
- The rules, relationships, objects and messages that flow through and between these systems, whether they are internal to the organization or are external to them (Joubert, 2010).

As knowledge assets evolve and flow through the organization, they constantly change character and form. Knowledge assets in different states have different requirements, react differently and have a different effect and value proposition to the organization. They represent a very broad set of entities and sometimes it is very difficult to pinpoint every knowledge asset relevant to the organization, as well as categorize, describe, govern, plan and design them to be of optimal value. Knowledge assets are in a constant state of flux and getting a design handle on them will be very difficult.

There are different approaches to classify knowledge resources. One of them is the categorization of knowledge into codified and tacit; specialist vs. common knowledge; know how, know why, know who and know what; and sometimes it is very common to identify the knowledge resources as intellectual capital which consists of several inter-related types of resources:

Human capital – capabilities, skills, experience and creativity of the employees whose development is very important: to have a working environment which enables and supports creation and sharing of knowledge; the individuals to have deepened knowledge for performing their working tasks and the company to use what the employees know more;

Structural capital – organizational capabilities, organizational structure and system of incentives with which the organization can meet the market demands, i.e., achieve its strategic objectives. They comprise of: hardware, software, databases, structures, processes/ standards, administrative systems, best practices, trainings, seminars, trademarks, patents and everything else from the organizational capability which supports the employees' productivity. An important characteristic of the structural capital is that it is explicit, it is owned by the company and its size is very important for the company;

Resources in knowledge about the market and the competitors – knowledge about the market, clients, partners, competitors, i.e., knowledge about the value that is created through the connections with the other entities with which the company conducts its business. These comprise of processes, tools and techniques that support the rise of the customer base and its development is heavily dependent on how quickly the organization responds to the market signals, if it involves partners in all the stages of the new product development and if it offers new solutions that the customers could practically use (Mentzas, Apostolou, Abecker & Young, 2003, O'Sullivan, 2005, and Stewart, 1999).

Some authors name the social capital as part of the intellectual capital as well. It is the system of values, beliefs, norms and rules which define the socially acceptable behavior, mutual trust and networks on which the interactions among the individuals within the organization are based and which enable the individuals to act collectively in order to achieve the organization's strategic objectives and to establish relations with other entities outside their organization (McElroy, Jorna, Van Engelen, 2006).

One has to have in mind that the knowledge that the organization possesses in one moment is not, per se. enough to generate a basis for a long-term sustainable competitive advantage. This advantage comes from the ability to effectively apply the existing knowledge to generate new knowledge and to take action through which the organization could gain competitive advantage from the knowledge. The advantage is sustainable because the more the company knows, the more it can learn. The sustainability can be achieved if the organization already knows something which in a unique way completes the newly gained knowledge with which there is a possibility for synergy of knowledge that other competitors don't have. The new knowledge is integrated with the existing one so that insights could be built and a more valuable knowledge is created and therefore the companies could search for new ways of learning and experimenting which can add new value to the existing knowledge through synergy from a combination.

There are several different views with respect to the processes through which the sustainable knowledge-based competitive advantage occurs. According to some authors, it is a process of organizational learning that could be defined as:

- A process for improvement of the actions that the economic entities take based on knowledge and understanding (Fiol & Lyles, 1985);
- Information and knowledge processing that results in change of behaviour Cyert & March, 1963 and Miller & Friesen, 1980);
- Process of responding to changes in the internal and external environment of the organization by detecting and correcting errors (Argryis & Schön, 1978),
- Based on an organization's experience, a process or an ability that enables it to maintain or advance its performance(Levitt & March, 1988).

The activities that comprise the organizational learning are: knowledge acquiring (development or creation of skills, insights, relations); knowledge sharing (dissemination of knowledge that certain individuals gained from others); application, use of knowledge (knowledge integration so that it is assimilated, becomes widely accessible and could be generalized for new situations), and its conversion into organization resources (organizational memory) such as databases, procedures and systems that could be used for organizational advancement (Njuguna, 2009).

Aspects of Knowledge Important for the Competitive Advantage

If the perspective of organizations as stocks of knowledge is to be of use, one needs to go beyond the simplistic proposition that knowledge leads to performance and so firms should invest in increasing their knowledge stocks. While two firms may have the same amount of knowledge, they almost always differ in the type of knowledge that the stocks consist of.

While there have been a few attempts to specify dimensions of knowledge other than its quantity, there is a paucity of studies looking into the performance effects of variation in type of organizational knowledge. There is a need to explore the different properties of organizational knowledge and the effects they have on organizational attempts to succeed in the long run. Knowledge could be analyzed and assessed with regards to the degree of its breadth and depth, complexity, fungibility, transferability, tacitness, codifiability and ability to be diffused within and across firms and whether the knowledge is: tacit or articulable, esoteric or generally known, exploratory or exploitative, declarative or procedural, and architectural or component.

There are several dimensions of organizational knowledge related to the sustained competitive advantage:

- Tacitness of organizational knowledge leads to sustained competitive advantage by making it difficult for rival firms to develop similar knowledge.
- Tacitness inhibits the enhancement of competitive advantage by making it difficult to either replicate organizational knowledge over time or transfer it across business units within the firm.
- Sustained competitive advantage is a function of the combination of architectural and component knowledge.
- Exploitative knowledge leads to decreases in returns variability.
- Exploratory learning increases the chances of competitively superior returns, and hence, a sustained competitive advantage.

Managing Critical Knowledge Assets: Achieving and Sustaining Organizational Competitive Advantage

- Organizational competence leads to sustained competitive advantage by providing economies of scope in implementing related diversification strategies.
- Organizational competence leads to sustained competitive advantage by providing adaptive abilities.
- The importance of organizational competence increases as the rate of environmental turbulence increases.
- Sustained competitive advantage is a function of combinations of breadth and depth of organizational knowledge (Narasimha, 2000).

The Impact of the Four Pillars of a Knowledge Management System on the Sustainability of the

According to DeNisi, Hitt and Jackson (2003), the sustainable knowledge-based competitive advantage is generated through a process of knowledge management (KM), or leveraging relevant knowledge assets to improve the efficiency, effectiveness and innovation by which a company achieves its. The KM process is comprised of: gaining knowledge, its selection, internalization and use (Holsapple & Joshi, 2003). According to a model developed by Stankosky, KM is about leveraging relevant knowledge assets to improve effectiveness, efficiency, and innovation. Knowledge assets are the new factors of production, and require management processes that stitch together leadership, organization, technology, and learning, all operating in harmony. All four need to be operational, and leaving out any one of them is detrimental to the competitive advantage of nations and organizations.

As mentioned before, the four principle areas (pillars) under which the elements or the subsystems of KM in organizations are:

Leadership/management – environmental, strategic and enterprise-level decision-making processes highly influenced by knowledge as strategic assets/resources. It is important that within every organization the leaders:

- Advocate the importance of learning and knowledge in an organization,

- Design, implement, and oversee an organization's learning infrastructure,
- Manage relationships with external knowledge providers,
- Provide ideas to improve the process of knowledge creation in the organization,
- Design and implement a knowledge codification approach,
- Measure and manage the value of knowledge,
- Manage the organization's professional knowledge managers,
- Lead the development of learning and knowledge strategies, focusing the organization's resources.

Leadership provides the ground for establishing an effective and efficient knowledge management system throughout the entire organization. It is not only used for providing the basic guidelines, but also for ongoing support for knowledge management practices.

Organization – operational aspects of knowledge assets, including functions, processes, formal and informal organizational structures, control measures and metrics, process improvement and business process reengineering. The organization comprises of all the systems and subsystems within the enterprise which is broadly defined to include its environment, relevant stakeholders, and the platform for the knowledge management system.

Learning – organizational behavioral aspects and social engineering in order to identify and apply the attributes necessary for collaboration and a learning organization. The analysis of learning related to knowledge management is less concerned with individual learning processes than with the system or organization as a whole. The primary focus of attention is the organization as a framework for individual action. Organizational learning differs from learning by individuals in that it involves the needs, motives and values of various members of the organization. Learning implies the development of knowledge which leads to a new collective understanding. This collective understanding influences behavior since the acquisition and interpretation of knowledge brings about changes in cognitive maps; which in turn affects the range of potential behaviors.

There are levels of learning within an organization. The first level of learning has often been referred to as adaptive learning or single-loop learning. The next level of organizational learning involves not only behavioral adaptation, but also changes in deeper cognitive structures. Significant changes occur in the relationship between the organization and its environment, necessitating more than a simple process of adaptation. Reconstructive learning or double-loop learning involves questioning organizational norms and values which seem unchangeable; setting new priorities, and conducting evaluations of these norms. As a result of learning, the internal value systems may have to be restructured. The organization's frame of reference can only continue to develop if existing structures are changed and the behavioral repertoire is modified. Learning is essential for managing the strategic knowledge assets because it forms the values and the behavior that is supportive of KM practices and processes.

Technology – various information technologies peculiar to supporting and/or enabling knowledge management strategies and operations. Many organizations employ IT in one form or another to manage their knowledge, but also for capturing tacit knowledge and then storing it in repositories. IT is not just about databases or information repositories. It should be understood less in its capacity to store explicit information and more in its potential to aid collaboration and co-operation between people. Technology provides the infrastructure for the KM system.

We can name several technologies commonly used for the purpose of managing the strategic knowledge assets within an organization:

- Intranet infrastructures – provide basic functionality for communication (e-mail, teleconferencing), as well as storing, exchanging, search and retrieval of data and information;
- Document and content management systems – handle electronic documents or web content respectively through their entire life cycle;
- Workflow management systems – support well-structured organizational processes and handle the execution of workflows;
- Artificial intelligence technologies – support search and retrieval, user profiling and matching of profiles, text and web mining;
- Business intelligence tools – support the analytic process which transforms fragmented organizational and competitive data into goal-oriented knowledge and require an integrated data basis that is usually provided by data warehouse;
- Visualization tools – help to organize the relationships between knowledge, people and processes;
- Groupware and collaboration software – supports the time management, discussions, meetings or creative workshops or work groups and teams;
- E-learning systems – offer specified learning content to employees in an interactive way and thus, support the teaching and/or learning process.

These four building blocks give the structure and enable the functioning of the KM system. All of them must be present in any enterprise management-engineering framework that has knowledge assets as the prime factors of production and also, they are mutually dependable and supportive.

The Knowledge Management System

The knowledge management system within any company performs several functions:

- Knowledge assurance – process of validation and verification of the knowledge in order to provide its quality and reliability.
- Knowledge generation – formation of new ideas through interactions between explicit and tacit knowledge. As defined by Ikujiro

Nonaka (1994), it consists of socialization (tacit to tacit), externalization (tacit to explicit), combination (explicit to explicit), and internalization (explicit to tacit). There are five modes of knowledge generation: acquisition; dedicated resources; fusion; adaptation and knowledge networking.

- Knowledge codification – a process of conversion of tacit knowledge into explicit form and its representation in easy accessible media for further use. It involves systematization, categorization, classification, summarization, collection and organization of knowledge, information and data and their suitable representation.
- Knowledge transfer – a culture-based process (considered as informal or "invisible") by which adaptive organizational knowledge that lie in people's heads is exchanged with others. Formal knowledge transfer is another basic process by which documents, data, or other types of resources is captured and stored in formats and media that allows for retrieval by others when needed. This process seeks to organize, create, capture or distribute knowledge and ensure its availability for future users and is more than just a communication process. There are several methods for knowledge transfer: best practice meetings; critical incident interviews or questionnaires; expert interviews; expert systems; information exchanges; internships; job aids; job rotation; knowledge audits; knowledge fairs; knowledge maps; lessons learned debriefings; mentoring; skills inventory; storyboards; storytelling; training etc.
- Use of knowledge – making knowledge operational and actionable for effective decision making. It involves engagement of the available knowledge resources for making informed decisions, taking appropriate measures, follow-up, control and improvement of processes, practices, etc.

These functions are mutually interconnected and enable the seamless functioning of the knowledge management system within the organization. The driving forces behind the knowledge management could be categorized as:

1. External driving forces:
- Globalization of business and fierce international competition, where only the most efficient and effective survive by being efficient, effective, and innovative in operations, marketing and production of products and services;
- Sophisticated and more demanding customers who require new features of products and services, better fulfillment of individual needs, higher quality and quicker response;
- Sophisticated competitors which continuously implement innovations in products, services and processes;
- Sophisticated suppliers who improve their capabilities and can participate in creating and supporting innovations to deliver sophisticated products.

2. Internal driving forces:
- Bottlenecks in enterprise effectiveness which have moved from visible and tangible sites to knowledge-intensive work areas, thereby imposing the need for better understanding, expertise and intelligent behavior;
- Increased technological capabilities;
- Understanding of how human cognitive functions (understanding, mental models, associations) affect decision making and performing knowledge intensive-work.

3. Other ongoing developments that will affect knowledge management further:
- Economics of ideas;
- Information management and technology;
- Cognitive science;
- Shifts in bottlenecks;
- New customization requirements for sophisticated customers etc.,
- Macroeconomics and policies that deal with valuing and taxing intangibles on the balance sheets of nations and organizations (Wiig, 2000).

Managing Critical Knowledge Assets: Achieving and Sustaining Organizational Competitive Advantage

The competitive advantage brings added value to the companies and the process of creation of this value within the knowledge-based organization could be described as a sequence of three knowledge processes:

- <u>Generative process</u> in which the knowledge is produced through goal-oriented activities for problem solving
- <u>Production process</u> that manifests the knowledge in a form of product or service
- <u>Representative process</u> which transmits the manifested knowledge to the customers.

However, this stylization of the linear sequence is overly simplistic and does not take into consideration the huge intensity and complexity of the interactions between the actors in the business systems which characterize the modern organizations. The relationships are not sequential, but reciprocal and simultaneous and they constitute a thick and complex network of cooperation in which the customers, the suppliers, competitors and other entities are included in an integrated and partnering system of knowledge generation in which most of the knowledge is tacit.

This complex network of networks converts itself into different abilities out of which some are idiosyncratically synergistic, cannot be imitated and cannot be surpassed – inherent core competencies and part of them can easily be copied and surpassed – secondary or auxiliary competencies. The competencies could be developed and advanced through learning (learning by doing, learning to learn etc.) or through gathering knowledge from external sources (absorptive capacity of the organization). The process of value creation connects numerous organizations which mean that a very larger set of capabilities is at stake. The mutual relations no longer come from the complementarily or the proximity between different sets of resources or couples of agents. They are a result of broader systemic forces in the environment which advance or maintain certain regimes, rules, conventions, forms of cohesion or bundles of market and non-market relations which generate even thicker and tighter networks. These "families" of forces are called sources of structural competitiveness i.e. sources of external economies or diseconomies of the system of processes that define the business system on a mesa level. It means that the business systems that learn are embedded in the wider economic system that learns and in which the focus is less on the allocation of the existing resources and is more on the creation of new value, products and services through innovation and learning and this economic system has the ability to increase its rate of learning. In fact, the notion structural competitiveness is an adequate term for representation of the plethora of regimes, rules and broader characteristics of the learning economy i.e. its economic, political and social system that enable effective collective learning in the business system and influence the capacity of companies to learn and transform themselves (de la Mothe & Paquet, 1988).

Conclusion

Creating and sustaining competitive advantage is the core of strategic management. The organization that aims at building a competitive advantage that cannot be easily eroded by environmental forces must focus on building organizational assets and capabilities that are valuable, rare, and not easily imitated by competitors. One of the central bases for achieving competitive advantage is the organizational capability to create new knowledge continuously and transfer it across various levels and parts of the organization. It involves a constant process of learning from a company's internal and external environments to creatively manage tomorrow's opportunities/threats as competently as they manage today's business.

The knowledge management process facilitates the effective utilization of employees' creativity and enhances organizational innovativeness and adaptiveness. Learning and innovative companies are able to find the means to deliver a given set of customer benefits at lower costs than competitors or provide customers with a bundle of benefits its rivals cannot match. They act as adaptive organizations that are able to sustain competitive advantage by assimilating new sources of technologies, skills, and core competencies.

Managing Critical Knowledge Assets: Achieving and Sustaining Organizational Competitive Advantage

References

Amit, R., & Schoemaker, P. J. H., (1993), Strategic Assets and Organizational Rent, Strategic Management Journal, Volume 14, Issue 1, pp.33–46.

Argyris, C and Schön, D. A., (1978): Organizational Learning: A Theory of Action Perspective Reading, MA: Addison-Wesley.

Barney, J. B., (1991), Firm Resources and Sustained Competitive Advantage, Journal of Management, Vol. 17, Issue 1, pp. 99–120.

Bell, D. (1973), The Coming of Post-Industrial Society: A Venture in Social Forecasting. Basic Books.

Bixler, C. (2005), Developing Foundation for a Successful Knowledge Management System" in ed. Stankosky M. A., Creating the Discipline of Knowledge Management: The Latest in University Research, Elsevier 52 – 54.

Boisot M., (1998), Knowledge Assets, Securing Competitive Advantage in the Information Economy. Oxford: Oxford University Press.

Cyert, R. M., & March, J. G., (1963), A Behavioral theory of the Firm, Englewood Cliffs, NJ: Prentice-Hall.

de la Mothe, J., & Paquet, G., (1998) Structural Competitiveness and Interdependencies: Regional Patterns in eds Dunning, J. H., & Boyd, G. Structural Change and Cooperation in the Global Economy. Edward Elgar Publishing.

DeNisi, A, S., Hitt, M. A., & Jackson, S. E. (2003), Managing Knowledge for Sustained Competitive Advantage, John Wiley and Sons,. 9 – 10.

Fiol, M. C., & Lyles, M. A., (1985), Organizational Learning, Academy of Management Review, Vol. 10, No. 4, pp. 803-813.

Fiol, M. C., (1991) Managing Culture as a Competitive Resource: An Identity-Based View of Sustainable Competitive Advantage', Journal of Management, Vol. 17, No. 1, 191 - 211.

Graen, G. B., (2008). What is a knowledge-driven corporation? Graen, G. B., & Graen, J. A. Knowledge-driven Corporation: Complex Creative Destruction. Information Age Publishing

Grant, R (2000), Shifts in the world economy: The drivers of knowledge management, ed Depres, C and Chauval, D Knowledge Horizons: The Present and the Promise of Knowledge Management, Butterworth Heinemann, 28-30

Holsapple, C. W., & Joshi, K. D., (2003) A knowledge management ontology, eds Holsapple, C. W., Handbook on Knowledge Management 1: Knowledge Matters, Springer, 104-109

Ishikawa, I., (2006) The Source of Competitive Advantage and Entrepreneurial Judgment in the RBV: Insights from the Austrian School Perspective, SMG

Working Paper No. 5/2006. Center for Strategic Management and Globalization, Copenhagen Business School.

Joubert, F. (2010), Knowledge Assets in Enterprise Architecture. University of Stellenbosch.

Levitt, B. & March, J. G., (1988) Organizational Learning, Annual Review of Sociology, Vol. 14 319-340.

Madhani, P., (2009) Resource Based View (RBV) of Competitive Advantages: Importance, Issues and Implications', Indian Management Research Journal, Vol. 1, No. 2.

McElroy, M. W., Jorna, R. I., & van Engelen, J., (2006) Rethinking Social Capital Theory: A Knowledge Management Perspective, Journal of Knowledge Management Vol. 10, No. 5, 124 – 136, Emerald Group Publishing Limited.

Mentzas, G., Apostolou, D., Abecker, A,. & Young, R (2003), Knowledge Asset Management: Beyond the Process-centred and Product-centred Approaches. Springer.

Miller, D. & Friesen, P. H., (1980), Momentum and Revolution in Organization Adaptation, Academy of Management Journal, Vol. 23, No. 4, 591-614.

Narasimha, S., (2000), Organizational Knowledge, Human Resource Management, and Sustained Competitive Advantage: Toward a Framework, CR Volume 10, Issue 1, 123 – 135.

Njuguna, J. I., (2009) Strategic Positioning for Sustainable Competitive Advantage: An Organizational Learning Approach, KCA Journal of Business Management Vol 2, No 1, 32 – 43.

Nonaka, I., (1994) A Dynamic Theory of Organizational Knowledge Creation, Organization Science, Vol. 5, No. 1, pp. 14 – 37.

O'Sulivan, K (2005) Leveraging Knowledge Management Technologies to Manage Intellectual Capital in ed. Stankosky M. A., Creating the Discipline of Knowledge Management: The Latest in University Research, Elsevier

Peteraf, M. A., (1993) The Cornerstones of Competitive Advantage: A Resource-Based View', Strategic Management Journal, Vol 14, No. 3, 179-191.

Porter, M. A., (1979) The Structure within Industries and Companies' Performance, The Review of Economics and Statistics, Vol. 61, No. 2, pp. 214-227.

Porter, M. A., (1998), The Competitive Advantage of Nations, 2nd Ed, Palgrave.

Stewart, T. A., (1999) Intellectual Capital: The New Wealth of Organizations Currency & Doubleday.

Wiig, K. M., (2000), Knowledge Management: An Emerging Discipline Rooted in a Long History in eds Depres, C and Chauval, D Knowledge Horizons:

Managing Critical Knowledge Assets: Achieving and Sustaining Organizational Competitive Advantage
The Present and the Promise of Knowledge Management, Butterworth Heinemann, 10 – 12, 22.
World Bank Institute (2007) Building Knowledge Economies: Advanced Strategies for Development. The World Bank.

Success Factors from the Frontline of Knowledge Management (KM)

Steve Newman

NASA (retired), Arlington, Virginia, USA

Introduction

This is a story based on personal experiences in implementing knowledge management programs at National Aeronautics and Space Administration (NASA) during the period from 1995 to the present. It provides practical guidance to develop and implement an effective Knowledge Management (KM) program. The fundamental concepts and approach presented are broadly scalable and can be applied across, or within, any government, commercial, or academic enterprise. This chapter provides a brief history and background of two remarkable KM success stories. In addition, it presents an empirically derived "KM Success Factor Model," a detailed work breakdown structure (WBS) and real examples to support the practice of developing and implementing a KM program.

History and Background

In mid 1990s, under the auspices of the "Reinvention of Government" and NASA's experiment with the "Faster Better Cheaper" hypothesis, long accepted and trusted government standards were being "trashcanned." The "Advance Quality" (AQ) team at NASA's Office of Safety and Mission Assurance (SMA) had the task of identifying "industry best practices" that could be used in lieu of government standards. Their benchmarking led to a treasure trove of design, manufacturing, and operational best practices, tools, and techniques employed by

Success Factors from the Frontline of Knowledge Management (KM)

some of the leaders in aerospace, electronics, and the automobile manufacturing sector, to include Motorola, Lockheed Martin Skunk Works, Ford, Boeing, Honda, and Orbital Sciences.

In 1995, as a NASA "early adapter" of internet functionality, a static portal called the "Advance Quality Tool Box" was deployed. This was the beginning of my NASA's KM journey.

Over the next few years I led my AQ team in conducting special studies and reviews of a number of high consequence NASA spaceflight programs. Each assessment was documented in a hard-bound report containing best practices and lessons learned for future NASA spaceflight programs. Seeking to identify common themes and structure within this body of knowledge led, in 1998, to the development of a framework I called the Process Based Mission Assurance (PBMA) model. This was also a pivotal time in my professional career as I entered the NASA Graduate Study Program and elected to begin a Doctoral program in Systems Engineering at The George Washington University (GWU). During my first semester, I discovered an elective called "Knowledge Management." It sounded intriguing, appeared to be another systems discipline, and a complement to my core studies -- so I signed up. This elective course was built, in-part, around a theoretical KM framework called the "Four Pillars Model" (Leadership, Organization, Technology, and Learning) developed by Professor Mike Stankosky and his colleagues (Baldanza and Stankosky 2000).

I soon realized that the Four Pillars provided a strategic guidepost to assist me in efforts to accomplish PBMA goals of distributing, disseminating, and institutionalizing aerospace SMA best practices and lessons learned. My KM journey at NASA then moves forward with a mission, clear objectives, and a theoretical underpinning which leads to the first of two KM success stories that follows:

KM Success Story 1: Process Based Mission Assurance (PBMA)

The emphasis of Process Based Mission Assurance (PBMA) is on sharing and using "industry best practices," and voluntary standards. PBMA grew up as a systematic attempt to codify and share best practices across the aerospace industry and to establish a "learning organization." The PBMA's vision grew from a hard-bound case study document into a multi-functional web-based resource.

My principal creative collaborator was NASA colleague Stephen M. Wander. Additional important contributions were made by Paul Benefield, Zachary Kantzes, and Don Vecellio from the ARES Corporation. Another important concept, incorporated into the early PBMA design was the idea that "work takes place in conversation," derived from Professor Marc Addleson, at George Mason University (Addleson 2001).

In 1998, development began on the PBMA-Knowledge Management System (KMS) web-based infrastructure, with the formal deployment of NASA's first fully-operational Agency-wide KMS in April 2000. The PBMA-KMS supported program management, engineering, and Safety, Mission & Assurances (SMA) communities.

Note: In 2011, after ten years of continuous operation, the PBMA-KMS was re-structured and absorbed into a new knowledge management system deployed at the NASA Safety Center. 700 plus PBMA-KMS CoPs continue to function under new management.

The PBMA-KMS provided users with a way to access work-process relevant documentation using a user-friendly, work-intuitive knowledge architecture (KA). PBMA KA included: requirements, planning, processes, and checks and balances spanning the nominal systems engineering life-cycle. Each of the 40 cells within the framework was populated with relevant documents and video nuggets (structured video capture) that are typically one to three minutes in length providing subject matter expert discussion of key takeaways related to a specific topic.

In October 2000 the PBMA KMS offered NASA's first web-based collaboration functionality. PBMA Communities of Practice or "work groups" – a name selected to avoid early KM jargon and to emphasize the objective of performing work more effectively. CoP implementation was supported with Center Rollouts and the first of annual CoP workshops in September 2001.

Success Factors from the Frontline of Knowledge Management (KM)

For the first time, using the PBMA-KMS, NASA provided a way to collaborate using the internet through a CoP or "Work Group." The Work Groups provide a way to break down geographical and organizational stovepipes and most importantly transfer files that were too large for the NASA email infrastructure to handle such as high resolution photographs from the International Space Station (ISS).

Other functions of the PBMA-KMS included:

- A Knowledge Registry (KR) – a site where individuals could upload biographies, detailed work experience, and contact information and then search for and connect with other experts. The goal of the KR is to network problem owners with problem solvers across the Agency. The KR had moderate success but was truly ahead of its time – encountering suspicions that management was gathering information for reduction in workforce planning or employee union concerns about who is and who is not an "expert," to simple cultural inertia - reluctance to share and network:
- A Secure Web Meeting that served NASA through 2010 as a secure alternative to the fragmented implementation of WebEx across the Agency.

Notable for this case is that it underscores the reality that KM is a multi-dimensional undertaking that requires elements of:

- Strategic Planning
- Business Process Engineering/Re-Engineering
- Workflow Analysis & Process Mapping
- System Engineering
- Information Technology
- Management Sciences
- Organizational Behavior Disciplines
- Human Capital Management

The PBMA development story was fraught with challenges, to include:

- developing collaboration technology in-house, before commercial products were available

- implementing web-based functionality before Agency security policies were in place
- implementing a KM program from an operational /functional organization (Safety & Mission Assurance (SMA)) – not from the Information Technology (IT) organization
- succeeding in the face of intense inter-center bureaucratic bickering

In spite of its challenges, PBMA-KMS was a huge success and honored and recognized within NASA as well as by external entities such as eGov.

KM Success Story 2: The Integrated Risk and Knowledge Management System (IRKMS)

In 2006, after 32 years of Federal service at Federal Aviation Administration and NASA, I joined the ARES Corporation and had the opportunity to continue working in the KM field supporting David Lengyel, the driving force behind the NASA Exploration Systems Mission Directorate (ESMD) Integrated Risk and Knowledge Management (IRKM) program.

Note: In 2011, with changes in NASA's strategic direction and the end of the Space Shuttle Program, the NASA ESMD organization was absorbed into the Human Exploration and Operations (HEO) Directorate. Accordingly, after five years of operation, the ESMD IRKM is in an evolutionary transition toward a new HEO KM program.

Dave had coupled KM with the critical programmatic risk management function within the ESMD, just as the PBMA-KMS team had married KM to the NASA SMA mission. The foundation of IRKM is Continuous Risk Management (CRM), a technical management process that is part of the systems engineering discipline. CRM requires an iterative identification and evaluation of events that could prevent the achievement of objectives coupled with proactive implementation of measures to control or mitigate those risks.

Success Factors from the Frontline of Knowledge Management (KM)

A novel aspect of the IRKM approach is using risk records from the CRM process to initiate an assessment of what knowledge to transfer to risk owners to help them solve their problem and then following-up to capture the actual strategy or measures used to mitigate the risk.

The IRKM Program further innovates by employing robust face-to-face (FTF) elements as well as web-based functionality and elements. The web-based implementation resides in a secure NASA internet domain called the Integrated Collaborative Environment (ICE). Within ICE the IRKM employs both portal and wiki functionality. IRKM makes extensive use of the PBMA community of practice to interact with a broader Agency audience including those who do not have access to ICE.

The IRKM portal provides access to current events and serves as a gateway to the IRKM Knowledge Based Risks (KBRs), a signature feature of IRKM. KBRs is a highly structured video of one or more Agency experts discussing a specific risk issue, embedded challenges, solutions, and lessons learned. Each KBR also has an associated knowledge bundle of relevant documents.

Within the ICE domain IRKM:

- Sponsor's implementation of Group Systems ThinkTank, a powerful brainstorming and group collaboration tool suite used in decision support training.
- Conducts extensive training and outreach for an ICE-based collaboration wiki tool that has ignited interest in use of the wiki environment across the ESMD organization.
- Contains a risk management implementation tool suite called Active Risk Manager (ARM) that supports operation risk management across ESMD.

The IRKM Program FTF elements that support KM work at NASA are:

- deploying quarterly workshops
- conducting knowledge sharing events
- hosting knowledge cafés
- conducting focused training and outreach "road show" activities

Other functions of the IRKM include:

- Continuous development of original content (risk management case studies, white papers, conference papers) that become FTF training material and is deployed on the portal or wiki.
- Work process awareness through Rapid Business Process Analysis (BPA) – as a necessary step in effectively implementing KM technology.
- Work process improvement in the general sense – applying "Rocket Science" tools to accomplish rapid work process improvement.

The IRKM implementation represents innovation and evolution of KM practices at NASA while extending (and validating) key ideas from the PBMA-KMS implementation, such as: focus on work, work processes, and work process improvement as well as bundling information around topics and the use of video capture.

KM Success Factor Model

The "KM Success Factor Model's development is based on a critical examination of the PBMA and IRKM programs; an ongoing engagement with The George Washington University KM community; and examinations of various KM theoretical models. This model is flawed and imperfect – as all models are - but strives to capture the right content, organized in a reasonably compact and concise framework, with an explicitly stated set of goals.

Context of Enablers and Challenges

As shown in Figure 1, the KM Success Factor Model consists of an embedded Force-Field diagram that depicts challenges and enablers impinging on core KM processes that strive to deliver the desired results – more effective performance – whether it is organizational learning, higher profits, innovation, or increased quality and safety.

Success Factors from the Frontline of Knowledge Management (KM)

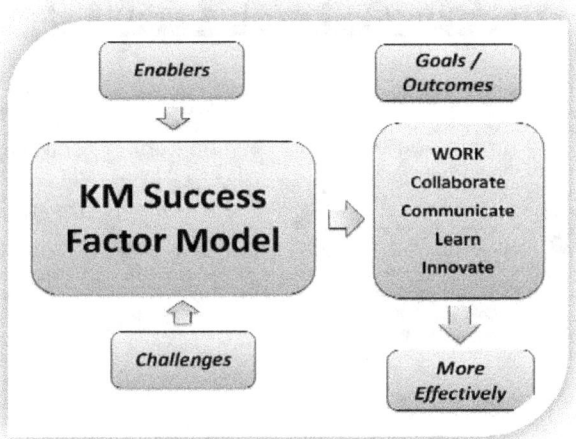

Figure 1: Context

Enablers are the driving needs of the modern workplace including the overwhelming need to find ways to work more effectively in a virtual team context. Other enablers include the cultural orientation of the workforce which is made up of an increasingly large number of individuals whom have always had access to the internet and a growing array of increasingly capable digital gadgets, this certainly calls for a more "open government" to serve as another enabling force. On the constraint or challenge side of the equation, one confronts forces that retard KM implementation including foremost - information security and enterprise security management. Security has a legitimate and important role to play (discussed later) but when it becomes over-zealous it can strangle a fledgling KM program still in the nest. Other KM program killers include internecine conflict – bitter feuds within organizations to consolidate power and influence.

The Model and Descriptive Matrix

The KM Success Factor (SF) Model is shown in Figure 2 below.

Steve Newman

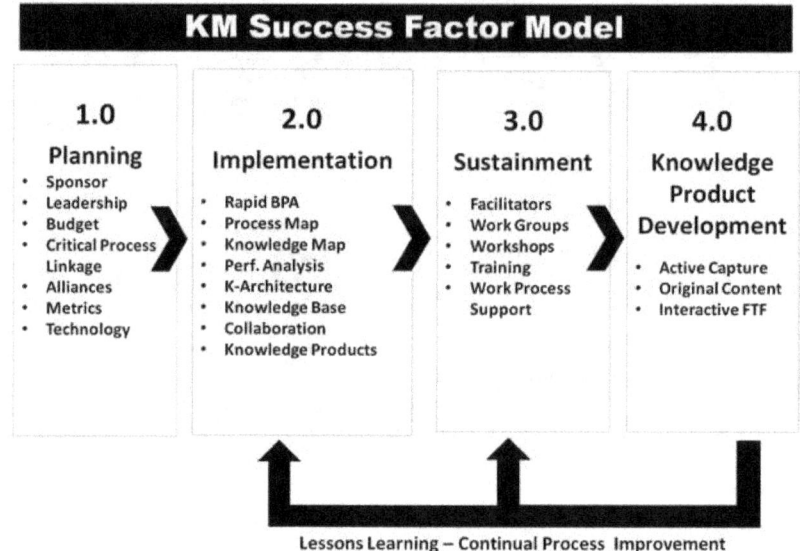

Figure 2: KM Success Factor Model

Part 1 contains seven SF planning activities. These activities help establish the environment in which a KM initiative can succeed addressing strategic vision and leadership as well as financial, political, and technical needs and issues.

Part 2 contains eight SF implementation activities. The activities include work process analysis, and performance analysis necessary to inform development of tailored knowledge architectures that are then employed in developing a knowledge-base, collaboration functionality, and development and deployment of knowledge products.

Part 3 contains five SF sustainment activities. These activities provide the infrastructure of work groups, workshops, and training that enables facilitators, embedded within organizations to provide bottoms-up work process support.

Part 4 contains three SF knowledge product development activities. Knowledge products can be electronically formatted entities (documents, audio, and video) that enable storage within the knowledge base and reuse.

Success Factors from the Frontline of Knowledge Management (KM)

Knowledge products can also be interactive experiences that transfer knowledge through discussion and conversation such as Café's, workshops, and Brown Bag events. Knowledge products are broadly defined as activities that capture and codify knowledge and/or create knowledge and/or enable transfer of knowledge. As shown in figure 2 the continuous learning loop delivers knowledge products back to the implementation and sustainment domains as needed in response to performance analysis and/or facilitator identified work process needs. The individual SFs within the model are introduced in Table 1 with a high level description of sub-elements, actors, and actions. The remainder of this chapter takes the reader through the details of each success factor.

Table 1. KM Success Factor Model

Success Factor	Element	Actions / Description
\multicolumn{3}{c}{Planning}		
1	Sponsor	AA / SAI / HEOMD Box Leads
2	Leadership	Establish a strong leadership team with "horsepower" in the community – providing sustaining support and budget advocacy
3	Budget	Provide baseline budget allocation through Strategic Integration and Analysis Division
4	Critical Process Linkage	Establish links to a critical business process including risk management, resource planning, project development, and operations
5	Alliances	Forge internal and external organizational alliances (programs, projects, functional offices, security, CIO, External Affairs, - other Governmental agencies, industry, universities)
6	Metrics	Establish metrics to gauge progress
7	Technology	Portals, CoPs, Wikis, Project Support Applications
\multicolumn{3}{c}{Implementation}		
8	Rapid Business Process Analysis	Conduct work process analysis to support development of work unit or enterprise knowledge architecture
9	Process	Develop a work unit or enterprise knowledge map incorporat-

	Mapping	ing all stakeholders, inputs, outputs, and identifying flow of information
10	Knowledge Mapping	Develop work process-specific knowledge maps identifying critical work process elements, including identification and location of knowledge and resources required to effective execute
11	Performance Analysis	Analyze available work process performance metrics to identify gaps or needs.
12	Knowledge Architecture Development	Based on previous steps, develop knowledge architecture that will support both capture as well as transfer of knowledge
13	Implement Knowledge Base	Using Knowledge Architecture develop portaland begin populating with relevant content including documents, audio, and video knowledge products.
14	Implement Collaboration Functionality	Using Knowledge Architectures implement CoPs and wikis.
15	Implement Knowledge Products	Based on preparation and tailoring analyses identify, develop and/or deploy knowledge products
Sustainment		
16	Facilitators	Establish KM facilitators within organizational work processes.
17	Work Groups	Establish a KM Implementation Team (work group) comprised of facilitators and KM initiative leadership. Engage in bi-monthly teleconferences and webinars.
18	Work Shops	Conduct annual face-to-face workshops
19	Training	Conduct KM product development training / including KBR development, and implementation of web based collaboration,
20	Work Process Support	Extend and integrate KM implementation with continuous process improvement activities
Knowledge Product Development		
21	Active Capture	Conduct video, laptop brainstorming, live event knowledge capture. Ensure issues of security, privacy, and approval are addressed.
22	Original Content	Develop original content (Develop / Tacit to Explicit / Video)
23	Interactive Content	Develop and implement face-to-face (FTF) knowledge transfer events

Success Factors from the Frontline of Knowledge Management (KM)

KM Success Factors

The sections that follow provide a work breakdown and more detailed descriptions of each of the specific success factors along with implementation examples and lessons learned from the NASA PBMA and IRKM programs.

Planning

Implementing an effective knowledge management program requires an enterprise-level strategic commitment combined with a top-down planning approach.

SF-1. Sponsor

The sponsor represents the budget advocacy, with budget decision authority for the project and is not typically involved in implementation activities. The sponsor must be intellectually on-board with the KM concept and has the responsibility of showing results and return on investment (ROI) to senior managers to sustain the project as well as supporting the Leader/Manager in dealing with organizational political conflicts. The sponsor's job is easier if there is a linkage between them and at least one or more core enterprise work processes. For example, The NASA Associate Administrator for Safety and Mission Assurance (SMA) sponsored the PBMA, while the Exploration Systems Mission Directorate, Integration Office Director served as the sponsor for IRKM.

SF-2. Leadership

The KM initiative leader would typically reside within the sponsoring organization. The leader would, ideally, be supported by KM facilitators or points-of-contact within program and projects. Facilitators would participate in bi-monthly teleconferences and annual workshops as part of the organization's KM implementation team.

Making the Case for KM

The KM Program leadership and management team must be capable of selling the concept, acquiring a multi-year budget, and building a constituency of stakeholders. They must be aggressive, technically savvy and politically aware. An example from a PBMA budget request in the early stages:

"The PBMA-KMS is a Knowledge Management System for Safety and Mission Assurance (SMA) that supports the Presidential Management Agenda, the NASA Strategic Plan in the area of Information Technology, and e-NASA."

Notice how this directive touches every political base available and underscores strategic alignment with the Agency's Safety and Mission Assurance mission.

KM leadership plays a key role in making the case for KM in as many ways as relevant to the organization. Simply posing questions (see Figure 3) is often an effective way to stimulate discussion and consideration of a KM initiative.

Brain Drain
- Will the retirement of a large segment of the workforce (Baby Boomers) result in critical process vulnerabilities? Has important tacit knowledge been captured?

Lessons Learned
- Does the organization have an effective process for capturing and transferring lessons learned (and adaptation of best practices)?

Collaboration
- Can the organization effectively communicate and collaborate across complex geographic, organizational, and contractual boundaries?

Culture
- How can KM "products and services," (e.g., Case Studies, storytelling) help in defining and shaping cultural norms and behaviors.

Resilient Teaming
- How can a KM program enable effective telecommuting when secure exchange of sensitive information is a requirement?
- How can a KM program enable continuity of operations when the local business offices are inaccessible for extended periods of time?

Decision Support
- How can KM serve as the means to integrate information more effectively, support evaluation of alternatives, and maintain a record of decisions.

Innovation
- Can innovation by boot-strapped by increased communication, collaboration and horizontal visibility across the enterprise?

Figure 3. Rationale for KM

Administrative

In addition, the KM initiative lead and supporting team would be responsible for developing an integrated KM Program Plan as well as developing and managing the annual budgets. It also may become necessary (recommended) to develop policies and procedures for implementation and use of communities of practice, wikis and other web-based tools. Other functions include routine reporting, coordination and organization of face-to-face events, to include workshops and knowledge sharing events. Most importantly, is the responsibility to maintain engagement and dialogue with all key stakeholders.

SF-3. Budget

The recommended approach is to start small – get moving with $150K to $500K minimum from the sponsor. Then try to augment that budget with contributions from other organizations directly benefiting from the KM project implementation. It's astonishing to look at the amount of money many DOD organizations spend on KM and/or the large staffing some organizations throw at the effort. PBMA and IRKM both had start-up budgets under $250K per annum with very small (two or three) civil servants working part-time on the effort.

You really can buy it by the scoop – especially if you are leveraging an in-place IT system and web domain. A modest start-up budget may be augmented with a "fee for service" arrangement with programs receiving direct implementation support (e.g., knowledge capture facilitation, training, content development, video recording, portal implementation of content).

Further, many "knowledge products" are relatively low cost to orchestrate and execute such as collaboration work groups, Brown Bag Events, webinars, process improvement activities. The desired end-state is for individual work activities to routinely conduct KCT events and routinely develop KCT products within existing budgets. Some of the higher-end KCT products (Case Studies and video production) that may become part of the institutional knowledge base do require a higher level of planning, and resourcing.

SF-4. Linkage

This might be called strategic linkage – unquestionably one of the most important keys to success for KM implementation. Linkage implies connection with specific, high value activities and work processes within an organization. When approaching managers to discuss KM, start with "I am here to discuss how I can help your critical work processes be more effective in leveraging the emergent internet technology." In the case of PBMA it is all about NASA-wide safety and mission success. In the case of IRKM it is all about more effectively managing risk across ESMD.

SF-5.   Alliances

Internal

Another must-do is forging alliances with key stakeholders (see Figure 4) – especially those organizations that have the ability to disrupt or delay your implementation. For example, the IT security, human resources (human capital) and even potential competitors – individuals and/or organizations that may have, or believe they have responsibility for some aspect of your KM initiative. Forging an early alliance is always the best way to head off destructive organizational warfare. Bottom-line: Identify all potential stakeholders and engage in a positive win-win dialogue and partnership.

PBMA was implemented before the Agency had a chance to develop and implement IT security and EA policies and procedures. Accordingly, partnerships were also forged with the CIO to enable the PBMA to be their pathfinder in developing IT security and implementing Enterprise Architecture Certification. A partnership with Human Resources was important in implementing the Knowledge Registry because of both privacy and employee union concerns. A partnership was developed with the Office of External Relations that had cognizance over determination of what is and what is not export- controlled information.

In the case of the IRKM, the need for internal partnerships was less acute because of the existing ICE internet domain with in-place policies. Important partnerships were developed with the Office of the Chief Engineer, the NASA Safety Center, Export Control officials, and many Center-based operational elements of ESMD.

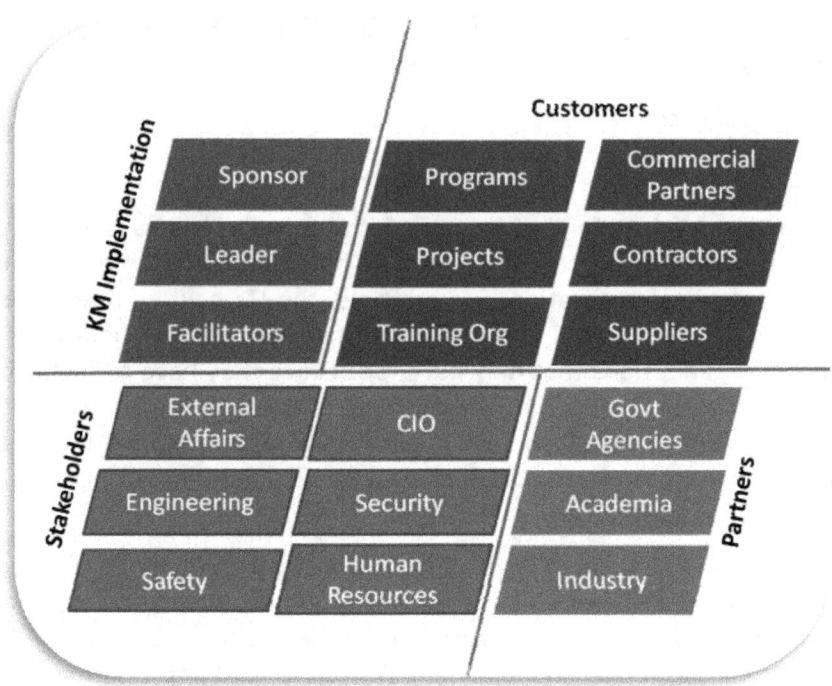

Figure4. Alliances: Customers - Stakeholders – Partners

External

In both the PBMA and IRKM programs great emphasis was placed on the importance of external alliances both to find new ideas (benchmark) and to validate the course of KM initiative implementation. IRKM developed strong alliances with key organizations across the government including the Federal Bureau of Investigation (FBI), Department of Defense (DoD), Defense Acquisition University (DAU), Federal Knowledge Management Work Group (KMWG), and the Undersecretary of Defense for Acquisition Test and Logistics (ATL). In addition, relationships were developed with the European Space Agency (ESA), German Aerospace Center (DLR) and the Japanese Space Agency (JAXA), exchanging best practices in implementing KCT. The IRKM team also maintained engagement with Aerospace Industries

Success Factors from the Frontline of Knowledge Management (KM)

Association of America (AIAA), and National Defense Industrial Association (NDIA) as well as KM leaders in the private sector.

Both teams also sought alliances and active dialogue with academic institutions involved with the development and evolution of knowledge management including The George Washington University, George Mason University, Old Dominion University, University of Missouri, and Pepperdine University.

SF-6. Metrics

KM is viewed in many large complex organizations as an enabling business practice, much in the same vein as the comptroller, the legal department, safety, accounting, program control or any other critical business services. In time, the question "What is the ROI for KM?" and will it go away? It will become as meaningless as asking for an ROI statement from building maintenance, security, safety, the comptroller, the legal department or any other essential and critical business service.

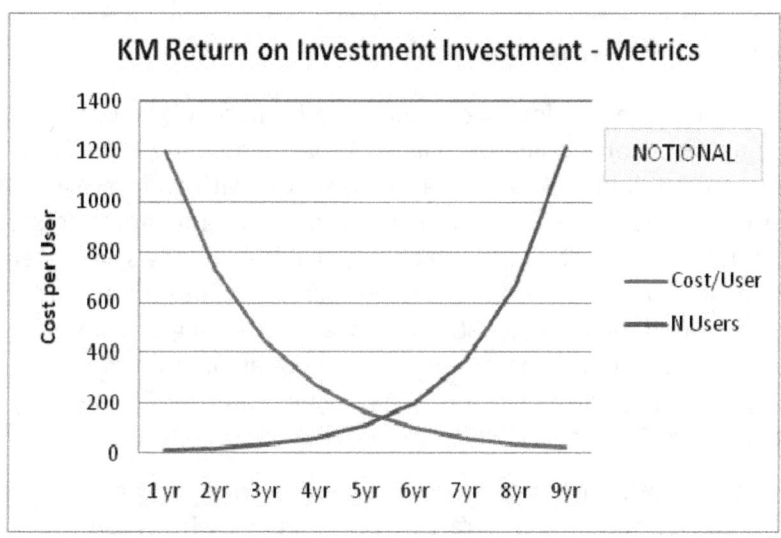

Figure 5. KM Return on Investment in IT Infrastructure

As stated previously, the goal is "more effective performance of work" within enterprise organizations, resulting in positive business outcomes. Business outcomes include cost containment, managing to schedule, fewer delays, shorter development time, higher reliability, first time quality, successful missions, accomplishing mission objectives.

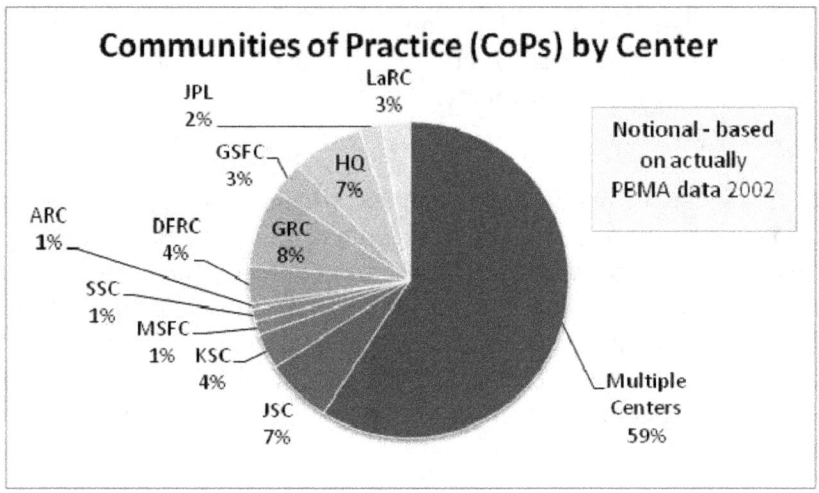

Figure 6. Cross-stovepipe Collaboration

I have found the previous wo graphics to be particularly useful in advocating for resource support. Figure 5, based on early PBMA CoP implementation data shows decreasing user cost with an increasing user base over time – the perfect IT investment dream. Another metric presentation approach, also graphical, (Figure 6) shows how people are starting to integrate/communicate across organizational and geographic boundaries in a collaborative way – breaking down stovepipe behaviors so often apparent in dysfunctional organizations. Sometimes, especially with a startup, KMS is valid and useful to employ activity metrics. Examples include:

- Collaboration Metrics: number of active wikis or communities of practice; numbers of strategic partnerships with NASA organizations, academic institutions, voluntary professional and standards organizations;

Success Factors from the Frontline of Knowledge Management (KM)

- Face-to-Face Knowledge Event Metrics: numbers of Café's, knowledge sharing forums, presentations at conferences, training events and workshops conducted at field centers;
- Web Resource Usage Metrics: hits, dwell time per visit, number of downloads, page views;
- Content Development Metrics: number of video nuggets on-line number in approval / number in production; number of best practice documents, lessons learned case studies,
- Web-Interaction Metrics: number discussion threads, number of items in discussion threads, number of blog entries.

SF-7. Technology

During the late 1990s, internet technology was a central, dominant element in KM systems and KM program development. In fact, the original PBMA collaboration environment was a "home-built" application called the Knowledge Information Center (KIC). Today, internet portal development software, collaboration "engines," and emergent social media applications are ubiquitous – technology capability is no longer an issue. Today's challenges involve navigating through a complex landscape of distributed internet servers and ever increasing security. User access is a non-trivial planning consideration.

Web Domain

In a complex organization one may discover component organizations are employing internet functionality residing in a myriad of domains provided by various entities including distributed institutional organizations (e.g., a NASA Center or an FAA regional office) and/or centralized Headquarters IT organizations. The web domain one chooses to employ will bind the degree to which it is possible to collaborate with organizations and individuals outside one's own organization. The fundamental issue is access and information type (public, sensitive, classified). The White House Open Government and Science, Technology, Engineering, and Mathematics outreach initiatives encourage the sharing of information. At the same time, in accordance with Federal laws, the responsibility exists to safeguard information identified as

Sensitive But Unclassified (SBU). The recommended approach to this dilemma is twofold:

1. Establish a secure domain to provide functionality (as noted above) that may involve sensitive but unclassified (SBU) information. NASA (in 2011) is moving to implement two-factor strong user authentication for such sites.
2. Identify and employ publically accessible web domains, still password protected, for collaboration with outside agencies, industry. Such sites would simply ground rule out sensitive content. This domain (or collection of domains) would be selected to support portals, CoPs and/or wikis.

The PBMA solution was to implement a publicly accessible knowledgebase while maintaining a highly secure community of practice environment approved by the Agency to contain sensitive but unclassified information. The CoP environment provided the founder the option of including any individual they approved consistent with Agency security policies. On the other hand, the IRKM wiki collaboration functionality was housed within the ICE domain and is accessible only by those individuals with an ICE account. As a consequence, the IRKM limited its ability to foster collaboration with outside agencies, industry, and academia.

Project Support Applications

A robust KM initiative will also serve to sponsor or advocate specialty program/project support applications on a case-by-case basis as required by programs and projects. Selected examples from the IRKM program are discussed below.

The Think Tank application is in use by many agencies across the Federal Government. The ESMD employed Think Tank to support team collaboration, decision making and "laptop brainstorming" in a knowledge capture mode. The Think Tank functionality also served as a key element in the ESMD decision support training initiative, assisting teams in brainstorming, prioritization, and alternative analysis. Of note, is the approach of integrating technology with face-to-face discussion and analysis – a powerful mix.

Risk management database applications were also deployed to assist in implementation of the continuous risk management process. It is important to note that risk records contained within the risk management databases provide important guidance in planning KM activities. In addition, risk databases can become knowledge-bases providing a historical program/project record of issues are encountered (and method of control or mitigation employed) throughout the life-cycle. The Quindi application has been used extensively to capture and integrate video, audio and PowerPoint presentations, screen shots, and whiteboards into an integrated product that can be deployed in a portal environment.

In late 2011, NASA established Internal Mobile Apps capability (apps@NASA) and NASA employees and contractors can now download mobile applications for Android, iPad, and iPhone platforms. The opportunity is to establish work productivity applications to support programs and projects. These applications provide anywhere access to critical NASA systems and tools to help perform work. The domain "apps@NASA" is hosted by the Center for Internal Mobile Applications (CIMA), which is a part of the NASA Enterprise Applications Competency Center (NEACC) in Huntsville, AL.

Social Media

Social media includes blogging, twitter, chat, threaded discussions and other emergent interactive web-based communication methods. Social Media is an area that has unrealized potential (at NASA) and within the work-centric KM Success Factor Model. In both the Both PBMA and IRKM implementation experiences (over a span of ten tears), the workforce has shown a reluctance to embrace blogging, face-book like applications (Knowledge Registry), tweeting, and other so called Web 2.0 capabilities. Part of the slow up-take has certainly been timing. But the real underlying causes are believed to be cultural and practical. The NASA culture is one wherein you are invited to state your views but you better have a carefully prepared presentation backed up with data - a popular NASA motto is "In God We Trust – all others bring data." Tweeting and blogging have just not taken hold as work tools. This reluctance might be overcome if there was a clear practical way to enhance the performance of work using the Web 2.0 tool kit.

Please note that the NASA public affairs organization have been highly engaged offering "Tweet Ups" for space launch events, important briefings, and other outreach activities – a way to conduct the work of public affairs - but this is the exception ... which tends to demonstrate a fundamental premise of the KM Success Factor Model – a successful KM project must first and foremost help people do work.

Implementation

There are eight SF activities in the implementation phase. These Success Factors interact as shown in Figure 7. Process and performance analysis helps define the knowledge architecture and knowledge gaps. The knowledge architecture, in turn, helps design the knowledge base structure and collaboration folder structure. The process performance analysis identifies knowledge gaps and needs and guides implementation of knowledge products.

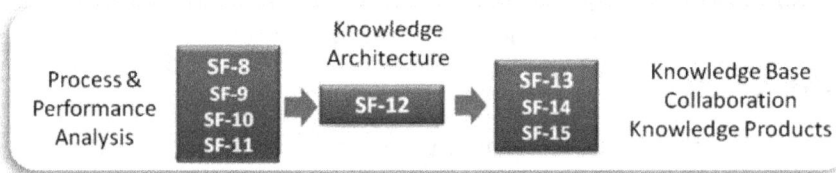

Figure 7. Interacting Elements of Implementation Process

SF-8. Rapid Business Process Analysis

Rapid business process analysis (BPA) implies a method of analysis that can be accomplished quickly – renewing (or creating) awareness of critical process elements, stakeholders, and flow. Rapid BPA consists of 10 Questions (see Table 2) to be an effective first step in developing the knowledge architecture that will serve as an important element in any successful KM program implementation.

Table 2. Rapid BPA - 10 Questions

Success Factors from the Frontline of Knowledge Management (KM)

	Rapid BPA – 10 Questions
1.	What is your product or service?
2.	Who is the direct customer?
3.	What comes in? – What goes out?
4.	How often do you deliver product?
5.	What information do you need to do your work?
6.	What people do you need to do your work?
7.	Who else benefits from your product?
8.	What rules & requirements govern the work?
9.	What checks and controls do you implement?
10.	Who is your boss or your sponsor?

Conducting Rapid BPA is most effective as a team activity using whiteboard, butcher paper, and a facilitator. At the end of the BPA session, all participants will ideally have reaffirmed their understanding (or for the first time really understood) work process goals, objectives, products, outcomes, and organizational values.

SF-9.   Process Mapping

A second step is developing a business unit critical process map. The Process Map provides a graphical depiction of the processes implemented in organizationally complex mission activity (see Figure 8). Process Mapping helps program participants and managers better understand and manage this complexity.

The process map will assist KM facilitators and project teams in understanding interactions and flow of information as well as products/deliverables between the program/project, and stakeholder organizations. For example, a typical NASA mission involves multiple centers, multiple agencies, multiple DOD elements, research laboratories, international partners, multiple spacecraft instruments, separate spacecraft-bus project office, separate launch vehicle project office,

USAF range safety managers, multiple contractors, and multiple subcontractors.

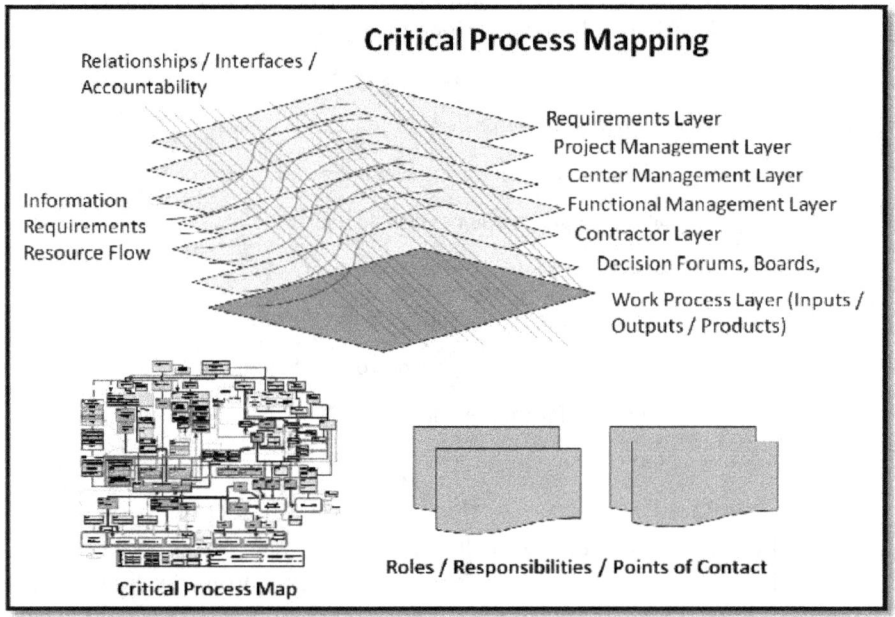

Figure 8: Critical Process Mapping

Information from rapid BPA along with additional research and discussion with stakeholders provides the basis to develop a process map and matrix. The utility of process mapping is underscored in NPR 8705.6B, "Safety and Mission Assurance (SMA) Audits, Reviews, and Assessments" that requires assurance process maps be included in all presentations made at the Safety and Mission Success Review, the Agency top readiness review chaired by the Chief Engineer and the Chief Safety Officer.

SF-10. Knowledge Mapping

The third step in the preparation process is development of knowledge maps that work in concert with critical process maps to identify process-critical information and individuals as well as the flow of information within the enterprise. A typical knowledge map will identify work process and products, knowledge needed to implement work

Success Factors from the Frontline of Knowledge Management (KM)

process, individuals within the organizations qualified to implement critical steps, depth of staffing, and gaps in capability.

SF-11. Performance Analysis

The fourth step in the preparation process is analysis of work process needs and/or knowledge gaps using available work process activity, performance metrics and issues. Consider, for example, the Fishbone analysis shown in Figure 9. The analysis examined over 100 separate risk issues identified in the NASA Constellation Program related to test and verification. This insight cued the implementation of knowledge product development including a systems engineering verification training event and multiple knowledge sharing webinar/workshops.

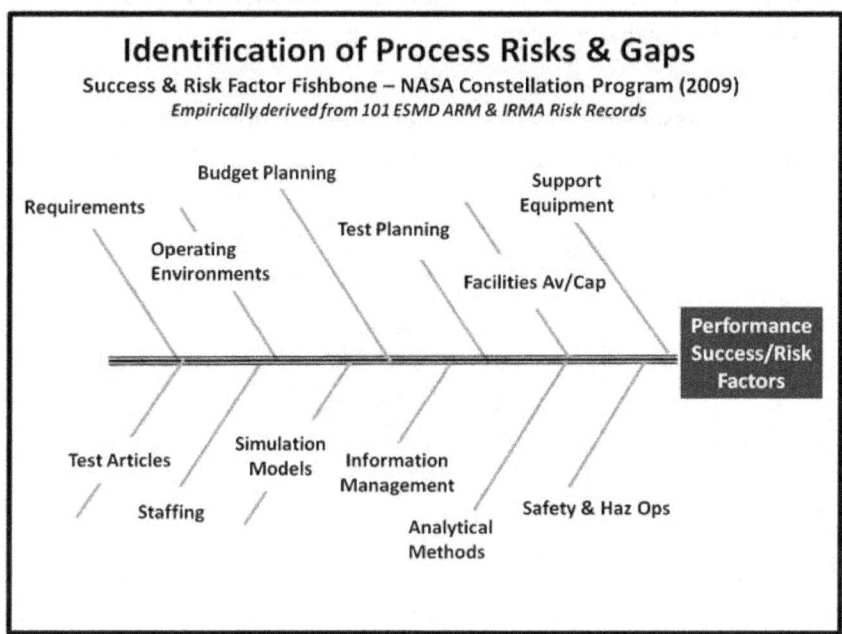

Figure 9. Process Performance Analysis

SF-12. Knowledge Architecture (KA) Development

At this point, one can begin developing one or more knowledge architectures. The KA is a crucial element in effectively implementing a KM initiative within any enterprise. A business unit specific KA serves as a basis for finding stuff, for communicating, codifying, storing, and using information within the enterprise. The KA structure is like a "saloon door" that swings both ways – enabling knowledge capture on one hand and providing an intuitive framework for transfer on the other.

The KA must be intuitive – must reflect the work process – must help work be accomplished. An important realization is that more than one KA will be relevant to an individual within an enterprise. At the same time, the number of different KAs will be limited to no more than two or three. Ideally, an individual could come to work on a given day and simply select the right graphical user interface for a given work activity. A framework implies a table or matrix graphical user interface (GUI), but with mouse-over, drop-down functionality it is possible to add additional navigational options.

The key is finding a structure so intuitive that people in the process will find the associated graphical user interface something they want to use. Several examples of knowledge architectures are presented below in figure 10.

Knowledge Capture & Transfer Frameworks

Universal 1
- Engineering Management
- Systems Engineering / Requirements
- Organization
- Communication
- Resources
- Technical Authority (SMA, Engineering)
- Schedule
- Design
- Manufacturing
- Test And Verification

Life-cycle Framework
- Design
- Design Verification
- Mfg/Assembly
- Mfg Verification
- Integration
- Sys Level Verification
- Operations

Strategic Framework
- Policies
- Processes

Tactical Framework
Eng Mgmt
Req Mgmt
SE&I
Technical

Functional
- Resource Mgmt
- Procurement
- Human Capital
- Organization
- Communication
- Technical Authorities

Milestone-Based (entrance/exit criteria)
Preliminary Requirements Review (PRR), Preliminary Design Review (PDR), Critical Design Review (CDR), and Operational Readiness Review (ORR).

Smart Shutdown
- Personnel Realignment
- Capability/Requirement Assessment
- Technology Realignment
- Facilities / HW / SW Realignment
- Contract Realignment
- Budget

PBMA	Formulation			Implementation				
	Pre Phase	Concept Devel.	Acq.	HW	SW	Mfg	Integ Test	Ops
Policies								
Plans								
Procedures								
Controls								
Verification								

Success Factors from the Frontline of Knowledge Management (KM)

Figure 10. Knowledge Architecture Examples

SF-13.   Implementation of Knowledge Base

Having established one or more process appropriate architectures one is prepared to implement a knowledge-base, typically deployed within a portal, portlet or series of web pages. The architecture or framework is then populated with relevant content including documents, audio, and video knowledge products.

SF-14.   Implementation of Collaboration Functionality

Today Community of Practice (CoP) technology is ubiquitous and competing systems have nearly identical functionality. The primary CoP engine for NASA over the past ten years has been the OSMA-sponsored PBMA with over 700 communities and 20,000 users. In the past year, PBMA CoPs have transitioned to a new engine under the direction of the NASA Safety Center called NSC Knowledge Now (NSCKN). Communities of practice generally fall into two categories. First is the "work group" – project oriented communities that typically follow a program/project life cycle. The second category is discipline oriented, sometimes referred to as a community of interest which is formed by groups of people from across organizational boundaries and often outside traditional or formal channels of communication who share a concern, a set of problems, or a passion about a topic. Primary CoP functionality includes: document library, media library, database, calendar, polling, threaded discussions, real-time chat, mailing lists, and action tracking

Wikis: Wikis are seen as the natural collaborative complement to Communities of Practices (CoPs) implemented within the framework of the existing Agency knowledge management systems. While CoPs deliver a wide range of work group functionality, including the means to manage documents, the Wiki functionality and rule set is uniquely oriented to controlled, change-managed, asynchronous, narrative (document) content development by a team of collaborators. Wikis provide teams an easy to use, flexible interface to collaborate on documents, conduct discussions, manage calendars, locate and share information, and, most importantly, work more effectively. Wiki characteristics include: ease of use; limited or no dependency on IT support programmers; owners can manage their content; security; allows development of intuitive work-process based information hierarchy and structure; provides the ability to work together in an asynchronous manner with automatic documentation of changes.

IRKM employed "Confluence" as its Wiki engine (within the ICE domain) to support virtual teams across the Directorate. In 2007, the intensive Wiki training was conducted at MSFC, KSC, JSC, and NASA HQ resulting in substantial engagement with over 330 Wikis spaces supporting 4000 active users.

SF-15. Implementation of Knowledge Products & Services

Having acquired an understanding of work process needs, knowledge gaps, and special requirements KM facilitators are now prepared to implement work performance support activities and develop focused knowledge products.

Knowledge capture and transfer methods and modalities range from the very simple (Brown Bag Lunch Speaker) to the relatively complex (Interactive Case Study). Table 3, below, identifies knowledge products and transfer events in the left-hand column. The columns to the right indicate: the relative development cost and complexity of the product or event; the demand on the user or participant's time; whether or not the knowledge is codified in an electronic format; and whether the product or event involves conversation, face-to-face interaction, hands-on interaction or storytelling, considered to be one of the most effective knowledge transfer modalities.

Table 3. Example Knowledge Products

Legend: H=high, M=medium, L= low / y= yes, n=no			
	Attributes	Digital	Interactive

KCT Products / Events & Functional Capabilities	Relative Development Cost, & Complexity	Demand of Time of User of Participant	Codified – Web Access Digital Transfer	Collaboration Capability	Conversation	Face-to-Face	Hands-On Interaction	Storytelling Dimension
Brown Bag Luncheon Speaker	L	L	n	n	y/n	y	n	y
Brown Bag + Video Recording	L	L	y	n	y/n	y	n	y
Process 2.0 Event	L	L	y/n	y	y	y	y	y
Laptop Brainstorming Event	L	L	y	y	y	y	y	y
P2.0 Training	M	L	y	n	n	n	n	n
Café Event	L	M	y/n	y	y	y	y	n
KCT Report	M-H	M	y	n	n	n	n	y
Knowledge Sharing Forum + video	M	L	y	n	y/n	y	n	y
Webinar	L	L	n	n	y/n	n	n	y/n
Webinar + Recording via Quindi	L	L	y	n	y/n	n	n	y
Email Push (pointer) Message	L	L	y	n	n	n	n	n
Video Nugget	M	L	y	n	n	n	n	y
KBR	H	L	y	n	n	n	n	y
Riskipedia	H	L	y	y	n	n	n	n
Case Study	H	L	y	n	y	y/n	y/n	y
Classroom Training Event	H	H	y	n	y	y	y	Y

A key takeaway to note is the opportunity to implement low cost, low time demand, KM activities (e.g., Brown Bag events, Process 2.0) in a routine manner within a given work process. As process enhancement needs are identified (e.g., – "we need to benchmark how DoD implemented affordability within their high technology projects"), one can then organize webinars and knowledge sharing events. Further on in the project implementation, where specialized knowledge needs are identified or the need exists to institutionalize or disseminate specialized knowledge, one can then consider development of video-based KCT products. Milestone events (e.g., PRR, PDR, CDR, ORR) also represent important opportunities to implement KM activities.

Sustainment

The eight sustainment activities include the infrastructure of work groups, workshops, and training that enables facilitators, embedded within organizations to provide bottoms-up work process support.

SF-16. Facilitators

Another critical success factor is establishing a network of embedded facilitators within implementing work processes. At NASA, facilitators will ideally be individuals with integration or systems engineering roles. Facilitators are typically asked to participate in bi-monthly teleconferences and annual workshops. Facilitators are called upon to serve as "knowledge flow managers" identifying their organizational information and work process needs as well as identifying best practices and lessons learned for transfer to other organizations, or identifying potential speakers for knowledge sharing forums.

PBMA Example: The PBMA-KMS early development phases include the establishment of "champions" at each facility/operating center across the organization or enterprise. The strategy includes formal, well-staffed, and well-funded rollouts at each operating center/facility followed by hands-on training/workshops which sought and facilitated customer/user feedback. These champions played a prominent role in the initial center deployment activities that were completed between November 2001 and March 2002. Center champions are called upon to assist in developing an SMA functional discipline knowledge map for their center as well as identifying potential candidates for videotape interviews (video nuggets) to capture tacit knowledge residing in center-based subject matter experts.

SF-17. Work Groups

The KM initiative leadership and network of facilitators provides the core work group. This core group would typically "tag-up" with a biweekly (sometimes monthly) teleconference. The work group members, individuals from their work processes and invited guest presenters engage in discussion, implementation planning, and exchange of lessons learned. The work group serves as the planning committee for subsequent workshops.

SF-18. Workshops

Workshops provide quarterly or annual opportunity for face-to-face interaction among core team members in a structured setting with presentations from sponsoring senior managers, guest speakers, facility tours, training and always exchange of lessons learned and best practices.

PBMA Example: On May 2001, a PBMA-KMS preview and workshop was held at NASA's Glenn Research Center (GRC) in connection with NASA's 2001 Assurance Technology Conference. During this workshop, "champions" representing each of the NASA Centers were trained in PBMA-KMS concepts and operation. In September 2001, the Center's PBMA-KMS champions assembled for the first workshop to discuss how best to develop and nurture communities of practice that span the NASA community. The workshop was designed to draw from the KM implementation experience of several leading US corporations and addressed knowledge management overview theory and practice, approaches to building communities of practice, sponsorship and linkage to enterprise strategic goals, and lessons learned in identifying formal and informal communities. The workshop provided a forum for discussion of center-specific strategies and issues for implementing communities of practice.

IRKM Example: In July 2011, the IRKM project implemented its 18th quarterly workshop providing attendees with a full agenda of science and technology keynote speakers, expert lessons learned presentations, and an embedded Defense Acquisition University (DAU) presentation of training material on Science and Technology Management. Previous workshops have ranged from a hands-on spacecraft integration and verification training class to expert presentations by leading figures in the Knowledge Management field. The workshops are always well attended. The forums invariably include extensive participant participation.

SF-19. Training

Training is an important element in sustaining a KM initiative. Training was developed within the IRKM program to assist facilitators in developing knowledge products, conducting knowledge capture events, and in conducting process improvement activities. IRKM training has included the courses shown in table 4.

Table 4. KM Implementation Training

KM Implementation Training	
Course Title	**Key Content**
Process 2.0 Facilitator Training	• Provides an overview of Process 2.0 and its benefits • Describes fundamental facilitation techniques as well as Process 2.0 tools and techniques
Web-Enabled Virtual Team Training (Communities of Practice)	• Provides an overview of virtual teaming and its benefits • Describes an approach to establish a virtual team • Provides an introduction to Wiki and NSCKN functionality
ThinkTank Technographer Training	• Provides instruction for using the ThinkTank (Group Systems) tool for interactive brainstorming, analysis and decision making
Knowledge-Based Risk (KBR) Training	• Provides comprehensive instructions on how to produce a KBR including planning, logistics, video-recording, post production, and web-portal implementation

SF-20. Work Process Support

The Success Factor Model places great emphasis on work process analysis and work process architecture development. It is natural for a mature KM project to ultimately address continuous process improvement bringing to bear the full range of tools and techniques.

Success Factors from the Frontline of Knowledge Management (KM)

NASA work teams have repeatedly implemented over the past three years the Process 2.0 (P2.0). P2.0 is a process improvement method that rapidly delivers sustainable results through implementation of simple but powerful concepts. Process 2.0 focuses on doing better work through a simple paradigm of plan-do-check-reflect. This methodology allows you to carefully manage the time of your participants, employs structure, and enforces discipline for team thinking. P2.0s are process-focused, collegial, structured reflection events. P2.0 events use critical process mapping, structured brainstorming techniques, and process failure modes and effects analysis to identify and address work process issues. The P2.0 method demands and enforces disciplined thinking to drive out actionable process improvements for the team. P2.0s have been used to assist a diverse set of team processes ranging from vibro-acoustic coupled-loads analysis, to the agency independent assessment processes, to a simple integration meeting gone awry. In every case, the result has been rapid, transparent, team-authored process improvement. P2.0 is a methodology that can be implemented at any point in a project life-cycle. Recommended events include:

- Start-Up activities set the stage for program/project success.
- Milestone-based activities are tailored to address program/project milestone needs (e.g., Preliminary Requirements Review (PRR), Preliminary Design Review (PDR), Critical Design Review (CDR), and Operational Readiness Review (ORR).
- Sustaining activities are important to implement anytime throughout the program/project life-cycle.

The training for Process 2.0 facilitators has been made available on the publically accessible NASA training web site.

Knowledge Product Development

As noted earlier, knowledge products can be electronically formatted entities (documents, audio, video) that enable storage within the knowledge base and reuse. Knowledge products can also be interactive experiences that transfer knowledge through discussion and conversation such as Café's, workshops, and Brown Bag events.

This section provides discussion of knowledge product development approaches and examples of products developed to address specific programs' and project needs. An approach to "Active Knowledge Capture" is described, followed by a discussion of original knowledge product development including specific examples and success stories for many of the knowledge products contained in table 3. The final sub-section provides implementation examples for several interactive, face-to-face (FTF) KCT events, also considered "knowledge products," in that they require planning, staffing, facilitation, and resource allocation just like development or deployment of other knowledge products.

There exists an enormous body of research (Prusak, Dixon and Hoffman 2010) devoted to knowledge transfer between individuals and within organizations. Individual knowledge is said to represent a deep, rich, contextual understanding of a subject. Organizational knowledge is said to include practices, processes, behaviors and know-how, communicated through interaction, conversation, cultural norms and learning modalities. Mindful of these insights, an important goal is to promote and maintain conversation and social interaction as part of every knowledge transfer product or activity. The blending of technology with FTF discussion is an increasingly viable option. Face-to-face modalities continue to provide perhaps the richest transfer opportunity. The role then of technology is to help tee-up the discussion by providing rich context through video and relevant documentation.

SF-21. Active Capture

Active capture implies a planned, structured, managed capture and codification activity resulting in an electronic record for inclusion in the HEOMD knowledge base. For example, an active capture activity may occur during a project progress milestone review or during any critical event in a project life-cycle. Other active capture events may include after action reviews with team members or planned studio sessions with work process participants.

Active capture often involves the use of video recording. Video content adds richness, the human element, and connects with the "You-

Tube" generation where video content is the expectation. Both PBMA and IRKM employed extensive video-based storytelling capture and transfer. Another example is an application called Quindi. Quindi allows one to capture and combine video, audio and PowerPoint presentations into an integrated product that can be deployed in a portal environment.

One of the most powerful techniques for active capture is Lap-top Brainstorming (LTB) using the Group Systems, Think Tank application to capture insights from the participants in their work processes. Participants in an individual session (locally and remote participating together) are connected to the internet and are able to develop and view aggregate input simultaneously. This capture process was successfully employed by IRKM for the Ares and Ares I-X projects. Integrated product team (IPT) participants were encouraged to provide mini-stories or vignettes from relevant to each of the thematic areas. In order to most effectively implement the LTB method one must develop a cadre of trained facilitators who would lead and interact with participants. The facilitator is supported by a technographer who "drives" the application and assists participants with login, drop-out, or operational issues. The facilitator employs a very careful time management protocol and adheres to the pre-established knowledge capture framework for the session.

Important administrative considerations for active capture include:

Training: Training is an important consideration for structured knowledge capture activities such as video interviews and production to ensure careful preparation, management of time, execution, and desired results.

Security: Federal law requires one to limit distribution of ITAR and Export Controlled information while, at the same time, Executive orders and Agency policy promote broad-based sharing of knowledge and lessons learned. The transfer planning scenario must carefully consider intended audience, access and information classification.

Privacy: When conducting video knowledge capture or conducting laptop brainstorming with a team of participants it is important to have established mutually agreed to ground rules and expectations, ideally documented in a signed consent form. For example, the form should address interviewee opportunity to review and approve video content or in the case of a Think Tank session – the opportunity to amend or revise their narrative.

Approval: It is also important to understand any other management review that will be required prior to implementation of the content as well as a clear understanding of the internet domain where the content will be accessible – internal intranet or public domain. If proper planning and preparation are conducted, one can avoid the delays of ITAR or legal review when moving to implement content on the internet or publically release a document.

Active Capture Examples:

Example 1: Ares I-X Knowledge Capture

The Ares I-X knowledge capture initiative (see Figure 11) provides a good example of a multi-faceted capture and transfer effort. The transfer element of the KCT process involved both face-to-face knowledge sharing events as well as web-based implementation of content. The web-based access has been provided through the Integrated Collaborative Environment (ICE) domain within the ICE wiki environment. The Ares I-X Knowledge Share Wiki features a video dashboard with "talking heads" of all Ares I-X IPT managers and team members, engineering and safety & mission assurance technical authorities, and launch control team members. Each video provides a discussion of best practices, lessons learned, cautionary notes, and suggested approaches for future projects. Other video content includes Knowledge-Based Risks (KBRs) – structured interviews with subject matter experts addressing specific technical risks (challenges) encountered in the Ares I-X project—examples include loads and environments, parachute test maturity, thrust oscillation, flight termination system, and heritage software. The document library includes access to the numerous bundled knowledge artifacts previously described.

Success Factors from the Frontline of Knowledge Management (KM)

Figure 11. Ares I-X Knowledge Share Wiki Poster

The Wiki also contains a directory with Ares I-X points-of-contact to enable follow-up discussions with content providers and subject matter experts. The Wiki also provides a variety of methods to easily access information including search, structured browsing, index, and tag clouds. Other features include a moderated drop-box providing the means for ICE users to post additional content related to the Ares I-X project.

Example 2: Knowledge-Based Risks (KBR) A KBR consists of a set of a video collage addressing a specific project risk issue (with broad / future applicability) along with a bundle of documents (white papers, articles, and presentations) related to the topic. The storytelling narrative describes how the risk was mitigated, special challenges, what worked or didn't work – specifically in terms of cost, cost savings, schedule, and technical performance. The KBR Poster is shown in figure 12.

Steve Newman

Figure 12. KBR Poster

SF-22. Original Content

The KM implementation team (facilitator and/or leadership) should be available to train, consult, and assist programs and projects in developing original content (knowledge products) relevant to their specific business activities. Ideally one would establish a small subject matter expert team to assist in periodically developing original knowledge products relevant to the execution of work processes, including case studies, news articles, analyses, Blogs, reports, and white papers. These products may be combined or bundled along with relevant documents, links, video content and references providing a rich resource to support critical process activity.

Example 1: Riskipedia Implementation:

Success Factors from the Frontline of Knowledge Management (KM)

Riskapedia is a Wiki-based resource (available within the NASA intranet ICE and NSKN domains) that provides extensive tools, techniques, best practices, videos, and lessons learned addressing the fundamental disciplines of risk management. Riskapedia is divided into three principal sections. The Risk Identification section provides taxonomies and checklists from multiple authoritative (web-based) sources for identifying typical system, programmatic, and integration risks. The Risk Assessment section contains a broad range of resources providing qualitative and quantitative tools and methodologies for analyzing, understanding, and communicating risks. Lastly, the Control and Mitigation section provides expert knowledge and guidance (new content) for mitigating and controlling risk in specific areas. The Riskipedia resource may become publically available in 2012.

Example 2: Risk Management Case Studies (RMCS)

RMCS's have been developed as multi-media interactive – FTF knowledge products. The case studies have the goal of placing small teams (5-8) of professionals in risk evaluation and decision-making situations using historical space program events. Case Studies are made available on the internet as a self study option but the training is typically delivered in an instructor-led environment using a large venue setting with breakout rooms or small group table configuration. The objective is ultimately to promote learning through enabling the conversation.

The SLWT case study addressed the many risks and challenges NASA Space Shuttle Program faced in developing the Super Lightweight Tank – a necessary achievement that enabled construction of the International Space Station in a high inclination orbit (see Figure 13). Looking into the future, engineers will face similar risks. Examining the critical thinking that made past programs successful will hopefully enhance the technical curiosity of engineers developing future space systems and make their programs equally robust.

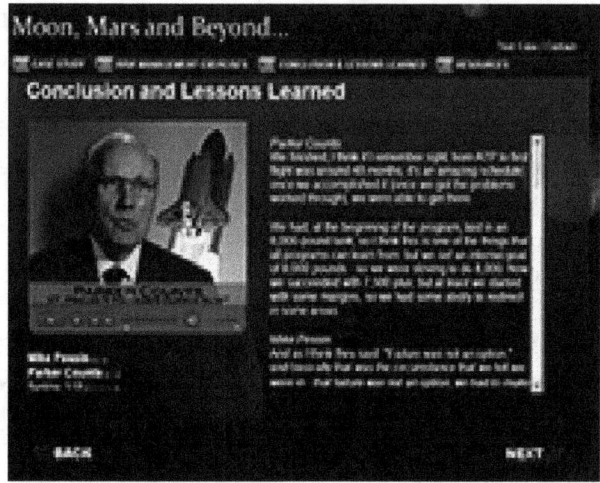

Figure 13. SLWT Case Study

Example 3: Email Push: Not all internet-based transfer activities are through the web. The email Push has been used by OSMA, APPEL, and ESMD to energize interest in newly developed content. OSMA publishes a Monthly Safety Message that highlights current knowledge products such as System Failure Case Study - providing a summary along with links to the full version. In the case of ESMD a quarterly message was transmitted to all-hands summarizing recent accomplishments and highlighting recently developed KBRs along with brief summaries and links to the web-based videos and document bundles.

SF-23. Interactive FTF

Some knowledge products are events that may not involve the use of any internet technology. The Brown Bag Lunch, the Café, and the Knowledge Sharing Forum are examples of interactive, structured knowledge product events designed to engage participants in conversation and thinking on topics relevant to work- process performance.

Example 1: Knowledge Café

The IRKM initiative has had great success deploying Knowledge Cafés to address specific challenges, issues or problems facing the organization. During 2008 – 2010, Cafés were conducted at Johnson Space

Success Factors from the Frontline of Knowledge Management (KM)

Center (see Figure 14), Marshall Space Flight Center, and NASA Headquarters.

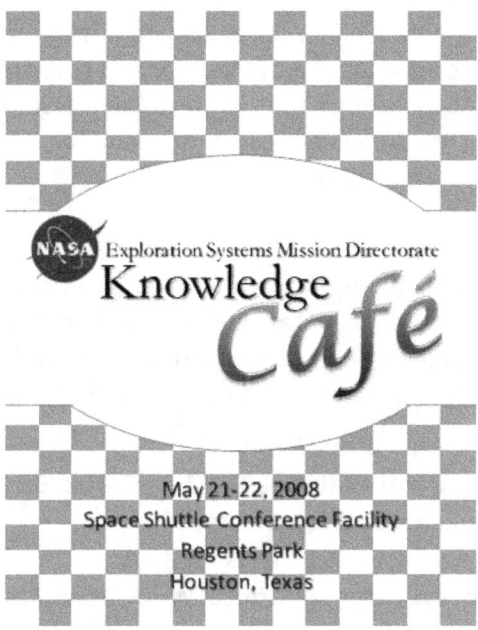

Figure 14: Knowledge Café Poster

The Café method, in brief, involves facilitated, time managed, small group brainstorming on a series of related issues while simultaneously accomplishing face-to-face social networking by remixing and rotating participants every 20 to 40 minutes. The product of a Café is a synthesized list of ideas (innovations, designs, processes, decision paths, etc.) on each topic area as well as a deeper understanding of the diversity of views on the issue.

Example 2: Knowledge Sharing Forum: The IRKM has sponsored and organized periodic (bi-monthly) knowledge sharing forums providing timely and relevant insights for programs and projects. Each forum is structured to showcase senior project leaders sharing insights on their personal project implementation successes and challenges. Events bring alumni from Apollo, Space Shuttle, and various other programs within NASA, the aerospace industry, and academia. Topics have included engineering management and systems engineering approaches, risk management, critical decision making, organizational issues, as well as cost and schedule challenges. The events have been broadly attended and seek, in particular, to engage emerging project leaders. In most cases, the events were video-recorded and the content made available through the ICE portal and NSCKN web site. The events were also made available as a webinar for participants across NASA unable to attend in person.

Conclusion

The KM Success Factor Model is an innovation in codifying a solution set of specific practices that can demonstrably result in a successful KM project. Amongst the success factors discussed in this chapter there is a subset that one may consider Critical Success Factors:

- Maintain A Work Centric Emphasis
- Pair Your KM Effort With One Or More Critical Business Processes
- Establish Stakeholder Partnerships
- Conduct Rapid Business Process Analysis
- Develop Process Maps For Critical Work Processes
- Develop One Or More Work-Based Knowledge Architectures
- Implement Web-Based Collaboration Functionality
- Place Strong Emphasis on Content – Remember – Content is King
- Develop Structured Video Content
- Laptop Brainstorming
- Focus On Structure, Conversation-Based Content
- Blend Face-to-Face With Technology
- Integrate The KM Initiative With Continual Process Improvement Efforts

Don't be afraid to change your approach - along the way make sure you continuously benchmark other organizations and borrow good ideas whenever you see them. Finally, be sensitive to organizational changes and periodically revalidate your alignment with emergent enterprise goals and objectives. Above all else, stay focused on the idea of KM as a means to help people work more effectively.

Success Factors from the Frontline of Knowledge Management (KM)

References:

Addleson, Mark, Presentation on 'The Future of Knowledge Management', Knowledge Management Roundtable, Arlington, Virginia, 2001

Baldanza, C. and M. Stankosky, "Knowledge Management: An Evolutionary Architecture Toward Enterprise Engineering," INCOSE March 2000.

Further Readings

Addleson, Marc, Nov NASA's COP (communities of practice) III workshop for process based mission assurance (http://pbma.hq.nasa.gov) in the Office of Safety and Mission Assurance. 'Organizational Change: the Path from Knowledge Work to Communities of Practice, 2003

Calabrese Frank, "A Suggested Framework of Key Elements Defining Effective Enterprise-Wide Knowledge Management Programs" Abstract of Dissertation, The George Washington University.

Denning Stephen, "The Seven Basics of Knowledge Management, International Review.

Davenport T.H. and L. Prusak, "Working Knowledge: How Organizations Manage What They Know", Harvard Business School Press, December 1997

Dixon, Nancy M., and Allen, Nate, and Burgess, Tony, and Kliner, Pete, and Schweitzer, Steve, Company Command: Unleashing the Power of the Army Profession, (2005)

Green, Annie (Author, editor), and Stankosky, Michael (editor), Vandergriff, Linda (editor), In Search of Knowledge Management: Pursuing Primary Principles, (2009) Emerald Group Publishing Limited

Liebowitz, Jay, (editor) Making Cents Out of Knowledge Management, March 2008, The Scarecrow Press Inc.ISBN: 0-8108-6048-1

Lengyel, David, M., and Newman, J.S, Managing Risk on the Final Frontier : Risk and Knowledge Management Combine to Support the Work of Rocket Science, Defense AT&L: May-June 2010

Newman, J.S., "Life Cycle Risk Management Elements for NASA Programs, A Program Manager's Guide to Faster / Better & Cheaper," Office of Safety & Mission Assurance, National Aeronautics & Space Administration, June 1997.

Newman J. S., "Process Based Mission Assurance" IAA-99-IAA.6.1.01, 50th International Astronautical Congress 4-8 Oct 1999/Amsterdam, The Netherlands, National Aeronautics and Space Administration (NASA) Washington, DC 20546, USA

Newman, J. Steven, D.Sc., NASA HQ, "The Knowledge Path to Mission Success: Overview of the NASA Process Based Mission Assurance Knowledge

Management System," Reliability and Maintainability Symposium (RAMS) 2002. Seattle, Washington. January 28-31 2002."

Newman, J. Steven, D.Sc., "PBMA-KMS Strategies for Thriving KM Programs - KM Myth-Busting, Space Shuttles, & Reindeer Tracking, Tales from the Front Lines of Knowledge Management." eGov 2005 Conference, April 21, 2005, Washington D.C.

Newman, J. Steven, D.Sc., "PBMA-KMS -NASA's IT Systems and Enterprise Architecture: The Present and the Future." Presentation to the NASA Small Business Solutions Conference, September 02, 2005 – New York City.

Newman, J. Steven, D.Sc., and Wander, Stephen M., "The Development of the PBMA-KMS –How We Did It," presentation to GSA, December 2005, Washington D.C.

Newman, J. Steven, D.Sc., and Wander, Stephen M., "KM for Improved Decision-Making and Program Management - A Pioneering Public Sector KM Case Study," eGov 2006 Conference, April 19, 2006, Washington, D.C.

Prusak, Larry, and Dixon, Nancy, and Hoffman, Ed, Panel Discussion Videotape - 16th ESMD Risk and Knowledge Management Workshop, Huntsville, Alabama, May 2010,
https://ice.exploration.nasa.gov/ice/site/km/llmn/

Sinclair, Niall, Stealth KM: Winning Knowledge Management Strategies for the Public Sector, (2006), Butterworth-Heinemann , ISBN: 075067931X, 9780750679312

Stankosky, M., editor (2004), Creating the Discipline of Knowledge Management: The Latest in University Research, Butterworth-Heinemann, ISBN 0-7506-7878-X

Wander, Stephen M., "The Evolution of Communities of Practice in NASA's Diverse Business Environment." Session 2-6, Strategies to Integrate Communities of Practice into Business Operations, eGov 2006 Conference, April 21, 2006, Washington, D.C.

KM Strategic Execution: How to Get Executive Attention

Patrice "PJ" Jackson

Lockheed Martin, Bethesda, Maryland, USA

Introduction

No executive wants their organization to fail. However, most executives fail to recognize how critical managing their knowledge assets is to the organization's bottom line. Successful organizations of the future will be those that are able to locate their knowledge assets in a split second, thus, demonstrating its ability to adapt to the complex environment of a global economy. Today's CEO must be cognizant that employee performance drives the bottom line and the successful leveraging of the collective knowledge of its employees or organizational knowledge delivers results.

Three hundred of the top scientific minds at a large defense Aero-Space company wanted to connect more than just once a year at their annual conference. They embarked on a journey that created a web-based community called the Fellow Collaboration Network (FCN). Over a period of three years, knowledge management (KM) principles and a KM Strategic Execution (KMSE) framework were applied to develop an environment that enriched their learning, allowed them to share and innovate collectively and produced a way for the next generation to engage, learn and be mentored by the brightest minds in the company.

KMSE is about a strategy that links what you know to what you need to accomplish. It is about people connecting to people, sharing and collaborating mission critical "know how" to increase performance and better decision making. KMSE is a journey that links what matters to executives to actions that matter to employees to deliver effective, efficient and innovation results. It is about leveraging knowledge to do things right, do things better and faster as well as the ability to create new things that align with the organization's critical competencies.

This is not about a "Big Bang" theory; this is about making it real and being successful. KM comes in all shapes and sizes, the key is to build your map with realistic expectations, make it personal to your organizational needs and make it scalable. This chapter documents how the FCN core team and its members learned and applied the KMSE framework, and comment on what went well, what could have gone better, and how it will be used again to build the International Collaboration Network community, to harness the brightest minds working in international business development.

Setting the Stage

In the context of this case study, KM is defined as the systematic leveraging of intellectual capital to increase organizational effectiveness, efficiency or to help the organization innovate. In addition, intellectual capital (IC) is characterized into three types; 1) human capital, which can be described as the skills and knowledge the people in the organization expose during the execution of their work, 2) organizational capital, which is found in the processes and documents, i.e., patents and procedures of an organization, and 3) relationship capital, which describes an intangible attached to the value of networks, between people who know who, and people who know how, to get their job done. The FCN case study addresses all three of these types of IC.

Harnessing the brightest minds in an organization can be a daunting task, however, when a Fellows program exists, the beginning is easy; as it starts with a list of participants from the program. Fellows are technical experts, scientist and engineers with advance degrees. They bring an expertise to work every day that is considered a critical knowledge asset to the mission of the organization. Sometimes they are the only person that knows how a particular task is accomplished and if they were not available, the program could be delayed in schedule, experience an increase in cost or worse, a reduction in quality to the customer. The prelude to having a Fellows program is for an organization to actually take the time to understand what critical knowledge skills give the organization their competitive advantage. For this organization, that task had already been developed and approved across the business areas. The hard part is the human process and getting people to share, collaborate and learn in a virtual setting.

Prior to nominating an employee to be a Fellow, the organization documents a list of competitive skills. An employee with a competitive skill is nominated with a set of recommendations on their value to the organization in their specialized field. A board of executive leaders then determines how many people are needed each year, in each competitive skill. Those chosen as the top one percent are the brightest minds and they are listed in a data base identifying their name, business areas and area of expertise. Until three years ago, the only interaction these Fellows had with each other was at an annual conference. The Fellows themselves declared that once a year was not enough. While most Fellows knew of each other, meeting once a year for three to four days was not the best way to leverage the potential of the brightest three hundred minds in the organization. There had to be a better way.

KM Strategic Execution (KMSE) Framework

KM is not a linear process; it is more a holistic metamorphosis. KM is the type of change that can best be described from a rear view mirror perspective. Looking back at the FCN, gives insight into a best practice that can be leveraged by others. KM is not random, but it is unique, and what works for one organization does not always work for another. Successful KM projects try to replicate their success, even in the same organization and fail. What research is starting to show is that there are patterns that emerge based on the core values of the organization and at the center of those core values are the leaders. In the fast paced world of business, executives are pulled between multiple priorities. Even when a project seems to be the most logical to pursue, if the business case is not solidly based on the organization's core values then it doesn't get the leadership's attention, it is just another nice thing that maybe someday we should investigate doing. It is for this reason that the KMSE framework is designed to address an organization at its core with three phases: a seven question baseline assessment, a four part strategic plan and a five phase execution path.

Seven Question Baseline Assessment

Someone somewhere is going to be given the task to start a KM initiative, and without any prior knowledge or expertise of the subject, their boss expects them to be successful. With these seven simple questions, you can start to baseline your KM effort and determine if you are aligned with a core value of the organization:

1. Why are you starting this KM effort? The answer to this question can help determine which direction the effort is headed: human capital, organizational capital, or relationship capital. Listen carefully for the core value that is being addressed: getting people to work together, being the first to innovate, being more competitive, or looking to place controls on getting things done right. This question usually sparks a lengthy discussion around many details that also help answer the other six questions;
2. Who is your most senior sponsor, and what is their desired outcome? It is important to know who is asking for the KM effort. Is it a mid-level manager or an executive vice president? It makes a difference. Not that both people aren't important, and may very well drive a successful project, but the higher up the person is in the organization the stronger their influence to ensure the effort is supported and remains a focus area. It is also critical to completely understand what the senior sponsor thinks the desired outcome is from the KM effort. One of the biggest false starts on any project can be through miscommunication between what one person thinks they are going off to do and those who actually execute the project;
3. What does your budget look like? KM isn't free. People will be spending time executing change and time is money. Be up front about what type of resources can be expended on the project and inquire if the budget is contingent on a plan being delivered and approved prior to execution of the plan. Many times sponsors put a small amount of budget in place for a team to develop

a KM plan of action. Once that plan is solidified, then there is an additional authorization of budget for the execution of the KM plan;
4. To which critical business objective or need is this linked? A strong alignment to a business objective or to a need that is lacking in an organization helps strengthen the value proposition of the KM plan. Traditionally, value in business is articulated in business objectives and what gets measured, gets done. When your business plan directs something to be accomplished, someone is measured against the delivery of that objective;
5. Who is your customer, are they internal or external? Let's face it, the KM plan will deliver something for someone, you may not know what yet, but knowing who will be the customer or user of what the KM plan delivers means there is an understanding of the voice and culture of the consumer. Are they flexible or focused? Are they internal or external to the organization? Does this customer look at success in the short term or over a long period of time? Does a breakthrough innovation mean more than incrementally controlled change? Be sure to have access to these customers, as you move forward you will want to get the customer involved in shaping and detailing the plan. The key is to have the customer engaged from the beginning so you can always calibrate your plan again what the customer will accept and deem successful;
6. How do you define KM? This question is focused at the KM project lead; the person who reports to the senior sponsor identified in question two. It is best to actually write out a definition for the KM project team and have the core team agree on the wording. Adding the definition into the project charter is also recommended. The project charter will be discussed later in this chapter under Employee Participation. Every word has meaning and getting everyone to agree on the definition of KM from the start will make the journey less confusing. A definition is like a monument for the team to refer to when the journey takes an unexpected turn. Referring back to the definition of KM, and either accepting what was written, or modifying it along the way, will

strengthen the KM plan and keep the team members moving forward together;

7. What is your desired outcome? Try to get the KM project team to agree on and define what outcome is acceptable. Many times a team takes on too much and never finishes. A smart way to think about the desired outcome is to first think big; what vision or overarching change is the KM project trying to accomplish. Then start small: identify actions that can make a difference today, tomorrow, next week, next month, next year. Then scale fast; use the KMSE framework to move the organization to a knowledge-based enterprise.

The amount of information gathered through these seven questions is priceless. Without this information, KM teams tend to wander and lose focus, wondering why the KM project was ever started. Document the answers and continue to refer back to them as time progresses. With the documentation of these questions, the first phase of the KMSE framework is completed. Now we move to phase two, the strategic plan:

Four Part Strategic Plan

1. Without a map, the road to your destination is circuitous. In KM, once there is an understanding of why the KM project is important, it becomes critical to ensure a map for success is developed. Four key elements of that strategy map are leadership, process, technology and learning. There is no cookie cutter or formula for this part, the uniqueness of the organization drives the amount of effort placed on each of these four elements. Leadership needs to set the vision for the KM effort. Documenting a Strategic Intent Statement explains an understanding of why KM is important to the organization: what valuable output matters, effectiveness, efficiency, innovation, or a combination of all three. Leadership sets its KM foundation by defining a personalized KM definition, assigning control and leadership, building and implementing an organizational KM policy. And, finally, leadership sets the direction and spells out KM goals and objectives and links them to a timeline in a KM maturity model;

KM Strategic Execution: How to Get Executive Attention

2. Processes are directly aligned to the core business objectives that are expressed in the organization's strategic plan. KM processes behave in a similar manner. KM processes need standards: identified process standards for knowledge capture, sharing, validating and reuse that are directly linked to the KM strategic intent statement. For example, if the objective is to get more people to work together, building networks that facilitate people, connecting people to people via social networks, sharing and learning, then a Community of Practice (COP) would be the selected KM process. Documenting a COP guidebook on how to plan, design and execute a successful COP is a standard KM process. If being the first to innovate is an objective, then having a standard innovation process in a shared environment that all staff has access to that detail a standard for submission would be appropriate. If being more competitive, or looking to place controls on getting things done right stands out as the organization's intent for KM, then developing a knowledge continuity process that captures critical program knowledge and facilitates the transfer of that knowledge to the next generation of workers would be yet another perfect example of standardized KM processes;
3. Technology enables execution of the organizational KM plan. Information technology (IT) should not drive the KM plan. IT is a connector and disseminator of the information that travels across an organization. It should be a goal that a holistic enterprise-wide technology plan is architected to enable and make operational the determined KM processes, one that aligns with the knowledge flow and the way work gets done. To gain the most return on invested IT capital, include a metrics component that can measure usage, network connections, employee adoption and overall performance, which in turn helps validate that the organization is institutionalizing KM and demonstrates increased effectiveness, efficiency and innovation;
4. A Learning Organization is the outcome of doing KM well. Organizations that value learning, also value diversity and inclusion. They create a nurturing culture where "need to share" is the default setting, rather than "need to know". These organizational

behaviors develop an environment that nurtures trust and relationship building, a fertile ground for KM and sharing knowledge across organizational boundaries. The development of a learning organization and the institutionalization of learning techniques support continuous learning and recognize that quality is valuable at every level of the organization from the most junior member to the Chief Executive Officer (CEO). One final point, learning organizations hold employees accountable; when you are part of a learning organization you are accountable for yourself and your personal growth, but also for the rest of the stakeholders in the organization. Only when you put the collective learning of an organization on the roadmap will the organization transform into a learning organization.

Five Part Execution Path

The KM strategy map lays out the journey that gets you from the current way of doing business to a future state. The maturity of a KM project develops over time, which is no surprise, since KM is a human endeavor and we all move at our own pace. Like most change efforts, KM matures and advances as each phase of the execution unfolds. By looking at each of the five phases of the execution path and determining how long your organization stays in each stage, determines the timeline for your KM project. It is critical to understand that success is not an overnight occurrence; real transformation can take three the five years if not more. Having an execution path helps manage the expectations and provide a clear view to the next phase. The execution path helps communicate to leadership and helps employees anticipate the journey. The five phases of the execution path are as follows:

Phase one of the execution path is awareness. An organization must first be aware they are in need of something before any true execution can take place. If KM has never been on the list of objectives, your organization may experience that information collection is ad hoc and chaotic; without a clear purpose. Experiences are not captured formally or informally; communities of practice neither cohesive nor identified. So much of the organization may be action-orientation,

KM Strategic Execution: How to Get Executive Attention

"ready-fire-aim," with little feedback, and superficial success criteria. For organizations in this state, knowledge walks out the door every day. Being aware that the management of intellectual capital; human capital, organizational capital and relationship capital is critical to the success and future of your organization is the first and most important step on the path to execution. When people are presented with a strong business case for change and are made aware of a valuable action, they tend to move forward. No timeline is detailed in this phase, you're either aware KM is valuable, or you are not. Getting traction may start at a grassroots level, but having executive support is the key to knowing you have traveled through the awareness phase;

Phase two is centered on pilot projects. Once an organization understands that KM is a valid business strategy and starts aligning identified critical knowledge with critical business objectives, the next logical step is to identify a focus area and apply the KM strategy to a small focused group. Identifying a pilot group is not always easy. Most people are busy doing work the current way and are not always that excited about change. People don't really fear change, they fear the unknown, and doing a pilot helps the organization understand the unknown. A simple way to pick a pilot group is by identifying gaps in current performance, and collective knowledge of the organization can be leveraged to make a difference. It could be in a program area, a corporate function, or a group of individuals that need to share. Learning what works well and what doesn't work well from these KM pilots is the key function of phase two. Once you start finding strategies that work, and can be replicated, then you move to make those successes standard processes. The Fellow Collaboration Network (FCN) is an example of a pilot group. In this step an organization may have several experiments in many areas of KM, or a few targeted projects. Do not assume this phase ends after a pilot ends, because new pilots for different strategies or difference user groups can be simultaneously active. The pilot phase is an experimental playground to try new techniques and tools and see what sticks. It is also the point when baseline measurements are identified and the start of tracking metrics. To show increased performance in effectiveness, efficiency and innovation there should be a baseline from which to track change and identify trends. Remember to refer to the answers in the seven baseline questions, particularity the core value that is being addressed: getting people to work together, being the first to innovate, being more competitive, or looking to place controls on getting things done right. The timeline for pilots can vary. Good rules of thumb are three to six months and then do an assessment to either continue or conclude the pilot. Some organizations, based on the size and participation of the pilot, may look at six to twelve months. A pilot, by nature, should be kept short, generally no longer than a year;

Phase three is taking successful pilots and moving that success into standard processes. Before moving a success into a standard process, it is important to first understand what success looks like in a KM pilot. When success is achieved in a KM pilot, document the learning and make them part of the standard communication system of your organization. It may be through a newsletter, or command media or through the actual changing of a guidebook or procedure manual. Make sure that the communication channels of your organization are getting the success stories on their front pages and include the details of what went well and why. This mass communication helps shape the new standards. Another way for success to be institutionalized is through the sharing of best practices at weekly KM "lunch and learn" sessions. This is a way to get others interested and start asking how they can adopt the KM best practice. Before long, these best practices become viral and then become a standard way of doing business. An example from the FCN is the project charter. When Community of Practice (COP) pilots were first set-up, not all required the COP to document a charter. Success varied over the first few years, but upon reflection and assessment of the pilots, it was clear those COPs that had a charter were more successful; therefore, the standard of a charter for COPs was established. The timeline for phase three is hard to nail down, because it is relative to the amount of time the first successful pilots take at your organization, how strong a communication network your organization has and how well your organizational culture adapts to change. At an enterprise-wide change level, think about effecting change and influencing behavior and you will quickly realize it will take significant time. The best way to describe the amount of time is to look for signs that your organization has started to mature in KM: the organization starts developing a learning culture, new technologies are invested in to document knowledge that can be quickly shared and located across the enterprise, expertise location systems connect people to people and people to information, knowledge capture and reuse become routine and are institutionalized. When the KM strategic plan evolves into a business case that the whole organization is aware of and the envisioned KM enterprise structure has started to emerge, it is a safe bet you have made it through phase three and well on your way to success;

Phase four is the ability to measure when KM processes are increasing performance in effectiveness, efficiency or innovation. Learning processes are embedded in core business processes and have become part of the way people and teams work. Learning from organizational knowledge is now a measurable goal. Metrics for linking performance to knowledge, innovation and performance improvement are tracked. Specific roles and responsibilities for managing the collective know-how are effectively resourced and maintained. An institutionalized learning culture emerges. The timeline for phase four starts with the pilots and matures in parallel with the process standards. It is critical to baseline what you are planning on measuring in phase two, so you can show the trends during phase four. In this phase, it is assumed that KM is part of the desired behaviors and addressed through annual performance incentives,

Phase five is working as a Knowledge-Based Enterprise (KBE). An enterprise that successfully adapts to change and demonstrates unconscious competence in knowledge, capture, sharing, collaboration, and re-use. New ideas flow freely and technology is seamless. A KBE is maximizing enterprise intellectual capital in all three areas: human capital, organizational capital and relationship capital. They have created an environment that supports collaborative knowledge sharing and mastered transforming enterprise knowledge into shareholder value.

Conclusion

KM Strategic Execution is about business, a strategy that links what you know to what you need to accomplish. It is about people connecting to people, sharing and collaborating mission critical "know how" to increase performance. The bottom line is that it is about better decision making. Once you have walked through the assessment questions, built the strategy plan and drawn out the path for execution, you are well equipped to get the attention and direction from the sponsor. Be sure to package the KM plan in a way that helps the leadership make a decision, one that is aligned to the organization's core values and can be accomplished. Unrealistic expectation can cripple a KM initiative. Getting executive attention can also be about timing, the best plan given to an executive at the wrong time can fail. In the case of the FCN, three month before the annual Fellows Conference the KM strategic plan for the Fellows was presented to senior leadership and the go ahead was given to make it happen. Based on the success of the FCN, the KMSE framework will be used again to build another community, the International Collaboration Network (ICN), which seeks to harness the brightest minds working in international business development.

References

Cameron, Kim. 2009. An Introduction to the Competing Values Framework. Control: 4. http://scholar.google.com/scholar?

Defense Acquisition University. 2005. "Community of Practice Implementation Guide," Version 2.0 February 8

Employee Participation, and Increased Organizational Performance – Building a Collaboration Network

Patrice "PJ" Jackson

Lockheed Martin, Bethesda, Maryland, USA

Introduction

People are busy, just ask them. Getting someone's attention is more difficult today than ever before. With the current state of information overload and the diversity of four generations with different work styles in the workforce, you really need to work hard to ensure employees are part of change initiatives. Some things are obvious, like in real estate, the price is tightly correlated to location, location, location and in KM success with employees is highly correlated to education, education, education. The problem is no one has time for more training, so how do you quickly get all the right people knowledgeable, prepare them for success and to inspire employees to participate. In the case of the Fellow Collaboration Network (FCN), this is their journey.

Collaboration Network Milestone Action Plan (MAP)

As long as people have traveled, maps have been used to get from point "A" to point "B" in the shortest time and with the least amount of obstacles. The same is true when it comes to building a collaboration network, a Milestone Action Plan (MAP) is critical to guide the journey. The MAP is a process designed to help emerging communities or collaboration networks build and sustain evolving, meaningful forums for creating, storing, and transferring knowledge and is an adaptation of the Defense Acquisition University Community of Practice Implementation Guide. The MAP process is divided into three parts; Part one, Plan the Foundation, is designed to get both leadership and community leaders on the same page. Participants identify their strategic intent and reasons for developing collaboration networks. This phase contains the educational process and the development of charters. Part two, Implement and Build, is designed to organize your collaboration network structure, knowledge assets and content. Part three, Operate Collaboration Network, is designed to focus on the management and success of the network.

Plan the Foundation (MAP.1)

Employees participate when you tell them to participate, when you entice them or when they care about the subject. The latter is the bull's-eye that brings the strongest participation and the core theme to building the FCN. The senior leadership approved the creation of the Fellows Collaboration Network and wanted it up and running in three weeks to coincide with the upcoming annual conference. Applying a KM principle of reuse, collaboration education has already been developed two years prior to the kick-off of the FCN. KM education had been an early pilot for the organization and had gone through various revisions until the organization was confident in the training, and felt it was flexible enough that every business unit could apply it to their specific needs. The training was called Community of Practice (CoP) Standards workshop, and was renamed to embrace the FCN's term Collaborative Network (CN) Standards – Understanding the Process to be Successful. The initial concept meeting was held to identify and establish the core group of community stakeholders and Subject Matter Experts (SME). A team was formed that served as the catalyst for standing up the community. The core team initiates the planning workshop by developing an agenda, identifying who should be at the session and ensuring a good representation of the community. Because the timeline for launching the FCN was short, the attendees were identified for the initial concept meeting and they would be the same attendees for the upcoming workshop. This initial concept meeting was a virtual Lunch and Learn meeting held during the one hour lunch time. A set of PowerPoint slides were used to get the attendees attention, to start getting them to care and, at the same time, get across some key points designed to get everyone on the same page prior to the actual workshop. The Lunch and Learn addressed theses overarching business challenges:

Point One-Why You Should Care

To achieve sustainable competitive advantage as the world's best ..., we must: shorten cycle times to decisions, reduce waste and rework, share a collective understanding of the customer and their needs and produce the right skilled workforce for now and the future. To sustain a competitive advantage there are knowledge challenges that must be addressed: complexity of information is overwhelming, how do we shorted the cycle time by getting the right knowledge to decision makers to enable them to make accurate and timely decisions? Not Invented Here syndrome is a plague of many of our business areas. How often do we look over the wall into a peer's business areas to see if what they are using as a standard could actually reduce time to deliver a product for us? Instead, we have multiple business areas creating similar technologies, rather than synergy around new and innovative ideas. Our expertise is our people, and the loss of their knowledge is devastating! For this organization, it is estimated that twenty percent of the workforce is eligible for retirement in five years, sixty to seventy percent over the following five years, which is upwards of ninety percent over the next ten years. How will we produce the right competencies to fill the right jobs without a plan?

Point Two – Why This Adds Value

The collaborative network is a key element of our KM strategy to move the organization horizontally toward becoming a knowledge-based enterprise. A collaborative network serves to connect people who share a concern, set of problems, mandate, or sense of purpose. They complement existing structures by promoting collaboration, information exchange, and sharing. Collaborative networks identify and connect talent horizontally across organizational, time, and physical boundaries. They enable the transformation of knowledge into action in a challenging, high-speed, interconnected environment. The issue is no longer about automating the individual, but automating the organization, connecting people and information. The social dynamics of trust, dialog, and motivation are more critical than technology. The benefits are quick access to subject matter experts (SME); timely sharing and reuse of knowledge; a forum for networking which provides community recognition around expertise; transference of best practices and lessons learned through general session, and developing mentoring relationships and talent through connections and individual sessions.

Point Three – We have a Plan

Employees don't fear change as much as they fear the unknown. Presenting the collaborative network building process as a structured, tried and true way of increasing organizational performance will set the expectation that the process has been used before and the organization knows what they are doing. Embarking on change with a map and a proven process empowers the employees with knowledge to trust that the time they spend developing the collaborative network will result in a better way of working and is worth the time and effort they put into the process. Knowing there is a plan, and the leaders will follow a structured path, reinforces that building a new collaborative environment to increase their performance is time well spent.

Setting Expectations

After presenting the three main points in the initial concept meeting, open discussion is ensued around the team's expectations for the FCN that will be addressed in the workshop. The following expectations are results of the open discussion:

- Solve our most difficult technical problems
- Finding solutions to challenges
- Tap into where the fires are located, find problems real time
- Determine most effective way for the Fellows to collaborate

Employee Participation, and Increased Organizational Performance – Building a Collaboration Network

- Think about how we want the Fellows to connect regardless of tool
- Choose the means to communicate what we've accomplished to other Fellows
- Increase awareness of Fellows across all business areas
- Be inclusive and not limit collaboration to Fellows only
- Investigate how to utilize other tools from across the organization
- Be cognizant of privacy issues
- Establish success metrics
- Establish a sense of team for those in the workshop
- Build a plan to move forward

This facilitated discussion is an exercise that starts to bond the employees to the plan and brings them into the mindset of the execution of the plan. Group discussions looking at the outcome of a process solidifies the collaborative network in the employee's mind and helps them start moving forward to delivering results.

Collaboration Network Workshop

An enterprise is what it knows! However, what it knows can be unknown, because often the act of knowing means searching for information and knowledge and/or people who know. Searching for information and knowledge, accounts for an average of thirty percent of wasted time spent on recreating information and rediscovering knowledge we can't find, which duplicates the effort due to the inability to leverage the existing skills, knowledge, and abilities of those who already know. This failure to know what the organization knows is due to the organization's structure, internal competition, and culture issues.

Collaborative networks help manage these challenges by accelerating problem solving, facilitating faster learning, maintaining and improving standards, increasing innovation and encouraging personal development. The FCN core planning workshop is conducted in one day with the core team members face-to-face and the support team virtually participating through a teleconference phone call and a shared desktop net-meeting to view the slides. Noteworthy, is reduction in time to conduct the workshop, as up until the FCN workshop, most community workshops required all members to be face-to-face and were, at a minimum, three days in length. The collaborative network workshop was condensed to accommodate the short turnaround for the launch of the FCN. The workshop brings together a diverse set of community stakeholders to discuss the community concept and to begin to formulate the purpose and intent of the community. Educating the attendees about the knowledge management and collaboration network value proposition provided them with foundational concepts to jump start their community. The workshop is designed to enlist the support of attendees in moving the whole enterprise horizontally towards becoming a knowledge-based organization as described in the KM Strategic Execution (KMSE) framework (Chapter 9). Subsequently, part of the workshop highlights the link back to the enterprise-wide KM strategic intent. An experienced Collaborative Network (CN) facilitator, who fills the roles of FCN champion and core team leader, is motivated to launch the FCN before the annual Fellows conference. The CN facilitator guides the interactive working groups to formulate identified outputs and starts the group on the road to becoming a vibrant collaborative community where people make a difference by sharing insight, ideas and capturing innovation. The success of the FCN workshop rests with the facilitator.

The workshop agenda is divided into overview, brainstorming, building the charter, the network structure, and next steps as follow:

Overview

The overview provides a practitioner introduction to KM and collaborative networks are presented as follows:

- KM History - Understanding the evolution of our enterprise civilization is the basis of understanding the cultural battles of a learning organization. Today's work cultures and applied work assumptions began to form with the agrarian society that focused our efforts on working the land and farming. As business evolved, we moved into the industrial age where we traveled to a factory and worked on an assembly line, soon automation began to make our work simpler and we built our work cultures around new ways of thinking. With the advent of the Internet, information technology catapulted us into the information age and the enterprise was born. Once again, our work culture shifted to one that was connected to virtually anyone anywhere, not just within our local business but globally as well. With each stage of this evolution, the cultural battles that emerged forged the new organizational structures and formed the boundaries through which each culture found comfort and complacency. Throughout the 1990s, knowledge emerged not as a power vehicle to hoard, but one that had more power if it was shared. People are now seen as the intellectual capital of an enterprise, and it is the capturing, sharing, validating and reuse of that intellectual capital to gain superiority and build innovation, which defines knowledge management in the knowledge age.

- Collaborative Network Value Proposition - Serve to connect people who share a concern, set of problems, mandate, or sense of purpose. Complement existing structures by promoting collaboration, information exchange, and sharing. Identify and connect talent horizontally across organizational, time, and physical boundaries.
- What Fuels an Optimum Collaborative Network (CN)?
- Visibility and Reuse – create a link between what has been developed in one place which can be useful in many others, if it were known and available.
- Mutual Support - when someone encounters a problem, they can count on the best knowledge of their peers, anywhere in the organization. The CN may be one of the few multi-faceted sources of knowledge, mentorship and advice for an individual's personal development.
- Company-Wide Learning – horizontally linking people who can learn from others' experiences everywhere, just as each of us now learn from our own local experiences,
- Collaborative Work - some problems are too complex for a single person or team in one central location, connecting people to people and people to information is key.

Patrice "PJ" Jackson

Roles and Responsibilities for Core Members

Sponsor – provides license to operate and can be an advocate within the organization to secure support and resources.

Leader – helps guide the direction of the CN and ensure it is providing value; can also serve as a referee to enforce ground rules and good conduct. It is actually best to have more than one leader, two or three works best. The rationale is that sometimes communities with a single leader come to be identified by that individual or personality. This can be a death sentence for a community, particularly if that individual goes away, loses the community's respect, lets their ego get in the way, stifles sharing, or becomes a bottleneck for getting knowledge out to the community.

Core team – effective management and sustainment of a community is enhanced by having a core team of three to seven individuals who can spend a more significant amount of time acting as an advisory board to help guide the community and serve as advocates within their respective departments.

Subject Matter Experts (SMEs) – such individuals can serve as a validation mechanism and as broader community mentors on specific issues. They can rotate in and out as needed a handful of times per year depending on the level of activity in their subject area.

Members – members typically vary their level of involvement – sometimes members are very active, at other times are lurking in the background, depending on their need for support and inclination to share.

Editor/Content Manger – works hand in hand with leaders and core team. This role might actually be filled by a leader or core team member. If the members have clear ground rules and expectations that they abide by in submitting content, the content manager's job is vastly easier. Division of labor might be distributed among multiple content mangers that are assigned discrete content areas for which they are responsible.

Facilitator – facilitation is a crucial role in those communities that engage in open discussions. Often discussions can ramble or become disjointed. Having an adept facilitator can keep members engaged in a constructive fashion and on topic, and can sense when a discussion has run its course and should be ended.

Assessing the Effectiveness of the Collaborative Network looks at its relevancy to today's and/or tomorrow's business needs. It ensures it has a sponsor to provide the license to operate, as well as a respected, passionate leader(s). The CN has identified a challenge shared by practitioners and builds a relationship of trust and respect through both face-to-face meetings and through a virtual meeting place that makes it easy to participate. The CN also provides recognition of expertise across the enterprise.

Brainstorming

During the brainstorming session, answers are captured for use during the charter development session to the following questions:

1. What are the critical issues/challenges facing the community?
2. Which of these issues/challenges can be improved by knowledge sharing?
3. How will solving these problems affect critical business issues?

Build the Charter

A charter describes the KM initiative, its rationale, its goals and its participants. The purpose of a charter is to align the expectations of all the contributors so that their energy focuses on the KM priorities.

Charter Development

During the charter development session a standard charter template is used. The charter outlines the following:

Purpose: identify the purpose/intent of the collaborative network; i.e., the collaborative network is focused on documenting, sharing, and transferring best practices;

Objective: identify the collaborative network objectives, i.e., the specific areas/issues that the collaborative network is interested in addressing;

Critical Business Issues: identify the critical business issues faced by the collaborative network;

Membership/Audience: identify the functional types the collaborative network is targeting or is trying to attract. Recognize that other employees may want to join this collaborative network and welcome their ideas and participation;

Measures of Success: list measures of success as determined by the collaborative network during the Workshop.

FCN Charter

The FCN charter addresses all three types of intellectual capital: human capital, organization capital and relationship capital. In the case of the FCN Charter, the core team develops a working document to collectively agree on their forward direction. The FCN Charter is as follows:

FCN Purpose: facilitate the interaction and integration of a multi-discipline group of people that have been recognized as leaders or experts within their particular domain or field in order to apply technical expertise more effectively to significant business and technical challenges.

FCN Objectives

- Increase the amount of cross domain and value added interaction across the corporation.
- Provide the physical and procedural infrastructure to facilitate collaboration.
- Provide the conduit for the flow of knowledge between Fellows and other forums in the organization.
- Facilitate collaboration between the Fellows to achieve optimal solution to technical challenges.
- Increase the amount of creativity and innovation to support business growth and improved performance on programs.
- Experiment with different knowledge co-creation and sharing approaches.

Employee Participation, and Increased Organizational Performance – Building a Collaboration Network

FCN Critical Business Issues

- Driven by collaboration, networks need to solve the really tough technical problems.
- Motivation for chief engineers and program managers to tap the expertise.
- Current lack of integrated communication between the Fellows.

FCN Membership/Audience

- All Fellows
- SME's and Future SME's (future Fellows)
- Internal Customers (Engineering, Business Development, Program Management)
- Corporate Engineering & Technology

FCN Measures of Success

- Number of interactions
- Number of experiments conducted
- Number of programs or business pursuits helped
- Customer feedback
- Number of supporting events (e.g., review teams, research and development, etc.)

Next Steps (FCN Network Structure)

During the last segment of the workshop, the attendees identify the core team members that drive the FCN and the launch, the resources to support the technical delivery of the FCN as well as the business rhythms of a weekly meeting until the conference and beyond. Additional SME are identified to leverage at the conference and get involved in testing the new environment. Finally, a documented development timeline details the next steps needed to design, build, populate and launch the FCN within three weeks.

Implement and Build (MAP.2)

Now that the blueprint and the foundation for the collaboration networks are laid, the next piece of the map is to establish the collaborative network structure. A logical, organizing structure is the cornerstone for building content that is useful and intuitive for the users. Great care should be taken to establish a viable structure, while still leaving room for growth. The team conducts an inventory of knowledge assets and performs knowledge mining and/or mapping to determine where the knowledge nuggets reside, who are the "keepers of the keys," etc. People are identified as editors or content managers for the collaborative network. Editors/Content Managers are responsible for monitoring both existing and new content within the collaborative network. To perform their job effectively, Editors/Content Managers must be trained how to use the collaborative network CN tool. In addition, they must learn the basics of content management. Be sure to take care to organize the content. Once an organizing structure has been created and it is determined where the knowledge resides externally, you must decide where each contribution belongs within the community. If an item easily fits within more than one topic area of the structure, choose a primary residence, and then cross-reference it to other topic areas. The addition of metadata tags helps to enhance the searching capabilities of your network. Identify and develop any content engineered specifically to support the collaborative network. Often during the needs analysis and knowledge mapping process, the core members identify knowledge gaps or areas where further instruction is beneficial. This content is created and submitted as frequently asked questions (FAQs), learning materials, or other forms of content.

For the FCN, the core team designed and delivered a simple architecture of files and a discussion forum on a web-based collaborative environment that facilitates social networking behavior to launch at the upcoming Fellows conference. The technology was still in prototype architecture, so the Fellows were considered early adopters and had the opportunity to help shape the technology for the organization.

Operate Collaboration Network (MAP.3)

Content is king! The ongoing main activity of the CN is to manage the content. Operating a collaborative network is an iterative process. Editors/Content Managers continually monitor both existing and new content (review, approve or deny content), feature content items to draw attention, check for outdated or inaccurate content, etc. Especially in the beginning, it is critical to facilitate the interaction within the collaborative network. The Facilitator is primarily responsible for encouraging the formation of relationships between members. The Facilitator helps to arrange and run meetings; make sure discussions, once posted, are answered; and link people with problems together with those who have answers. To gain employees attention it is wise to market the collaborative network, which can increase traffic and expand the network. Marketing the collaborative network can be accomplished in a variety of ways, from telling a friend, to passing out brochures at a conference, to e-mailing a news group, etc. Every member, especially those assuming leadership roles, serves as an ambassador for his/her collaborative network. Spread the word! As the network evolves, new issues arise and areas of focus can change. Part of the role of the CN Leader and Editor/Content Manager is to keep the community relevant to the needs of the members. One method of keeping content current/relevant is through research-related endeavors and potentially engineering content to close knowledge gaps. Each network may have a different method of determining the value or success of its endeavors. At some point, each community must take time to re-evaluate what has been accomplished asking questions related to the network's stated purpose and objectives.

On-Going Operations & Monitoring

A garden left unattended will wither and die, so too will a Collaborative Network. The best laid plan for a CN will only produce the beginnings of a new way of increasing organizational performance. Focused time needs to be applied to the ongoing operations and monitoring of a fully functioning CN to reap the fruits of the team's labor. One way of monitoring the CN is by performing a progress check between six and twelve months after the CN is up and running. The Early Progress Check List (EPCL) below contains useful questions you can facilitate though a group discussion with key players from the CN. Answers to these questions will help the CN Leader shape the future of the network and take the appropriate step to ensure continued success.

Patrice "PJ" Jackson

Early Progress Check List (EPCL)

Does the community have a common purpose? Is the purpose compelling to leadership, prospective members, and their functional managers?

1. Is the common purpose aligned with the enterprise strategy?
2. Is the right sponsorship in place; i.e., a respected leader who is willing to contribute to the community?
3. Do the functional sponsors agree with the community's scope, purpose, and membership?
4. Are core members and the community leader enthusiastic, content experts, and able to develop the community?
5. Do members' functional managers agree that time spent in the community is valuable?
6. Does the community have the right content experts to provide perspective and meaning to its membership?
7. Does the community have enough members to stay alive?
8. Are collaborative tools in place and easily accessible? Are members willing and able to use them?
9. Are needed resources available, i.e., webcasts, virtual meeting rooms, etc.?

Addition of Collaboration Learning Subject Matter Experts (SME)

For the FCN, the operational success was the core team members and the weekly FCN meetings. From the first concept meeting, the core team members had a vested interest in the success of the FCN. They stayed connected through the FCN and through a weekly call to talk through the ideas for moving the FCN forward. An additional member was added to the core team after the first year, a collaboration learning subject matter expert. This was an insertion of a new set of eyes and came with new ideas for adoption and awareness that catapulted the content of the FCN to the next level.

Increased Performance – Awareness, Adoption, and Advanced Users

The journey, up until now, has been about getting executives to pay attention to KM and to get the employees to participate in the effort.

Employee Participation, and Increased Organizational Performance – Building a Collaboration Network

By now, understand that for the work to get to increased performance does not happen overnight. Increased performance is tightly linked to the core value that is being addressed: getting people to work together, being the first to innovate, being more competitive, or looking to place controls on getting things done right, which link back to where the KMSE (Chapter 9) started during those original seven baseline KM assessment questions. Increased performance can only be realized if the current environment is baseline and goals are set for the value of doing work the new way. Applying the KMSE framework, gets you to the point of logical steps that have been taken to get the strategy and execution plan in place. Now, it is up to the employees to change their behavior and make the KM effort a success.

The Timeline

For the FCN, it was a three year process. Each year, a different focus became clear, but only in retrospect -- a rear view mirror perspective. The FCN did not go into the three years knowing the outcome. Once the three years had transpired, a pattern emerged around awareness efforts in year one, increased adoption in year two and by the third year, the Fellows were becoming advanced users, bringing new ideas to the core team members to accelerate the change and increase the value of the FCN.

Year 1- Awareness

Timing was tight, but the FCN launched three days before the annual conference. The focus was getting the word out about the FCN and raising awareness of why attendees should care about this new thing called a Collaboration Network. The core team, with help from the technical team, put the designed architecture in place and did a small group of user tests prior to the launch. The FCN core team attended the conference and two productivity coaches traveled to the Fellows conference and set up a multi-station tabletop help center, where the Fellows could learn "hands-on" about their new Fellows Collaboration Network. FCN posters were placed in walkways around the conference venue to encourage attendees to stop and learn about the FCN: Formulate Questions, Co-create Innovation and Nurture Learning. Over the next three days, the activity of 250 attendees generated 2,800 hits to the FCN from 495 unique users, which showed that employees not attending the conference were participating and the enterprise effect was happening. During the conference, twenty percent of the Fellows population became new members, signing up for a personal space and loading content in the FCN. The core team was pleased with the initial response and set out to focus on awareness goals to be accomplished by the next Fellows conference:

Reach and surpass FCN Tipping Point - get critical mass of Fellows to use the FCN, promote FCN as a value-add node for enterprise-wide collaboration and increase FCN marketing.

Lead cultural change through positive results - change the way we think about working together, get our Engineering communities to collaborate more, expand Fellows Action Teams. The Fellows Action Teams were an outgrowth of the conference, mini-FCNs, focused on one problem area. Five Fellows Action Teams were created the first year of the FCN.

Welcome all employees to participate in the FCN - engage more Fellows, leaders, Program Managers, Chief Engineers, SMEs, future Fellows, Innovators, Collaboration & Knowledge Creators/Sharers, across all our "generations", boomers, Generation X, Generation Y and Millenniums.

Provide online mentoring opportunities - be a member of a Fellows Action Team, learn about leading edge technologies Fellows are working on.

Find expertise among LM Fellows – search FCN discussion forums, document libraries, Blogs, Wikis, discover knowledge that Fellows are creating and sharing.

Learn from Fellows – increase FCN webcasts, technical papers, patents, stories, join online discussions with Fellows across the enterprise.

Employee Participation, and Increased Organizational Performance – Building a Collaboration Network

Year 2 – Adoption

Twelve months later, the FCN was once again a spotlight at the annual Fellows conference. This time the focus was on adoption, getting Fellows to sign up and participate not only at the conference, but all year long. In addition, this conference invited rising talent, employees who had the potential to become future Fellows; this addition made for an interesting mix of generational styles that fueled the adoption of the FCN. As in the previous year, two productivity coaches set up a multi-station tabletop help center where the Fellows could learn "hands-on" about their Fellows Collaboration Network and FCN posters were placed across the conference venue with the theme remaining FCN - Formulate Questions, Co-create Innovation and Nurture Learning. A general session workshop for FCN adoption was added so Fellows could bring their laptops and get adoption guidance. During the year, enterprise-wide productivity ambassadors were available through a queuing system, a list where Fellows could request personalized help and a collaboration ambassador, at their work site, would provide them personalized help. During the three days at the conference, one hundred new members to the FCN were added as well as goals set to increase FCN adoption over the next twelve months:

Set Up Fellows Technical Library - enables Fellows to post technical papers, articles, patent information, etc. onto FCN. Creation of a simple view for the library, and assigning a web part on the sub-page for that particular library is the easiest way to facilitate easy navigation and retrieval of data. Views allow for grouping, sorting, and filtering of data.

Create Blogs - leave the FCN Blog open to all Fellows to contribute, and for all US Employees to read only. This allows for any Fellow to post to the blog. All Fellows are encouraged to sign up to "Receive Alerts" for the FCN Blog.

Set Up Fellows Discussions – ask a Fellow, open to the entire US population to post to and interact with Fellows. Specific topics posted and tagged to show up for people searching for information. Having "topics" ready for reply posts allows for increased visibility of the FCN discussions. Fellows are encouraged to "Receive Alerts" on topics of interest to them. Core Team members have been instructed to turn on "Receive Alerts" for the entire discussion board in order to facilitate discussion and alert Fellows who may be interested in topics that have updates.

Create Webcasts - specific topics of learning presented by Fellows and webcast across the enterprise. The webcasts are achieved and viewable upon demand. As well as "What the Fellows Collaboration Network (FCN) Can Do for You" - a Webinar to learn how the FCN started and how to leverage the environment on another program.

Create FCN "Gardener" term Knowledge Broker/Facilitator - monitors the FCN Blog entries and determines when a blog discussion should be elevated to a Focus Space on the FCN. Look across enterprise at information resources, and identify connections that should be made between FCN entries and other employees and resources.

Update FCN Maintenance - develop a functional map of data and content, to provide alternate ways to navigate through the FCN. Consolidate data and content into smaller, more efficient entries and add meta-data, such as tags.

Deliver Cross-Generational Accelerated Learning Commentary Wiki - to capture and draw comments from both the Generation X future Fellows and the current Fellow attendees to demonstrate Web 2.0 collaboration on cross-generational knowledge transfer using FCN.

Update Security - leave permission for all community participants at "contribute." Allow core team members to have full permission. Create sub-sites for all Fellow Action Teams and provide full permission to team members for their sub-site.

Increase Collaboration Network Productivity - twice monthly provide productivity sessions on collaboration behaviors and share lessons learned, best practices and encourage participation. Advertise that CN sessions are eligible as training credits in Learning Management System (LMS).

Year 3 – Advanced Users

Advanced FCN users descended on the productivity team at the next annual Fellows conference, where it was apparent the students had become the teachers. Much of the baseline scenario remained the same, the venue was the same, but the difference was the FCN users; they had taken productivity to the next level all year long and were sharing it with the enterprise. Awareness of the FCN was at an all time high, fewer posters were needed in the third year. Adoption had reached over fifty percent of the Fellows and increased performance was visible in the daily activity on the FCN. Fellows Action Teams had grown to 18 strong in just a short three years. Each Fellows Action Team is directly aligned to a business need adding value to increased performance. Not one of the over four hundred attendees asked what the FCN was, instead this year's conference attendees had come as storytellers, each had a story about how they were using the FCN and what they had implemented to increase the users experience. Over one hundred attendees asked for FCN help on advanced subjects like managing lists, multiple calendars and tasks, embedding a video, displaying micro-blogging feeds as well as how to build custom pages for sub-teams. The user base had matured over the past three years, and now they were craving new capabilities like advance enterprise search and expertise location. An enterprise Search Challenge was part of the productivity team in the third year which added an estimated 250,000 additional documents indexed from library content, program summary reports, and business area newsletters. In the area of expertise location, a prototype for an enhanced white page was available for the Fellows to test. Over 165 conference attendees participated in the demonstrations which generated 61 feedback cards, 49 new pilot users and 74 enhancement suggestions. The Fellows had evolved from a group of bright minds to a force to be leveraged.

Conclusion

From the beginning of the KM scene, the debate has always been about the value between people, process and information technology (IT). In the case of the FCN, people and process were the nucleus. IT was never a focus, it was just the vehicle for the increased performance, which is tightly linked to the core value being addressed: getting people to work together, being the first to innovate, being more competitive, or looking to place controls on getting things done right. True KM pauses long enough to reflect and document what went well and what could have gone better. The FCN's willingness to be a pilot and stay the course over the three year journey coupled with leadership's support is all in the "what went well" column. The one thing that could have gone better, frankly, was the technology. The technology was slow to scale to the users' experience and is going to be converted to a new technology platform to keep up the pace with the advanced users. The good news is that the FCN is thriving. Their secret formula was simple: have a plan, adapt and be flexible, listen to the users, adjust along the way, and stay the course. The FCN enriches the learning of the Fellows and all who use the FCN. The Fellows network shares and innovates collectively and is a fertile network for the next generation to engage and be mentored by the organization's brightest minds – the Fellows.

References

Cameron, Kim. 2009. An Introduction to the Competing Values Framework. Control: 4. http://scholar.google.com/scholar?

Defense Acquisition University. 2005. "Community of Practice Implementation Guide," Version 2.0 February 8

The Cognizant Organization

Annie Green

George Washington University, Washington, D.C., USA

Introduction

> *"Any intelligent fool can make things bigger, more complex, and more violent. It takes a touch of genius -- and a lot of courage -- to move in the opposite direction."*
>
> - Albert Einstein

It has been said that organizations know a lot of things, but they don't always know what they know. Often times there is a wealth of information, but where it is, how to find it, where or who to call to get it, generally are obstacles that prevent sharing, which significantly impacts the performance of an organization. This is not something new, but a problem many organizations face. Organizations know expertise is available, but don't always capture it or know where to find it once it is captured. The most valuable asset in an organization is the collective skills and expertise of people. This "know-how" can be used when leverage when facing similar experiences is "lost" and unavailable for reuse and the ability to measure its contribution to performance is virtually nonexistent. It is more important than ever to establish effective paths to value intangible assets. It is imperative that today's organizations embark on a journey to establish a culture of sharing and a means to identify and value the contributions of intangible assets.

A core objective of intangible assets is the valuing of knowledge, a key outcome of the knowledge worker and the business environment. Identifying, quantifying, valuing, and maintenance of intangibles assets have proven to be a difficult task for the 21st century organization. Knowledge creation, capture, sharing, dissemination and valuing are an evolving and dynamic process. There is little to no focus on the process itself, because, traditionally, knowledge management (KM) does not have a 'systemic' approach; instead it is always associated with a disruptive process. A systemic approach to the identification, measurement and management of intangible assets is a complex venture. This chapter presents a cognitive theoretical model that uses systems engineering to develop methods that promote a more efficient and effective path to track intangible assets from its inception to its value -- or a thinking organization that is cognizant of its intangible assets.

Business value - The Inception

We are lost in the Knowledge era without a map. — (Allee 1998).

Knowledge is identified as the most critical resource of today's business enterprise. Yet, most businesses cannot clearly define this critical business value driver. Most businesses have not defined what knowledge is, its value, or the best approach to its valuation. Today's business does not have a reliable map of the territory. This shines a spotlight on the business requirement for organizations to become "intelligent" about their environments; to understand the intangible assets to be gained; and subsequently to know the intangible assets to be valued.

To move forward in the knowledge economy, businesses should look inward and rigorously scrutinize their business processes/practices to define the intelligent attributes that align with the organization's performance (Senge 1990). This discovery will provide the foundation a business needs to construct an intangible valuation system that aligns with business performance. This foundation facilitates the construction of a performance based cognitive system that:

- codifies business intelligence and places emphasis on the synthesis and simulation of its processes/practices;
- embodies features that are essential when modeling business activity; and
- provides definitions, attributes and constraints of business intelligence.

The Cognizant Organization

The challenge or major issues to building this foundation are (Newell 1990):

- modeling intelligence within the context of the business enterprise;
- identification of independent components of business intelligence,
- the ability to determine the importance of interactions between knowledge mechanisms, processes, knowledge, representation and goals of the enterprise that compose the basic concepts of intelligent systems.

To define and manage what an organizations knows and doesn't know must be structured within the context of the business enterprise. Intangible assets within the 21st century business enterprise are to be managed like traditional factors of labor, capital and raw materials (VonKrogh et al. 1998). To increase the probability of adding value, successful businesses have to articulate the link between their business strategy and what its workforce needs to know, share and learn to execute the strategy ((Zack 1999) (Allee 2000)). Strategy identifies the desired future state of the business, the specific objectives to be obtained, and the strategic moves necessary to realize that future (Boar 1994). Strategy includes all major strategic areas and the value chain ((Boar 1994) (Porter 1980) (Alter 1999)).

The value chain supports the business in identifying all the ways its intangible assets could or should bring value to the business ((Sullivan 2000) (McNair and Vandermeersh 1998)).

The value chain is a:

- "Unique combination of activities that together creates competitive value-added products or services for a company" (Koulopoulos 1997, 60)
- Describes business processes where each of the processes adds value (McNurlin and Sprague 1998, 82)
- Represents a systematically organized path of a product or service to customers ((Von Krogh et al.1998, 225) (Sullivan 2000)),

- Consists of tasks and activities that are organized into workflow applications that eliminate waste - unnecessary and redundant tasks and automation of routine tasks ((Koulopoulos 1997 60 - 61) (Alter 1999)).

The alignment of the organization's intangible assets with its vision and strategy, positions an organization to focus their resources and activities on objectives to achieve them faster or without unnecessary effort. The value chain is the systematic way to divide a firm into its discrete activities ((Porter 1985) (Alter 1999)). The value chain provides the alignment of business value to its subsequent valuation components. The value chain traces backward to the business objectives and traces forward to the discrete business value components. The value chain is the starting point of the valuation of intangible assets within the business enterprise.

The Framework of Intangible Valuation Areas (FIVA) [Figure 1] is an intangible asset taxonomy (Green 2008) that represents a validated set of business value drivers. The taxonomy sets the foundation to identify and link performance measurements/indicators to its intangible value drivers and subsequently capture measures to monitor and evaluate leading and lagging indicators. FIVA's foundation consists of the following eight value components:

Customer – economic value that results from the associations (e.g., loyalty, satisfaction, longevity) an enterprise has built with consumers of its goods and services.

Competitor – economic value that results from the position (e.g., reputation, market share, name recognition, image) an enterprise has built in the business market place.

Employee – economic value that results from the collective capabilities (e.g., knowledge, skill, competence, know-how) of an enterprise's employees.

Information – economic value that results from an enterprise's ability to collect and disseminate its information and knowledge in the right form and content to the right people at the right time.

The Cognizant Organization

Partner – economic value that results from associations (e.g., financial, strategic, authority, power) an enterprise has established with external individuals and organizations (e.g., consultants, customers, suppliers, allies, competitors) in pursuit of advantageous outcomes.

Process – economic value that results from an enterprise's ability (e.g., policies, procedures, methodologies, techniques) to leverage the ways in which the enterprise operates and creates value for its employees and customers.

Product/Service – economic value that results from an enterprise's ability to develop and deliver its offerings (i.e., products and services) in a timely manner that reflects an understanding of market and customer(s) requirements, expectations and desires.

Technology – economic value that results from the hardware and software an enterprise has invested in to support its operations, management and future renewal.

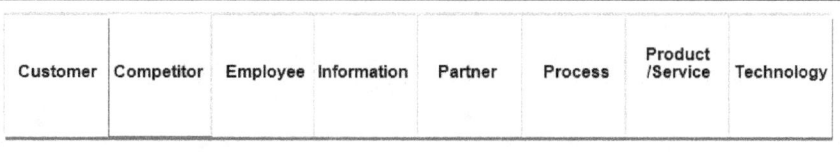

Figure 1 – Business Value Components (Value Chain)

Building up from the foundation - An Approach

To reason with knowledge, we first need to be able to represent it in a formal manner (Cawsey 1998).

FIVA defines business value components that contribute to intangible valuation. It is the base for "Business Reasoning, Analytics and Intelligence Network (BRAIN)." BRAIN [Figure 2] is a cognitive system for the business enterprise. Its purpose is to dissect the "thinking" system – a group of interacting, interrelated or interdependent elements forming a complex whole (The American Heritage Dictionary, 2nd College Edition 1984) – of a business enterprise into its interacting, interrelated and/or interdependent elements to create the organizational mind.

BRAIN leverages the current enterprise environment and integrates fundamental types of models to each other to provide a holistic approach to valuing intangible assets in a business enterprise environment. BRAIN's intent is to uncover the intelligence that currently exists so as to make decisions and act on those decisions – the thinking organization.

BRAIN links business value drivers and their intangible indicators to business operational and historical data. These business value drivers are correlated to determine the strength of the relationship between them. The correlation of the value drivers, intangible indicators and operational and historical data, provides intelligence into understanding the importance of interactions between intangible assets and business operations. This intelligence can be used to make decisions surrounding the development of improvement initiatives targeted at more efficient and effective operations of businesses.

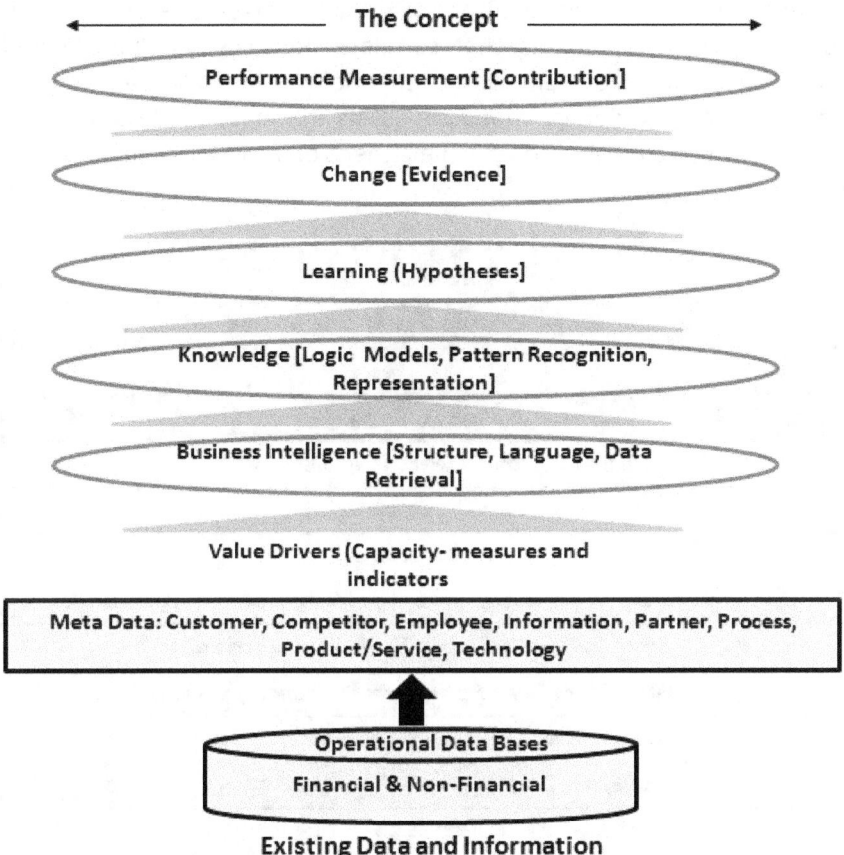

Figure 2: Business Reasoning, Analytics and Intelligence Network (BRAIN) Concept

BRAIN is the mind of the organization and the mind requires a physical existence. BRAIN is further developed into a system or tool that facilitates its analytics and outputs. This adds the engineering component to establish Engineering Business Reasoning, Analytics and Intelligence Network or E-BRAIN [Figure 3]. E-BRAIN provides a scientific enterprise system to identify solutions focused on innovation and improvements to business problems and inefficiencies. It identifies relationships between specific intangible value drivers, measures and indicators to uncover trends and patterns providing insights, opportunities and solutions. Being cognizant of thought patterns leverages businesses in creating models that simulate business intelligence and knowledge. Such a system would enhance business leaders' understanding and cognition of intangible assets that have successfully contributed or not contributed to achievement of strategic objectives and goals.

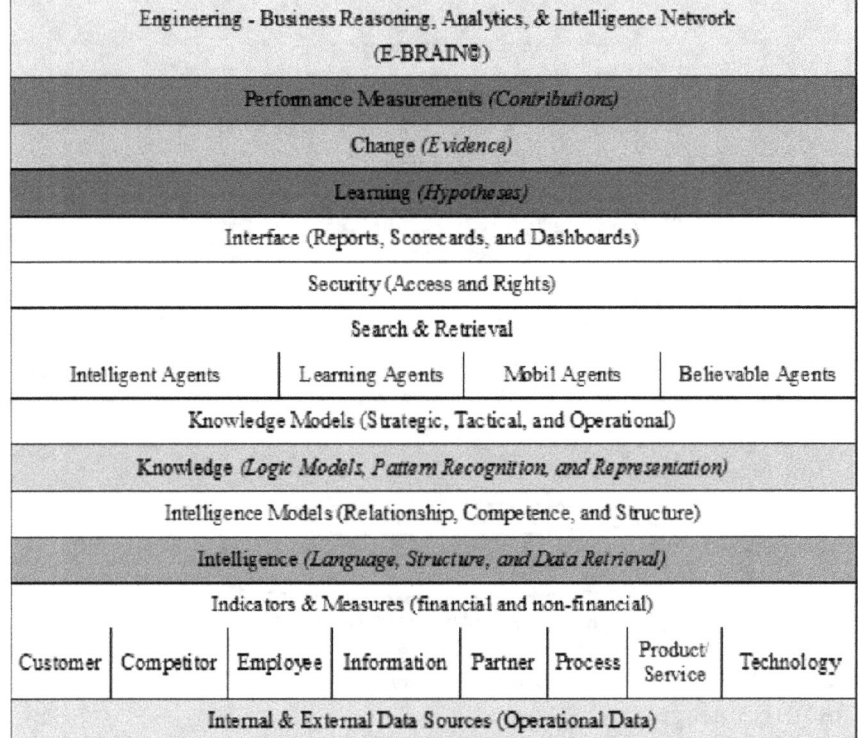

Figure 3: E-BRAIN Theoretical Performance-Based Intangible Asset Valuation System

The Components of E-BRAIN

E-BRAIN [Figure 3] takes a systems approach that requires businesses to think about and define a language for describing and understanding the forces and interrelationships that shape the behavior of intangible asset valuation (Senge 1990). It provides a systemic and holistic approach to intangible asset valuation through the integration of valuation components, characteristics, value drivers and technology-based components. E-BRAIN establishes a common language of valuation in the context of the business decision-making processes. Its approach establishes elements that promote cognitive learning from the data, information, intelligence and knowledge stored in operational and historical repositories.

E-BRAIN integrates:

1. Seven valuation components:

System – constructs a map that details the coherent picture of the value components that drive the performance of a business.

Cognitive – identifies business value drivers which support the understanding and construction of mental models that make sense of the business and what guides the decisions and actions of the decision-makers.

Intelligence – provides a view of negative and positive impacts on an organization's performance based on a body of information from which knowledge can be obtained by questions, by inquiries, predictions, explanations and prescriptions for control.

Knowledge – builds formal models based on rules or principles prescribing a particular course of action.

Learning – accumulates and analyzes information in the form of knowledge aligned with activities that may be well or badly performed.

Change – supports inquiry that results in thinking and acting that yields profound inner shifts in peoples' values, aspirations, and behaviors and outer shifts in processes, strategies, practices, and systems.

Performance Measurement – measures success factors from different perspectives, as well as perspectives of past, current, and future performance.

2. Nine distinctive characteristics:

Concept – building blocks that depict the diverse components of valuation within a business.

Structure – definition of relationships and orderings that exist between and amongst business concepts and the language and symbols which represent them.

Language – internal representation of data and external communication of value.

Data Retrieval – interfaces to external and internal data of the business enterprise.

Logic Models – transformation of business functions/conditions into a form that represents easily recognizable sets of objects in the real business world.

Pattern recognition – identification of similarities among differences, and differences among similarities.

Knowledge Representation – transformation of knowledge into a business fact.

Hypotheses – formulation of facts from relationships and orderings that are used for further investigation.

Evidence – assertion of validity into the simulation of business knowledge.

3. The eight intangible asset value components (Customer, Competitor, Employee, Information, Partner, Process, Product/Service, Technology) as defined above.

4. Six technology-based components:

Indicators & Measures (Database) – facilitates the capture of indicators and measures, known as capacity, to form a body of information.

Intelligence Models (Logic) – uses the body of information to cross-pollinate value drivers and construct a body of intelligence.

Knowledge Models (Logic) – uses the body of intelligence to identify events that can be symbolized and manipulated to determine a course of action

Search & Retrieval – the uses of classification technologies to retrieve, filter, and manage information in computers

Security (Access and Rights) – ensuring intelligence and knowledge have adequate protection from intrusion

Interface (Reports, Scorecards, and Dashboards) – visualization software that helps organizations view information, intelligence and knowledge in graphical form and perform analytics

Using operational data to drive intelligence

> "Not everything that counts can be counted and not everything that can be counted counts."
>
> - Albert Einstein

Operational data provides a wealth of information that serves as a source of understanding and addresses the problems that face the business in achieving its goals. The right set of operational data grows intelligence, which is the ability to comprehend, understand and profit from experience (Wiig 1994). The challenge is to be able to identify within a business domain and in common language, what measurements and indicators the business needs to know about its intangible assets.

E-BRAIN's initial layer contains measures and indicators or the "capacity" of the business. This "Capacity is the value-creating ability of an organization" (McNair and Vangermeersch 1998, 1). It is represented in four categories of diagnostic information (Drucker 1998):

1. *Foundation Information* -- routine measures such as cash-flow and liquidity projections which, when normal, basically do not tell much; however, when not normal, indicate a problem that needs to be identified;
2. *Productivity Information* -- measures that deal with performance of key resources. These measures must also include the total-

factor productivity, which means that they should provide the value of all costs, including the cost of capital. These measures incorporate such tools as economic-value-added analysis (EVA) and benchmarking to measure and manager total-factor productivity.
3. *Competence Information* -- measures associated with core competencies that link market or customer value with special skills and abilities of the producer or supplier of products and services,
4. *Resource-allocation Information* -- measures associated with the allocation of scarce resources, such as capital and performing people.

Drucker (1998) identifies the four categories of information to provide results that inform and direct business tactics and strategy development. E-BRAIN incorporates the basic economics of business within its structure by identifying a core set of intangible asset activities. It provides attributes that have a direct or indirect relationship with the identification of profit and value-adding activities on resources. Each activity and its attributes are mapped to the expense structure of the business and changes are reflected in the associated expense as activities are affected in operations. This aids decision making in effective management of intelligence and the ability to identify value and non-value adding activities to achieve an optimum level of organizational performance.

Capacity is defined for every value component. The union of the eight value components and capacity creates the "body of information" to engineer business intelligence. The body of information provides a common language for discussing and measuring capacity utilization. It provides a comprehensive approach to the engineering of business intelligence and supports a valuation system to measure the achievements of the business by using the capacity of an organization as its measurement of performance. Structures and functions are identified and defined as the conduit by which intelligence is achieved. Business measures and indicators are extracted from operational data and transformed into business intelligence, which aligns with objectives and goals.

The Cognizant Organization

The cross-pollination of value components provides multi-dimensional data that contributes to the diagnostics of productivity, competence and resource-allocation information. The cross-pollination of business value components constructs the following three categories of intelligence:

1. *Relationship Intelligence* – understanding of how the interactions between knowledge workers influence organization performance.
2. *Competence Intelligence* – understanding of how the abilities/proficiency of knowledge workers influences organization performance.
3. *Structure Intelligence* – understanding of how the organization's infrastructure environment influences organization performance.

The combination of relationship, competence and structure intelligence provides a "body of intelligence" to create knowledge. The modeling of business intelligence introduces a new level of abstraction that allows the conventional naming of these combinations and the elevation of them into strategic, tactical, and operational business models.

Evolving intelligence into knowledge

The "body of Intelligence" is further manipulated and summarized to uncover and model business knowledge. This, once again, introduces a new level of abstraction that allows visibility into the value contributions of intangible assets and the elevation of them into strategic, tactical, and operational forms.

E-BRAIN supports the levels of abstraction through the development of semantic networks and frames. Semantic networks and frames provide a simple and intuitive way of representing facts about objects (Stanfill & Waltz 1986). Both schemes allow the representation of categories of objects and relationships between objects, and draw simple inferences based on intelligence. Semantic networks are used in the definition of complex interrelationships and provide the foundation of a sophisticated inference system. Frames emulate the mental recall of images of a particular object and its related attributes by human thought. These knowledge models establish a foundation to plan for the future.

Learning from what is known

An organization learns when it adds to its store of information or body of knowledge through organizational inquiry (Argyris and Schoön, 1996). E-BRAIN simulates the comprehension of information, organization of ideas, analysis and synthesis of data, application of knowledge, and the ability to choose among alternatives in problem solving. E-BRAIN's capturing of intangible asset information, intelligence and knowledge follows the practice of econometrics. Econometrics is the developing and applying of quantitative or statistical methods to the principles of economics (Johnston and DiNardo 1997).

Econometrics focuses on applying analyses to time-series, cross-sectional, panel and multidimensional panel data. Time-series data contains observations over time; cross-sectional data contains observations at a single point in time; panel data contains both time-series and cross-sectional observations; multi-dimensional panel data contain observations across time, cross-sectional, and across some third dimension.

Econometrics combines economic theory and statistics to analyze and test economic relationships. Its methods use statistical procedures to estimate relationships for models defined on the basis of theory, prior studies, and domain knowledge. It combines numerical forecast output with subjective or judgmental input to refine forecast findings.

Quantitative statistics supporting econometrics and forecasting in E-BRAIN are:

Extrapolation – the use of historical data to forecast. Exponential smoothing applies the principle that recent data is weighted more heavily and averages cyclical fluctuations to forecast the trend from the data and to derive a forecast (Makridakis, Wheelwright and Hyndman 1998).

Quantitative Analogies – the identification of situations that are analogous to a target situation to be used to extrapolate the outcome of a target situation.

Causal Models – cause and effect models developed on the basis of prior knowledge and theory. Time-series and cross-sectional regression used to estimate model parameters or coefficients. Use theory and prior knowledge when defining causal variables. The key is to identify important variables, the direction of their effects, and any constraints (Allen and Fildes 2001).

Segmentation – identifying important causal variables, creating segments and their priorities to make forecasts.

The business enterprise is an ever changing large and complex venture that has an overabundance of internal and external information to gain insights and learn from. These insights and learning contribute to the business leader's improved decision making surrounding operational efficiencies. This new level of abstraction provides a "body of knowledge" to serve as the basis of the business leader's decisions.

Decisions in the knowledge economy require content and analysis to learn from and promote the future growth and renewal of a business. With the complexity of so much information and analysis, visualization software serves the purpose of measuring change for learning. A visualization interface helps the business to leverage information and perform analytics. The learning interface is created based on the intelligence and knowledge repositories that feed its structure using the inherent models that are defined within its structure.

Learning interfaces include professional reports, scorecards, and dashboards that provide strategic, operational, and tactical views as follows:

- Strategic reports, scorecards, and dashboards have a scorecard interface that supports business leaders in tracking performance against strategic objectives.

- Operational reports, scorecards, and dashboards have an interface that supports senior and supervisory workers to monitor and optimize operational processes.
- Tactical reports, scorecards, and dashboards have an interface that supports business managers in improving their understanding of the processes and activities for which they are accountable.

Driving change from what is learned

From the analyses and forecasting, the business has visibility into the value components that impact its effectiveness and efficiencies. The business begins change initiatives based on the results and findings of the analyses and forecasts. Change measures the progress towards achieving goals and the measurements of change are not just "hard" measures. Change practice can be grouped into three categories (Utsahajit 2009):

Employee Perception -- activities are focused on aligning employees' views toward changes in the business operations. These activities are centered on continuous learning through hands-on experience, both mentally and physically. Employee perception activities are directed at creating the readiness for change among employees by promoting the attitude of accepting changes as challenges and pathways to success at the customer, community and corporate levels. In addition, employees are encouraged to believe in the values of commitment, consistency and communication.

Team Development – activities are focused on creating a sense of excellence, trust, and collaboration among employees. The organization believes that successful changes, when employees embrace excellent quality, communicate truthfully among one another, and are willing to do everything possible to achieve mutual goals.

Environmental Improvement -- activities are focused on bringing changes into reality. These activities entail improvement both in the physical environment and the work atmosphere.

Although the measures are validated from their quantifiable and qualitative journey from value component to knowledge, resulting change initiatives can fail, because their delivery is not aligned with the impact on people. Include the "soft" measures, such as motivation, commitment, ownership and resistance to change, as these are the critical variable for feedback that can help a team reflect, learn and move forward (Senge et al. 1999).

Measuring the performance contributions of intangible assets

Performance measurement deals with the implementation of an organization's strategy (Kaplan and Norton 1996). A balanced measurement system is used to identify and control critical factors that lead to success. The measures for the performance measurement system are chosen based on the organization's vision and strategy (Kaplan and Norton 1996). The aim is to measure success from different perspectives, like customers, employees, processes, and financial, as well as from the perspective of past, current, and future performance, such that these different aspects of performance can be analyzed and managed (Okkonen et al. 2002).

Differences in the use of performance measurement depend on the time frame monitored. Performance measurement at the short-term or operative level is used for guidance, control, and managing quality, whereas in long-term strategic issues it has a dual role in implementing and updating strategy (Okkonen et al. 2002). Performance measurement ((Neely 1998) (Simons 2000), (Kaplan and Norton 1996)):

- translates strategy into concrete objectives
- communicates the objectives to knowledge workers
- guides and focuses knowledge workers' efforts towards achieving objectives
- controls whether or not the strategic objectives are reached
- use double-loop learning to challenge the validity of strategy
- visualizes how individual employee's efforts contribute to the overall business objectives

E-BRAIN is a cognitive theoretical intangible asset valuation model that integrates strategy, culture, and viability. This model starts with business value components and their capacity, which evolves into intelligence, knowledge, learning, change, and translates into performance measures. These performance measures identify and control critical factors that align with the ability of a business to meet its goal of identifying and controlling the value contributions of intangible assets to business performance.

The thinking organization

> *"To survive today's ongoing changes, we must be prepared to reconsider the very models on which our obsolete organizations are based"*
>
> – Toflter, Alvin , 1985.

E-BRAIN begins with operational and historical data and transcends through the cognitive layers of the organization mind [Figure 4] (intelligence, knowledge, learning, change and performance measurement). Each of these areas contains the elements that embody intelligence and subsequent knowledge within the context of the business enterprise. The cognitive components that drive E-BRAIN are:

Business Intelligence (Long Term Memory) – summarized static information that is used to determine patterns amongst data and information for use in decision making

Knowledge (Short Term Memory) – temporary buffer area that stores results of decisions until these results are encoded into the enterprise body of knowledge

Organizational Learning (Motor Productions) – functions that decode and analyze information to determine its value to the system

Change Management (Perceptual Productions) – functions that encode information from the environment into information for the system

This structure is used to disseminate knowledge to key stakeholders within the organization. The basic economics of business are applied to the structure by identifying a core set of value-adding activities, transformations, transactions performed by the business.

The Cognizant Organization

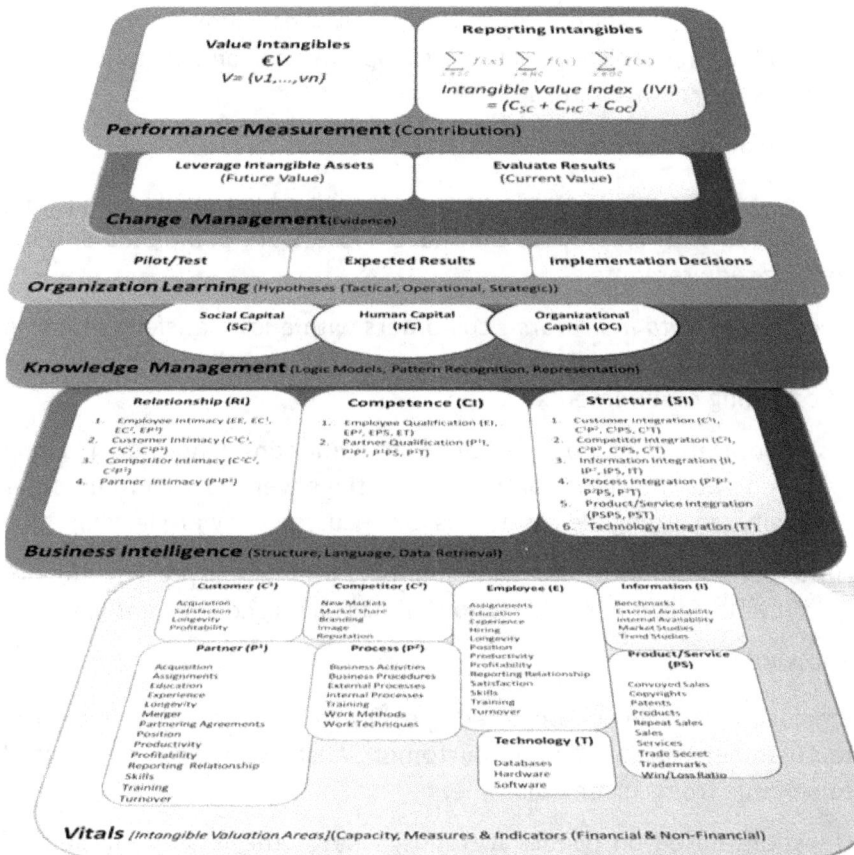

Figure 4: The Organization Mind

Below is an example that walks-through a single business "thought" from E-BRAIN's perspective. The example focuses on two business value components: Customer and Employee. It also focuses on one intangible indicator for each of these value components. An intangible indicator for a customer is their satisfaction with the services and/or products from the providing organization. An intangible indicator for an employee is the training they have received and apply in the performance of their work.

The cross-pollination of Customer/Satisfaction with Employee/Training indicators linked to operational and historical data presents the following results:

Relational Intelligence

Operational Data Indicators - customers with a high satisfaction rating are aligned with employees that have successfully completed specific training requirements

Operational Data Indicators - customers with a low satisfaction rating are aligned with employees that have not successfully completed specific training requirements

Historical Data Indicators - prior to implementing Employee Training Requirements, Customer Satisfaction ratings were low and Customer Longevity (an intangible asset) was low – customers were leaving

Historical Data Indicators - after implementing Employee Training Requirements, Customer Satisfaction ratings increased substantially

Knowledge

Employees that have completed specific Training are directly related to Customer Satisfaction and Customer Satisfaction is directly related to revenue from current customers.

Question: Based on historical trends, what is the financial impact of employees not being trained to support customers?

Action: Identify a pilot group of employees and train employees aligned with current customers that have a low satisfaction rating.

Learning

Monitor the results of the action to determine if the impact is favorable.

Change:

If favorable, implement a policy to ensure all employees receive and complete the required training.

The Cognizant Organization

Performance Measurement

The revenue gains from satisfied customers due to the increase longevity (customers not leaving) of current customers.

As demonstrated in the above example, BRAIN provides attributes that demonstrate recall and intellectual skills. This facilitates regression analysis, enabling a business leader to be cognizant of past practices and obstacles (lessons learned). In addition, it supports the dynamic capture of current transactions for continuous monitoring to support gut instinct (Gladwell 2005) and future forecasting (Davenport and Harris 2007).

Conclusion

> "There is nothing more difficult to take in hand, more perilous to conduct or more uncertain in its success than to take the lead in the introduction of a new order to things."
>
> - Macchiavelli, 1469 – 1527

The elusiveness of intangible assets all seems to stem from the complexity of its structure. The way to make a complex system simple is to decompose it into its primitive elements. Its view becomes more holistic and its construction more manageable. This paper is the culmination of the decomposition of a system that values intangible assets and could be the first step to measuring, valuing and managing this hidden asset that accounts for 85% of the value of an organization.

The value of intangible assets is viewed as critical to the success of a business. In past years, technology was not amenable to the new Information Technology (IT) strategies of today. In recent years, IT has offered businesses phenomenal ways to capture, store, retrieve and distribute information. Fortunately, businesses are now capturing and storing lots of data, unfortunately, access and retrieval of that data such that it is actionable in helping the business to deliver products/services faster, cheaper & better, is not a clear picture.

Businesses are searching for a way to leverage and reuse resources. In the last decade, businesses have jumped on board with Total Quality

Management (TQM), Computer Aided Systems Engineering (CASE), Business Process Re-engineering (BPR), Data Warehousing, and Data Mining, etc., with insignificant results. These IT strategies have been successful at increasing the IT budget with little or no effect on organizational performance. All of these IT strategies have included technology advancements and information. However, the third component to a successful process is not included – the human factor. Without the "know-how" of the individuals who process data into a usable form, the intangible assets gains of a business are virtually nonexistent.

References

Allee, Verna. 1998. The Knowledge Evolution: Expanding Organizational Intelligence, Oxford, UK and Waltham, Massachusetts, USA: Butterworth-Heinemann.

Allee, Verna. 2000. Reconfiguring the Value Network. Journal of Business Strategy. Vol 21, N 4, July-Aug. [Available from http://www.sveiby.com.au/Allee-ValueNets.htm.

Allen, P. G., & Fildes, R. 2001. Econometric Forecasting. In J. S. (Ed), Principles of Forecasting (303 - 362). Norwell, MA: Kluwer Academic Publishers.

Alter, Steven. 1996. Information Systems: A Management Perspective, 3rd Edition, Addison-Wesley.

Argyris, C., & Schon, D. A. 1996. Organizational Learning II, Theory, Method, and Practice. Reading, Massachusetts: Addison-Wesley Publishing Company.

Boar, Bernard H. 1994. Practical Steps for Aligning Information Technology with Business Strategies, How to Achieve a Competitive Edge, New York: John Wiley & Sons, Inc.

Cawsey, Alison. 1998. The Essence of Artificial Intelligence, Upper Saddle River, New Jersey: Prentice Hall.

Davenport, T. H., & Harris, J. G. 2007. Competing on Analytics: The New Source of Winning. Boston, MA: Harvard Business School Publishing Corporation.

Drucker, P. 1998. The Information Executives Truly Need. In H. B. Review, Harvard Business Review on Measuring Performance (pp. 1-24). Boston, MA: Harvard Business School.

Gladwell, M. 2005. Blink. New York, NY: Time Warner Book Group.

Green, A. 2008. A Framework of Intangible Valuation Areas: The Sources of Intangible Assets within an Organization. Germany: VDM-Publishing.

Johnston, J., & DiNardo, J. 1997. Econometric Methods, Fourth Edition. New York, NY: McGraw Hill.

Kaplan, R., & Norton, D. 1996. The Balance Scorecard, Translating Strategy into Action. Boston, MA: Harvard Business School.

Koulopoulos, Thomas M.1997. Smart Companies Smart Tools, Transforming Business Processes into Business Assets, New York: Van Nostrand Reinhold.

Makridakis, S., Wheelwright, S. C., & Hyndman, R. J. 1998. Forecasting Methods for Management, Third Edition. New York, NY: John Wiley.

McNair, C., & Vangermeersch, R. 1998. Total Capacity Management: Optimizing at the Operational, Tactical and Strategic Levels. Boca Raton, FL: St. Lucie Press.

McNurlin, B. C., & Sprague, R. H. 1998. Information Systems Management in Practice, Fourth Edition. New York, NY: Prentice Hall.

Neely, A. 1998. Measuring Business Performance. Why, What and How? London: Profile Books Ltd.

Newell, A. 1990. Unified Theory of Cognition. Cambridge, MA: Harvard University Press.

Okkonen, J., Pirttimaki, V., Lonnqvist, A., & Hannula, M. 2002. Triangle of Performance Measurement. Business Intelligence and Knowledge Management. Stockholm: Euram.

Porter, Michael E. 1980. Competitive Strategy, Techniques for Analyzing Industries and Competitors:.The Free Press.

Porter, Michael E. 1985. Competitive Advantage, Creating and Sustaining Superior Performance. The Free Press.

Senge, P. 1990. The Fifth Discipline: The Art & Practice of the Learning Organization. New York, NY: Doubleday.

Senge, P., Kleiner, A., Roberts, C., Ross, R., Roth, G., & Smith, B. 1999. The Dance of Change, The Challenges to Sustaining Momentum in Learning Organizations. New York, NY: Doubleday.

Simons, R. 2000. Performance Measurement and Control Systems for Implementing Strategy. New Jersey: Prentice Hall.

Stanfill, C., & Waltz, D. 1986. Toward Memory-Based Reasoning. Communication of the ACM, Vol 29, No. 12 , 1213-1228.

Sullivan, P. H. 2000. Value-Driven Intellectual Capital, How to Convert Intangible Corporate Assets into Market Value. New York, NY: John Wiley & Sons.

Toffler, Alvin. 1980. The Third Wave. London: Pan Books.

Utsahajit, W. 2009. Implementing Change Practice through Learning and Development: A Case Study of Kaeng Khol Cement Plant, Siam Cement Group, Thailand. NIDA Development Journal, Vol. 49, No. 2, pp 110-124.

VonKrogh, G., Roos, J., & Kleine, D. 1998. Knowing in Firms: Understanding, Managing and Measuring Knowledge. London: Sage Publication Ltd.

Wiig, K. M. 1994. Knowledge Management, The Central Management Focus for Intelligent-Acting Organizations. Arlington, Texas: Schema Press, LTD.

Zack, Michael H. 1999. Knowledge and Strategy. Oxford, UK and Waltham, Massachusetts, USA: Butterworth-Heinemann.

Keeping Abreast: A Knowledge Management (KM) Challenge for Information Technology Service Providers

Richard Donnelly and Christopher Durney

The George Washington University, Washington D.C., USA

Introduction

This chapter presents a specific knowledge management challenge— how organizations that provide information technology (IT) services acquire and manage new knowledge to help them keep abreast of rapid technological change. We present evidence that these organizations develop formal systems to find, acquire, process, use, and evaluate information about technological change. IT service providers (ITSPs) do this in recognition that without knowledge of emerging technology they could not otherwise provide their core services effectively. For an independent private sector ITSP, the inability to keep abreast of technological change would mean the decline and the eventual demise of the firm out of failure to compete successfully. For internal service provider units, failure to keep abreast could drive the organizational parent to outsource the most sophisticated services and perhaps eventually abandon the unit altogether; rather than tolerate a loss of effectiveness in the parent's mission.

Organizations exist and perform their work in relationship with their external environments. If significant changes occur in their external environment, organizations within that environment must adapt appropriately to maintain their relationship to their external environment (Morgan 1986; Stinchcombe 1990; Eisner 2003). This dynamic adaptation is at the heart of organic models of the organization that have emerged in the last forty years and that stress the relationship of organizational learning, strategy, and adaptability (Burns and Stalker 1968; Galbraith 1977; Kanter 1984; Morgan 1986; Senge 1990; Yeo 2005). ITSPs face this learning challenge because of their high dependency on environments that change dramatically through the advance of the enabling technologies.

Rapid change of any kind causes environmental turbulence and a high level of ambiguity in the external environment (Daft and Lengel 1986). Even the best run organizations chafe under conditions of high ambiguity. It is well established that environmental ambiguity can limit organizational success (Stinchcombe 1990; Galbraith 1977). Accordingly, getting the right information—"the news"—about the ambiguity becomes a critical goal of organizations facing rapid change (Stinchcombe 1990). In times of severe environmental turbulence, organizations gather and process more information about the environment and develop more lines of inquiry into it (Daft and Lengel 1986; Lozada and Calantone 1996). This tends to lead to the development of more formal knowledge systems to acquire and process that information; as organizational management tries to improve its ability to navigate forward.

The formal systems used by organizations to keep abreast of rapid technological change are essentially knowledge management systems. They involve five aspects: A) finding the information, B) acquiring it, C) processing it into productive knowledge, D) making use of the knowledge to stay competitive in a technologically dynamic environment, and E) evaluating the knowledge gained. We explore these five aspects of keeping abreast within the context of the ITSP industry, an industry that is famously undergoing rapid technological change driven by both incremental and disruptive technological advances.

Rapid Change in the IT Industry

An ITSP's core competency is to help customers manage their business information through the design and implementation of information

Keeping Abreast: A Knowledge Management (KM) Challenge for Information Technology Service Providers

systems, telecommunication networks, and computer hardware. The ITSP may be a viable independent organization that derives all of its revenues from the services it provides, or it may be a unit internal to a larger organization that is funded as a budgetary line item of its organizational parent. Independent ITSP businesses are consultancies and service providers that compete through sales and marketing campaigns or through a proposal process. Captive internal units serve only the parent company or agency and perform assignments as commissioned by the management of the parent. Such internal units exist in both the private and public/non-profit sectors. Whether protecting the profit stream of an ITSP business or preserving the legitimacy of an internal ITSP unit, the challenge of keeping abreast is a key concern of the ITSP managers. Any ITSP that fails to manage knowledge on relevant technological change faces the threat of falling behind its competition or into obsolescence, sometimes irreversibly so. This is the "making it real" challenge.

ITSP managers are flooded every day with information about new products and services appearing in the market. They must wade through voluminous technical and semi-technical discussions and specialized advertisements to decide which trends and products match the internal needs of their organizations and allow them to offer real business value. IT is ubiquitous in today's business environment, so that all managers in all industries can benefit from keeping abreast of IT developments. But this is discretionary, at least to some degree. Managers and IT professionals in organizations whose core business is providing IT services face a much greater challenge. Keeping abreast is essential to survival for these individuals.

The sustained pace of rapid change in IT—from the incredible growth of power of the microprocessor to the vast amount of information now being produced and circulated over the Internet—is well documented (Gilder 1989; Wurman 1990; Gantz, et al., 2008). Below are three examples that illustrate the kinds of rapid change in the IT environment which create the demand for effective Keeping-Abreast Knowledge Management (KAKM) systems. The first example is a large multi-year system development that extended in duration well beyond the product improvement and product development cycle times for the enabling technologies. This example represents a challenge to management at several levels, not just to ITSP managers. The second example is the change in a particular class of tools (programming tools) used routinely in IT systems, so that using last year's tool is tantamount to building-in obsolescence. This example represents a challenge to technology managers and senior professionals in IT. The third example is the cascading effect of a significant growth in capability or practice in the industry (e.g., the Internet) on the design of services provided. This example represents a challenge to innovation managers, new product/service developers, system architects and security personnel.

Example 1: Line-Item Changes on a Large Federal IT Support Contract

Large IT support contracts have been the primary mechanisms by which U.S. Federal Government organizations procure and implement new information systems and technology. These contracts can be very large in size—support contracts in the $100 million range which are common and many get much larger—and can take up to two years or more from the time the procurement is first announced to the time it is awarded. The period of performance is often lengthy as well; lasting from three to seven years or even more after award.

On one such federal IT contract, the planning and procurement procedure took three years from the time the request for proposal (RFP) was issued to the time the agency awarded a five-year IT support services contract. The contract included 58 separately priced hardware and software products, some of which were (by then) newer versions of products that had been solicited in the original RFP. Other line items in the contract were entirely new and had not been part of the original RFP requirements.

Four years later, a review of the contract revealed that there were 63 separately priced hardware and software product line items on the contract. Only ten of these products were still being sold in the version originally specified in the contact. Of the products from the original contract that were still listed, 28 were specified in new versions (often several generations past the original version). Sources within the ITSP holding this contract indicated that the change from one version to the next had a fairly small impact on perhaps, a quarter of the new version cases. In the other three-quarters of the cases, however, the changes in versions represented added capabilities or product structure changes that led to a measurable impact on the project. Finally, 25 of the products listed on the original contract were completely new, and required a formal identification, evaluation, selection, and approval process as contract performance was underway.

Example 2: Changes within a Particular Class of Tool

The rapid pace of technological change affecting ITSPs can also be seen in the history of change within a specific class of software tool. Looking at software programming tools; for instance, one can find a complex lineage in which major changes take place on a regular basis. The growth of new tools from existing ones increases the complexity of tool choices, including selecting among some tools that are incurring only incremental change, some that call for full replacement, and some that represent the emergence of entirely new products. As an illustration, the timeline in the Wikipedia article, "Timeline of programming languages" (Wikipedia 2012), shows that through the six decades from 1950 through 2010, approximately 47 programming languages emerged in each decade. Not all of these languages were viable at the same level of scope and applicability and some faded out within only a few months. Still, the constant emergence of new programming languages every year is another indicator of the pace of change experienced by ITSPs. And it illustrates the vast array of information that must be reduced to knowledge, at least cursorily, in order to assess its potential relevance.

Example 3: The Effect of the Interaction of Changes within the IT Environment

A third example of rapid change in IT faced by ITSPs is the complementary or cascading changes that occur as change in one area drives changes in related areas. Between the years 2000 and 2011, the number of users on the Internet grew an estimated 528.1 %, from approximately 360 million users in 2000 to approximately 2.3 billion users in 2011 (Internet World Stats 2012). In addition to increased number of users, the complexity of the computing environment also increased with the addition of smart phones, tablets, social networking software, and other products.

This exponential growth in users and the products they use can reasonably be assumed to have resulted in a concomitant rise in IT security vulnerability. Indeed, in late 2010, Panda Security's anti-malware laboratory reported that over the first ten months of the year, the lab had detected new malware, including viruses, worms, Trojans and other threats, that accounted for 34% of all malware created to that point. That is, the amount of malware threatening computer systems grew by a third in just ten months (Panda Security 2010).

In response to this rate growth, an increase in security products over the same period would be expected. That this did indeed occur is illustrated in "Probably the Best Free Security List in the World." The list which has been compiled over a number of years and is continuously updated by Gizmo's Freeware, identified well more than 700 security products in over 25 categories as of May, 2012 (Gizmo's Freeware 2012). While no single Chief Information Systems Security Official (CISSO) would be expected to know all the software products available, the sheer size of the available knowledgebase demonstrates how interacting elements of the technology environment can magnify the keeping-abreast challenge.

These three examples demonstrate the huge scale and breadth of the knowledge management challenge ITSPs face if they are to keep abreast of rapidly emerging technical developments.

Five Challenges of Keeping-Abreast Knowledge Management (KAKM) Systems

This section explores in detail the five key dimensions of this KAKM challenge: A) where to find the information, B) how to get the information into the organization, C) how to process the information into productive knowledge, D) how to put that knowledge to use, and E) how to evaluate the usefulness of the knowledge.

Keeping Abreast: A Knowledge Management (KM) Challenge for Information Technology Service Providers

A) Finding the Right Information—Knowing Where to Look

The first step in the Keeping-Abreast Knowledge Management (KAKM) system is to determine where to find the right information that will make a difference to the organization in fulfilling its mission.

The organizational environment is made up of multiple sectors, all of which have impact on the organization. Duncan (1971) differentiates between the internal environment (the organizational, decisional-making components) and the external environment. He lists five components of the external environment that are critical for organizations to monitor—customer, supplier, competitor, socio-political, and technological. Subsequent writers have added refinements to the sectors, but the basic idea remains. For ITSPs, it is clear that technological change is a pre-eminent matter. But changes important to the organization can arise in any of the sectors. For instance, changes in governmental regulations or in the economy could have an effect on an organization's competitive position comparable in impact to the effect of new technological discoveries.

Where do ITSPs look to get information about changes arising in the technological sector? Clearly, the technological sector itself is the primary source. Reading the technical and scientific literature, tracking patents and patent applications, interacting with technology developers at conferences and shows, perusing product literature and comparative analyses, engaging technical consultants and employing up-to-date professionals; all are potentially relevant. An effective KAKM system will recognize, though, that information about technological changes and their effects may also be detected from discussions with customers, suppliers, or competitors, from monitoring emerging regulatory concerns and socio-economic trends, and so on. The best ITSPs will identify multiple sources of information that, when monitored together, will produce the knowledge needed to adapt to rapid technological change.

With multiple sources of information to access and with limited resources and limited capacity, organizations must choose the sources they deem most important. Only information that helps the organization answer the questions that constrain its success really matter (Stinchcombe 1990). Therefore, organizations must decide, whether by explicit or implicit choice, which of the external sources matter most. Then they must commit their resources to getting the news about those areas.

In the process of matching the information need to the right information source, ITSPs may look for different sources for different information-gathering phases. For instance, organizations may undertake a fairly high-level scanning phase that builds cognitive awareness of innovations in a particular area—for example, security or programming languages—followed by a more intensive phase in which they search for information that will help evaluate the products for use (Ashton and Stacey 1993; Auster and Choo 1994, Mortara, et al., 2010). The first phase may concentrate on mass media and Internet searches to lay out the basic terrain of the developing area. As the intensity and depth of the search increases, it is natural for ITSPs to extend the search to incorporate interpersonal sources such as networking, attendance at trade shows, and so on (Bunn and Clopton 1993, Mortara, et al., 2010).

B) Getting Information about Changing Technology into the Organization

After deciding in the first step where to look for the right information, the second step is finding mechanisms for getting the information into the organization.

In order to reduce or remove the uncertainties that the organization perceives as critical constraints in pursuing their mission, organizations structure themselves to collect relevant information in as timely a way as possible (Stinchcombe 1990). The mechanisms employed vary according to the kind of uncertainty, the source of the information about the uncertainty, and the selected channels for getting the information to the organization's information processing units. Some of the mechanisms for getting technological information into the organization evolve naturally from the nature of technical staff and how they communicate.

Keeping Abreast: A Knowledge Management (KM) Challenge for Information Technology Service Providers

A key role in organizations dependent upon technology is the Technology Gatekeeper. These are professional employees who enhance information gathering by personally spanning the boundary between the internal knowledge base of the company and external knowledge sources (Allen 1977). Allen's research reveals the existence of a two-step gatekeeping process: 1) information gathering, and 2) dissemination. The gatekeeper is the kind of technologist who tends to be well acquainted with information sources outside the immediate organization. These individuals are naturally inclined to seek out these sources, reading more literature, attending more conferences, participating in more information exchanges. In the age of the Internet, the gatekeeper, or "idea scout" (Whelan et al. 2011) is more likely to get initial information about developments from Internet sources rather than interpersonal ones. Still, interpersonal "scouting visits" play a role in ensuring that the information gathered is thoroughly discussed and understood with other experts outside the organization. And the gatekeeper maintains long-term, stable relationships with the professional acquaintances and related sources in the external community (Allen 1977; Mortara et al. 2010).

Accordingly, the gatekeeper's colleagues within the ITSP count on the gatekeeper to know the latest trends in the environment. A short cut to finding new information for many employees is to simply ask the gatekeeper. It is interesting to note that gatekeeping activity can be encouraged by management but that real gatekeepers emerge instinctively and are discovered, not assigned. Simply appointing someone to the gatekeeping position does not ensure the expert authority and wide array of professional relationships necessary for the gatekeeper to fulfill the function adequately (Nochur and Allen 1992). Such self-selection by gatekeepers limits management's ability to structure this aspect of the KAKM system.

When the need for relevant information on technological change becomes more urgent, the gatekeeper's role proves inadequate to meet the information demand. As the pace of change increases, ITSPs send agents into the field in various ad hoc roles to make first-hand observations. The best agents go on to develop useful personal relationships externally, holding frequent meetings and attending face-to-face presentations with people who hold the information needed (Ashton and Stacey 1995; Mortara et al., 2010). Unlike gatekeepers, who emerge naturally from the pool of technologists, these agents can be appointed by management and assigned specific liaison duties. ITSPs rely heavily on partnerships with vendors as a source of information, assigning vendor liaisons particularly to those vendors perceived to be market leaders in the areas in which the firm does its business. ITSPs may also set up relationships with suppliers who are not the market leaders as a means of reducing their vulnerability to changes from unexpected directions. In addition, those suppliers seeking to oust an industry leader and take over that position are often fertile sources of comparative analyses, uncovering subtleties of competing approaches that may be highly instructive to the ITSP.

Similarly, agents may be assigned to develop relationships with key customers. The major responsibility of customer relationship managers is to attend to the satisfaction of key customers who use or might in the future use the organization's services and products. Furthermore, an ITSP's best users are often those who push the current technology and services into new areas and understand the need for experimentation and appropriate risk-taking. These lead customers (or lead users) provide valuable information about the future usefulness and direction for the ITSP's products and services (Von Hippel 1986). The customer liaison is, thus, a key mechanism for gathering and disseminating user-sourced information back into the ITSP. A simple and obvious prescription for enhancing information gathering is to get as many sensors 'out there' as possible. Thus, staff learning programs, when enforced and tied into professional competency models, provide great flexibility and potential for bringing required new information into the organization. Such programs cause everyone—all the individual agents—in the ITSP to play a role in the keeping-abreast challenge, and they also establish an expectations baseline for learning. The result is that the entire staff becomes conditioned to the challenge of continuously keeping up with new ideas and technologies.

C) Processing Information into New Knowledge

ITSPs knowledge on information technology represents a core competency. ITSPs, like other technology-based organizations, build their competitive strength through their ability to learn continuously and take advantage of that learning (Senge 1990; Eisner 2003; Yeo 2005). The company's knowledge base is one of its key assets and it must continually add to the knowledge base by sucking in ideas from outside its frontiers and by making sure that they circulate inside the company (Micklethwait and Woolridge 1996). By the nature of technology and technological information, the mere collection of information is found to be inadequate preparation for its effective use. The new ideas brought into the organization through the collection mechanisms discussed above require further processing before they become the knowledge necessary to help the organization adapt effectively to changing technology.

In describing the elements of an intelligence system for science and technology, Ashton and Stacey (1995) detail three elements of the processing necessary to convert source information into productive knowledge for the organization. These activities include:

1. Developing the analysis results
2. Ensuring that the information is correct, current, and complete
3. Interpreting the business significance, by evaluating the meaning this information has for the firm (Ashton and Stacey, 1995).

Three means for taking source information and developing it into organizational knowledge that can be internalized by the organization are research, study, and experience (Kerssens-Van Drongelen et al. 1996).

One type of research is organizationally approved scanning that is assigned formally to a scanning unit. The scanning unit is responsible for monitoring the external environment, finding important information in it, processing the information for its value, and delivering that information to the appropriate decision makers.

While scanning units are structured to focus on the external environment, they also consume valuable organizational resources in doing so. Many ITSPs cannot afford a stand-alone scanning unit so they add it as a specific responsibility within an existing unit. For instance, ITSPs in the federal sector, the enterprise architecture function is expected to analyze the current and future environments, develop a "target" enterprise architecture comprising business, performance, data, and technical views of the architecture, and develop sequencing plans to move from the current environment to the envisioned one. A critical element in the success of such architecture work is scanning the external environment for those developments and trends that need to be incorporated into the target architecture. The Federal Segment Architecture Methodology (FSAM) published by the U.S. Office of Management and Budget (OMB) (Office of Management and Budget 2008) requires that federal architects review the state of the internal and external organizational drivers before beginning the annual architecture update activities.

Cohen and Levinthal (1989, 1990) regard the internal research and development (R&D) organization as a primary source of the learning that builds the organizational knowledge base and increases the organization's ability to absorb even more new learning (its absorptive capacity). Firms sometimes invest in R&D for the learning experience the research activity provides the company. Does R&D function this way for ITSPs? In most situations, R&D labs not only produce learning but are often expected to produce new value through the development of new products. In ITSPs, services predominate over products; thus, R&D activities undertaken by ITSPs focus primarily on how new services can be developed around emerging new technologies. Such an approach implies, in turn, a way to get the learning on these new services out of the R&D lab and into the hands of the people responsible for delivering the services in daily operations.

Related to internal R&D labs are: a) internal projects taken on to increase internal learning and b) the establishment of technology labs for testing new software and products, especially in mixed configurations. An example of an internal project would be an ITSP's implementation of Web 3.0 tools for outreach to their own customers. Following successful implementation, Web 3.0 tool implementation then becomes a new service offering to help those customers with their own outreach activities. Similarly, placing Web 3.0 tools in a technology lab in which the tools can be exercised and demonstrated also provides more intimate knowledge of the tools, their peculiarities, and their possible uses. Walking customers through a technology lab environment in which new capabilities are available for review often results in new ideas for how the tools can support the customer's mission.

The concept of Communities of Practice (CoP) has developed within the knowledge management community as a means of explaining how individual knowledge can grow into something larger and more useful for the organization. CoPs are groups within the organization that share a context of meaning and sense-making about the 'know how' aspect of knowledge (Brown and Duguid 1998). This sense-making role gives the CoP a communal knowledge that is greater than a single individual's knowledge store. A CoP can play a key knowledge processing role by 'warranting' the information it finds to be worthwhile and useful to the organization (Brown and Duguid 1998). As a group, the community tests information received and ensures that the information is correct and actionable. Information that cannot be converted into productive knowledge is of little use to the community's members.

CoPs may be explicit or implicit; the key is that the community has a shared sense of what its members know, how they know it, and why sharing the knowledge is important for them in their organizational role. However, to become a meaningful part of the KAKM system, implicit CoPs must become more explicitly recognized by management as playing a vital role in the knowledge processing activity of the ITSP. A challenge for ITSP' managers is how to identify these communities and optimize the sense-making that they do automatically for the whole organization.

Two important aspects of the processing of information into knowledge are the evaluation of the knowledge and processing it for delivery to other users within the ITSP. Evaluation of new knowledge is largely informal within ITSPs. No standard evaluation frameworks exist that might aid in the evaluation process. From the point of view of identifying innovations for potential adoption, the criteria that Rogers (2003) describes as important to successful innovation—relative advantage, compatibility, complexity, trialability, and observability—might be taken as, at least, an informal framework for evaluating emerging technologies. After all, these attributes still seem to function reliably, even when only implicitly, in influencing the adoption of new technology.

Regardless of how the new knowledge is evaluated, the scanning unit, whatever its form, must judge what to pass on, what to store, and what to discard. The judging is a combination of the results of the evaluation, the current organizational situation, and the demands of the external environment. Results, deemed to have organizational value, must then be packaged in the most accessible way possible. Potential dangers, when processing information for delivery, include the following:

Misinterpretation—recommendations are not warranted by the information.

Inaccuracy/uncertainty—output of analysis is wrong or too uncertain to be of value.

Short-term orientation—preoccupation with short-term pre-empts consideration of longer-term issues.

Lack of acceptance—results are not accepted whatever the reason (politics, lack of understanding, etc.).

Diversified business—multiple relevant environments make analysis too complex.

Misperceptions—narrow, limited or invalid perceptions of the external environment (Diffenbach 1983).

D) Using the New Knowledge

In the spirit of 'making it real', it must be acknowledged that information accessed and processed into knowledge does not always make its way into actual use. Many monitoring and scanning processes, although intended to provide information for organizational decision making, do not ensure this expected final step (Hambrick 1982; Jain 1984). Unless the information gets to the people that are equipped to take advantage of it, the KAKM system will not achieve its purpose (Whelan, et al. 2011). Some participating functions are even prevented from doing so by organizational politics (Lenz and Engledow 1986; Davenport, et al. 1992). Knowledge that is not used productively by the organization is eventually lost, along with the resources spent in gathering information and processing it. Three ways in which knowledge can be used productively are the following.

Getting New Knowledge into the Planning System

Much of the literature discusses the use of such information in the decision-making processes of the organization (Fahey and King 1977; Jain 1982). In this capacity, the information serves as early warning alerts and decision support to identify potential technological threats (monitoring developments in specified areas or identifying overall patterns and trends) and to identify opportunities for technology investment (Ashton and Stacey 1995). Maier (1992) reported that nearly 88% percent of the 131 firms surveyed indicated that results of scanning were matched with planning in at least some way, although nearly 80% admitted that they did not have a formal link between scanning and strategic planning.

A number of considerations go into the delivery of any new knowledge to decision makers. First, the information must be processed, packaged, and delivered to decision makers when it is needed. When the use is in the strategic planning process, this means that the information must arrive prior to or during the process. However, technological advances do not necessarily correspond to neat planning cycles.

Second, the accuracy of the information is important. Forecasts on emerging technology will generally be beset by ambiguity, which increases when the causality of environmental events cannot be established with certainty (Daft and Lengel 1986). Even when a strong case can be made that a particular emerging technology will likely become a success, there are too many confounding factors that come into play to guarantee success. This harsh reality may leave technologists satisfied, but planners are generally conservative in nature and want a solid basis for making planning decisions. Thus, a compromise must be struck between the planners' desire for certainty and the scanners' understanding that the information delivered will always be partly conjecture.

Third, the media chosen to deliver the information depends on the type of information, the intended audience, the cost, the urgency of the need for the information, and user preferences (Ashton and Stacey 1995). Depending on the amount of uncertainty and ambiguity in the information itself, the delivery can range from rich media such as one-on-one conversations and live presentations to less rich media, such as formal reports and documents (Daft and Lengel 1986).

Incorporating New Knowledge into New Products and Services

New knowledge can be incorporated into new products and services (Allen 1977; Leonard-Barton 1995) thereby helping to realize the potential value of the KAKM approach. These new products and services may be engendered outside the formal planning processes. Pitt and MacVaugh (2008) instruct technology management to nurture the processes, both formal and informal, by which acquired knowledge is converted into new product development. Technology managers may create the conditions for this kind of knowledge sharing, but it cannot be legislated or made a formal system. Managers have to understand that at the start of a new development effort, they should encourage the informal exchanges of tacit and explicit knowledge in an open communicative atmosphere. Too much control too early will cut down on the positive effects of the newly acquired knowledge (Richtnér and Åhlström 2010). Still, without the influx of new knowledge into the organization, and without that knowledge making its way to the technical staff, the impetus for new ideas and innovative services must be blunted to some degree.

Using New Knowledge to Build Organizational Responsiveness

Finally, information can be used to build absorptive capacity. For high-technology firms, the corporate technical knowledge base represents an organizational asset that allows for the continuance of the core competency and that can, itself, be a source of competitive advantage (Edvinsson and Sullivan 1996; Whitaker 1996). If the knowledge base is compromised, whether by loss of personnel or by failure to keep abreast of emerging technology, the effect is a depletion of core competency.

The use of new knowledge in building absorptive capacity happens informally in the exchange and processing of information that occurs intuitively in CoPs. However, knowledge transfer must be managed actively if the knowledge is to become part of the foundation for future learning. Delivery of information for absorptive capacity can take a number of forms, including training, presentations, knowledge databases, and personnel exchange programs.

E) Evaluating the Value of the New Knowledge

In an era of extreme cost consciousness, the ITSP must try to determine how well the keeping-abreast activity is actually providing the expected benefits to the organization. Measurements of the value of the information gained through the KAKM system are important for justifying on-going management commitment to the system (Mortara, et al. 2010). In any measurement system, the expectations for the system need to be quantified, targets need to be established for each measure, information needs to be gathered and compared to the target, and judgments need to be made about the efficacy of the system.

As with much knowledge management, the value of the information gained through a KAKM system is difficult to quantify (Andone 2009; Mortara et al. 2010). The best measure would be to be able to attach specific KAKM system outputs to positive organizational outcomes, thus demonstrating clear return on the keeping-abreast investment.

But these connections are fragile, at best. The desired outcome—that the organization keeps abreast of emerging technology—is not easily itself quantified. No industry standard exists for how an organization measures whether it is sufficiently up-to-date. And if organizational success at keeping abreast is hard to define, the connection with the information coming from the keeping-abreast system will be certainly hard to demonstrate.

Related benefits may be substituted for keeping abreast value per se. For instance, when a firm invests in the establishment of a technology laboratory, the organization's senior managers tend to want some indication of the return on investment. To provide some feedback of this sort, one ITSP we observed sent new customers a questionnaire asking: 1) if the new customer had visited the technology lab, and 2) if so, did the visit have any impact on their eventual decision to employ the company's services. The organization's Chief Technology Officer (CTO) told us that the positive feedback from customers was included in the annual report of technology lab activities that was submitted to senior management and was used as justification to continue funding in the next year. However, the CTO also admitted that this metric had little to do with the effect that the lab had on keeping the firm's staff up to date on new technology.

Measuring activities and outputs from the keeping-abreast system is easier but less meaningful (Andone 2009). The organization can measure the amount of papers written, the number of new technologies scanned and evaluated, the number of conferences attended, the number of CoP meetings held, and the number of new patents generated. However, these measures tell very little, if anything, about the value of the information produced by the KAKM activities for the organization.

To some extent, the measure that counts the most appears to be a qualitative judgment that is held in the mind of the scanning system sponsor. This sponsor is a senior manager with scope and budget to support the scanning activity in its current form. Should the sponsor leave the organization or begin to look for a more quantitative rationale for supporting the keeping-abreast activity, the benefits of the system, and often its very existence, can quickly be called into question (Lenz and Engledow 1986; Mortara et al. 2010).

There is evidence that the more intense a firm's commitment to aggressive use of technology, the more it sees scanning as a necessity (Maier 1992). However, developing better value measures for the effectiveness of keeping-abreast systems should help make a stronger, more objective case for the value of these approaches.

A Portfolio of Keeping-Abreast Approaches

Nine Keeping-Abreast Approaches

While a sequential view of information processing has been presented, it is important to remember that information processing is actually an iterative activity. For instance, evaluation may go through several steps. As a trend is found to have applicability for the ITSP, progressive information finding and processing will occur, with interim decisions—to gather more information, test the current information, or dismiss the trend as finally not significant, for instance—being made at meaningful points. In addition, at several points gap analysis will occur to help determine the potential value of the new information (Lozada and Calantone 1996) with new information sought to fill the gaps as they are identified. Similarly, the various mechanisms for collecting, processing, packaging, delivering, and using keeping-abreast information are not likely to be observed in stand-alone fashion.

Our studies of keeping-abreast knowledge management (KAKM) practices have involved developing an extensive framework of expected behaviors based on the existing literature. This framework was then used in constructing an interview guide. Several open-ended questions allowed for the exploration of several new behaviors identified by interviewees and these new behaviors were then added to the framework. We used interview-based case studies to explore the keeping-abreast approaches used by ITSPs (e.g., Durney and Donnelly 2004).

Thirty-one ITSP organizations were involved in the study. Eight of the subject organizations were in the public sector, nine provided IT services for internal end-users only, and fourteen provided IT services for external customers as their core revenue-generating business. The government's ITSP organizations had between 100 and 500 technical personnel and between $25 million and $67 million in IT budget. Four of the nine internal ITSPs were in this same size range, while five had greater than 500 employees and IT budgets larger than $70 million. Four of the external ITSP organizations had revenues under $500 million and fewer than 1,000 employees, while ten were larger than 1,000 employees and had annual revenues in excess of $500 million. Seven of the external ITSPs had a customer focus primarily the government market, while the other seven had either a split focus, or favored the commercial sector.

In our structured interviews, we asked a number of questions about the keeping-abreast behaviors we expected to find. As the early interviews progressed, we added to the list of approaches, revisiting the initial organizations to confirm or deny existence of the newly identified approaches. As expected, we found a variety of keeping-abreast approaches in ITSPs, with each approach differing from the others in the nature of the information sources, acquisition channels, processing and storage approaches, and delivery strategies used.

Based on our case studies of this selection of ITSPs, a list of keeping-abreast approaches includes the following:

- Vendor relationship programs
- Technology gatekeepers
- Staff learning programs
- Communities of practice and interest
- Customer relationship programs
- Formal scanning units
- Technical laboratories
- Internal projects
- Research and development

Keeping Abreast: A Knowledge Management (KM) Challenge for Information Technology Service Providers

The selection of nine approaches for inclusion in the portfolio, at this time, does not preclude the expansion of the portfolio in the future, should new keeping-abreast approaches emerge (Whelan et al. 2011; Mortara et al. 2010).

ITSPs blend some or all of these keeping-abreast approaches together to form a dynamic and integrated organizational response to the keeping-abreast knowledge management (KAKM) challenge. The specific characteristics of this keeping-abreast "portfolio" for each ITSP can be captured and analyzed, leading to a keeping-abreast "profile" that is unique for each organization. This profile is based on the degree of commitment the ITSP's management has regarding the various knowledge management approaches.

Measuring ITSP Commitment to Keeping-Abreast Knowledge Management

The more convinced ITSP management is about the importance of a particular approach to keeping-abreast knowledge management (KAKM)—the customer relationship manager, the vendor liaison, a technology gatekeeper, a community of practice (CoP) and so on—the more resources the ITSP commits to that approach. This commitment of resources is visible in explicitly stated goals, objectives, and expected outcomes for the particular approach, in defined processes, in capital investments in equipment and software, in recognized organizational status for participants, and in assigned personnel.

For instance, a common keeping-abreast approach is the vendor liaison. The vendor liaison develops a relationship with a vendor who provides information about product directions, emerging product strategies, potential new customer requirements, ideas from other product users, and so on.

Of course, we should note that the vendor relationship is important for reasons other than keeping abreast. For instance, the vendor may provide marketing and sales leads to the ITSP through the vendor relationship. The vendor may even partner with the ITSP on certain customer engagements, even to the point of adapting the product line for certain important customers. Furthermore, the relationship is important to the vendor as well, since the vendor needs to have a ready supply of technicians in the external environment who are prepared to help customers make the best use of the vendor's products.

As vendor relationships gain in significance for the ITSP, the ITSP tends to commit more organizational resources to support the role. The management of the ITSP provides the vendor liaison with goals and expectations, time, expenses, and other resources to help the vendor liaison manage the vendor relationship effectively. Often, these vendor relationships will even include contractual agreements between the ITSP and the vendor. In return for this corporate commitment, the vendor liaison is expected to make knowledge about the vendor's plans and directions available to those who need it in the organization.

Thus, at the higher levels of interaction, the ITSP naturally develops an increasing amount of definition and organizational structure to deal with the various aspects of the vendor relationship. In the data accumulated from the case study interviews with ITSP managers, this organizational commitment to a specific keeping-abreast approach appears to fall along a continuous spectrum, from an absence of commitment at one end up through increasing levels of organizational structure, resources, and articulated goals and expectations that are assigned by the ITSP to the keeping-abreast activity.

Based on our observations of ITSPs, we have articulated five keeping-abreast commitment levels for each of the nine keeping-abreast approaches. While each specific approach has its own specific conditions at each level, the commitment levels can be universally defined as:

- *None* - the ITSP does not support this approach
- *Ad hoc* - the ITSP uses the approach, but only temporarily, often in reaction to some external event
- *Basic* - the approach has some continuity and definition, but is fairly limited in organizational expectations, structure, personnel, and other resources

Keeping Abreast: A Knowledge Management (KM) Challenge for Information Technology Service Providers

- *Structured* - the approach has continuity and permanence in the ITSP. Processes, structures, and expectations exist for the approach and personnel are assigned with continuing responsibility for the approach
- *Integrated* - the approach is integrated with the other keeping-abreast approaches through some form of linkages

Using these generic commitment levels and adjusting them for the different approaches based on our observations of ITSPs, we have developed a keeping abreast—commitment levels framework (Tables 1 – 3). The keeping-abreast commitment levels framework provides a means for comparing keeping-abreast behaviors among various ITSPs.

Table 1. Commitment Levels Framework: Keeping-Abreast Approaches—Commitment Levels Framework (1)

Category Rating	Vendor relationships	Gatekeepers	Staff learning
Intent	"Get the news first" from the source of the changes.	Bridge internal and external in key areas.	Develop keeping-abreast responsibility within each staff member.
Elements	Vendor liaisons. Formal commitments. Certification programs. Business leads received. Links to other communities. Site visits. Education programs.	Identified gatekeepers. "Yellow pages" of technical specialists. Incentives for gatekeeping activity. Technical career path with senior technologists at top.	Professional development programs. Competency models for understanding career progression. Professional networking.
0: None	Few or no formal relationships. (Note: this can be a result of a formal decision to endorse an open architecture.)	No gatekeepers apparent.	No formal program.
1: Ad hoc	Some relationships exist with key vendors, but on basis of *ad hoc* personal	Several people acknowledged for their expertise in important areas. Called upon as	Learning program is hit-or-miss, training in response to specific needs (new

Category Rating	Vendor relationships	Gatekeepers	Staff learning
	relationships.	needed for events. No formal recognition or role.	project, personnel retention, etc.). Limited formal networking
2. Basic	Some rules in place. Appointment of liaisons is corporate decision and documented. Structured expectations between vendor and ITSP.	Some corporate recognition of areas of expertise of key gatekeepers. Some resources and some expectations exist for gatekeepers to keep up.	Some continuity throughout the year. Elements in place but significant variability in enforcement. Rewards exist for professional networking.
3: Structured	Vendor liaison program as part of overall strategy. Resources available. Vendor learning programs are part of overall learning program.	Gatekeepers receive resources, including some free time for learning. Some systems exists for directing inquires and findings. Role of senior technologists has corporate status.	Learning program, enforced and regular; resources available to support the learning programs, competency models and career paths are used. Networking is fairly pervasive.
4: Integrated	Vendor program tied into direction of the company. Findings from vendors fed into strategic planning processes. Relationships between vendors and CoP/I, tech lab, and other keeping-abreast components.	Senior technology officers have acknowledged role within the organization, e.g., CTO, senior technology partners, etc. CTOs are linked to other elements of KAKM structures and roles.	Active ties with strategic planning and direction setting. Competency models integrated with communities of practice (CoP). Professional networking is part of practice.

Table 2. Commitment Levels Framework: Keeping-Abreast Approaches—Commitment Levels Framework (2)

Category Rating	Communities of practice/interest (CoP/I)	Customer relationships	Formal Scanning Unit

Keeping Abreast: A Knowledge Management (KM) Challenge for Information Technology Service Providers

Category Rating	Communities of practice/interest (CoP/I)	Customer relationships	Formal Scanning Unit
Intent	Stay in touch with a particular subsector through group social structures.	Take the lead on important developments from key customers.	Responsible for scanning and evaluating technology trends and providing input to planning.
Elements	Defined workgroups and membership. Documentation of role. Gathering, processing, warranting, and dissemination of knowledge gained. Resources available for supporting group.	CRM programs. "Lead users" identified and relationships developed. Regular feedback sought and used to improve services. Integration of customers input with planning.	Clear responsibility for monitoring developments and evaluating technology. Assigned staff, reporting relationship and integration with planning process.
0: None	No acknowledged CoP/I exist.	No formal program.	No formal group.
1: Ad hoc	Sporadic brown bags about hot topics; *ad hoc* workgroups created around specific issues.	Customer needs occasionally included in strategic planning but without system. Customer proposals drive learning.	Group brought together when needed to provide input to planning process.
2. Basic	A few key workgroups/CoP/I meet regularly. Some reporting back to the larger group. Some resources exist for bringing the group together. No formal role in planning.	System exists for identifying customer needs. Some expectations exist for customer managers. Customers may participate in some product evaluation. Customer feedback sought and used.	Group exists on continuous basis. Scanning responsibility may be assigned as either core or additional responsibility. No real tie to other planning processes or expectations.

Category Rating	Communities of practice/interest (CoP/I)	Customer relationships	Formal Scanning Unit
3: Structured	Formal, continuous CoP/I. Warranting of knowledge for dissemination to larger group. May arrange for formal presentations to rest of staff. Supporting resources provided.	Customers input actively sought as part of overall strategy. Resources available for support of CRM program. Some sort of service level contracts exists between IT staff and key customers.	Group exists with clear scanning responsibility as one of its main charges. Planning looks to the group for input on regular basis.
4: Integrated	CoP/I integrated with labs, planning, KM, staff learning. Costs covered. Responsible for the stewardship of new knowledge in the subject area.	Customers become partners in research and Shared programs for keeping abreast, integrating suppliers and CoP as appropriate. Formal "lead users" programs exist.	Group is hub of scanning for organization. May coordinate input from CoP and other sources. Will be integrated with tech lab and R&D.

Table 3. Commitment Levels Framework: Keeping-Abreast Approaches— Commitment Levels Framework (3)

Category Rating	Tech Labs	Internal projects	R&D
Intent	Have a central locus for the exploration of new products and ideas. Allow experimentation and hands-on feel.	Understand the product as applied in real life. Transfer new skills to other work.	Create the future rather than keep abreast of it. In applied research, test the new products and ideas before buying in.
Elements	Hardware and software made available to staff. Dedicated lab staff available for help and research. Formal budget and organizational struc-	Projects intentionally selected for learning. Lessons learned collected and shared. Staff seeded into other projects.	Internal research and R&D projects and experiments. Process for choosing projects and awarding resources. Joint R&D with competitors or

Keeping Abreast: A Knowledge Management (KM) Challenge for Information Technology Service Providers

Category Rating	Tech Labs	Internal projects	R&D
	ture and role.		customers.
0: None	No lab. Note: Several subjects mentioned that they intentionally did not fund labs because they did not see a way to recoup their investment.	Internal IT projects are not part of ITSP' framework.	No R&D.
1: Ad hoc	Labs developed as needed, usually in response to specific project needs, then go away.	Learning from projects is recognized after the fact, not as planned use of project. Feedback is sporadic, random.	Rare applied research projects for spot issues. Operational capability demonstration (OCD) for proposals treated as applied research.
2. Basic	Some continuity. Hardware and software exist; budget resources available. No FTE assigned on a permanent basis.	One or two major projects may be undertaken with the expressed (primary or secondary) purpose of building knowledge and competency for the ITSP.	Research program is documented; research budget exists for a limited amount of research projects. Research is sometimes broader than focused on a specific project.
3: Structured	Lab has budget, assigned FTE's, mission, and measurements. Policies and procedures are in place for lab use.	Internal projects are intentionally undertaken to develop learning for transfer. Staff have structured ways to get involved in such internal efforts. Lessons learned are shared.	Avenues exist for individuals to propose research ideas. Research budget exists for key projects. Rewards exist for winning research projects. Research results are shared.
4: Integrated	Director of lab has senior technical role in strategic planning.	Most new ideas tested internally in some capacity as	Research centers exist; customers and partners are invited to

Category Rating	Tech Labs	Internal projects	R&D
	Lab is integrated with other organizational learning. Knowledge products from lab are "pushed" to end-users. Multiple labs may exist. May be centralized or diversified by BU.	means to gain new knowledge. Staff from internal projects is used to seed other projects. Integrated with CoP/I and tech labs.	participate in research projects; customers can propose research topics. Research can be sponsored by other keeping-abreast approaches—CoP/I, tech lab, vendor and customer representatives. Formal feedback.

We have used the keeping-abreast commitment framework to compare and evaluate the keeping-abreast approaches of a variety of ITSPs. Our findings, to date, constitute case research, so we do not claim statistical validity of these findings. Nonetheless, we believe these findings point to effective approaches to managing knowledge on emerging technologies of relevance to ITSPs.

Recommendations for ITSPs in Managing Knowledge about New Technology

No single knowledge management approach will enable an organization to keep abreast of rapidly changing technology. The dynamic dimension of knowledge use suggests multiple integrated methods are better than one single method in responding to a complex, rapidly changing external environment. In our experience, ITSPs must find multiple ways for getting keeping-abreast information into the organization, evaluated, and disseminated to the staff that needs it in their daily decision making.

ITSP managers should do whatever can be done to encourage the free flow of information through the organization. Free information exchange really appears to be an enabling condition for effective keeping-abreast knowledge management activity. Incentives and rewards must support information sharing and collaboration. Without this

Keeping Abreast: A Knowledge Management (KM) Challenge for Information Technology Service Providers

support, keeping-abreast information will be lost and the benefits of any KAKM system will be diminished.

ITSPs must help the organization manage the knowledge gained through keeping abreast activities in integrated ways. The most robust KAKM systems that we have observed have best practices discussions and methodology databases alongside the vendor databases and the internal discussions about products. These systems seem oriented to reduce internal uncertainties that arise not only from external technological sources, but also from internal sources, including the dissonance that can arise from multiple voices competing for attention from various sides of the issue.

While managing multiple approaches, we advise ITSPs to focus on at least one approach to bring it to the integrated-level of commitment (see Tables 1 – 3, above). Our observations suggest that achieving the integrated level of commitment on at least one of the keeping-abreast approaches represents a threshold that, once passed, strengthens the keeping-abreast commitment throughout the entire ITSP.

Because of the large volume of information coming into the organization when the approaches in the keeping-abreast portfolio are working at high levels, the ITSP manager must develop some rules of thumb for determining what is of value and what is not. Some information will be immediately recognized as useful by specific practitioner communities and should receive appropriate near-term attention. Other information will appear to have only more general applicability but may be of potential value in the future. Such information should not be allowed to clutter the knowledge management system or dilute the attention paid to the directly relevant information, but should usually be retained in some retrievable manner for possible future use.

Finally, keeping abreast is an on-the-margin activity, and every expenditure commits money and resources that could be used for other investments. Therefore, ITSP managers should attempt to maximize the on-the-margin contributions of each individual within the organization—staff learning activities, CoP, and technology gatekeeping are approaches that offer the possibility of splitting the cost between the ITSP corporate margin and the individual's margin. The manager must be careful not to be exploitative in following this advice, however. Rewards and recognition for individual contributions must be real and substantive.

Conclusion

Keeping abreast is a knowledge management challenge for ITSPs. The extent to which they commit resources to respond to this challenge is determined to a great extent by how close the IT services they provide are to the core of the organization's business. Building management commitment will always be a success factor for effective keeping-abreast knowledge management. ITSP managers who believe that keeping abreast is critical to organizational success must constantly argue that case to the senior managers who make the key budget decisions affecting the organization's keeping-abreast commitment levels. Obviously, the more any of the keeping-abreast approaches can be shown to be producing measurable business value for the organization, the greater the likelihood that senior managers will provide the required resources.

References

Allen, Thomas J. Managing the Flow of Technology. Cambridge, MA: MIT Press, (1977).

Andone, Ioan I. "Measuring the Performance of Corporate Knowledge Management Systems." Informatica Economica 13 4 (2009): 24-31

Ashton, W. Bradford and Gary S. Stacey. "Technical Intelligence in Business: Understanding Technology Threats and Opportunities." International Journal of Technology Management 10 1 (1995): 79.

Auster, Ethel and Chun Wei Choo. "How Senior Managers Acquire and Use Information in Environmental Scanning." Information Processing & Management 30 5, (1993): 607-618.

Brown, John Seely and Paul Duguid. "Organizing Knowledge." California Management Review 40 3 (1998): 90-111.

Bunn, Michele D. and Stephen W. Clopton. "Patterns of Information Source Use Across Industrial Purchase Situations." Decision Sciences 24 2 (1993): 457-478.

Keeping Abreast: A Knowledge Management (KM) Challenge for Information Technology Service Providers

Burns, Tom and G. M. Stalker. The Management of Innovation. London: Tavistock, 1968.

Cohen Wesley M. and Daniel A. Levinthal. "Absorptive Capacity: a New Perspective on Learning and Innovation." Administrative Science Quarterly 35 (1990): 128-152.

Cohen, Wesley M. and Daniel A. Levinthal. "Innovation and Learning: The Two Faces of R&D." Economic Journal 99 (1989): 569-596.

Daft, Richard L. and Robert H. Lengel. "Organizational Information Requirements, Media Richness and Structural Design." Management Science 32 5 (1986): 554-570.

Davenport, Thomas H., Robert G. Eccles, and Laurence Prusak. "Information Politics." Sloan Management Review 34 1 (1992): 53-65.

Diffenbach, John. "Corporate Environmental Analysis in Large US Corporations," Long Range Planning 16 3 (1983): 107-116.

Duncan, R. B. "Characteristics of Organizational Environment and Perceived Environmental Uncertainty." Administrative Science Quarterly 17 (1972): 313-327.

Durney, Christopher P. and Richard G. Donnelly. "A Portfolio Approach to Keeping Abreast of Emerging Technology." Proceedings of the International Association of Management of Technology 2004 International Conference, Washington, District of Columbia (2004).

Edvinsson, Leif and Patrick Sullivan. "Developing a Model for Managing Intellectual Capital," European Management Journal 14 4, (1996): 356-364.

Eisner, Alan B. "The Effects of Rapid Environmental Change on Competitive Strategies: An Organizational Learning Perspective." Academy of Strategic Management Journal 2 (2003): 33-48.

Fahey, L. and W. King. "Environmental Scanning in Corporate Planning." Business Horizons 20 4 (1977): 61-71.

Galbraith, J. R. Organization Design. Reading, MA: Addison-Wesley, 1977.

Gantz, John F., Christopher Chute, Alex Manfrediz, Stephen Minton, David Reinsel, Wolfgang Schlichting, Anna Toncheva. "The Diverse and Exploding Digital Universe: An IDC White Paper." IDC (2008). Retrieved on May 1, 2012.

Gilder, George. Microcosm. New York: Simon & Schuster, 1989.

Gizmo's Freeware. "Probably the Best Free Security List in the World." Accessed on May 1, 2012.

Hambrick, D. "Environmental Scanning and Organizational Strategy." Strategic Management Journal 3 2 (1982): 159-174.

Internet World Stats. "World Internet Usage and Population Statistics December 31, 2011." Updated April 28, 2012. Accessed May, 1, 2012. www.internetworldstats.com/stats7.htm

Jain, Subhash C. "Environmental Scanning in U. S. Corporations," Long Range Planning 17 (1984): 117-128.

Kanter, Rosabeth. The Change Masters. New York: Simon and Schuster, 1984.

Kerssens-Van Drongelen Inge C., Petra C. de Weerd-Nederhof, and Olaf A. M. Fisscher. "Describing the Issues of Knowledge Management in R&D : Towards a Communication and Analysis Tool." R & D Management 26 3 (1996): 213.

Lenz, R. T. and Jack L. Engledow. "Environmental Analysis Units and Strategic Decision-Making : A Field Study of Selected 'Leading-Edge' Corporations," Strategic Management Journal 7 1 (1986): 69-89.

Leonard-Barton, Dorothy. Wellsprings of Innovation. Boston, MA: Harvard Business School Press, 1995.

Lozada, Hector R. and Roger J. Calantone. "Scanning Behavior and the Process of Organizational Innovation." Journal of Managerial Issues 8 3, (1996): 310 - 325.

Maier Jerry L. Environmental Scanning for Information Technology: An Investigation of How Firms Assess the Information Technology Component of the External Business Environment. Ph.D. Dissertation. Auburn University. 1992.

Micklethwait, John and Adrian Woolridge. The Witch Doctors. New York: Random House, Inc., 1996.

Morgan, Gareth. Images of Organization. California: Sage Publications, Inc., 1986.

Mortara, Letizia, Ruth Thomson, Chris Moore, Kalliopi Armara, Clive Kerr, Robert Phaal, David Probert. "Developing a Technology Intelligence Strategy at Kodak European Research: Scan & Target." Research Technology Management 53 4 (2010): 27-38.

Nochur, Kumar S. and Thomas J. Allen. "Do Nominated Boundary Spanners Become Effective Technological Gatekeepers?" IEEE Transactions on Engineering Management 39 3 (1992): 265-269.

Office of Management and Budget, Federal Segment Architecture Methodology (FSAM), 12/8/2008

Panda Security. "One third of all computer viruses that exist were created in the first 10 months of 2010." Accessed May, 1, 2012. http://press.pandasecurity.com/news/one-third-of-all-computer-viruses-that-exist-were-created-in-the-first-10-months-of-2010.

Keeping Abreast: A Knowledge Management (KM) Challenge for Information Technology Service Providers

Pitt, Martyn, and Jason MacVaugh. "Knowledge Management for New Product Development.". Journal of Knowledge Management 12 4 (2008): 101-116.

Richtnér, Anders and Pär Åhlström. "Top Management Control and Knowledge Creation in New Product Development." International Journal of Operations & Production Management 30 10 (2010): 1006-1031.

Rogers, Everett. The Diffusion of Innovations, 5th edition. New York: Free Press, 2003.

Senge, Peter. The Fifth Discipline. New York: Doubleday, 1990.

Stinchcombe, Arthur. Information and Organizations. California: University of California Press, 1990.

Von Hippel, Eric. "Lead Users: a Source of Novel Product Concepts." Management Science 32 7 (1986): 791-805.

Whelan, Eoin, Salvatore Parise, Jasper de Valk, and Rick Aalbers. "Creating Employee Networks That Deliver Open Innovation." MIT Sloan Management Review 53 1 (2011): 37-44.

Whitaker, Randall. "Managing Context in Enterprise Knowledge Process." European Management Journal 14 4 (1996): 399-407.

Wikipedia contributors, "Plagiarism," Wikipedia, The Free Encyclopedia, Updated April 29, 2012. Accessed May, 1, 2012.

Wurman, Richard Saul. Information Anxiety. New York: Bantam Books, 1990.

Yeo, Roland K. "Revisiting the Roots of Learning Organization: A Synthesis of the Learning Organization Literature." The Learning Organization 12 4 (2005): 368-382.

Transformational Leadership and Knowledge Management: It's Effect on Organizational Innovation and Performance

M. Birasnav[1], Mirghani Mohamed[2] & Anjum Razzaque

[1]New York Institute of Technology - Bahrain campus.
[2]Applied Knowledge Sciences, Inc., Leesburg, VA, USA

Introduction

It is important to identify the kind of leadership styles that enable and prepare employees to adapt to technological change. New technology implementation is a continuously changing process that is carried out by organizations that focus on achieving and sustaining a competitive advantage. New technology implementations support improvements to customer service, delivering quality products, and enhancement of employees' skills within organizations (Schepers et al. 2005). Research studies have found that various leadership styles, for example, charismatic leadership (Wang et al. 2005), transformational leadership (Humphreys 2001), and transactional leadership (Appelbaum et al. 1998) are related to technology implementation.

Knowledge Management (KM) and Leadership Style

An organization's technology infrastructure is essential for implementing knowledge management (KM). It is reasoned that with the support of a KM infrastructure, KM processes create organizational knowledge, which identifies significant and positive variations on the organization's competitive advantage. It is important to establish a KM supportive culture within the organization that promotes KM concepts and encourage employees to be involved in KM processes. Organiza-

Transformational Leadership and Knowledge Management: It's Effect on Organizational Innovation and Performance

tional leaders have a responsibility to implement KM processes within their organizations. It is also incumbent of the organization leaders to know that the kind of leadership style they possess is related to KM technology implementation. Politis (2001) found that self-management leadership behavior, transformational leadership, and transactional leadership are significantly and positively related to the behaviors and skills that promote knowledge acquisition. However, leadership behavior related to organizing work, work relationships, and work goals, discourages employees' knowledge acquisition skills. Among transformational leaders, Crawford (2005) found that they are capable to implement activities that encourage employees to become involved in KM processes, such as information acquisition, creation, and application. Consequently, involvement in the KM process supports firms to deliver innovative products and consequently, improves firms' performance (Darroch 2005; Gloet and Terziovski 2004; Malhotra 2005; DeCarolis and Deeds 1999). Therefore, it is evident that in the knowledge-based economy, improving organizational innovation and performance is necessary to ensure success of today's organizations. Though research studies widely examined the role of transformational leadership (Aragon-Correa et al. 2007; Garcia-Morales et al. 2008) and the role of KM process (Darroch 2005; Gloet and Terziovski 2004) on organizational innovation and organizational performance, to date, there has been no research study conducted to analyze the role of KM processes in the relationship between transformational leadership and organizational innovation and between transformational leadership and organizational performance. This chapter presents a first step in this direction, as it conveys the process applied in analyzing the role of the KM process in relationships among transformational leadership, organizational innovation, and organizational performance through a conceptual model (Fig. 1).

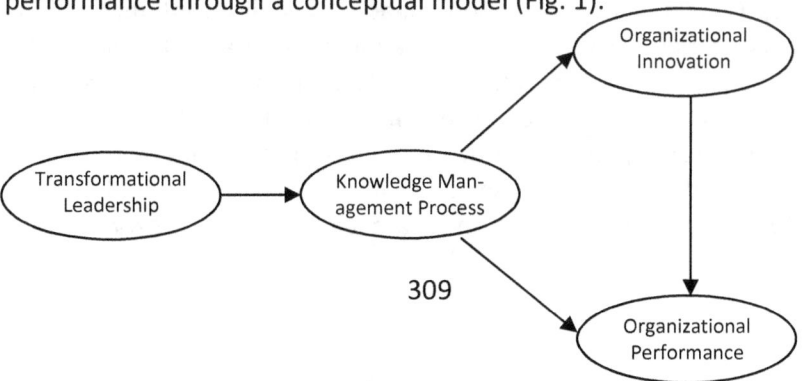

Figure 1: Mediation Role of Knowledge Management Process

Transformational Leadership

Early studies claimed that leadership is a personality trait that leads to success; so one can assume that leaders are born (Ogbonna and Harris 2000). However, Kim (2007) has quoted that a great leader is not born or self-made, but he/she is developed by mentors. Widespread criticism towards this theory led researchers to consider style- and behavior-oriented leadership approach (Ogbonna and Harris 2000). The role and processes of leadership set direction, create alignment, and foster commitment among employees, which leads an organization to make leadership a source of competitive advantage (Kim 2007). Transformational leaders encourage their followers to achieve astonishing work outcomes and to develop self-leadership skills through mentorship and empowerment (Bass 1990; Kelloway et al. 2000; Bass and Riggio 2006; Lowe et al. 1996). Transformational leaders are charismatic leaders as they inspire their followers to be members of shared goals and vision, thus, encouraging their outcomes to be more innovative, and solve problems using a participative style to achieve finer results (Bass and Riggio 2006). This leads employees to perceive transformational leaders as effective and satisfying and employees have a tendency to identify with their leader (Bass, 1990). Transformational leaders have certain behaviors, which are described through four components: (1) idealized influence, (2) inspirational motivation, (3) intellectual stimulation, and (4) individualized consideration (Liu and McMurray 2004). Transformational leaders' idealized influence helps followers to behave in a way that leaders serve as role models by showing a high sense of morality towards their followers. They are risk takers and random; their behavior improves followers' tolerance towards uncertainty; and their leadership style is more adaptive to changing conditions (Nemanich and Keller 2007). Inspirational motivation component inspires and motivates followers and expresses to them a powerful futuristic vision (Bass and Riggio, 2006; Pillai et al. 1999). Intellectual stimulation encourages creativity and innovation through trying new approaches and looking at problems from multiple dimensions. Through individualized consideration, transformational leaders invest time mentoring their followers. They accommodate individual differences by supporting a two-way communication channel. Their behavior of succeeding in a supportive atmosphere with effective listening is essential and is a tool they use to commit tasks to followers in order to develop their skills (Bass and Riggio 2006; Pillai et al. 1999).

Knowledge Management (KM)

Since the 90s, businesses have embraced KM to link people, process, and technology to achieve the best out of information, collaboration, and experiences with an agenda of accomplishing better organizational growth rate and performance level (Guptill 2005). KM is considered a tool that helps to sustain competitive advantage in the turbulent market environment (Joia and Lemos 2010). According to Wickramasinghe et al. (2005) businesses have shifted their focus from being manufacturing-oriented (valuing physical assets) to service-oriented (valuing knowledge assets). Knowledge exists in the form of two types: (1) tacit and (2) explicit. Tacit knowledge is difficult to imitate, more valuable, and cannot be fully utilized (Jimes and Lucardie 2003). In contrast, explicit knowledge is evidence-based, easy to manage, documentable and distributable (Jimes and Lucardie 2003; Mansingh et al. 2009). Knowledge has immense potential to achieve and sustain a competitive advantage and an organization's strategies should be formulated to manage knowledge to properly utilize it within an organization. KM is defined as "the management function responsible for regular selection, implementation and evaluation of knowledge strategies that aim at creating an environment to support work with knowledge internal and external to the organization in order to improve organizational performance" (Maier 2005, 433). According to Riano (2010), knowledge is classified based on: (1) know-what, (2) know-how, and (3) know-why. A KM process architecture consisting of the activities of acquiring knowledge, documenting knowledge, transferring knowledge, creating knowledge, and applying knowledge, create and utilize organizational knowledge and intellectual capital (Filius et al. 2000; Bate and Robert 2002). Knowledge acquisition is an activity of acquiring knowledge from inside and outside of an organization. Knowledge documentation pertains to knowledge storage and retrieval, i.e., storing, organizing, and retrieving knowledge in the forms like databases, documents, and codified knowledge. Knowledge creation refers to the creation of both tacit and explicit knowledge through the process of socialization, externalization, combination, and internalization (Nonaka 1994). It should be noted that Knowledge creation is the most valuable activity in medical decision making. Knowledge application is where systems like Decision Support Systems and expert systems, allow individual employees to utilize knowledge possessed by another. While most firms concentrate on capturing or utilizing existing knowledge resources, some organizations, like, Ernst and Young, concentrate on sharing knowledge to ensure all the employees receive the new knowledge (Bate and Robert 2002).

Organizational Innovation and Performance

Organizational innovation is an essential activity for organizational survival and growth, and it must be a major focus in the current turbulent economic environment of today's organizations. Organizational innovation is defined as "the application of ideas that are new to the firm, whether the newness is embodied in products, processes, and management or marketing systems" (Weerawardenaa et al. 2006, 39). Innovation is measured based on the assessment of new production or service rates and changes in internal procedures from previous years (Miller and Friesen 1983). Organizational learning, or learning from past history, plays a key role in organizational innovation (Razzaque and Karolak 2010). Coupled with transformational leadership, organizational learning facilitates organizational innovation, and this relationship is extended to predict organizational performance (Aragon-Correa et al. 2007). According to Antony and Bhattacharyya (2010), organizational performance is defined as "a measure of how well organizations are managed and the value they deliver to customers and other stakeholders (p. 43)." Products or services which are very rare, valuable, and inimitable in the market have potential to positively affect firm performance. Evaluating return on assets, internal resources, and main products or services' sales growth rate of an organization over the past is the way researchers measure performance with reference to their potential competitors (Aragon-Correa et al. 2007).

Transformational Leadership, Knowledge Management, and Organizational Innovation

The knowledge management process has enough potential to play a mediator role in the relationship between transformational leadership and organizational innovation.

Transformational leaders divert employees from routine works, encourage finding creative solutions to ambiguous job-related problems, and keep them more adaptive to new environment (Nemanich and Keller 2007). These behaviors encourage employees to acquire information inside and outside of the organization that creates an external knowledge that has a certain impact on the innovation process (Frishammar and Horte 2005). Crawford (2005) found that transformational leadership behaviors have positive associations with information acquisition. Linking information acquisition with innovation, Frishammar and Horte (2005) have provided enough evidences that acquiring information about the competitors and needs of customers is a prime element for the success of innovation.

Similar to knowledge acquisition, documenting knowledge is an essential stage of the KM process. According to Filius et al. (2000) it involves activities related to documenting knowledge generated during brainstorming sessions and documenting learning from successes and failures of any kind of project carried out by organizations. Success and failure are the outcomes of risk-taking behavior executed by the transformational leaders. Therefore, documentation is necessary for recording these successes or failures to be taught to followers for use on future projects. Thus, transformational leadership is positively associated with information preservation (Nemanich and Vera 2009). Accordingly, a firm's innovation is enhanced by further developing followers' innovative behaviors through organizational learning (Aragon-Correa et al. 2007; Crawford 2005).

To improve an organizational innovative capability, an employee's knowledge must be transferred to other employees within the organization or other units of the organization. Shortening the time to share or transfer the right knowledge can help organizations reduce employees' time spent acquiring knowledge to perform work. However, knowledge sharing and transfer requires significant investment in a technological infrastructure, built for knowledge sharing and transfer. In addition, the transformational leadership style is more effective for sharing knowledge than other leadership styles (Bryant 2003). It has been found that employees, who work under transformational leaders, perceive that new technology is very useful for achieving organizational goals, especially when leaders clearly explain the purpose of implementing the technology (Schepers et al. 2005). It is believed that sharing the right knowledge during brainstorming sessions or quality circles increases the chances to improve employees' innovative behaviors. It has also been found that knowledge sharing improves technological innovation (Ipe 2003; Scarbrough 2003).

Involvement in the knowledge creating process enables employees to generate new and different ideas and knowledge from their experiences (Bryant 2003). The four behaviors of transformational leadership correlate with information creation (Crawford 2005) and transformational leaders are the sources for new idea development and encouraging employees to create and implement their ideas through new process and product development. (Birasnav et al. 2011). Researchers have confirmed that the linkage between knowledge creation and innovation leads to improvement of firm innovation (Baldwin and Hanel 2003; Dougherty 1992; Mascitelli 2000). Knowledge sharing and knowledge creation require motivation at the individual and team level, which places emphasizes that employees should be rewarded for sharing and creating knowledge. Transformational leaders often provide monetary or non-monetary rewards to employees to motivate them to create knowledge and to share (Bass and Riggio 2006). Similarly, transformational leadership correlates with knowledge application (Crawford 2005) and it has been found that transformational leaders encourage employees to apply knowledge generated during job-related problem solving to make decisions. Overall, transformational leaders establish a KM infrastructure, and an innovation-supportive culture, to improve organization innovation (Jung et al. 2003).

Transformational Leadership, Knowledge Management, and Organizational Performance

The knowledge management process has enough potential to play a mediator role in the relationship between transformational leadership and organizational performance.

It has been proven that transformational leaders increase sales performance by implementing human capital-enhancing human resource management (HRM) practices, (Zhu et al. 2005). Their major aim of implementing HRM practices is to improve knowledge and skills. Knowledge creation occurs through the assessment of employee performance when transformational leaders initiate and transform new ideas into new products. Knowledge creation is motivated through offering rewards to develop new ideas and knowledge from personal experiences shared within a team (Bryant 2003). Assessing employees' performance is an activity of HRM that transformational leaders implement within the organization (Zhu et al. 2005).

The transformational leaders' behavior positively affects knowledge acquisition attributes (Politis 2001). Knowledge acquisition attributes have a positive association with organizational performance. In other words, they predict firm profitability, on-time delivery, and quality (Inkpen 1998; Politis 2002). Particularly, it has been found that transformational leaders encourage documentation of knowledge through increasing employees trust level (Podsakoff et al. 1996; Renzl 2006). It is understood that documented knowledge is shared and creates new individual and organizational knowledge that has potential to affect firm performance. Leaders encourage sharing of ideas by offering solutions to others' problems within a team especially when they are rewarded financially or through non-financial appraisals (Bryant 2003). Transformational leadership has a positive association with knowledge sharing, because of their behavior to act as mentors to their followers and, consequently, employees attain all the benefits related to human capital enhancement (Birasnav et al. 2011). Further, knowledge sharing and human capital enhancement have positive associations with firm performance (Zhu et al. 2005; Singh 2008; Lauring and Selmer 2011). However, knowledge is better applied when an organization has systems to convert ideas into innovative revenue generating products and services (Bryant 2003).

Overall, leaders have positive associations with KM process implementation, which aids their effectiveness at improving organizational performance, by allowing them to motivate all employees, establish an equal opportunity environment, and develop measures where they ultimately reward their employees for their performances (Singh 2008). Mohamed et al. (2004) proposes a KM system approach that explains the positive impact of KM process principles on cross-functional team performance and has significant association with financial and non-financial firm performance.

Relation between Organization Innovation and Performance

Organizational innovation is positively related to performance. The rate of innovation of an organization decides its survival and growth in the market. In general, innovation is classified as exploratory (radical) innovation and exploitative (incremental) innovation. Damanpour (1996) considers organizational innovation as the development of new products, services, technologies, managerial systems, plans, and procedures. Further, Aragon-Correa et al. (2007) defines organizational innovation based on the rate of introduction of new products or services and the rate at which organizations change their internal operating practices with reference to their competitors. Since firms have to face extensive numbers of competitors in the markets, uncertainty in the introduction of new technology, and uncertainty in market needs, organizations must improve its innovativeness (Han et al. 1998). Like a new idea replaces the old, innovations replace organizations' image in the market, and it is obvious that firms that are not innovative, reduce themselves of the overall performance level. Supporting these notions, Lin and Chen (2007) found that both exploratory and exploitative innovation has potential to positively affect firm performance. From a research study conducted among sixty nine organizations, Hull and Rothenberg (2008) found that innovation rate has explained significant variance on firm's profitability. It is also proved among Korean firms that creativity has significant association with non-financial performance such as improving product quality and customer satisfaction (Lee and Choi 2003). It is also evidenced from Lee and Choi's research findings that innovations are related to corporate performance.

Conclusion

It is witnessed in many firms that they strive to identify new ways that help to improve their return on assets, sales volume, quality of the products, and to reduce cost. One of the ways, nowadays, that many firms concentrate is increasing the rate of radical and incremental innovation, which supports firms to survive in today's competitive environment as well as facilitate the capture of a significant percentage of market share. In this direction, this chapter carried out a review of literature based on a conceptual model that explained the antecedents of innovation and performance, and findings are summarized based on the relationships mentioned in the model. It is identified that transformational leadership and KM process are the antecedents of organizational innovation and performance in the turbulent economic environment in which many firms survive.

It is transformational leaders who encourage their followers to acquire knowledge, transfer knowledge, document knowledge, create knowledge, and apply knowledge. Creating a new knowledge increases innovation rate of a particular company. Subsequently, it builds intellectual capital pool. It is even witnessed in many companies, for example, Microsoft, Oracle, Dell that possess more number of patents to date because of the creation of new and unique knowledge. This is viable only when leaders create a vision for the future of the organization, develop human capital, and motivate employees. Since transformational leaders do perform these activities along with the implementation of KM programs, firms deliver strong financial performance. Therefore, focus-shift is required in the HRM practices, particularly, in training given to their human capital. For example, transformational leadership development programs should be conducted among employees who possess human capital instead of traditional training.

Importantly, it is required to examine the conceptual model and propositions stated in this chapter. This examination would help organizations to identify at what extent their leaders are involved in implementation of KM process and the extent at which KM process helps to increase innovation as well as performance. In this direction, Multifactor Leadership Questionnaire (Bass and Avolio 1995), KM process measure (Filius et al. 2000), and organizational innovation and organizational performance measures (Aragon-Correa et al. 2007) can be used to examine the proposed model in future.

There seems to be a further study of focusing on KM infrastructure such as corporate culture and new technology implementation, for example, cloud computing, in addition to the conceptual model. It is reasoned that transformational leaders focus on establishment of supportive culture to implement KM process in their organizations.

References

Antony, J. P. and Bhattacharyya, S. (2010), "Measuring organizational performance and organizational excellence of SMEs - Part 2: An empirical study on SMEs in India", Measuring Business Excellence, Vol. 14 No. 3, 42-52.

Appelbaum, S. H., St-Pierre, N. and Glavas, W. (1998), "Strategic organizational change: the role of leadership, learning, motivation and productivity", Management Decision, Vol. 36 No. 5, pp. 289-301.

Aragon-Correa, J. A., Garcia-Morales, V. J. and Cordon-Pozo, E. (2007), "Leadership and organizational learning's role on innovation and performance: Lessons from Spain", Industrial Marketing Management, Vol. 36, pp. 349-359.

Baldwin, J. R. and Hanel, P. (2003), Innovation and knowledge creation in an open economy: Canadian industry and international implications, Cambridge University Press Cambridge, UK.

Transformational Leadership and Knowledge Management: It's Effect on Organizational Innovation and Performance

Bass, B. M. (1990), "From Transactional to Transformational Leadership: Learning to Share the Vision", Organizational Dynamics, Vol. 18 No. 3, pp. 19-31.

Bass, B. M. and Avolio, B. J. (1995), The Multifactor Leadership Questionnaire, Mind Garden, Palo Alto, CA.

Bass, B. M. and Riggio, R. E. (2006), Transformational Leadership, Lawrence Erlbaum Associates, Mahwah, New Jersey.

Bate, S. and Robert, G. (2002), "Knowledge Management and Communities of Practice in the Private: Lessons for Modernizing the National Health Service England And Wales", Public Administration, Vol. 80 No. 4, pp. 643-663.

Birasnav, M. Rangnekar, S. and Dalpati, A. (2011), "Transformational leadership and human capital benefits: The role of knowledge management, Leadership & Organization Development Journal, Vol. 32 No. 2, pp. 106-126.

Bryant, S. E. (2003), "The Role of Transformational and Transactional Leadership in Creating, Sharing and Exploiting Organizational Knowledge", Leadership & Organizational Studies, Vol. 9 No. 4, pp. 32-44.

Crawford, C. B. (2005), "Effects of transformational leadership and organizational position on knowledge management", Journal of Knowledge Management, Vol. 9 No. 6, pp. 6-16.

Damanpour, F. (1996), "Organizational complexity and innovation: Developing and testing multiple contingency models", Management Science, Vol. 42 No. 5, pp. 693-716.

Darroch, J. (2005), "Knowledge management, innovation and firm performance", Journal of Knowledge Management, Vol. 9 No. 3, pp. 101-115.

DeCarolis, D. M. and Deeds, D. L. (1999), "The impact of stocks and flows of organizational knowledge on firm performance: An empirical investigation of the biotechnology industry", Strategic Management Journal, Vol. 20 No. 10, pp. 953-968.

Dougherty, D. (1992), "A practice-centered model of organizational renewal through product innovation", Strategic Management Journal, Vol. 13 No. S1, pp. 77-92.

Filius, R., de Jong, J. A. and Roelofs, E. C. (2000), "Knowledge management in the HRD office: A comparison of three cases", Journal of Workplace Learning, Vol. 12 No. 7, pp. 286-295.

Frishammar, J. and Horte, S. A. (2005), "Managing External Information in Manufacturing Firms: The Impact on Innovation Performance", Journal of Production Innovation Management, Vol. 22, pp. 251-266.

Garcia-Morales, V. J., Matias-Reche, F. and Hurtado-Torres, N. (2008), "Influence of transformational leadership on organizational innovation and performance depending on the level of organizational learning in the pharmaceutical sector", Journal of Organizational Change Management, Vol. 21 No. 2, pp.188-212.

Gloet, M. and Terziovski, M. (2004), "Exploring the relationship between knowledge management practices and innovation performance", Journal of Manufacturing Technology Management, Vol. 15 No. 5, pp. 402-409.

Guptill, J. (2005), "Knowledge Management in Health Care", Journal of Health Care Finance, Vol. 31 No. 3, pp. 10-14.

Han, J. K., Namwoon, K. and Srivastava, R. K. (1998), "Market orientation and organizational performance: is innovation a missing link?", Journal of Marketing, Vol. 62, pp.30-45.

Hull, C. E. and Rothenberg, S. (2008), "Firm performance: The interactions of Corporate social performance with Innovation and industry differentiation", Strategic Management Journal, Vol. 29, pp. 781-789.

Humphreys, J. H. (2001), "The relationship with support for E-Commerce and emerging technology", Journal of Management Research, Vol. 1 No, 3, pp. 149-159.

Inkpen A. C. (1998), "Learning and knowledge acquisition through international strategic alliances", Academy of Management Executive, Vol. 12 No. 4, pp. 69-80.

Ipe, M. (2003), "Knowledge Sharing in Organizations: A Conceptual Framework", Human Resource Development Review, Vol. 2 No. 4, pp. 337-359.

Jimes, C. and Lucardie, L. (2003), "Reconsidering the tacit-explicit distinction - A move toward functional (tacit) knowledge management", Electronic Journal of Knowledge Management, Vol. 1 No. 1, pp. 23-32.

Joia, L. A. and Lemos, B. (2010), "Relevant factors for tacit knowledge transfer within organisations", Journal of Knowledge Management, Vol. 14 No. 3, pp. 410-427.

Jung, D. I., Chow, C. and Wu, A. (2003), "The role of transformational leadership in enhancing organizational innovation: Hypotheses and some preliminary findings", The Leadership Quarterly, Vol. 14 No. 4/5, pp. 525-544.

Kelloway, E. K., Barling, J. and Helleur, J. (2000), "Enhancing transformational leadership: The role of training and feedback", Leadership & Organization Development Journal, Vol. 21 No. 3, pp. 145-149.

Kim, S. (2007), "Learning goal orientation, formal mentoring, and leadership competence in HRD - A conceptual model", Journal of European Industrial Training, Vol. 31 No. 3, pp. 181-194.

Lauring, J. and Selmer, J. (2011), "Multicultural organizations: Common language, knowledge sharing and performance", Personnel Review, Vol. 14 No. 3, pp. 324-343.

Lee, H. and Choi, B. (2003), "Knowledge Management Enablers, Processes, and Organizational Performance: An Integrative View and Empirical Examination", Journal of Management Information Systems, Vol. 20 No. 1, pp. 179-228.

Lin, C. Y. and Chen, M. Y. (2007), "Does innovation lead to performance? An empirical study of SMEs in Taiwan", Management Research News, Vol. 30 No. 2, pp. 115-132

Liu, L. and McMurray, A. J. (2004), "Frontline leaders - The entry point for leadership development in the manufacturing industry", Journal of European Industrial Training, Vol. 28 No. 2/3/4, pp. 339-352.

Lowe, K. B., Kroeck, K. G. and Sivasubramaniam, N. (1996), "Effectiveness Correlates of Transformational and transactional Leadership: A Meta-analytic Review of the MLQ Literature", Leadership Quarterly, Vol. 7 No. 3, pp. 385-425.

Maier, R. (2005), "Modeling knowledge work for the design of knowledge infrastructures", Journal of Universal Computer Science, Vol. 11 No. 4, pp. 429-451.

Malhotra, Y. (2005), "Integrating knowledge management technologies in organizational business processes: Getting real time enterprises to deliver real business performance", Journal of Knowledge Management, Vol. 9 No. 1, pp. 7-28.

Mansingh, G., Osei-Bryson, K. M. and Reichgelt, H. (2009), "Issues in knowledge access, retrieval and sharing - Case studies in a Caribbean health sector", Expert Systems with Applications, Vol. 36, pp. 2853-2863.

Mascitelli, R. (2000), "From Experience: Harnessing Tacit Knowledge to Achieve Breakthrough Innovation", Journal of Product Innovation Management, Vol. 17 No. 3, pp. 179-193.

Miller, D. and Friesen, P. H. (1983), "Strategy-making and environment: The third link", Strategic Management Journal, Vol. 4, pp. 221-235.

Mohamed, M., Stankosky, M. and Murray, A. (2004), "Applying knowledge management principles to enhance cross-functional team performance", Journal of Knowledge Management, Vol. 8 No. 3, pp. 127-142.

Nemanich, L. A. and Keller, R. T. (2007), "Transformational leadership in an acquisition: A field study of employees", The Leadership Quarterly, Vol. 18, pp. 49-68.

Nemanich, L. A. and Vera, D. (2009), "Transformational leadership and ambidexterity in the context of an acquisition", The Leadership Quarterly, Vol. 20 No. 1, pp. 19-33.

Nonaka, I. (1994), "A Dynamic Theory of Organizational Knowledge Creation", Organization Science, Vol. 5 No. 1, pp. 14-37.

Ogbonna, E. and Harris, L. C. (2000), "Leadership style, organizational culture and performance: Empirical evidence from UK companies", International Journal of Human Resource Management, Vol. 11, No. 4, pp. 766-788.

Pillai, R. Schriesheim, C. A. and Williams, E. S. (1999), "Fairness Perceptions and Trust as Mediators for Transformational and Transactional Leadership: A Two-Sample Study", Journal of Management, Vol. 25 No. 6, pp. 897-933.

Podsakoff, P. M., MacKenzie, S. B. and Bommer, W. H. (1996), "Transformational Leader Behaviors and Substitutes for Leadership as Determinants of Employee Satisfaction, Commitment, Trust, and Organizational Citizenship Behaviors", Journal of Management, Vol. 22 No. 2, pp. 259-298.

Politis, J. D. (2001), "The relationship of various leadership styles to knowledge management", Leadership & Organization Development Journal, Vol. 22 No. 7/8, pp. 354-364.

Politis, J. D. (2002), "Transformational and transactional leadership enabling (disabling) knowledge acquisition of self-managed teams: The consequences of performance", Leadership & Organization Development Journal, Vol. 23 No. 4, pp. 186-197.

Razzaque, A. and Karolak, M. M. (2010), "Building a Knowledge Management System for the E-Health Knowledge Society", Journal of Economic Development, Management, IT, Finance and Marketing, Vol. 2 No. 2, pp. 23-40.

Renzl, B. (2006), "Trust in management and knowledge sharing: The mediating effects of fear and knowledge documentation," Omega, Vol. 36 No. 2, pp. 206-220.

Riano, D. (2010), "A Knowledge-Management Architecture to Integrate and to Share Medical and Clinical Data, Information, and Knowledge", in Riano, D., ten Teije, A., Miksch, S. and Peleg, M. (Eds), Knowledge Representation for Health-Care: Data, Processes and Guidelines, Springer Berlin / Heidelberg, pp. 180-194.

Scarbrough, H. (2003), "Knowledge management, HRM and the innovation process", International Journal of Manpower, Vol. 24 No. 5, pp. 501-516.

Schepers, J., Wetzels, M. and de Ruyter, K. (2005), "Leadership styles in technology acceptance: do followers practice what leaders preach?", Managing Service Quality, Vol. 15 No. 6, pp. 496-508.

Singh, S. K. (2008), "Role of leadership in knowledge management: A study", Journal of Knowledge Management, Vol. 12 No. 4, pp. 3-15.

Wang, E. Chou, H. and Jiang, J. (2005), "The impacts of charismatic leadership style on team cohesiveness and overall performance during ERP implementation", International Journal of Project Management, Vol. 23 No. 3, pp. 173-180.

Weerawardenaa, J., O'Cassb, A. and Julian, C. (2006), "Does industry matter? Examining the role of industry structure and organizational learning in innovation and brand performance", Journal of Business Research, Vol. 59, pp. 37-45.

Wickramasinghe, N., Gupta, J. N. D. and Sharma, S. K. 2005. (2005), Creating Knowledge-Based Healthcare Organizations, Idea Group Publishing: Hershey, PA.

Zhu, W., Chew, I. K. H. and Spangler, W. D. (2005), "CEO transformational leadership and organizational outcomes: The mediating role of human capital enhancing human resource management", Leadership Quarterly, Vol. 16 No.1, pp. 39-52.

Cyber-and Semantic Technology Integration for Knowledge Awareness

Lakita Conley-Ware

New York Institute of Technology, Vancouver, BC, Canada

Introduction

Organizational rule-of-thumb strategies or heuristics and departmental expertise provide the knowledge and intelligence for an organization. However, in many organizations where knowledge is captured, it is isolated in specialty databases or uploaded to an inconsistent maze of cyber sites which utilize an array of web technologies. Such storage provides access to potential knowledge at a data or at best an informational level. Cross subject integration as a way to provide meaningful knowledge and a way to "connect the links" across an organization are difficult to create using conventional technical methods. An understanding of the cyber technology network in conjunction with a meaningful set of models that transverse across the cyber highway and corporate repositories, can provide an avenue for the future of the knowledge focused organization. The objective of this chapter is to illustrate how the model called the Anatomy of Cyber-Technology©, in conjunction with heuristic driven semantics and social media, can provide a technical path called "socialnomic." This technical path can greatly assist in building sustainable knowledge awareness in an organization.

The Data to Knowledge Problem Domain in an Organization

Today, across many organizations, private and Government, there is an atrophy of expertise in an organization's professional staffing population. The departure of the baby boomer subject matter from the business community, the lack of a collection mechanism to store organizational heuristics or lessons learned and the continued use of organizational data silo repositories have contributed to the loss of organizational knowledge. In general, products designed strictly to elicit knowledge from experts do not typically include comprehensive processes. These products have a tendency to be biased, toward the experience of the knowledge elicitor. Traditional knowledge management (KM) practices have not been able to illustrate professional perspectives integrated with an expert's mental aggregates which comprise their non-biased mental ontologies. In an organization, these mental ontologies incorporate the heuristics of their professional day-to-day operations. These ontologies tend to reside only within the private data sources of the organizational experts. At best, many organizations manage to build linkages between data points in organizational warehouses and repositories which are, typically, loosely defined in a traditional relational database format. However, this format does not provide meaning to these data points. A structure is needed that would provide a technical mechanism to capture the intellectual capital, heuristics and implicit knowledge from the experts as well as any cross pollination of organizational division knowledge. Such a system would then support areas of on-going knowledge sustainment in an organization.

Knowledge by Many Different Understandings

There appears to be varying definitions of the term knowledge. For the purpose of this chapter, knowledge is an integrated concept, consisting of experiences, values, contextual information and expert views. Knowledge can originate from an expert and/or the "knower". In organizations, knowledge is embodied in the firm's documented repositories and intellectual capital of its staff (Davenport 2000; Miller and Morris 1999). There are three types of knowledge which were defined during the early explorations of Artificial Intelligence/Expert Systems. They are explicit, heuristic and tacit knowledge. (Hayes-Roth 1983)

Knowledge Management (KM) embodies the capture, acquisition, elicitation, organization, transfer and utilization of knowledge for leveraging relevant knowledge assets. These assets are aimed at improving effectiveness, efficiency and innovation of an organization (Cook and Brown 1999; Stankosky 1999, 2005). There are two key strategies for KM – collaboration and codification. KM systems are used for identification and representation of knowledge using methodology tools such as ontology (Stankosky 1999, 2005; Davenport 2000). Ontologies, taxonomies and graphical visualizations are all types of technologies that can support the elicitation of knowledge.

Knowledge driven technologies can support the packaging of semantics. Semantics can be used to wrap current cyber-technologies which promote social interaction and avenues for knowledge sharing. Here begins the building of a cyber-knowledge network.

Many organizations have moved to the utilization of social networks and blogs to capture intellectual capital. However, the connections between different types of social networks and blogs are only through hyperlinks. In the Web 1.0 and 2.0 World, there are no automatic linkage mechanisms to integrate content as a way to gain knowledgeable intelligence. For instance, content in Facebook, Blogsters and Daily-Booth can only be connected by use of a hyperlink that only provides the reader the ability to make assumptions about the connections between layers of unstructured text and images

The Cyber Generation Knowledge Professional (CGKP) vs. the Traditional Knowledge Expert/Engineer

The traditional knowledge expert utilizes a tool set built on heuristic libraries and codified-to-non-codified implicit and tacit knowledge. These information oriented systems are configured in a range of structured components – from relational databases to taxonomically configured data dictionaries.

The CGKP has to redefine traditional knowledge engineering methodologies to meet the extremely aggressive changes that pertain to the cyber world. This professional must be versed in an array of cyber-technologies, as well as an expert in many traditional knowledge base technologies. The typical CGKP is intimate with the foundations of the cyber and social technologies. However, no one person can be a true expert in all the technology categories that encompass cyberspace. The CGKP can apply traditional knowledge engineering skills to new networks when working with the subject matter expert (SME), but they also need to understand the versatilities and changes that take place in the cyberspace technology industry. Therefore, utilization of tools that educate these experts on cyberspace technology is critical. One tool that provides for the exploitation of cyber technologies is the Anatomy of CyberSpace © (ACS). (Conley-Ware, 2010) The ACS explores the use and technical features of cyberspace technologies. Example are: virtual worlds, social media, gaming, multimedia with 3D and video-to-text chat systems, all of which represent ways to capture knowledge.

The CGKP must have a better understanding of the KM technologies which can be viewed as a continuum of information. This continuum can support knowledge growth and, provide a path that starts with data and continues to actionable intelligence. The continuum begins with the movement of data-to-data and incorporates KM directed technologies. These include:

- meta-data repositories that have feeds from entity extractors
- data warehouses and data marts
- content and records management systems

From data-to-data in the continuum, it moves to data-to-metadata then metadata-to-people and people-to-people. Under the data-to-metadata, the umbrellas of technologies that utilize or collect knowledge are:

- taxonomies and ontologies
- the semantic web and structured databases that can store RDF schemas(resource description framework) link analysis tools with feeds to entity extractor
- business intelligence technologies such as expert systems and decision support systems

- cloud architectures for structured and unstructured data (all in support of the big data needs)

People-to-metadata are the set of technologies that provide for search and discovery of data and knowledge. Such technologies are:

- informational search and retrieval applications such as FAST, SHAREPOINT or GOOGLE Search Appliance or open source option, i.e., Soir Lucene
- faceted or navigational search tools
- data mining and pattern matching systems
- image recognition search tools
- visualizations such as link analysis and statistical measuring tools
- business analysis applications such as CRMs

There are also People-to-People technologies that deal with unstructured data and provide person-to-person interactions. Such technologies are:

- two way messaging systems like instant messaging and Sametime
- social medias applications found in cyberspace like Facebook and MySpace
- blogs, micro blogs and wikis
- social media applications: social bookmarking, i.e., Delicious.com, social news, i.e., DIGG, social networking, i.e., Facebook, Friendster, Twitter, Social Video"ing"- i.e. YouTube
- big data portals designed for advanced collections and collaboration
- audiopedia applications
- video and audio collaboration tools
- virtual world applications

In using People-to-People directed technologies, semantics can provide a pathway between the types of content that can be launched in an array of cyber networks. However, the CGKP must understand social media in terms of capturing, discovering and disseminating knowledge.

Cyber-and Semantic Technology Integration for Knowledge Awareness

The modern day CGKP needs to be skilled in repeatable knowledge life cycles, processes that allow for the use of cyber educational tools, such as the Anatomy of CyberSpace© and the more sophisticated ways to elicit knowledge from the subject matter experts. Just as important, they need to be able to elicit the personal knowledge base from explorers of knowledge that leave their foot print on blogs, wikis and other forms of expert driven social media. This array of skills can be obtained through the use of advanced knowledge acquisition tools as well as the utilization of various sophisticated knowledge processing methodologies. This multi-disciplinary background allows CGKPs in the corporate arena to provide the level of knowledge sustainment which is needed in today's Knowledge-Centric Organizations.

Understanding Cyber Technology: The Anatomy of CyberSpace© (ACS)

The Anatomy of Cyberspace© with its assorted ontologies are Internet directed tools that can be used to provide organizational intelligence. This intelligence, in the form of knowledge, can only be acquired through extensive experience with cyberspace technologies or collaboration with Internet subject matter experts (SMEs). Before discussing how this tool can be used for cyber-technology knowledge exploration and exploitation, there needs to be some discussion on what is the Anatomy of CyberSpace© (Conley-Ware 2010).

There are a variety of texts and Internet sources available that discuss cyber-technology. There are static visualizations and information highways that focus on Web 2.0 and other advanced technologies. Several of these have been designed to visually mimic various subway transit systems. However, it should not be assumed that these public visuals can be used to show cyber-technology relationships, integrations, technology linkages, or technology embedding factors for various cyber technologies. Some cyber applications have moved to creating labels for country versions of specific cyber-pipes, i.e., Google US, Google China, etc. None of these tools; however, explore their overall operational processes and how they function with other Internet technologies.

The Anatomy of Cyberspace© is interactive and a dynamic knowledge model that closes the gap in understanding cyber technologies; from how applications and relationships work to technology linkages where possible. It was built as a key resource product for a research knowledge-driven methodology which explored new ways of knowledge. The ACS consists of a layer of knowledge models, all configured in a series of ontologies as a way to provide user insight into cyber-technology integration points. It also provides some understanding on possible hidden locations of cyber-back-doors. Though comprehensive, at the time it was originally built, information collection and analysis must be on-going for the ACS in order to keep pace with the rapid evolution of advanced IT technology for the Internet. Therefore, the Anatomy of Cyberspace© is a "living tool" that must parallel the deployments of new Internet technologies.

When evaluating the new advances in cyber technologies, it is often difficult to determine the origins for its usage. Such questions as

- Is it the new technology?
- Is it the integration of an old with a new technology?
- Is it the morphing of an existing cyber-technology?

During this tool's early research analysis and development, the researcher determined that cyberspace technologies could be classified and grouped into the following technology focused services:

1. Online communications service
2. Online information service
3. Online media service
4. Online educational learning or e-learning services
5. Level 3 Internet application service: Web 2.0, public business interactive portals, multi-level web applications, e-business, e-auctions
6. Online virtual communications and
7. Online social network services

Each of the seven service areas in the ACS include the names of the technology, the technology description as described above, the current URL and where applicable, the active links for demonstrations.

Cyber-and Semantic Technology Integration for Knowledge Awareness

These seven services provide a pathway for the primary cyberspace technologies, which are classified and grouped into the following:

- Embedded technologies and the associated applications
- Morphed technologies
- Integration of technologies
- New technologies (Conley-Ware, 2010)

Each arm of the ACS is broken down into components that cover descriptions of the technology features and/or examples and/or explanations of its existence and/or interactive components of a given feature:

- The online communications arm breaks cyberspace technologies into categories and from there into the most popular applications in these categories. Some of which are email: gmail, cox mail, yahoo mail, Comcast mail, AOL and hotmail. Other technologies are unified communications and collaborations, instant messaging engines, blogs of various types and chat networks.
- The online informational arm covers technologies such as those focused on video and photography, RSS feeds, personal profiling, blackboards, wikis, forums and Level 1 of Web 1.0 directed site.
- Online media works around the details of YouTube and other Video or imagery directed services.
- Online education and E-Learning includes computer based-training media, WebCT, the interactive classroom and video internet.
- On-line social network services refer to online communities which reflect social media networks based in various countries.
- The On-line virtual communications arm consist of online gaming, 2D virtual communities, augmented realities, 3D virtual communities with avatars and 3D virtual communities without dimensional communities.
- The large and more diverse arm is Level 3 – Web 2.0 public business applications, which include items such as craigslist, eBay, Amazon and various other electronic businesses.

All these areas of cyberspace offer socialization features to the 21st century cyberspace surfer. For instance, games represent social gaming technologies that may or may not connect to other related applications, but they do offer a social connection for those in the gaming community. ACS allows a user to transverse several layers deep to explore the many avenues of various gaming cyber communities. Figure 1: The Anatomy of Cyber Technology, provides a visual of the top seven services and some of the secondary extensions.

The three types of knowledge are used for the steps associated with the cyber-technology collections:

- Explicit knowledge collection - codified and documented
- *Tacit knowledge collection* - the expert's heuristics
- *Implicit knowledge collection* - collaborative knowledge from diverse backgrounds

The layers of maps and models illustrated in Figure 1 are the results from the original research exploration for the knowledge collection. The sources of reference for explicit knowledge were the various brand names and cyber technology types that were identified in the original research for the construction of ACS, all from a vendor and user perspective. Tacit knowledge came from research investigations and experiences of numerous long-time users of the Internet (long-time users are equal to at least 5 to 10 years of experience with at least 5 of the cyberspace services identified from the Anatomy of Cyberspace©). This user information was collected and codified over the course of the three years in which ACS emerged. Implicit knowledge collection originated from group interviews with seasoned 19 to mid-20 year olds that consider themselves cyberspace "geeks". Here, cyber geeks are defined as a college graduate or high school graduate that played 10 or more hours of computer on-line games and other cyber network activities per week for at least 1.5 to 5 years. These geeks had activity recorded in social networks 4 out of 7 days a week. Random interview questions to these geeks covered cyberspace gaming, various cyber- technology integration, virtual world participation, social networking and technology hybrids. All interview information was researched and validated using vendor material and other technology

Cyber-and Semantic Technology Integration for Knowledge Awareness

documentation prior to its inclusion in the development of the Anatomy of Cyberspace© (Conley-Ware 2010) knowledge model.

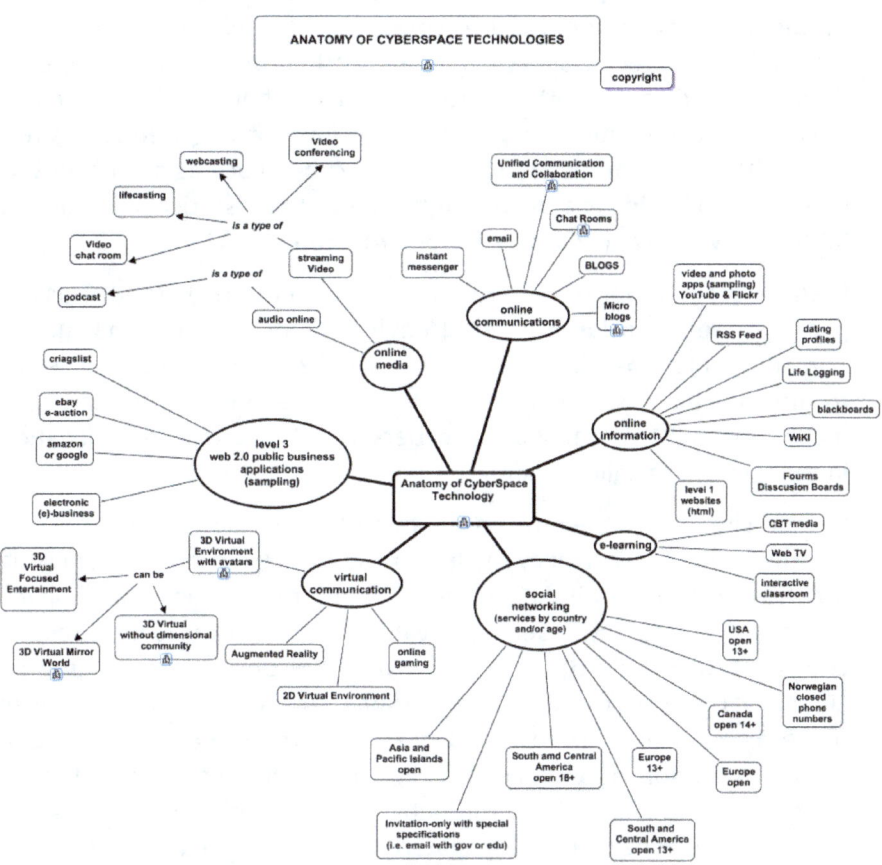

Figure 1: The Anatomy of Cyber Space ©: Cyber-Technology Understanding

To better understand some of the collections in these services, the following is a breakdown of sub-layers under the Online virtual communications arm of the ACS. There are several components to Virtual communications. The one described in this extraction is 3D Virtual Communications with avatars.

The virtual 3-D Internet environment starts with communications from one person to the next through an animated character. These animations are called avatars. The goal of this virtual world is to imitate or mimic that which represents everyday life. In many cases today, these avatars are used to represent a fantasy life of a real world individual. Since the characters are all virtual, real world laws and policies appear to be non-existent. In this virtual world an individual's avatar can maintain and function at a super human level, if the user so desires. These 3D virtual worlds are listed within cyberspace as semi-free services. The following is a list of only some of the historical and current 3D Virtual World applications listed in ACS today:

MetaVerse: A player must create a parallel to the real world. This application creates a fantasy world environment to mirror imaginative human interactions. Avatars can be customized to disguise themselves from other players. This is associated with Second Life which is the most famous 3D virtual world in cyberspace. It had its central location in a virtual space called Linden.

Second Life: This is the most in-depth and diverse of the avatar driven communities. The currency in this virtual world can be profit making for those that travel in Second life. The currency is in Liden dollars. This type of currency is semi-equivalent to American dollars. Second Life is a broad multi-tier social network. It is operated or hosted by Linden Labs Incorporated. Organizations, academia and other businesses can develop virtual environments to promote online real world life collaboration, interactive training or virtual activities and functions. A Second Life grid environment is how a world within this application is developed and propagated. Speech and real-time text enabled environments are also available to a developer:

- www.secondlife.com.
- RocketOn: This is an online virtual gaming environment.
- There.com: This is an avatar based online gaming and chat room virtual world. This system retired in 2010.
- Real Extend/Open Sim Project and platform: This provides a user with open source code for the purpose of creating plugs into Sec-

ond Life without having Second life membership. This would be considered a 3D Web. www.realxtend.com.
- OLIVE/platform: Formerly one half of the There.com. This platform utilizes with Forterra, a 3D software development tool which provides the ability for organizations to build 3D worlds within an intra- and extra-net environment. http://www.forterrainc.com.
- Vivify Focus: This is a 3D avatar which can be used with Facebook and AIM. The browser plug-in program site is www.vivaty.com (This site became inactive with a total closure during the spring of 2011).
- VSIDE: This originally was owned in part by AOL and the other owner was Dopplerganger, Inc. This is an avatar based environment which is directed to a teen audience. It is a virtual party house for teens. www.vside.com.
- Worlds.com: The Company by the same name created this virtual world. This is one of the oldest virtual world locations (on the Internet- founded in 1994). This is a 3rd party platform having associations with Red Light Center. World.com has grown from just having limited avatars to being very Second Life looking. It allows users to create their own avatars, share experiences in various communities and teleport throughout the World.com virtual environment. Worlds.com current "claim to fame" is its ability to take its users from the one dimensional web page experience, to the virtual experience of various web page environments. Instead of a browsing a movie listing and looking at clips, a user can attend a movie clip with other avatars. Users also have "chat" and video in this virtual world. www.world.com.
- A World of My Own (AWOMO): This is a gaming portal where the only communication is via the gaming avatar. This is a UK based development environment. http://www.awomo.com.
- Cybertown First: This is one of the early generation avatar environments. It came online in 1998, but has not been supported with development updates for more than 5 years.

- HiPiHI China: This is a parallel application out of China. It is comparable to America's Second life. All dialogue is in Chinese. www.hipihi.com/index_english_html.
- Twinity 3D: This is an avatar application that is a cross between mirror imaging 3D and imaginative (metaverse). All real tours and metaverse experiences are focused in Germany. The content is in English. This is a social and dating oriented virtual world environment. It offers 3D chat across many of its communities. Users can attend parties, build their own apartments, and visit virtual locations from Miami Beach, Florida to virtual London, England. http://twinity.com.

As of 2011, many of these long time virtual worlds are still in operation.

The ACS has been designed to provide the user with an understanding of the cyberspace world as a way to accomplish a variety of technology driven tasks. Such a tool can provide knowledge to the organizational users that are attempting to integrate collaborative knowledge via cyberspace that is sustainable and repeatable into the organization's structure.

Traditional vs. Changes in Knowledge Acquisition through Representation Tools

With organizational knowledge quickly being moved between cooperate data silos, Internet clouds and other knowledge gathering tools within the social media networks, direct collaboration for knowledge exchange has moved to textual socialization. This means that an organization has additional layers of capture and elicitation to make available to their Informational Technology (IT) divisions. Usage of a knowledge format can support these collection and gathering processes.

Knowledge life cycle model formats are evolving models. There are no universal knowledge models that have been adopted across the IT industry. However, there are stages that must be incorporated into any KM life cycle process. The stages start at acquisition and go through representation. These are critical steps when capturing and utilizing

Cyber-and Semantic Technology Integration for Knowledge Awareness

knowledge. The building of a knowledge model is one of the primary steps in any knowledge representation. One must remember that this effort is only as successful as the steps associated with effective knowledge acquisition (Tiwana 2002; Davenport 2000). These steps are critical when dealing with the utilization of knowledge in a cyber network. Most of the techniques used for knowledge capture (also called elicitation) have evolved from expert system methodologies (Milton 2003). Knowledge acquisition takes place during the generation and organization phases of a KM life cycle. To get to a point where knowledge representation can be broken down and implemented accurately in a cyber network, the acquisition process must include: knowledge acquisition, capture and elicitation (KACE).

Data repositories and warehouses, knowledge bases containing codified knowledge, online organizational applications that contain implicit knowledge and the standalone manual repositories of the SME's tacit knowledge only provide minimal organizational support for the type of KACE process needed to develop meaningful knowledge representation systems. Even the emergence of cloud technology has not been able to handle the capture and needs of knowledge representation. The new mode of operation for KACE is the Internet's social media network. However, the "galactic" scope of knowledge encapsulated in cyber applications is still in their infancy stages within organizational structures. To transition to a more flexible structure that utilizes cyberspace technology, knowledge representation practices must be incorporated and understood by the traditional Knowledge Architect/Engineer as well as the CGKP.

A historical relevant understanding of knowledge representation is the following:

> "A multidisciplinary subject that applies theories and techniques from three other fields:
> 1. Logic provides the formal structure and rules of inference.
> 2. Ontology defines the kinds of things that exist in the application domain.

3. *Computation supports the applications that distinguish knowledge representation from pure philosophy "*

(Sowa 2000).

The beginning of knowledge representation must start with the raw form of the knowledge – the data. At this level, the data is typically represented in the form of a model: the entity-entity or entity-attribute. One or both schemas can be propagated into a schema that depicts the relationships between the model types. Another type of model can be created as an outgrowth of the entity-attribute model. It is the conceptual model. Data is parsed together by mapping informational fragments into human thoughts in the conceptual model. A more structured format is to store these conceptual models in traditional relational databases or knowledge driven repositories such as ontology networks (OWL- web ontology language or RDF- resource description framework) or object-oriented dominant systems. There are a number of ways to represent knowledge in its various forms, but there must be a technical mechanism built into the systems to eliminate silo farms and redundancy pathways from developing over time. These models have a number of structural formats which can be used to represent knowledge. All are dependent on the overall knowledge elicitation process. The following is a list of the more common tools used to represent structures of knowledge:

Hierarchy Tool - A structured expression in a sub-layer which is mapped on a vertical or horizontal plane.

Laddering Tool - This is used to build taxonomies and ontologies of knowledge nodes. Once a methodology has been selected, this technique is also advantageous for decision networks and building goal trees.

Matrix-based Tools - This requires building tables where the x-axis outlines the problem domain and the y axis supports all the possible solutions that have been postulated by the knowledge engineering team (i.e., SME, Knowledge experts/engineers, and knowledge architects).

Cyber-and Semantic Technology Integration for Knowledge Awareness

Network Diagram Tools - This shows nodes connected by arrows. The nodes can represent any type of concept, attribute, value or task, and the arrows between the nodes any type of relationship.

Diagramming Tools - This relates to the design of concept maps, state transition networks, event diagrams and process maps. The use of this technique becomes important in capturing the "what, how, when, who and why" of tasks and events. (Epistemic, 2000; J. D. Novak 2006)

Other less popular techniques include, but are not limited to sorting and constraint processing

Current explorations have potential with the use of "Big Data" clouds that utilize some ontology model as a way to store knowledge. Such representations of this kind still have a developmental cycle to conquer.

Organizations employing CGKPs can explore utilizing knowledge driven methodologies that explore effective KACE tools. One such experimental KACE to be used as a representation methodology is the Differential Diagnosis (DD) Knowledge Life Cycle Methodology. This experimental methodology explores the use of the medical DD process model as a legitimate and reliable model for the capture, elicitation organization and utilization of knowledge. (Conley-Ware 2010). This knowledge can be subject based or organizational based. The data sources can be structured as well as unstructured. The key is the use of a SME or an Organizational Knowledge Expert. Details of this methodology can be reviewed in the research under Dr. Conley-Ware, Medical Differential Diagnoses (MDD) as the Architectural Framework for a Knowledge Model: A Vulnerability Detection and Threat Identification Methodology for Cyber-Crime and Cyber–Terrorism (Conley-Ware 2010).

Ontologies to Support Knowledge Modeling as a Representation Media for Cyberspace

Like other KM oriented concepts, ontologies had its origin in the 1980s as an outgrowth from the Artificial Intelligence industry. One of the most accepted and consistent definitions across academic research, the commercial industry and the DODIIS ontology 2006 working group is:

"An Ontology is a semantic information model that defines a set of entities by their properties and constraints and then explicitly specifies the relationships between those entities. Therefore, ontologies can provide the framework for semantically reconciling disparate information into a unified context (unified body of knowledge) *(ARL, 2007)*. Since 2009, Ontology building applications and tools have been part of the leading edge technologies used by business intelligence specialists. A definition presented by Dave McComb, President of Semantic Arts, Inc., is that:

> *"An Ontology is a formal description of the meaning of the information stored in a system. It resembles a conceptual model, but goes much beyond a conceptual model in that the formal definitions allow the system to infer class membership based on prosperities."*
>
> - *Semantic Arts, Inc., Nov 2009*

Additionally, inference engines running on ontologies allow users to extract and integrate information stored in distributed systems.

The focus of an ontology is to explicitly describe the "what" of an object. Ontologies are important to the development and maintenance of taxonomies. A broad ontology can be used to generate taxonomies (Conley-Ware, 2010). A taxonomy can provide the terminology for each object of a domain in one or more of the following formats:

- thesaurus
- object ambiguity also called fuzzy logic
- dictionary format

The structure of information in these formats is typically hierarchical. However, in a knowledge driven paradigm, the hierarchical format must be structurally flexible. The concept of poly-hierarchy would more appropriately meet the needs for taxonomies that are knowledge driven. When considering Web 2.0 functionality, the building of folksonomies can also be added to the construction of subject matter expert (SME) derived taxonomies. Web 2.0 provides an avenue for those specialty vocabularies that are only traceable in specific Web 2.0 taxonomies. For instance, Twitter gurus have special notations that are not universally seen in other social media applications. This unique dictionary of words or folksonomy can be added to a traditional formatted taxonomy to provide an understanding across web and traditional applications. This could be part of a taxonomy-to-ontology integration tool.

When using implicit and tacit knowledge in a knowledge driven paradigm, there needs to be a way to capture and represent the knowledge. The use of ontologies and taxonomies provides such a component (Conley-Ware, 2010).

The use of ontology supports other data-to-knowledge specifications outside of the scope of knowledge types. There are cases where developing ontologies can be critical in defining data sets and associated structures needed for problem-solving methods, domain-independent applications, or algorithms that support rule generation for knowledge driven systems. This type of ontology can be built to support horizontal and vertical departmental requirements across an organization. Such ontologies are called "semantic ontologies" and can be used to support knowledge management systems (KMS) where there needs to be an analysis as a way to define the meaning of information (Warren, 2006). The semantic approach involves the integration of taxonomies. In the works by Kitamura-Obfkmm and Mizoguchi in 2004, an ontology based knowledge methodology described a production system which had ontologies as part of its system's core. In their work, ontologies were used to capture functional information as a way to determine specifications for production environments (Kitamura-Obfkmm 2004). In the research by Conley-Ware, decision trees were used in conjunction with the ontologies. Knowledge was captured and fed into the decision trees. The knowledge gathered from these two activities (ontologies and decision trees) was then structured hierarchically for operational research use (Conley-Ware 2010). Other types of ontologies can be used to provide linkages between components of an organization, i.e., association ontologies, ordered list ontologies, weighting ontologies (blog: by zazi0815, 2010) and others. However, not all of these are recommended for the needs of a knowledge driven organization, particularly in a discussion on the organizational needs of Web 2.0 technology.

For an organization to successfully incorporate knowledge driven semantics using ontologies for cyber technologies, there must be a move away from the normalization of a static bureaucracy process to the adaption of processes that are agile. These processes should be able to adjust to the changes as knowledge evolves and, thus, better mirror the needs of the structural and dimensional changes in the ontologies. Management teams in organizations can also promote the "think tank" concept of behavior with their knowledge workers. This is a great way to sponsor creative thinking at a group level. This better leverages the ability to build implicit knowledge ontologies that are sustainable even after the group's experts move to other areas.

Linkages between Organizational Information from Web 1.0 to Web 3.0

An Informational Ontology for 'WEBS' Understanding the use of ontologies for a knowledge driven organization utilizing cyber technologies, provides the necessary path "to connecting the links" for understanding the knowledge of organizational experts. To begin to illustrate how ontologies can be used for organizational cyber knowledge sharing, there needs to be an exploration of an ontology which explains the integration between Web 1.0, 2.0 and 3.0. Figure 2: An Ontology for the Webs is a depiction of the interconnections between the three web environments.

This Web Cycle Ontology was constructed through the application of knowledge search methodologies in the research by Dr. Conley-Ware (Conley-Ware 2010). The integration between Web 1.0 and Web 2.0 is very drastic - Web 1.0 starts and ends at the HTML web page. Interactive cyber communication for Web 1.0 occurs at email messaging and internet chatting. Web 1.0 was equivalent to a one-way transfer, it was very informative and not interactive. There were online communities of practice (CoP) created in the early stages of web portals, but

Cyber-and Semantic Technology Integration for Knowledge Awareness

they were more indicative of primitive chat rooms than true CoPs. In general, these portals did not utilize organizational knowledge from the experts. The focus was on informational postings covering specific topics within an organization.

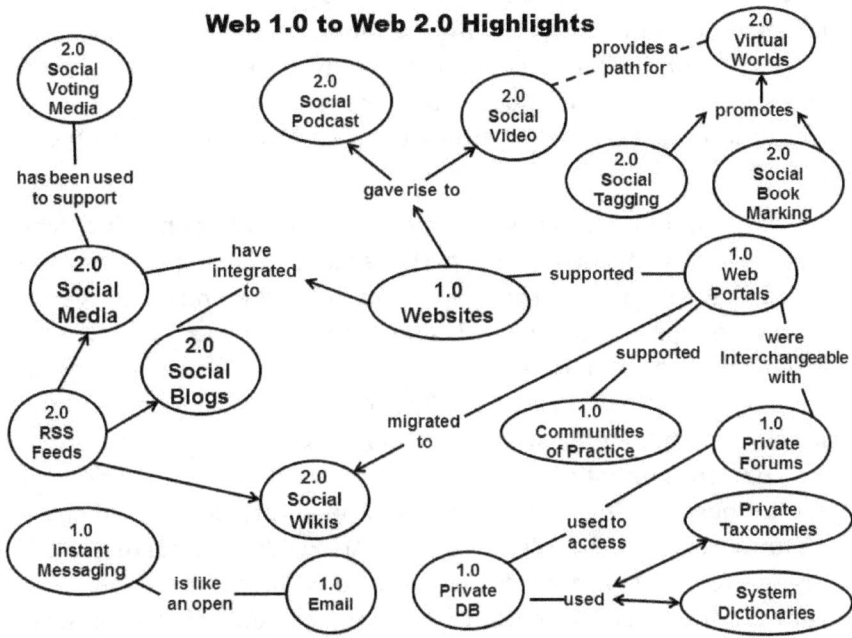

Figure 2: An Ontology for the Webs

This is in contrast to Web 2.0, which spans ones imagination for interactivity with the bubble of social media that has taken over the Internet. Web 1.0 was very privately directed. There were closed web sites and very passive modes of communication. This informative cyberspace environment was great as an online library hub, but it did nothing for those that wanted to experience real-time interactive collaboration. For an organization, Web 1.0 provided a landing field to market an area of speciality and it provided informational packages to members of the organization via its Intranet or Extranet. The early stages of sales organizations in Web 1.0 were about their ability to capture the reader as a customer. The environment of Web 2.0 looks at how to exploit these services by providing an "at your Internet door experience" via a web service and RSS feeds. Web 2.0 moved away from portals and composite online applications to multi-level interactive experiences by way of social media and 2D/3D virtual worlds. Images in Web 1.0 were very static. However, they slowly morphed into 3D interactive dynamic imagery with the more advanced technologies of Web 2.0 – for instance avatar technology. Interactive dashboards, video such as YouTube and video integrated with photographic imagery to interactive white boarding brought a new frontier to the dynamics of Web 2.0.

Web 2.0 is about interactive communication and connecting cyberspace surfers with self made experts called bloggers. The idea of privacy has become a critical commodity in the second phase of Web 2.0 with the boom in social media via applications like Facebook, Myspace and Twitter. Web experts such as Tim O'Rielly (www.oreilly.com) now have to compete with Web 2.0 self-made experts like blogger, Darren Barefoot, who publishes a blog by the same name (www.darrenbarefoot.com). There are parallels and similarities from the offerings in Web 1.0 and Web 2.0. The library online card catalog taxonomy structures in Web 1.0 gave rise to Web 2.0 textual tagging and then folksonomies which can be used with advanced web search engines. Knowledge or content management applications running in web portals grew-up in Web 2.0 to be wikis. Online encyclopedias morphed into the well known components called Wikipedia and Intellipedia.

Social media has extended the way a cyberspace publisher expresses information and knowledge through new and artistic ways of mapping unstructured data – i.e., the birth of the Word Cloud. A site called Wordle (www.wordle.net) was launched as a cyberspace toy for creating word clouds. It has now become a new way to provide knowledge in presentations, videos and in standard word documents. One such word cloud is illustrated in Figure 3: A Word Cloud.

These word clouds take paragraphs of unstructured data and narrows it down to what appears to be key words in the form of an artistic rendering of words. Upon viewing, the reader gets the overall point of

Cyber-and Semantic Technology Integration for Knowledge Awareness

the text at a glance. This is great for knowledge representation; however, it does provide variances for knowledge collection in cyberspace that may be difficult.

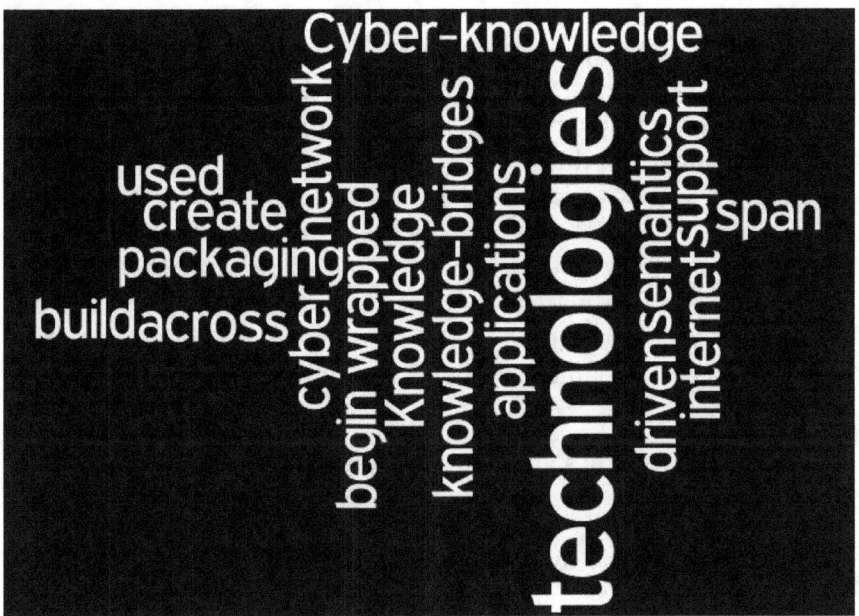

Figure 3: A Word Cloud

Web 2.0 left a lot for users to do if the goal was to understand more than the "big picture" regarding one's level of expertise. The knowledge expert in Web 2.0 needs to have an account on Twitter, Facebook, LinkedIn and several others, in addition to having a blog and web site to really be interactive while also supporting KACE needs. There is the utilization of Application Programming Interfaces (APIs) which provide the owner of the knowledge the ability to link the sites together. However, to a consumer of expert knowledge within cyberspace, the work required to play "hopscotch around the Internet" as a way to gain a percentage of knowledge from an expert can take longer than a series of personal interviews. With the birth of Web 3.0, a path is provided for various "buckets" of knowledge discovered by the Internet surfer to be "mashed" together.

Web 3.0 provides the most intimate connection between the seeker of knowledge and the knowledge expert beyond the scope of the personal interview in cyberspace. Just as Web 1.0 has bridges to Web 2.0, Web 2.0 has pathways to Web 3.0. The connections between these web worlds can be best understood through the construction and utilization of an ontology. The semantics depict the relationships between the bridges in the Web 1.0 to Web 2.0 ontology as depicted in Figure 2: An Ontology for the Webs. The semantics provide meaning between the bits of data, as well as a user's ability to transverse across and down an experts understanding of the same data. This ontology, used in conjunction with the ACS, can provide a non-sophisticated SME with the necessary tools needed to start moving from their paper intensive SME environment in their organization's use of cyber knowledge.

Knowledge Drivers for CyberSpace: A New Definition for MASHUP – Socialnomics

This section explains how the concept of MASHUP can be used to drive cyber technology and semantic network integration. Earlier in the chapter, there was an extensive discussion on structures called ontologies and taxonomies and how semantics played an important role in the development of these structures. These factors provide the foundation for the MASHUP of these technologies using a semantic network. In order to drill into the playground of these technologies, there must be some discussion on what is meant by a semantic network. It is a composite of semantic technologies woven together in support of a technical solution that utilizes knowledge with any combination of the following:

- ontologies
- taxonomies
- knowledge trees or models
- inference drivers based on rules from business and experts

Cyber-and Semantic Technology Integration for Knowledge Awareness

- extracted content and semantic search engines (i.e., search with an understanding of why a particular search was requested) (Another name for this is intelligence searching)

The use of a semantic network for the foundation of a collaboration environment has been under consideration by organizations since the social media boom on the Internet. One such organization is the New York Times. In October of 2010, the New York Times launched a partners'hip with the International Press Communications Council, to create an environment for the publishing community which could provide a framework for language commonality and meaning diversity. It was called rNews (Sandhaus 2011). The senior architect of the organization's IT semantic platform, Evan Sandhaus, saw that the standard RDF model used to build ontologies did not take into account the differences in naming structures for like or similar datasets. This was also true of the standard RDF model utilized as the concept for ontology-to-taxonomy integration. rNews would provide a communication framework of terms, though spelled the same, might have different meanings based on the word in English or another language. This also included the understanding of the word based on the sector of journalism that used the word. This particular semantic network would work as a bridge across various areas of journalism, as well as the language barriers that exist in the cyber world today. (Sandhaus 2011) As of 2011, it could not be validated if this work had been launched into all the organization's operational factors utilizing ontologies.

Semantics, in general, are the toughest barrier for any organization to develop when trying to support the building of a knowledge driven community. With the integration of Internet content, the use of semantics provides a new dimensional challenge. This is particularly true for a traditionally structured-data-directed organization, as well as those organizations that have created their own intra-social network like IBM or sectors of the Department of Navy (DON). Within the participants of the KM focused area of FOSE (The (Federal) Knowledge Management and Cloud Computing-2011), there are those that still believe in the enterprise ontology or taxonomy paradigm. Many organizations have departmental specialties that range from the intellectual capital in the infrastructure departments to the subject matter experts in the organization's core services. The vocabulary and understanding of the vocabulary can differ in each of these areas in an organization; therefore, requiring a need for multiple taxonomies. The explicit knowledge that is already codified and lives in the corporation's structured data bases today is often merged into the ocean of "on-the-spot" knowledge captured from the Internet's social media applications. Many specialty personnel within an organization currently support their own outside interest that goes beyond their employer's domain. The Sr. Architect for semantics at the New York Times, Evan Sandhaus has his own specialty semantic Twitter followers (Sandhaus 2011). Others have their own specialty blogs, wikis or video chat channels on YouTube. Many times the expert's outside social media platforms have an impact on the dissemination of knowledge in their organization.

Organizations must begin to think outside the cyber "box" to capitalize on the range of knowledge representation tools that are available in cyberspace. They must also look at ways to build bridges between these channels of knowledge. By using the cyber tools available, organizations can begin to capture knowledge from their organizational SMEs by way of their heuristics driven blogs, wikis, tweets and social network sites. They can even discover hidden messages in video chat messages inside a technology driven game.

One way to look at this dimensional integration is what this author calls the Mashup of technology or in short, Socialnomics. This is the socialization of an expert's content within social media. Socialnomics has several critical areas of use. The first is a pseudo – cloud infrastructure, under the umbrella of cloud computing. Cloud computing provides an individual or an organization everything that is available in their network in one environment. It provides a place for what has been called SaaS (software as a service) and a set of infrastructure concepts for IT that can possibly downgrade the number of server farm silos that currently do not contain any collection of cyberspace knowledge.

Cyber-and Semantic Technology Integration for Knowledge Awareness

Cloud computing could provide the ability to share instant messages, emails, application accounts and various other forms of unstructured and non-textual media with others without logging into numerous portals and applications. Even though, cloud computing currently has been detailed at the infrastructure layer and not much at the "connect the concepts," "knowledge bites" or "validation of content" layer, it can be a significant asset in a semantic network environment. This environment would first provide an easy and effective way to manage KACE for existing organizational data, as well as cyberspace collaboration and knowledge representation. Additionally, it would provide a means to collect and utilize paths of related knowledge through knowledge bridges that are supported by a semantic network backbone. Even in forward thinking organizations like IBM, knowledge users have many tools at their disposal, i.e. internal wikis, instant messaging, internal blogs, portal, internal slide sharing and others (IBM, FOSE 2010), but there are no network streams that direct users from one source to the next as a way to collect related knowledge or information. On the Internet, a user can follow someone on Twitter and then connect and be a follower of the same person's Facebook, but that does not guarantee that the Facebook content is the same as that followed on the Twitter thread. Using the Socialnomic concept, a private cloud technology would include an organization's view of collaborative spaces, like an internal Twitter and Facebook, visualization software services, a knowledge repository that has a very open architecture with an inference engine driver to support organizational business and subject matter experts' rules and an image library that could be coupled with a tagging library. All would be running on a semantic network backbone. The semantic network would provide a Socialnomics user the opportunity to do semantic explorations and get back feeds that reflect knowledge that has been codified, in addition to an expert's heuristics and any 'group think' from streaming twitter subject matter feeds.

The idea of a private, public or hybrid cloud is not new and many have been built by industry as of 2011. The difference is the concept of a private cloud that has a one-way pipe out to the Internet. The idea dates back to the 1990's concept of an intranet and extranet. Organizations had their private network space called an intranet and then they had a common shared space with the Internet, the Extranet. The complications of publishing and the types of information that had to be driven through content management structures did not provide an appealing use for the end user. The structure of the extra, intra (formerly called a portal) net did not provide an opportunity for knowledge expression and collaboration like it is experienced in cyber social media today. Cloud technology can possibly enable information technology groups to be scalable and agile in the services that they offer to support in an intranet social unit.

The Socialnomic concept would provide a level of confidence in the knowledge utilized, because it would require a validation footprint for all knowledge contributed by any level of expert. This is not a change in the current cyber world architecture, but it is a different way to harness cyber-technology than is currently being used today. The level of confidence of the information and knowledge type would be relatively high due to the validation systems that would be required prior to publication to the cloud. How do you validate a twitter feed one might ask? You do not, but twitter feeds would be categorized as expert, opinion or collaborative thoughts.

For the use of imagery, photographic or graphical, a tag would be required to be published with each image by an organizational user. This tag could be folksonomic, linguistic based on language or traditionally taxonomic. All tag types would be handled by the semantic network backbone. The backbone would also include semantic ontologies that would require maintenance by a semantic technology network team. A conceptual view of a Socialnomic network is illustrated in Figure 4: The Socialnomic Concept.

Cyber-and Semantic Technology Integration for Knowledge Awareness

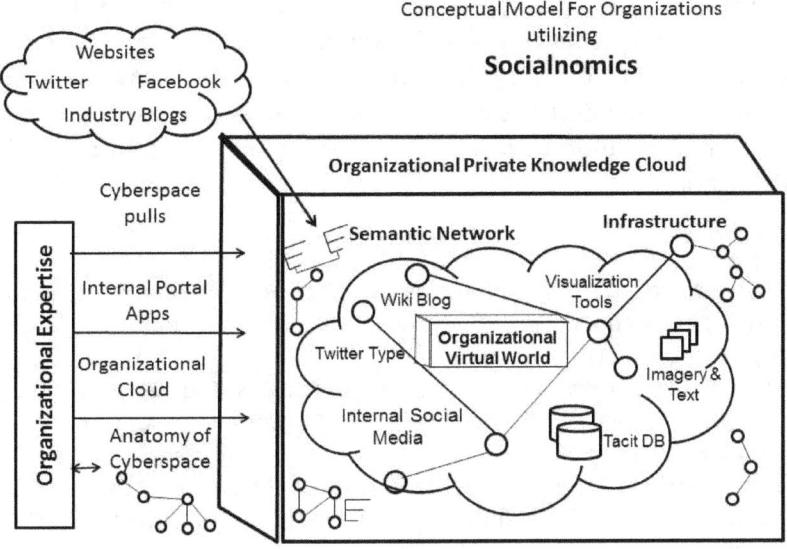

Figure 4: A conceptual view of Socialnomics

The reality of such a network is not that far in the distance future. Companies are already moving to cloud computing, DOD is looking to decentralize the number of data farms across the services. Innovators in government knowledge management shops such as the Navy, US State Department, US Aid and others who are key contributors to yearly national Knowledge Management conferences (FOSE, KM 2011) and innovators of WEB 2.0 are working and implementing parts of this puzzle today. The next step is to provide an architectural, financial and agile plan to move to this new type of Mashup forward.

Conclusion

The backbone of knowledge management systems and tools, in conjunction with agile methodologies and expert directed methodologies, provide the foundation for the cyber – semantic integration platform. The actual operational construction of the Socialnomic structure requires detailed architecture. This article provides the groundwork as well as the concept for the next step in building such architecture. This is a way to harness the fast moving technologies of cyberspace by key organizations (Government and Commercial). Such a technology as Cyber-Semantics is critical in order to capture the knowledge that is provided in the heuristics of historical mission SMEs and IT gurus, both of which are important to the long-term growth and stability of any organization.

References

BarefootDarren, DarrenBarefoot.com, Blogs on Social Media, 10. 2010 to 6, 2011, Blogs about Web 2.0, 4/ 2009 www.darrenbarefoot.com, (accessed date, May 2011)

Cook,S.D.N and Brown, J.S , Bridging Epistemologies: The Generative Dance between Organizational Knowledge and Organizational Knowing, Organizational Science 1999.

Conley-Ware, Lakita, "Medical Differential Diagnosis (MDD) As the Architectural Framework for A Knowledge Model", (PhD. Diss., The George Washington University School of Engineering, 2010.

Davenport, Thomas and Laurence Prusak; Working Knowledge: How Organizations Manage what they know; (Massachusetts: Harvard Business School Press; 2000), Chapter 3-7.

Epistemic, Epistemics.co.uk/notes/2000.htm, Knowledge Models, (accessed date, March 10, 208).

Applications International Corporation (SAIC), 2/10/2010 (May 14, 2011)

Hayes-Roth, Frederick, Building Expert Systems, Massachusetts: Addison Wesley 1983.

HiPiHi Co.,Ltd. Hipihi. 2005. http://www.hipihi.com/en/ (accessed date May 16, 2011)

Jonathan Feinberg. Wordle. 2009. www.wordle.net (accessed date May 16, 2011)

Kitamura, Y and Riichiro Mizoguchi, "Ontology-Based Functional Knowledge Modeling Methodology and Its Deployment", Engineering in the Age of Semantic Web Proceeding (EKAW), The Institute of Scientific and Industrial Research Osaka University, October 2004, 99-155.

Linden Research, Inc. Second Life, www.secondlife.com (May 14 2011)

Metaversum. Twinity. 2011. www.twinity.com (accessed date May 16, 2011)

Miller, William and Morris, Langdon, "Fourth Generation R&D: Managing Knowledge, Technology and Innovation", (New York: John Wiley and Sons, 1999).

Cyber-and Semantic Technology Integration for Knowledge Awareness

Milton, Nick Knowledge Acquisition; www.epistemics.co.uk/Notes/63 0-0.htm 20 November 2003, Reviewed 28 April 2007.

Milton, Nick Knowledge Acquisition; www.epistemics.co.uk/Notes/63 0-0.htm20 November 2003, Reviewed 28 April 2007.

Novak, Joseph and Alberto, The Theory Underlying Concept Maps and How to Construct and Use them, Florida Institute for Human and Cognition , original 2004, ,2006, 2008 revision.

O'Reilly,Tim, What is Web 2.0: Design Patterns and Business Models for the Next Generation of Software, 2005, www.oreilly.com (accessed date June 2011).

O'Reilly, Tim Web 2.0 Expo 2009, New York Experience Notes, December 2009

Sandhaus, Evan, Semantic Web Meetup:Learn About rNews, April 2011 New York Times.

Semantic Arts Inc. (2009 November). Upper Ontology. White Paper.

Sowa, Jon, Knowledge Representation Logical, Philosophical and Computational Foundations, Public Grove, Brooks 2000.

Stankosky, Michael, "Creating the Discipline of Knowledge Management", 1999, 2005.

Tiwana, Amrit; The Knowledge Management Toolkit, (New Jersey: Prentice Hill PTR), 2002.

Worlds.com. Worlds. 2010. www.worlds.com (accessed date May 16, 2011)

zazi0815, July to December 2010, comment on various types of ontologies, (i.e., association ontologies, ordered list ontologies, weighting ontologies), smiy.wordpress.com., June5,2011, http://smiy.wordpress.com/tag/ordered-list-ontology/.

Improving Healthcare Quality Using Web 4.0 Decision Making

Anjum Razzaque, Mirghani Mohamed[1] & M Birasnav[2]

[1] Applied Knowledge Sciences, Inc., Leesburg, VA, USA
[2] New York Institute of Technology - Bahrain campus.

Introduction

The recent ubiquity of social networking tools and the appearance of the semantic web can have direct effects on improving the quality of medical decision making. These social networks facilitate the improvement of healthcare (HC) service quality, but only if used as knowledge management's (KM) collaborative systems that promote synergy, transfer and sharing of relevant knowledge. This merger through software in the cloud infrastructure is a pre-requisite for the future sustenance of e-health that can materialize in the next decade.

HC staggers in its service quality causing a rise in patient mortality rate, HC costs and medical errors (DeMarco 2010; Bodenheimer and Fernande, 2005; Hrg 2008; Chernichovsky and Leibowitz 2010; Kozer, Macpherson and Shi 2002). Most frequently ignored medical errors are diagnostic errors. One out of every 10 diagnoses in the US, is concluded incorrectly (Campbell 2010) costing $55.6 billion annually (Chicago Injury Attorney Blog, 2010). Forty out of every 100 Americans visit the emergency room (ER) where evidence-based quick decision making is very critical (Kopun, 2010). Most clinical Decision Makers (DMs) either lack the support of or are without a HC knowledge management system (KMS). Abundant HC literature, related to decision support, fails to show the importance of HC KM in facilitating medical decision making. Clinicians are asked to: (1) gather and interpret information, and (2) implicitly or explicitly bridge the daily inferential gap even when lacking evidence needed to reason a decision (Jalal-

Karim and Balachandran 2008). This is possible through sharing experiential knowledge among HC physicians to improve medical decision-making quality (Liu et al. 2008). HC KM is a new pitch facilitating decision making through its infrastructure and processes (Zhang 2008).

Knowledge (KM) Process, Infrastructure and Architecture

Since 1997, KM is proposed as a passionate Healthcare (HC) topic. Nonetheless in 2001, it was reported again that KM is a soft area in HC since these organizations are information rich but knowledge poor, i.e., slow at embracing KM. They need to understand the importance of a KM infrastructure (Perrott 2008).

The KM perspective is composed of a KM architecture that is made up of four elements, aimed at improving organizational processes, i.e., collaboration and decision making, performance and learning. The four elements of KM architecture are: (1) knowledge components, (2) KM processes, (3) information technology (IT) and (4) organizational aspect, knowledge components and KM process being the main components. Knowledge component defines knowledge. (Rajesh, Pugazhendhi, and Ganesh 2011), i.e., relevant information processed and the power to act and make decisions. Knowledge is either explicit or tacit. Explicit knowledge can be articulated and is reviewable; whereby, tacit knowledge resides within experts' actions and experiences. In a knowledge hierarchy, data is required to create information, i.e., relevant data analyzed and processed for meaning; and information is required to create knowledge (Hick, Dattero and Galup 2007). Tacit knowledge exists everywhere (Hick, Dattero and Galup 2007). Information is organized data with patterns made out of it while knowledge is manipulated information for applicable decision making (Hsia et al. 2006). Knowledge can be transformed from data rather than from information and data is also attainable directly from knowledge (Hick, Dattero and Galup 2007). KM turns data to information, to knowledge within KM processes to enrich an organization to compete (Hsia et al. 2006).

KM has become a tool to sustain an organization's competitive advantage (Antonio and Lemos 2010). This interdisciplinary business model manages knowledge through its processes (Wickramasingha, Gupta and Sharma 2005). This process involves acquisition, creation, filtrations, storing, sharing and exploiting of knowledge. IT refers to its related support infrastructure like database, network, etc. (Rajesh, Pugazhendhi and Ganesh 2011) and a pre-requisite for KM success and sustenance of development (Mohamed, Stankosky and Mohamed 2009). As in the case of this research, HC organizational structure is: (1) its structure, (2) shared corporate culture and (3) human resource management (Rajesh, Pugazhendhi and Ganesh 2011). To facilitate medical decision making, building KM infrastructure is indispensable for sustaining tacit knowledge sharing (Frid 2000).

KM infrastructure is aided by three elements: (1) technical support, (2) organizational culture and (3) organizational structure. Knowledge sharing has a mediating effect between KM performance and KM infrastructure (Jie & Zhengang 2010) where knowledge sharing facilitates medical decision making since a balance of both knowledge types are compulsory for decision making (Abidi, Cheah and Curran 2005); (Baskaran et al. 2005). Knowledge sharing is measured across two entries: (1) explicit knowledge sharing and (2) implicit knowledge sharing. Implicit knowledge sharing is sharing of know-how, know-where and know-who as well as education and training-based expertise. Explicit knowledge sharing involves business proposals and reports, methodologies, business models, knowing each-others' failures/successes and business knowledge obtained from medical resources like newspapers, journals, etc. (Lin and Chang 2008). As per the scope of this research, our interest lies in the concept of socialization where tacit knowledge is converted to tacit knowledge, e.g., sharing experiences (Ciccarese et al. 2005); (Nemati et al. 2002). Technical support here is referred as to a KMS. Five components can serve as pre-requisites for building a successful KM know-how being: (1) Community of Practice (CoP), (2) content management, (3) knowledge transfer, (4) performance outcome tracking and (5) technology infrastructure (Perrott 2008).

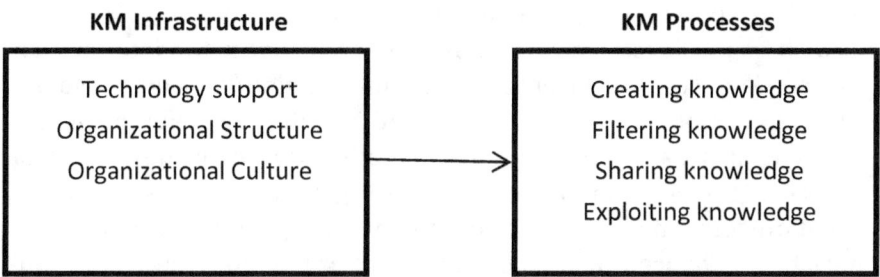

Figure 1. KM Architecture Model

A HC KMS infrastructure needs to be incorporated. It is composed of processes, tools and techniques with KM activities through a comprehensive nursing KMS framework. HC KMS is a new trend to facilitate an e-health environment, i.e., a solution to current HC information overload crises. This is possible through KM technologies and applications that improve access and transfer of e-Health knowledge to all HC professionals of all levels (Hsia et al. 2006). Even though research has stressed KM architecture through the seven layers mirroring the OSI model, KM referential model, KM spectrum and Ovum KM tools architecture model, this work considers the KMS architecture model for its simplicity and since it is based on three useful services (infrastructure, knowledge and presentation) facilitated by KM technologies. The infrastructure services establish the elementary technology stand for KM implementation based on storage – knowledge repository, e.g., data warehouse and knowledge server and communication, i.e., between users, collaboration among users and workflow management. Knowledge services are reinforced by technology solutions to encourage knowledge flow, generate new knowledge and warrant ease-of-access to knowledge repositories. Here new knowledge is refined, created/discovered or new tacit knowledge is codified/articulated. In addition, knowledge is shared/transferred amongst organizational members using technologies/KM tools like social networking analyses, also referred to as collaboration tools like social computing (an emerging research area) (Chua 2004). Organizations share knowledge to stay competitive (Hick, Dattero and Galup 2007). Also knowledge is re-used here, i.e., captured, packaged, distributed and applied via technologies like content management and conceptual mapping, based on search capabilities. The presentation services boost the interface between knowledge seeker and the information/knowledge source through personalization (i.e., seeker attains interest/preference-based content also based on content/assigned/attributes values and business context. For example, e-mail – intelligent, agent, personalization, solution sets, and user rules to handle messages). Visualization is to facilitate enhanced means to understand retrieved knowledge (Chua 2004).

Social Networking Enables Knowledge Sharing

Even though social networking studies have been matured since decades in the field of sociology and anthropology, there is still an opportunity to test its theories and assumptions concerning structures and behaviors using web-based/virtual and real-time tools available today. These tools also provide new computational models and data to test the online-social networks. Social networks are now a next generation web. Such a move is paving the way for decision making, organizing, innovating and Web 2.0 (Oinas-Kukkonen, Lyytinen, and Yoo 2010); (Jie and Zhengang 2010). Such social computing attracts investments, e.g., $6 billion in 2007, in the US itself, since 60% of social computing companies reside in the Silicon Valley like Linkedin, for professional networking, and FaceBook, for friendship (Ala-Mutka et al. 2009).

Since 1990s, CoP was utilized in the business world but new in HC (Bentley, Browman and Poole 2010). The new art of practice is the merging of members of differing CoPs to work together in a collaborative environment in the hope to improve the outcome of activities (Oborn and Dawson 2010). The importance of community as a knowledge resource, achieved new heights when knowledge was realized as embedded and constructive through social information relationships and social interactions share common practices and where organizational boundaries do not apply. This person-based network is where people help each other in solving problems. Here, sense is made through storytelling and knowing, which is practice-based and community-based. Here, knowledge, people, infrastructure and organizational processes support CoPs and are defined as structured informal environments where knowledge is like practical experience to theoretical concepts amongst CoP members. A CoP is important because knowledge is un-separable from context and communal conversations between knowledge seekers and contributors share interests bound by informality and context during knowledge sharing and applying common practice (Plan and Leidner 2003). CoPs have become valuable for work-based problem solving by seeking knowledge. A CoP is knowledge driven so content defines and gives value to a virtual community. This Knowledge is willingly shared. It is important to investigate why individuals do or do not-share knowledge when given a choice. This means understanding motivations that facilitate a knowledge sharing behavior. Once these motivations are understood, one could be able to inspire knowledge sharing. This is possible through social theories like: (1) social cognitive theory (SCoT) and (2) social capital theory (SCT).

SCoT defines human behavior as an interaction of personal factors, behavior and social network. Participants join a community as a social group; hence, their behavior is partially shaped, controlled, and influenced by such a group (Chiu, Hsu and Wang 2006). SCT is the good will created through social interactions that facilitates taking action and intellectual capital (created by the interaction of personalized retainers) is socially and contextually embedded knowledge. Intellectual capital builds social capital between retainers. SCT and intellectual capital are important organizational resources and advantageous when co-evolving. Intellectual capital is developed by considering the tacit-explicit knowledge type and the analyzing of the social-individual knowledge dimension (Mansingh, Osei-Bryson and Reichgelt 2009). These theories motivate knowledge sharing. Communities are social concepts, sharing experience with three key factors: (1) shared traditions and rituals, (2) hold a sense of belonging in a group, and (3) shared moral responsibility. Such communities are formed on common grounds like professional disciplines or interests and gain value through member participation. Virtual communities (e.g., online forum, virtual CoP or bulletin board) interact through communicated systems rather than face-to-face. Tacit knowledge is shared through interpersonal means while structured process or technology facilitates the sharing of explicit knowledge. In a social network, the interaction between inter-relationships facilitates direct proportionality with knowledge sharing; hence, cost effective, faster and easier (Chang and Chuang 2010).

Web 3.0 Cloud Computing and Social Networking Support E-Health

E-Health organizations are gaining attention and are becoming a norm, since it assists with the improvement of HC quality. Now, HC is transforming into a knowledge community, bonding with hospitals, clinics, customers and pharmacies to share knowledge within and across boundaries. Hence, new challenges are reported as being: (1) how to integrate various knowledge bases so HC professionals can have one centralized access and (2) how to manage knowledge effectively by exercising IT tools (e.g., a KMS can be implemented and e-portals can integrate medical knowledge into clinical workflows) (Hsia et al. 2006). With the advent of e-health as not only a technical development but an attitude, ways of thinking and mindsets where networking is utilized to improve ICT-based HC locally and globally, such that, HC services are enhanced or delivered virtually, or in other words via the Internet and relevant technologies (Eysenbach 2001).

On the Internet, social computing will continue flourishing to fast-track e-health; with technology advancing to Mobile 2.0 and social web where things think using sensors, i.e., cloud computing (i.e., internet joint with computing). In this mobile domain context, awareness will grow and artificial intelligence will support social computing with systems integrated with human bodies and brains for real time monitoring and support. In HC, social computing can make global HC information available at all levels through a large-scale collaborative system to systematically gather massive amount of knowledge for patients, clinicians and researchers to improve scientific discoveries, research and development (R&D) and discover new disease therapies. This is how HC quality will be facilitated. However, there are issues like identify theft, privacy invasion risks and unclear data ownership which call for further research. Social computing is also enhancing decision making. Since 2006, there has been a shift from Web 2.0 to Web 3.0

mobile social computing raising growth of mobile devices. Web 2.0 is dependent on cloud computing and combinations of its techniques with techniques of the semantic web to open the door to a more revolutionary web. Web 3.0 is costly and high in yield. Semantic related innovations pave a path for Web 3.0 with cloud computing being the most focused with major investments going towards its infrastructure (Ala-Mutka et al. 2009).

Leadership Facilitate KM Processes and Infrastructure

Since communities have no reward systems to influence knowledge sharing and motivation is important to sustain participation (Chang and Chuang 2010), the role of leadership is important to investigate. Senior management contributes to a knowledge-sharing environment by applying tacit and explicit knowledge for problem solving (Hick et al. 2007). Leadership inspires to motivate to contribute and; hence, facilitate organizational performance (Birasnav et al. 2009). Early studies characterized leadership as a personality trait for being a successful leader. Hence, one could assume that leaders are born (Ogbonna and Harris 2000). In order to understand what leadership is, it is first better to consider the fortune of wisdom stressing that a great leader is not born or self-made but developed through mentoring (Kim 2007). Widespread criticism towards this theory gave birth to style and behavioral leadership approaches (Ogbonna and Harris 2000) (Bass 1990). The roles and processes of leadership set direction, create alignment and foster commitment within groups so an organization makes leadership a source of (Bass and Riggio 2006) organizational competitive advantage (Kim 2007). Leadership is of two types: (1) transactional and (2) transformational (Bass, 1990). Those leaders who lead using social exchange, e.g., rewarding their followers for productivity (Lowe, Kroeck and Sivasubramaniam 1996) harvest transactional leadership. However, transformational leaders – a finer leadership performance (Bass 1990); (Kelloway, Barling and Helleur 2000) - encourage their followers to not only achieve astonishing outcomes but also develop their own self-leadership skills through mentorship (Bass and Riggio 2006) to empower them rather than make them dependent (Lowe, Kroeck and Sivasubramaniam 1996).

Transformational leaders, are charismatic leaders, inspiring their followers to be members of shared goals and vision as well as encourage their outcomes to be more innovative and problem solving, e.g., through either directive or participative, so as to achieve finer results (Bass and Riggio 2006). Employees see transformational leaders as effective and satisfying, since employees want to identify with them (Bass, 1990); (Lowe, Kroeck and Sivasubramaniam 1996). On the other hand, employees feel they lack in their intelligence under the leadership of transactional leaders (Bass and Riggio 2006). Leadership is not only a definition pertaining to those at the top (Kelloway, Barling and Helleur 2000) but occurring at all levels with an organization by all employees, as this is also the core notion of transformational leadership (Bass and Riggio 2006). Leadership within an organization supports knowledge processes, i.e., by rewarding employees who create new knowledge and share knowledge to improve organizational performance. This reward boosts up an employee or increases his/her salary; hence, effecting human capital benefits through such a KM process (Birasnav, Rangnekar and Dalpati 2009). It has been reported that when it comes to transformational leadership, ample theories apply suitably to create an atmosphere for KM where organizational employees are productive when having the freedom to create, share and test ideas to generate superior levels of innovation. However it is transactional leadership that motivates knowledge application. Even though both types of leadership are required to effectively manage knowledge, every individual tends to exhibit one form of leadership more than the other (Bryant 2003).

Framework to Improve Healthcare Decision Making

Current literature states that clinical decision making lacks knowledge sharing (Jalal-Karim and Balachandran 2008) as well as CoP (a KM tool), a new and soft area in HC research; since KM is new to HC (Hsia et al. 2006). It has been observed that ample current literature focused on theories like SCT or SCoT exisits to motivate knowledge sharing. On the other hand, other research stresses virtual CoP improve not only knowledge sharing but knowledge creation. Current research has failed to consider, holistically, the composition of all KM processes working in harmony with the KM architecture to better facilitate medical decision making motivated also by leadership. Holistic thinking is inspired through the fact that any KM project should grasp human and technical aspects, balanced and interactive, acting as one rather than two separate dimensions. Figure 2 illustrates the system-thinking model, which functions to integrate other models described in this work.

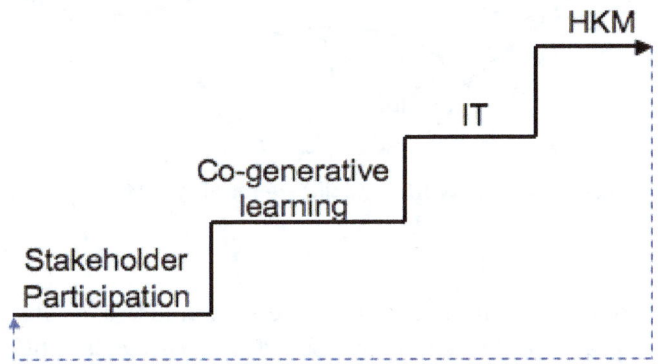

Figure 2. Route towards achieving HC KM from a holistic point-of-view. *Source: Chowdhury (2007)*

Figure 3, a conceptual framework as a proposed holistically mapped out, grounded in theory solution, and a key to improving medical DM quality

The following propositions are planned for future empirical testing so KM tools like a virtual CoP can facilitate the enhancement of the quality of medical decision making within cross-functional environs, being: (1) leadership plays a positive role towards KM architecture and KM infrastructure and medical decision-making quality, (2) KM processes and KM infrastructure have a positive impact on medical decision-making quality and (3) KM infrastructure plays a positive supportive role on KM processes.

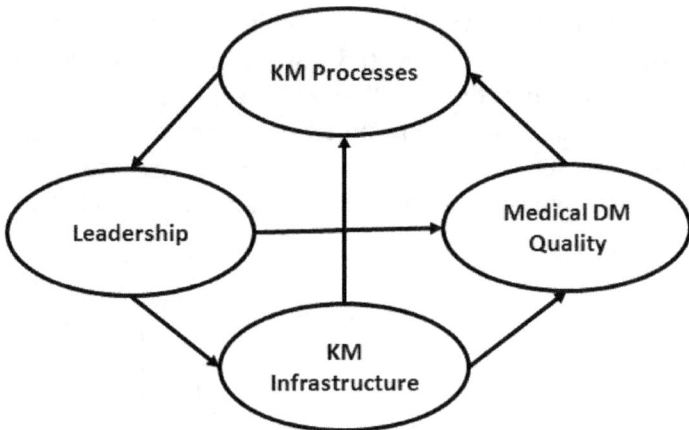

Figure 3. Conceptual framework to facilitate medical DM.

Conclusion

With HealthCare, a complex service oriented industry, quality in decision making lags behind when compared with rising HealthCare costs versus high patient mortality and dissatisfaction rates worldwide. This work contributes to the knowledge society, its proposed conceptual framework, grounded in theory that considers the importance of healthcare knowledge management, infrastructure and KM processes, as well as the influencing role of leadership, to facilitate medical decision making quality in the e-health environments taking into consideration the futuristic perspective of Web 3.0 social computing and social networks with virtual CoP as a KM tool. Pertaining to the HC KM study, future work should better understand the challenge of clinical decision-making processes and measures in their impact on patient satisfaction. Also identified theft, privacy invasion risks and unclear data ownership call for further research with the advent of Web 3.0.

References:

Abidi, S. R., Cheah, Y. and Curran, J. (2005). A Knowledge Creation Info-Structure to Acquire and Crystallize the Tacit Knowledge of Health-Care Experts. IEEE Transactions on Information Technology in Biomedicine, Special Issue on Knowledge Management in Healthcare , 9 (2).

Ala-Mutka, K., Broster, D., Cachia, R., Centeno, C., Feijóo, C., and Haché, A. (2009). The Impact of Social Computing on the EU Information Society and Economy.Retrievedfrom http://ipts.jrc.ec.europa.eu/publications/pub.cfm?id=2819 [Date retrieved March 2012]

Antonio, L & Lemos, B. (2010). Relevant factors for tacit knowledge transfer within organisations. Journal of Knowledge Management, 14(3): 410-427.

Baskaran, V., Bali, R. K., Arochana, H., Naguib, R. M., Dwivedi, A. N. and Nassar, N. S. (2005). Towards Total Knowledge Management for Healthcare: Clinical and Organizational Considerations. 26th Annual International Conference of the IEEE EMBS. San Francisco, CA.: In IEEE Press.

Bass, B. M. (1990). From Transactional to Transformational Leadership: Learning to Share the Vision. Organizational Dynamics , 18 (3), 19-31.

Bass, B. M. and Riggio, R. E. (2006). Transformational Leadership Second Edition. Mahwah, New Jersey, USA: Lawrence Erlbaum Associates, Inc., Publishers.

Bentley, C., Browman, G. and Poole, B. (2010). Conceptual and practical challenges for implementing the communities of practice model on a national scale - a Canadian cancer control initiative. BMC Health Services Research , 10 (3).

Birasnav, M., Rangnekar, S. and Dalpati, A. (2009). Enhancing Employee Human Capital Benefits through Knowledge Management: A Conceptual Model. Global Journal of e-Business & Knowledge Management , 1, 20-26.

Bodenheimer, T. and Fernandez, A. (2005). High and Rising Health Care Costs. Part 4: Can Costs Be Controlled While Preserving Quality?. Ann Intern Med, 143(1): 26-31.

Bryant, S. E. (2003). The Role of Transformational and Transactional Leadership in Creating, Sharing and Exploiting Organizational Knowledge. The Journal of Leadership and Organizational Studies, 9 (4), 32-44.

Campbell A. (2010). Diagnostic Errors- An Often Overlooked but Common and Dangerous Type of Medical Error Retrieved from http://www.oklahomainjurylawadvocate.com/medical-malpractice/reducing-diagnostic-surgical-errors/ [Date retrieved October, 2010]

Ciccarese, P., Caffi, E., Quaglini, S. and Stefanelli, M. (2005). Architectures and tools for innovative Health Information Systems: The Guide Project. International Journal of Medical Informatics. International Journal of Medical Informatics , 74 (7-8), 553 - 562.

Chernichovsky, D. and Leibowitz, A. A. (2010). Integrating Public Health and Personal Care in a Reformed US Health Care System. American Journal of Public Health, 100(2): 205-211.

Chicago Injury Attorney Blog, 2010. US Medical Malpractice Costs Averaging About $55.6 billion Yearly Retrieved from http://www.uslaw.com/library/Personal_Injury [date retrieved]_Law/US_Medical_Malpractice_Costs_Averaging_556_Billion_Yearly.php?item=890968.

Chua, A. (2004). Knowledge management system architecture: a bridge between KM consultants and technologists. International Journal of Information Management, 24, 87–98.

Chang, H. H. and Chuang, S.-S. (2010). Social capital and individual motivations on knowledge sharing: Participant involvement as a moderator. Information & Management, 48 (1), 9-18.

Chiu, C.-M., Hsu, M.-H. and Wang, E. T. (2006). Understanding knowledge sharing in virtual communities: An integration of social capital and social cognitive theories. Decision Support Systems, 42, 1872–1888.

DeMarco, B. 2010. Alzheimer's Reading Room. Retrieved from http://www.alzheimersreadingroom.com/2010/03/cost-of-healthcare-worldwide.html [Date retrieved March 2012]

Eysenbach, G. (2001). What is e-health? Journal of Medical Internet Research, 3 (2), e20.

Frid, R. J. (2000). Infrastructure for Knowledge Management. San Jose, CA, USA: Writers Club Press.

Hicks, R. C., Dattero, R. and Galup, S. D., (2007), A Metaphor For Knowledge Management: explicit islands in a tacit sea. Journal of Knowledge Management, 11(1), 5-16.

Hrg, S. 2008. Rising Costs, Low Quality in Health Care: The Necessity for Reform Retrieved from http://finance.senate.gov/library/hearings/download/?id=191d240c-fa6b-4f70-b985-b74bc560d322. [Date retrieved November 2011]

Hsia, T.L., Lin, L.M., Wu, J.H., and Tsai, H.T. (2006). A Framework for Designing Nursing Knowledge Management Systems. Interdisciplinary Journal of Information, Knowledge, and Management, 1, 95-108.

Jalal-Karim, A and Balachandran, W. (2008). Interoperability Standards: the most requested element for the Electronic Hea1thcare Records significance. 2nd International Conference – E-Medical Systems, 29-31 October 2008, E-Medisys2008, IEEE, Tunisia: In IEEE Press.

Jie, X., & Zhengang, Z. (2010). Research on the Relationship between Knowledge Management Infrastructure, Knowledge Sharing and Knowledge

Management Performance. Management and Service Science (MASS), 2010 International Conference on, (pp. 1-4). Muhan.

Kelloway, E. K., Barling, J., and Helleur, J. (2000). Enhancing transformational leadership: the role of training and feedback. Leadership & Organization Development Journal, 21 (3), 145-149.

Kim, S. (2007). Learning goal orientation, formal mentoring, and leadership competence in HRD A conceptual model. Journal of European Industrial Training, 31 (3), 181-194.

Kopun F. 2010. Doctor heeds siren call of emergency room Retrieved from http://www.healthzone.ca/ health/article/863043. [Date retrieved November 2011]

Kozer, E' Macpherson, A. and Shi, K. (2002). Variables Associated With Medication Errors in Pediatric Emergency Medicine. PEDIATRICS, 110(4): 737-742.

Lin, C. and Chang, S. (2008). A relational model of medical knowledge sharing and medical decision-making quality. Int. J. Technology Management, 43 (4), 320-348.

Liu, C, Jiang, Z, Zhen, L. and Su, H. (2008), A bilateral integrative health-care knowledge service mechanism based on MedGrid, Medline, 38(4), 446-460.

Lowe, K. B., Kroeck, K. G., and Sivasubramaniam, N. (1996). Effectiveness Correlates of Transformational and transactional Leadership: A Meta-analytic Review of the MLQ Literature. Leadership Quarterly, 7 (3), 385-425.

Mohamed, M., Stankosky, M. and Mohamed, M. 2009. An empirical assessment of knowledge management critically for sustainable development. Journal of Knowledge Management, 13(5): 271-286.

Nemati, H. R., Steiger, D. M., Iyer, L. S. and Herschel, R. T. (2002). Knowledge warehouse: an architecture of knowledge management, decision support, artificial intelligence and data warehousing. Decision Support Systems, 33, 143-161.

Mansingh, G., Osei-Bryson, K.-M. and Reichgelt, H. (2009). Issues in knowledge access, retrieval and sharing – Case studies in a Caribbean health sector. Expert Systems with Applications, 36, 2853–2863.

Oborn, E. and Dawson, S. (2010). Learning across Communities of Practice: An Examination of Multidisciplinary Work. British Journal of Management, 21, 843–858.

Ogbonna, E. and Harris, L. C. (2000). Leadership style, organizational culture and performance: empirical evidence from UK companies. Int. J. of Human Resource Management, 11 (4), 766–788.

Oinas-Kukkonen, H., Lyytinen, K. and Yoo, Y. (2010). Social Networks and Information Systems: Ongoing and Future Research Streams. Journal of the Association for Information Systems, 11 (2), 61-68.

Perrott, B. E. (2008). Knowledge management from an industry perspective. Journal of General Management, 34 (1), 33-70.

Plan, S. L. and Leidner, D. E. (2003). Bridging communities of practice with information technology in pursuit of global knowledge sharing. Journal of Strategic Information Systems, 12, 71-88.

Rajesh, R., Pugazhendhi, S. and Ganesh, K. (2011). Towards taxonomy architecture of knowledge management for third-party logistics service provider. Benchmarking: An International Journal, 18 (1), 42-68.

Wickramasingha, N, Gupta, J. N. D. and Sharma, S. K. (ed.) (2005). Creating Knowledge-Based Healthcare Organizations, Hershey, PA: Idea Group Publishing

Zhang, X. 2008. Understanding the Conceptual Framework of Knowledge ManagementinGovernmentRetrievedfrom http://unpan1.un.org/intradoc/groups/public/documents/un/unpan030557.pdf   [Date retrieved November 2011]

Afterword

"Making It Real" extends and expands on The George Washington University (GWU) mantra: "Theory to Practice... a Continuum," coined to define the GWU Knowledge Management (KM) academic and real world journey initiated in 1998, accredited in 2000, and still going strong in 2012. Edited and led by Dr. Annie Green, an initial and veteran theorist/practitioner of the GWU KM program, this third book contains strong author representation from many members of GWU's Institute for Knowledge and Innovation (IKI) community.

The 14 chapter articles contribute a universe of usable methodologies, tools, and multiple real world applications vital to creating usable knowledge enabled environments for public, private, and academic enterprises. This text spans the power of "Story Telling narratives" used to transfer knowledge before and even post written language to today's globally connected digital world of "Socialnomics" and Web 2.0 and 3.0 participants. Mechanisms are presented for managing and valuing the "Intangible Knowledge Assets" recognized and inventoried by only a minuscule number of enterprises. A learning interlude, when the reader can "connect the dots," is offered by optimizing the flow of knowledge driven by the "Number of Individuals in a Given Group" and influenced by their cultural traits, attitudes and behavioral patterns. Ways and means for "Transferring and Preserving Organizational Knowledge," with the highly mobile and often transitory national and international workforce, reflects the realities of an interlocking global citizenry riding the currents of economic demands. These early themes in the book trend toward the "theory" aspects of KM. Later chapters transition the reader quickly into real world enterprises where organizational, leadership and technology challenges are faced in applying and implementing sound knowledge management principles and practices. Examples range from NASA programs to unidentified (but clearly representative private sector corporate settings),

Francesco A. Calabrese, D.Sc.

and continue with IT services, Cyber security and Health Care markets/applications all profiled to emphasize the transition from theory to (real world) practices.

These summary "Afterword" reflections might well have ended here, but the GWU- IKI Community experiencing a decade of somewhat amorphous but continuing resistance to the perceived management of human cognition, often identified as a "knowledge generating engine" in Homo sapiens, also seeks to project what might lie ahead in the accelerated sweep of global knowledge sharing. To that end it seems appropriate to briefly explore the "AfterWARD of this Afterword."

AFTERWARD: The preparation of these musings shared time in September 2012 with the 30 year anniversary of the newspaper USA TODAY. The anniversary theme was "USA TOMORROW, September 14, 2042, the Next 30 Years." Of the multiple "futures type articles" presented, several resonated with themes in "Making it Real." The linchpin connector piece dealt with lifelong learning, highlighted by the theme: "Keeping it Real." That seemed to be a great segue to the Future from the Past (Theory to Practice… a Continuum) and the Present (Making it Real). "Keeping it Real" 1* was dubbed a "constant" defined as: "Teachers and other students will be central to learning. The human element is really important" [emphasis added]. The human involvement may seem obvious, but too often the notions of identifying, crafting, validating, packaging, sharing and verifying knowledge and its transfer is attributed to non-human trappings. There are important ancillary influences to be sure, i.e., Leadership commitment and support; Organizational forums, processes, recognition and rewards; Technology widgets, gadgets, tools, virtual environments, algorithms, Web 2.0, 3.0, 4.0… n.0 ad infinitum! The "reality" in GWU, IKI's knowledge centric world is that when all three of these elements exist in a robust and sustainable measure they will engender Learning as the fourth element in a harmonious Universe, [i.e., GWU's Four Pillar KM Framework] 2* driven by human intellect to achieve greater results of Efficiency, Effectiveness and Innovation facilitated through knowledge sharing and collaboration!

Afterword

That same article 1* made note that "... you want learning to be as much fun as it is to play a video game..." The inference, in my opinion, supports the basis for the strong emphasis now emerging on "Virtualization through Visualization" reminiscent of the historical cliché that "a picture is worth a 1,000 words." That appears consistent with the real world emergence of virtual classrooms hosting tens of thousands of globally distributed "learners," who are selecting from a catalogue of free online courses taught by star professors from around the world." There was also a reference to one such course in mathematics where students are challenged to apply course principles in rescuing the Apollo 13 astronauts. That "failed NASA mission" made into a movie [available in DVD] is one of the top 10 inspirational films of all time. It is also replete with multiple visually enhanced learning and knowledge acquisition and transferability events. The real world saga was followed at the time of its occurrence by billions of viewers worldwide through continuous TV coverage. But the full learning /knowledge transfer experience is best acquired by watching the film and being an attentive and knowledgeable "virtual participant" with both the astronauts in the spacecraft capsule and the mission control facility experts as they struggle and eventually bring the crippled spacecraft to a safe splashdown.

The USA TOMORROW, September 14, 2042 Anniversary edition also references the following:

That: "Once again USA TODAY is reinventing storytelling......" [emphasis added]. 3*

That: "Often it takes a crisis to precipitate a transformation..." [an experienced truism to achieving success in many KM program implementations]. 4*

That: "Cars won't fly, but they'll amaze......" [In their "intelligent systems evolutions" once humans can cede auto pilot control]. 5*

That: "Millions of people may become astronauts; a jaunt across the globe will take only a few hours flying at 'radical' speeds ....." [in fact the first unmanned, private sector space shuttle round trip to the Space Station has already occurred]. 6*

Francesco A. Calabrese, D.Sc.

That: "…reading, writing, and digital delivery has increased interest in reading. It seems more fun, exciting and cool to read on a new device…….." [all positives to encourage and sustain lifelong learning]. 7*

But the coincident happenstance of USA TODAY's anniversary is only one dot in a universe where organizations like the World Future Society, Apple, Google, Amazon, Facebook, Twitter, YouTube, Cable TV, etc., etc., exist, proliferate and, on the negative side, lead humans (the ultimate knowledge source) to the situation graphically portrayed on the cover of Newsweek-- March 7, 2011 "Brain Freeze – How the deluge of information [a level below several derivates of knowledge] paralyzes our ability to make good decisions" (Sharon Begley) 8*. The emphasis here is on every day decisions by every day humans on: "buying a car, choosing a healthcare plan, figuring out what to do with your 401(k), etc., …….." It is these unintended consequences which demand that there be a "counter force" striving to "Keep it Real" by filtering the tsunami of information so the "[right] actionable knowledge flows to the [right] people at the [right] time within the [right] levels of human intellectual capacity." That is the continuing challenge for those of us struggling in the uncharted seas of global knowledge riptides, and this text, "Making it Real," is a helpful "flotation device" to set us on the correct bearing and keep us on course throughout the tumultuous knowledge inundation voyage of this 21st century.

Enough of my preaching! We need action now, and my wish is that this book, so artfully brought together by Dr. Green, will serve as a platform for concerted action by you, the readers. Anne is an excellent point of contact, since she is a leader of the KM Educational Forum and a member of The George Washington University's Institute for Knowledge and Innovation, both of whom are dedicated to advancing the discipline and practice of KM. My wish is for all of us to add to our wealth by leveraging the relevant knowledge around us for both the common good, as well as our own.

Sincerely,

Francesco A. Calabrese, D.Sc.
The George Washington University

Afterword

Co-director, Institute for Knowledge & Innovation

References:
USA TODAY, September 14, 2012. A world where grades will be left behind. Learning will be free, tailored, high-tech and a whole lot of fun. Keeping it Real, according to Sebastian Thrun: Teachers and other students will be central to learning "The human element is really important" Mary Beth Marklein (p. 6F).
Stankosky, Calabrese, Baldanza – A Four Pillar Framework, KM Model, 2000.
USA TODAY, September 14, 2012. The future of news: You - Once again, USA TODAY is reinventing storytelling, David Callaway (p. 2F).
USA TODAY, September 14, 2012. Dissatisfaction will usher in changes, Newark mayor says, Newark Mayor Cory Booker is a champion of social media - "Often it takes a crisis to precipitate a transformation." Susan Page (p. 2F).
USA TODAY, September 14, 2012. Cars Won't Fly, But They'll Amaze - Ford's top executive [Bill Ford] says tech will drive the industry, Chris Woodyard (p. 8F).
USA TODAY, September 14, 2012. Millions of people may become astronauts, [Richard Branson] Ben Mutzabaugh (p. 9F).
USA TODAY, September 14, 2012. The words that fly off the page 'Change,' 'choice,' - In reading, writing and digital delivery. [Gina Centrello, president and publisher of Random House Publishing Group] Craig Wilson (p. 15F)
Newsweek, March 7, 2011. I Can't Think, The Twitterization of our culture has revolutionized our lives, but with an unintended consequence – our overloaded brains freeze when we have to make decisions. Sharon Begley (p. 28-33).
The Futurist Magazine, September/October 2010.
a. Prospects for Brain-Computer Interfacing, Patrick Tucker (p. 7-8).
b. Wisdom Facing Forward, What It Means to Have Heightened Future Consciousness, Tom Lombardo (p. 34-42).
c. Foresight for the World's Youth, Edward Cornish (p. 44-46).
d. Tried and True: Technological Transformation - From Paper to Disk to Cloud, Cynthia G. Wagner (p. 60-61).
The Futurist Magazine, November/December 2010.
a. Hooked on Noise - Many young people spend hours listening to music on portable devices, Rick Docksai (p. 7-8).
b. TweetPatrol, Deploying Social Networks to Solve Public Safety Issues, Patrick Tucker (p. 8-9).

Francesco A. Calabrese, D.Sc.

c. Tapping the Cognitive Surplus - "The sudden bounty of accessible creativity, insight and knowledge is a public treasure..." Clay Shirky (p. 21-22).
d. Tomorrow's Interactive Television - The iPad and its successors could revolutionize television, John M. Smart (p. 41-46)
e. Outlook 2011, forecasts for the Decade Ahead in 13 Subject Areas (a nine page pull out).

The Futurist Magazine September/October, 2012 – The 22nd Century at First Light

Are You Smarter Than a Sixth-Generation Computer?, Tests for measuring non-human intelligence development, Richard Yonck (p. 6-7).

The New Age of Space Business - By the 2020s and beyond we could see a historic expansion of human activity in space, Joseph N. Pelton (p. 15-19).

Serving Justice with Conversational Law - Digitized, semantic legal-expert systems will allow more people to access and understand the law, David R. Johnson (p. 21-24).

Major Transformations to 2100: Highlights from the TechCast Project, Laura B. Huhn, William Halal and 12 Scenario Authors (p. 33-55).

www.ingramcontent.com/pod-product-compliance
Lightning Source LLC
Chambersburg PA
CBHW072131220426
43664CB00013B/2211